SQL SERVER
T-SQL COMPREHENSIVE
VERSION 2012

Pindaro E. Demertzoglou, Ph.D.

Alpha Press – Albany, New York 2014

ISBN-13: 978-0-9883300-4-7
ISBN-10: 0988330040

Printed in the United States of America

Library of Congress Control Number: 2014915309

This publication, its supporting materials and the accompanying database is an information product published for general reference and sold as is. It does not offer legal, accounting, psychological, or tax advice. The publisher and author disclaim any personal responsibility or liability, directly or indirectly, for information presented in this publication. The purchaser or reader of this publication assumes all responsibility for the use of the materials and information contained within. The author and publisher made every effort to prepare this book with care and accuracy. However, they assume no responsibility for errors, inaccuracies, non-working code, or omissions. The material in this book is presented for educational purposes only.

About the Author

Pindaro's relationship with databases started with DBase III back in 1991, continuing with all versions of MS Access since early 1993, and working with MS SQL Server, MySQL, Oracle, and IBM DB2 for a number of years. From then on, he is still in love with all of them. After twenty years, he still works with data, information processing, integration, and dissemination.

Pindaro is currently a faculty member in the department of Information Systems at the business school of Rensselaer Polytechnic Institute in Troy, New York where he is teaching databases and business analytics for the last fifteen years. Pindaro also completed and collaborated on a myriad of database projects for organizations or in collaborative efforts between the University and various corporations.

Pindaro's interests in information science, transactional systems, and analytics focus on creating more efficient and flexible organizations. The idea is to accomplish more with fewer resources and in less time leaving a small footprint on the environment. Pindaro's education includes a BS from the American College in Thessaloniki Greece, an MS, MBA, and a PhD in the United States. He received national and international distinctions for his work in the field and faculty awards for his teaching methods.

Nevertheless, the majority of the author's experience came from participating in a multitude of industry projects. There, everything has to work efficiently, reliably and above all be acceptable by the people of the corporation. Theoretical knowledge, though useful, takes a second place in these cases. A solid application and strong promotion within the organization are the primary success factors.

Dedication

This book is dedicated to my thousands of students for the continuous inspiration throughout the years.

Acknowledgments

I would like to express my gratitude and say a big thank you to all the teachers around the globe for their effort, patience, and time they devote to their students.

I would like to thank the faculty and staff of the American College of Thessaloniki, Greece who made this college a prestigious and internationally recognized institution. Specifically, I would like to express my deepest appreciation to the former president of the college, Dr. William McGrew and the head librarian Mrs. Pat Kastritsis for their decisive and unrelenting guidance and help to their students. Pat is no longer with us today but the difference she made in my life is propagated to the thousands of students I taught over the last fifteen years in New York. She will live through my own students and the students of my students who receive the same values and attention as the ones I received from Dr. McGrew and Mrs. Kastritsis.

Moreover, I would like to express my deepest appreciation to the staff and faculty of Rensselaer Polytechnic Institute, Troy, NY, United States for the collegiate atmosphere and continuous support in my efforts. I would also like to thank Dr. Shobha Cengalur-Smith, my thesis chair form the State University of New York, Albany United States, who for five and a half years guided me step by step through my research endeavors on databases. I do not know how she did it but she was always there for amazing but lengthy and intricate discussions on databases and their role in organizations.

I also would like to thank very much my student Mr. Travis Scavone for all his feedback, spelling edits, and code edits he provided. He has a keen eye for detail and he caught errors and omissions that I missed in my multiple reviews.

Finally, I really want to thank all my students who with their tens of thousands of questions on databases over the last fifteen years gave me the spark to think and rethink a multitude of points from different perspectives and learn a lot as a result.

BRIEF TABLE OF CONTENTS

DETAILED TABLE OF CONTENTS

PREFACE: HOW TO USE THIS BOOK

1. How to download the free version of SQL Server 2012 Express

1. Go to the URL below. Just in case the URL is not valid anymore, search for "SQL Server 2012 Express download" on the web and multiple links will come up. We are looking to download the "SQL Server Express with Advanced Services" version.

https://www.microsoft.com/en-us/server-cloud/products/sql-server-editions/sql-server-express.aspx#fbid=EEeRCp8EQvJ

2. From the available versions click to download "SQL Server Express with Advanced Services." The following screen will come up. To determine if you have a 32 or 64 bit system go to "Control Panel/System and Security." Then click "System" and have a look at the system type that you have. Select the language and click download.

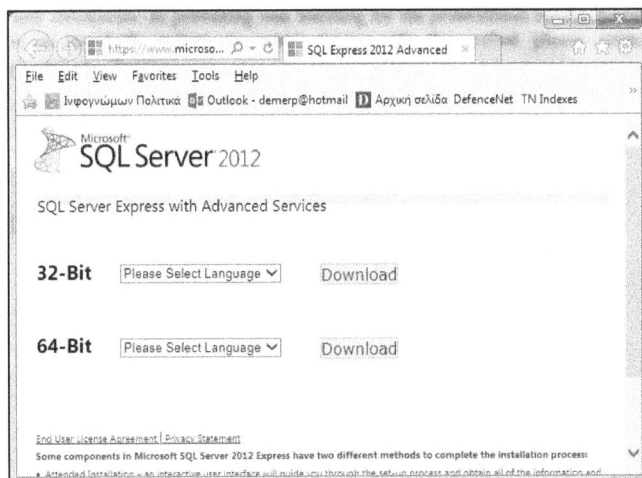

3. Follow the download and registration steps to save the SQL Server file in any folder on your system. The name of the file should be SQLEXPRADV_x64_ENU. Even if the name of the file changes, we are always looking to download the Express Edition with Advanced Services.

2. How to install SQL Server 2012 Express

1. Start the installation
Double click on the SQLEXPRADV_x64_ENU.exe file to extract its contents and start the installation. It happened to me that when the file had downloaded it did not have the .exe extension. If this is the case with you, you can simply add the .exe extension to it and it will work fine.

2. **Click** on **"New SQL Server stand-alone installation or add features to an existing installation."**

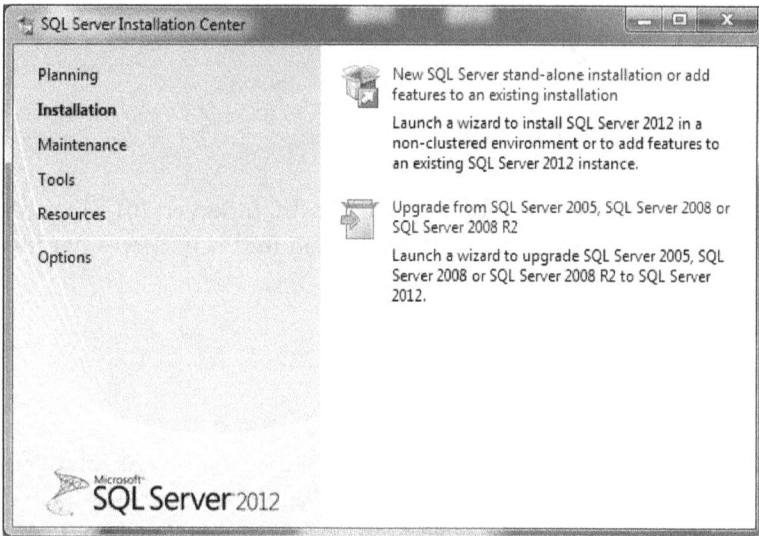

3. Accept the license agreement and **click next**.

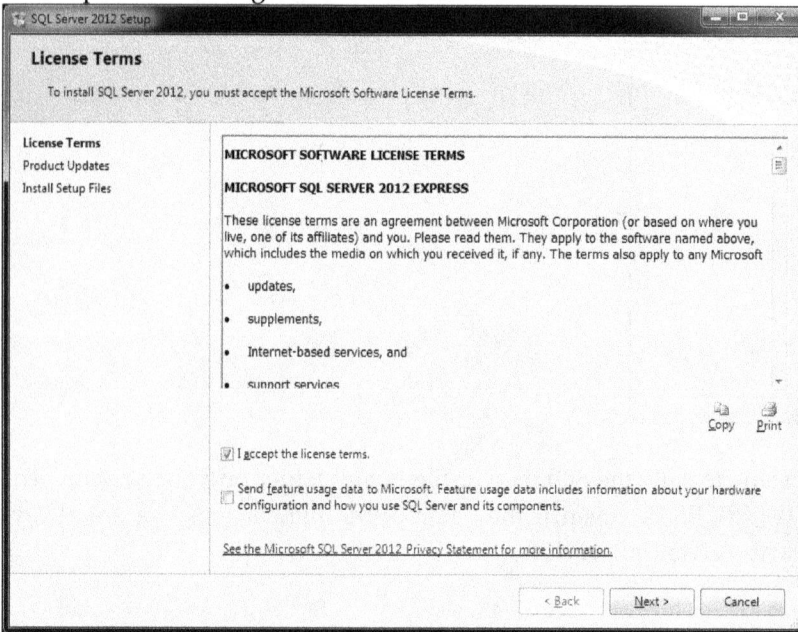

4. If prompted, allow the installation of any updates.
Click Next in the following screen to install updates.

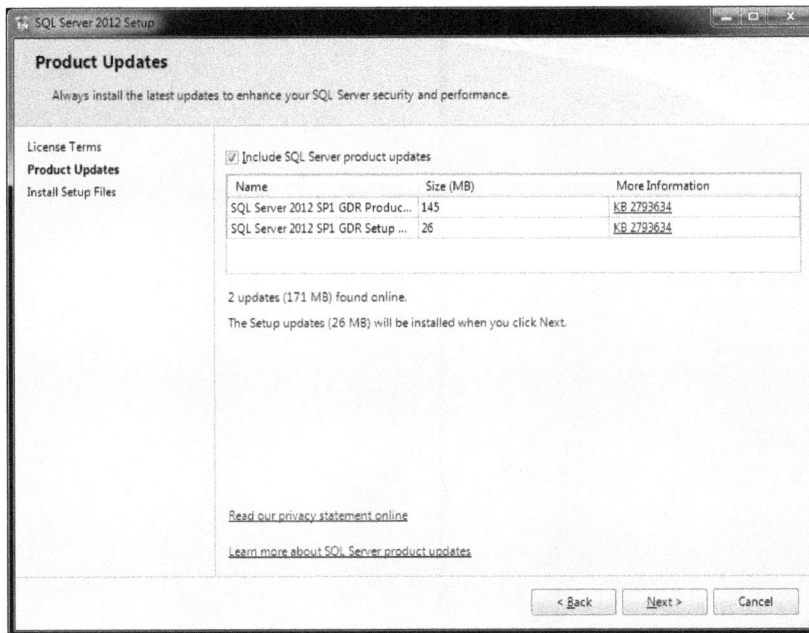

5. Select the features to install as in the following screen and click next. The features might be preselected by the software. You can also change the installation directory in this screen.

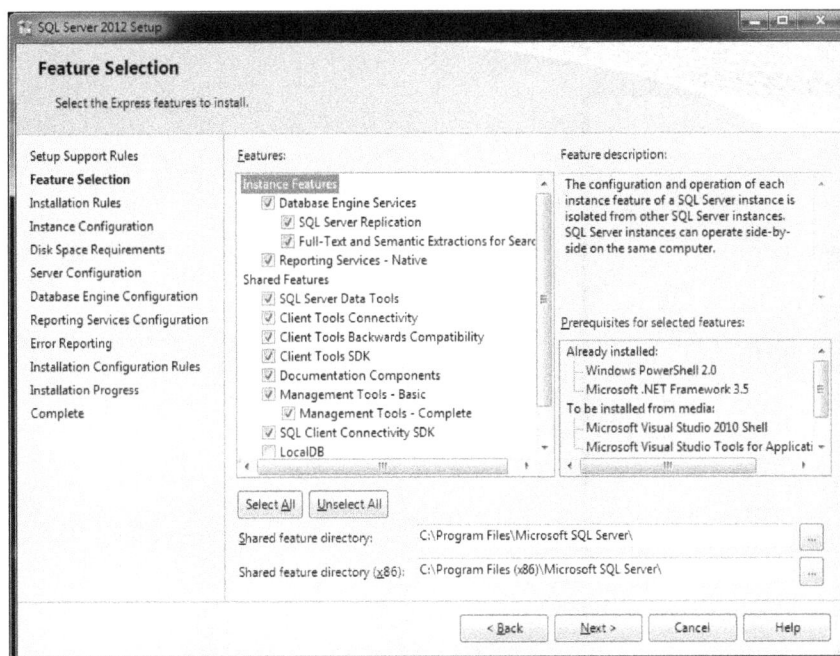

6. For the instance configuration screen just **click next**.

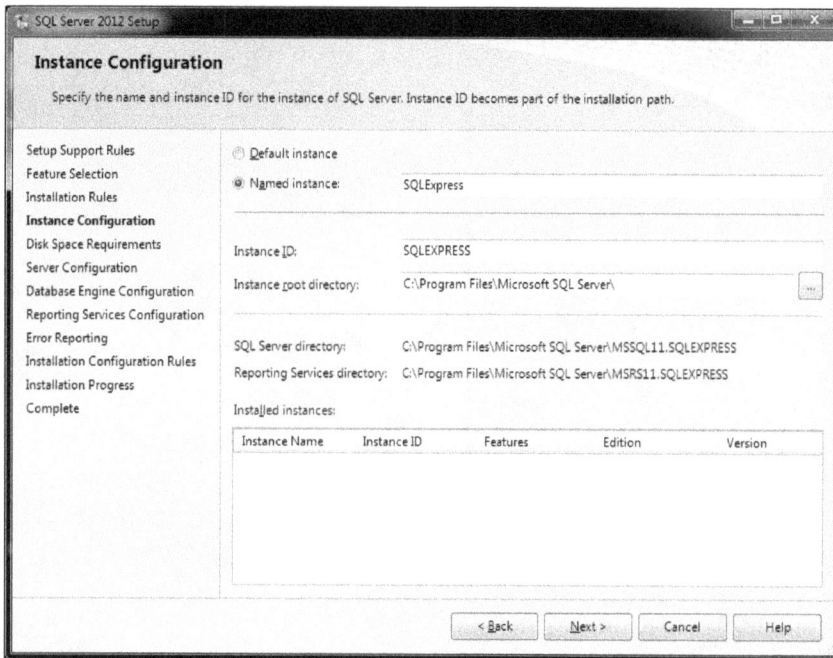

7. For the server configuration screen change the "Startup Type" for the SQL Server Browser from "Disabled" to "Automatic." The SQL Server browser allows SQL server to be "discovered" from client connections. **Click next**.

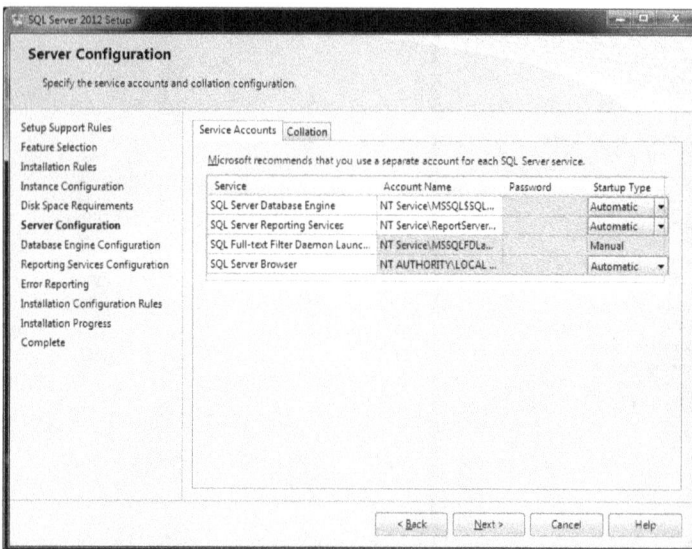

8. For the Database Engine Configuration screen below perform three actions: First, for authentication mode click on "mixed mode". This choice allows us to use SQL server specific accounts instead of windows accounts only. Second, specify a password for the SQL Server System Administrator account. Third, if it is not already there, add the current user as a SQL Server Administrator. **Click Next**.

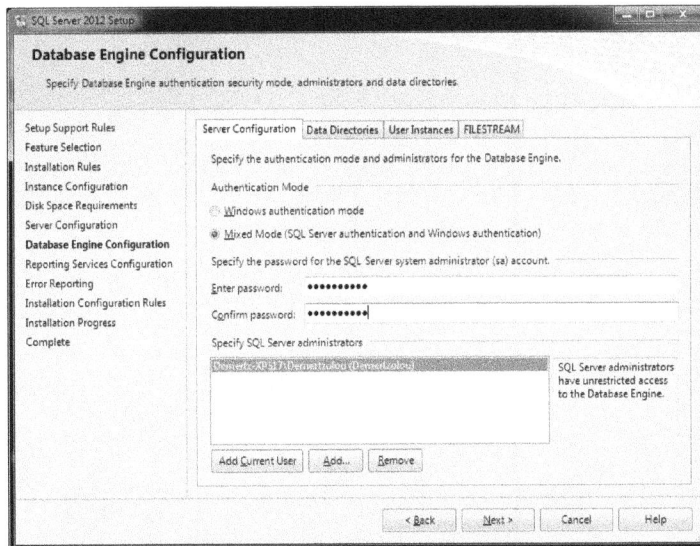

9. For the Reporting Services Configuration, leave the choice to "Install and Configure" and **click Next**.

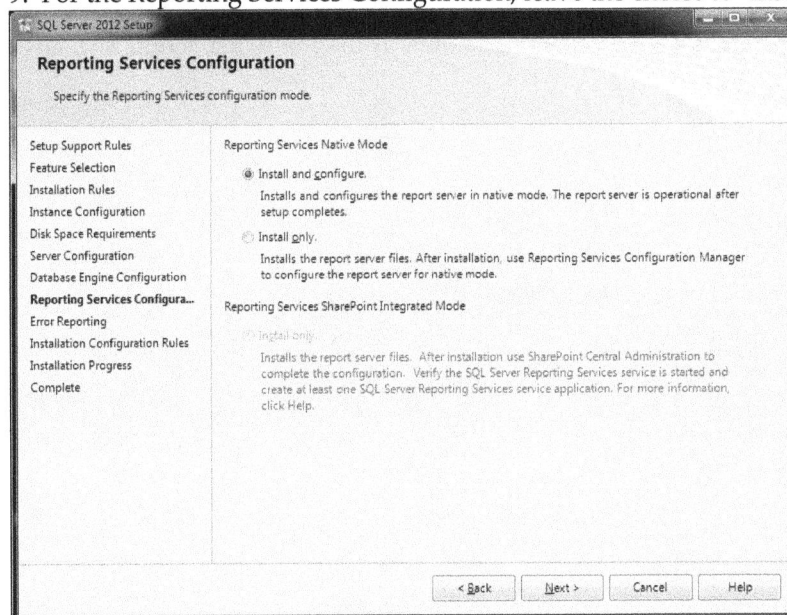

10. For Error Reporting in the following screen, decide if you want to send error reports to Microsoft and **click Next**.

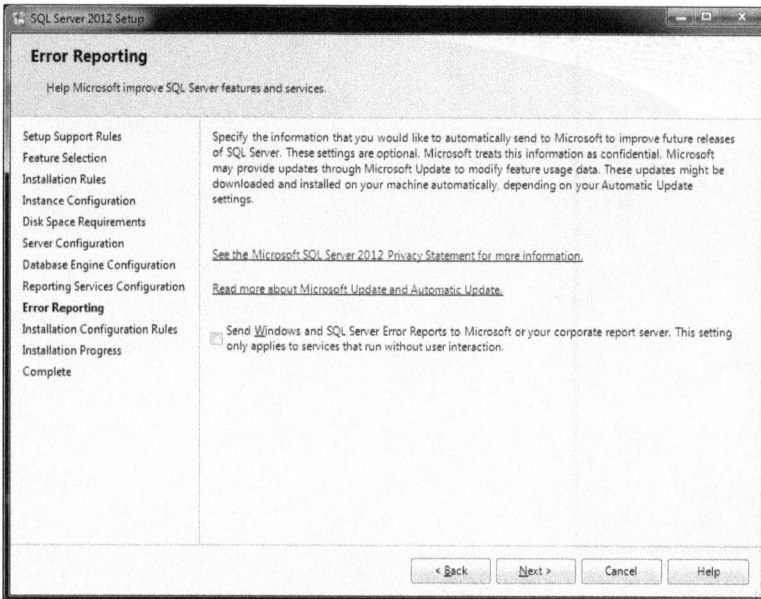

11. Wait up until the installation of SQL Server is complete as it is shown in the following screen and **click Close**. You are done.

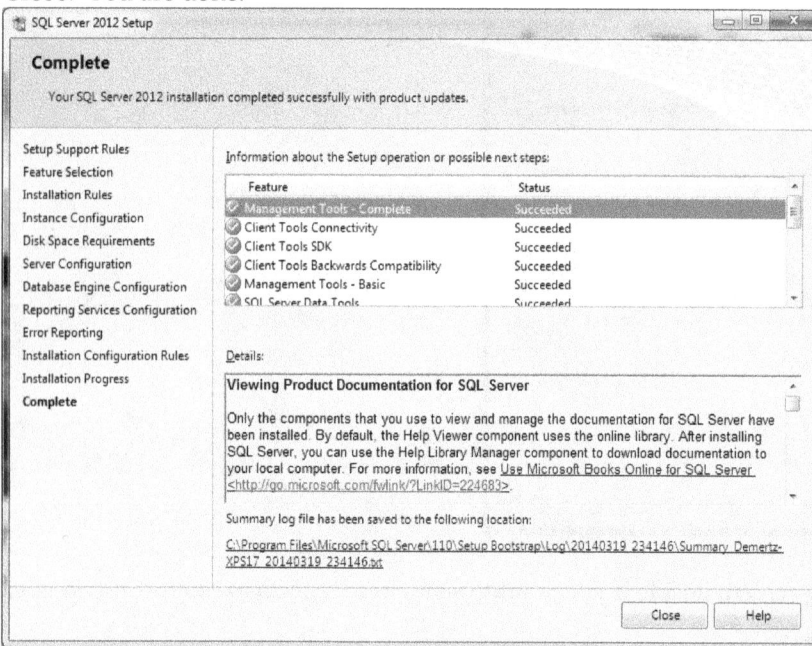

3. How to download the sample database

To download the sample database for the book and stay connected with the latest news and updates please go to http://www.databasechannel.com/Products/default.html, and click on your book link to access its resources. Just in case you have any trouble at all downloading the sample database, please email us at alphapress@hotmail.com and a real human being will answer your question.

4. How to load the sample database to your SQL Server Express Instance

1. Move the database you have downloaded to the folder C:\Program Files\Microsoft SQL Server\MSSQL11.SQLEXPRESS\MSSQL\DATA. This is the folder in which SQL Server stores its database files. Our own file structure appears below and the pasted SQLServer2012_TSQL.mdf is highlighted:

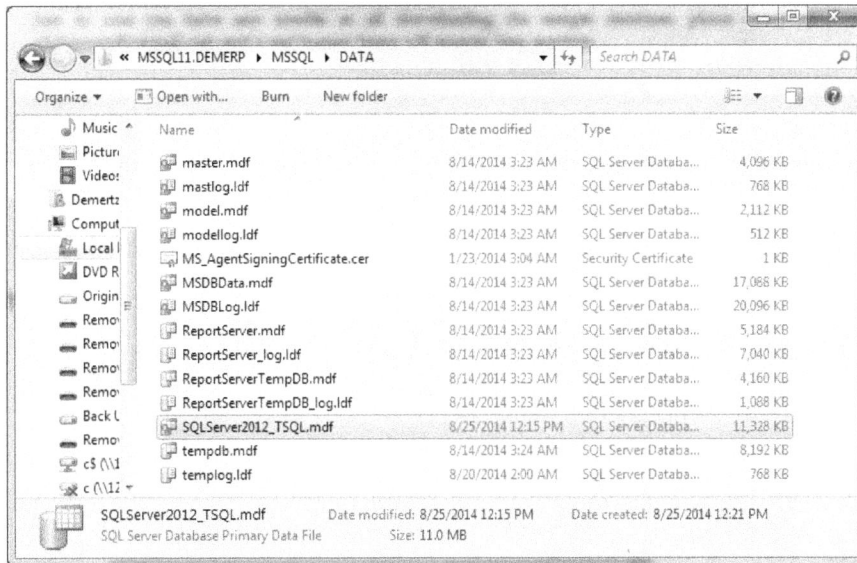

2. Start MS SQL Server Management Studio and click on the databases node to expand it. Your database structure should look close to the one below: Our goal now is to make the "SQLServer2012_TSQL" database to appear in the database list so that you can work on it.

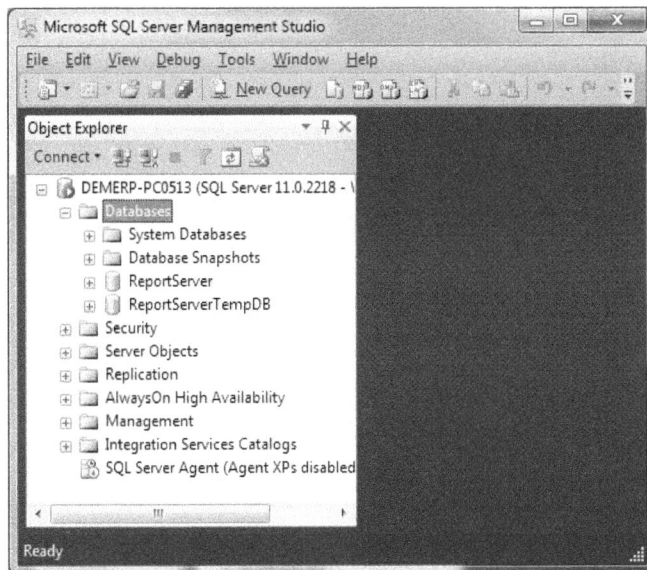

3. Right click on "databases", and select "attach". The following screen will come up:

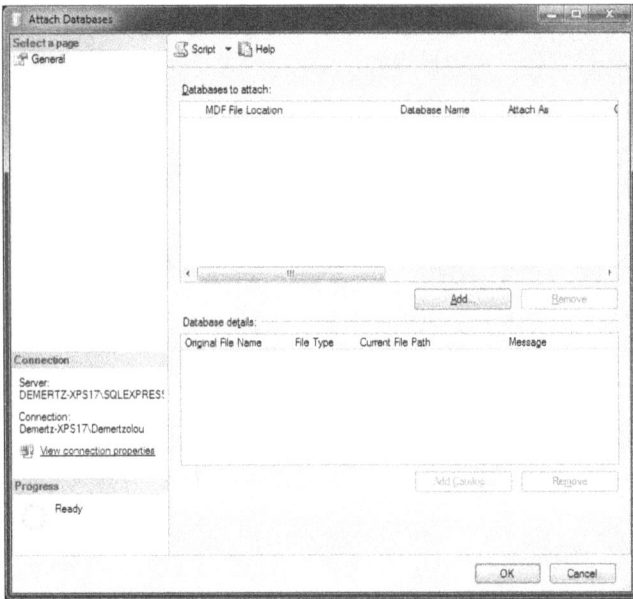

4. Click **Add**. The following screen will come up. Click on the SQLServer2012_TSQL.mdf database file to select it and then click **OK**.

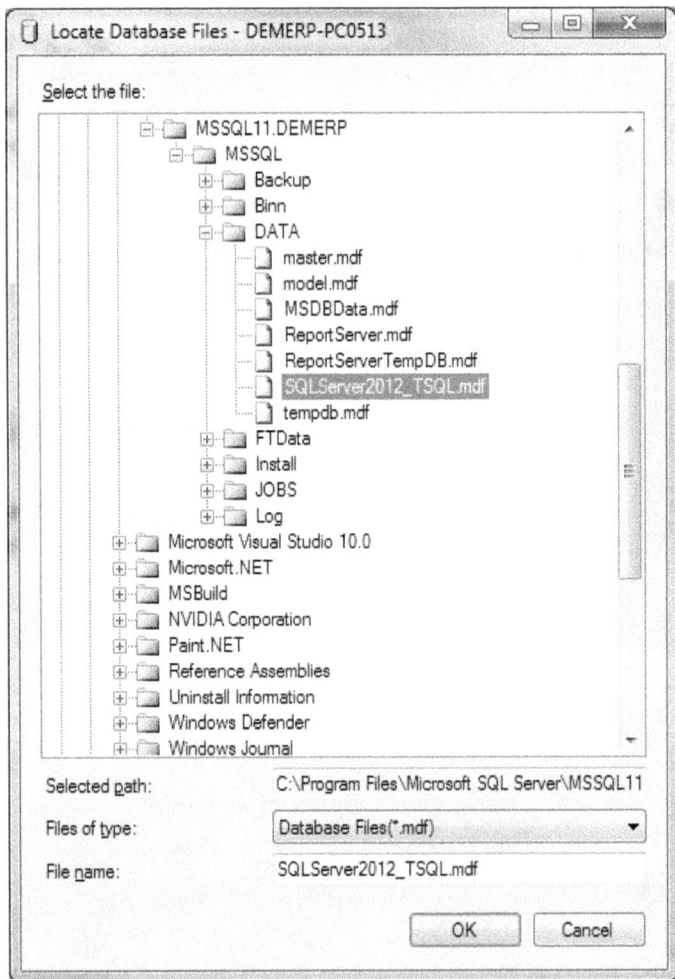

5. At this point your screen should look like this:

xxii

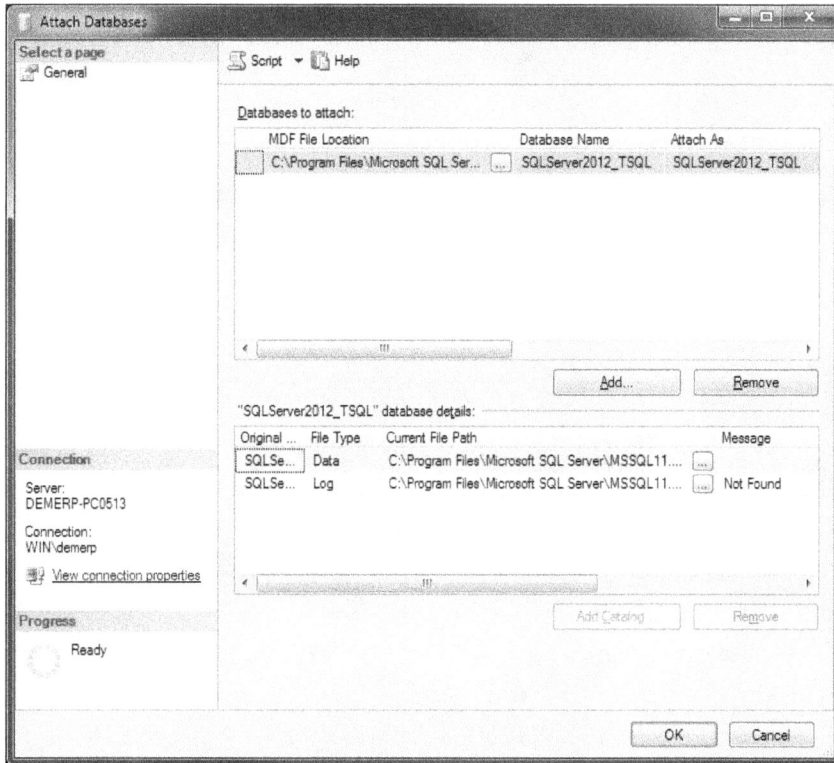

6. Select the the log file as shown in the screen below and and click "Remove".

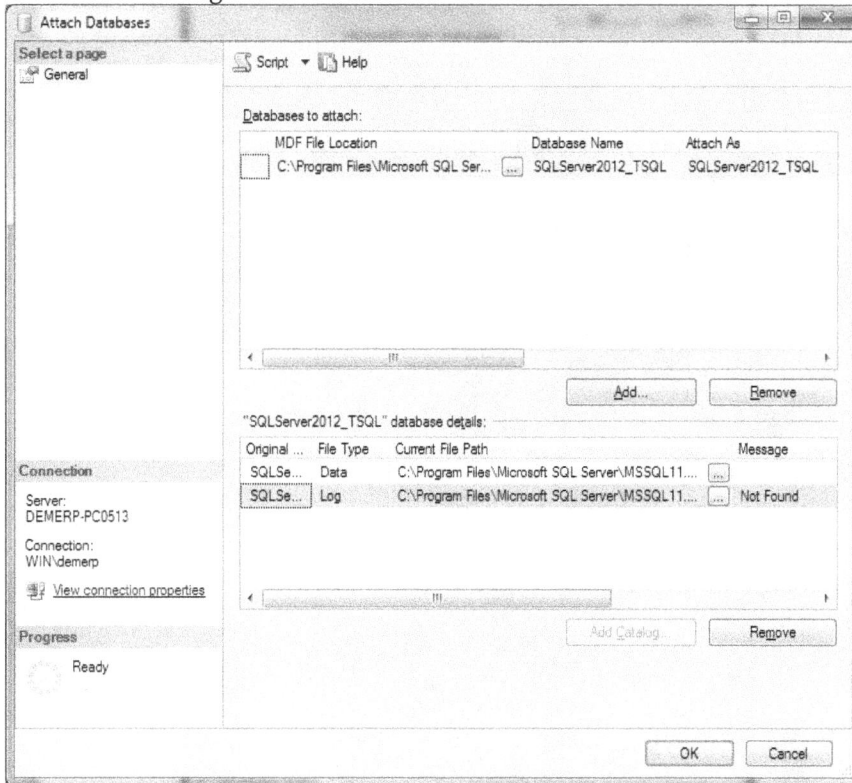

7. Your screen should now look like the one below.   Click OK again to attach the database.

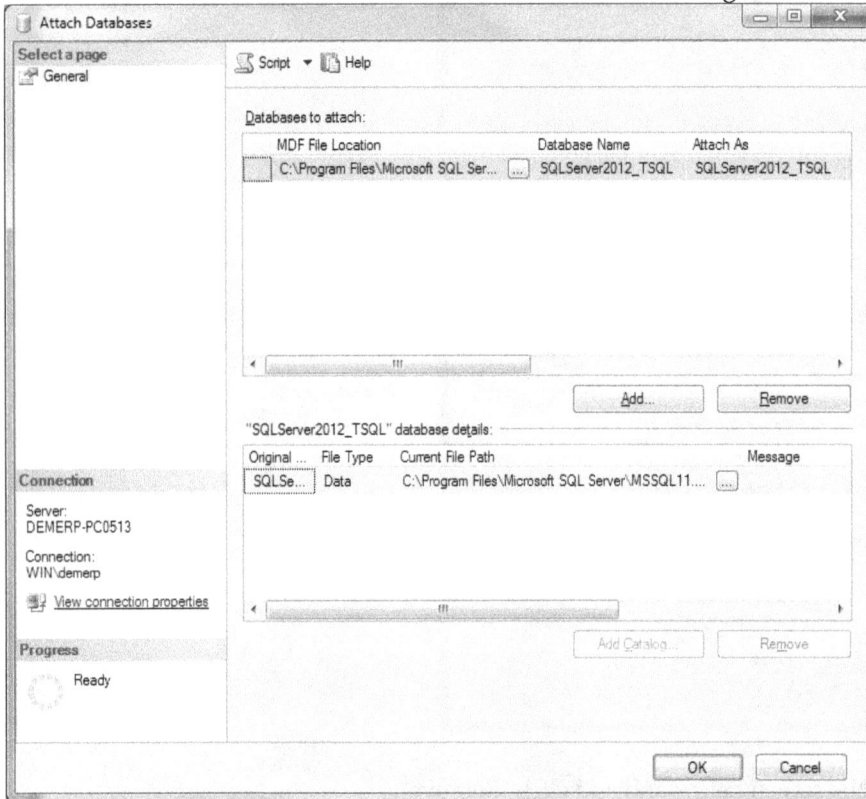

8. Your database structure should now look like the one below: Your database is ready for use.

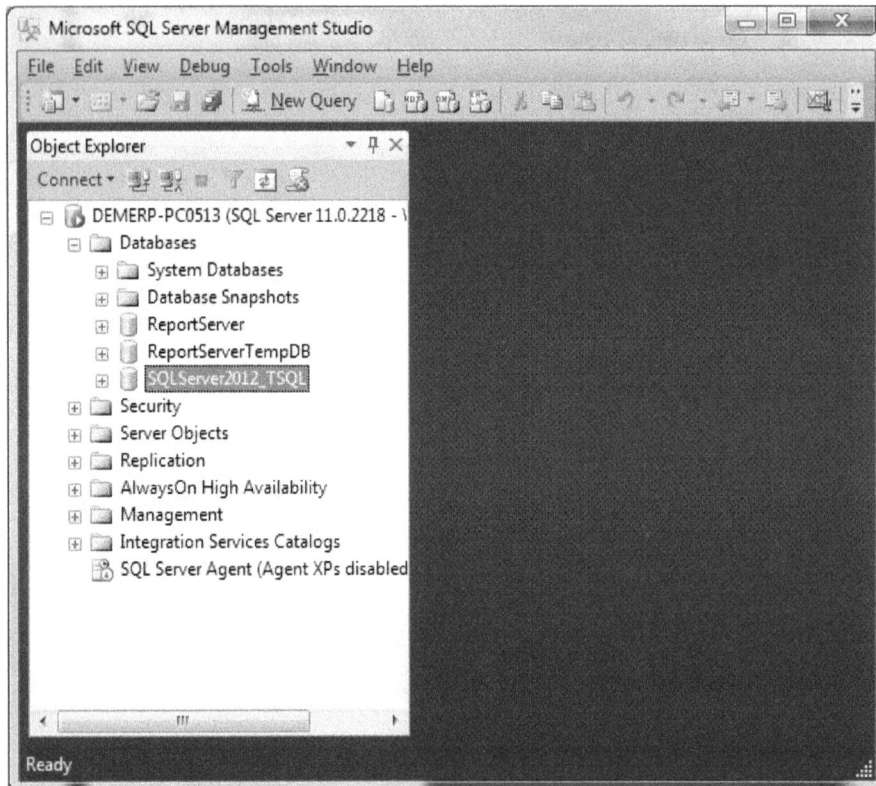

5. How to start working with the book examples

In the SQL Server Management Studio environment click on the button "New Query" on the toolbar or enter Ctrl-N. This will create a new query window in which you can run all the examples of this book. Make sure that the database you are working on is the "SQL Server2012_TSQL" one as it is shown in the "available databases" textbox in the image below.

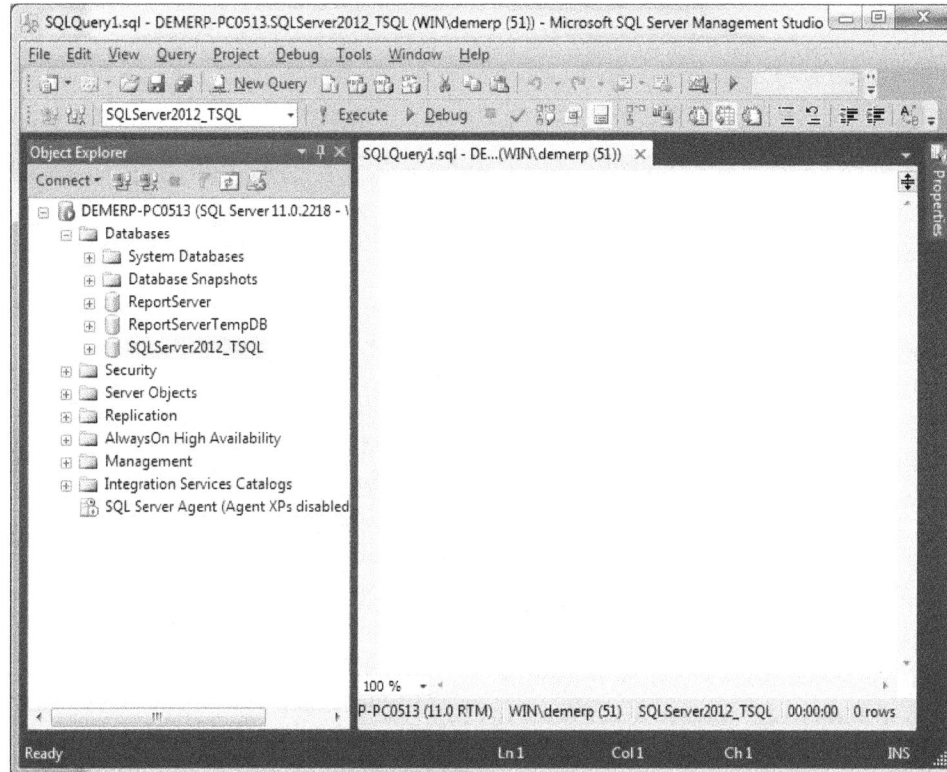

CHAPTER 1
SQL FOUNDATION FOR BUSINESS

6. The origins of SQL

SQL stands for Structured Query Language and it is the standard language for manipulating relational databases. It was developed by IBM in the mid-seventies and at that point it was named SEQUEL standing for Standard English Query Language.

SQL is based on the Relational Database Model officially defined in June 1970 by E. F. Codd in his amazing paper "A Relational Model of Data for Large Shared Data Banks." In his article Dr. Codd explained the need for a new relational model and language for maximum independence from specific programs and system platforms. To this end the goal set more than 40 years ago has been achieved and SQL is used in a multitude of platforms and database servers.

IBM continued its work on SQL throughout the 1970s and introduced SQL/DS in 1981, and DB2 in 1983. The problem was that Oracle was successful in releasing a relational RDBMS in 1979 beating IBM in its own game by two years. Sybase and Microsoft formed a partnership to produce their own RDBMS and they worked together up until version 4 of their product. After that, Sybase and Microsoft continued to produce their own databases with Sybase working on their SYSTEM products and Microsoft on their SQL Server versions. Today all commercial vendors face severe competition from open source relational databases like Postgress SQL.

> **A tribute to Dr. Codd**
>
> Dr. Codd joined IBM in 1949 and he worked on numerous projects such the logical design of computers and operating systems. He will be remembered for his creation and work on the relational model of databases in 1970 and relational algebra in 1972. Dr. Codd continued his work on SQL and in 1981 received the extremely prestigious Turing Award for his work on database systems. He is considered the father of modern relational databases.

SQL is endorsed by the American National Standards Institute (http://www.ansi.org), and is used by MS SQL Server, dBase for Windows, Paradox, MS Access, INGRES, SYBASE, Oracle, IBM DB2, and other database software. The American National Standards Institute has the role of maintaining SQL, and periodically publishes update versions of the SQL standard. All major database systems comply with the ANSI standards such as SQL-89 and SQL-92 but the constructs and expressions used in a particular environment might be somewhat different because many of the RDBMS were developed prior to standardization and also commercial vendors introduce proprietary features to gain a competitive edge.

7. What is SQL

SQL is a fourth generation, non-procedural computer programming language. By non-procedural we mean that we are looking at the end result and not the sequence of lines of code. In traditional programming, lines of code execute in sequence, one after the other, to produce the end result. In SQL, a section of code at the end of the SQL statement might execute before a section of code in the beginning of the SQL statement.

The next important characteristic of SQL is that it works to manipulate relational database management systems (RDBMS). These RDBMSs like IBM DB2, Oracle, MS SQL Server, and PostgressSQL, usually constitute the data layer of the corporation's transaction processing system or at least that should be the case. These transactional databases should be highly normalized which means they consist of a large number of entities with fewer attributes in them or in other words, they consist of many tables with fewer fields in them. It is the job of SQL to manipulate data from multiple tables at the same time. However, in today's working environment transaction processing systems often consist of several relational databases and a host of other heterogeneous data sources (text files, hierarchical files, spreadsheets, etc.) which result in vast amounts of inefficiency for the corporation.

8. SQL in its role as Data Definition Language (DDL)

These SQL statements are further divided into two main categories: In the first category, we have SQL statements we use to create database objects such as tables, indexes, and relationships. In this case we call the SQL code Data Definition Language (DDL). The DDL language supports only three statements which are the CREATE, ALTER, and DROP statements. The ability to use SQL to create database objects does not represent just one additional way to work with a table. By using pure SQL statements, we can understand the inner structure of the objects we are creating. We can also use our knowledge of SQL to enter the realm of other databases like PostgresSQL or MySQL to create objects independent of any design interface, and we can create and delete temporary objects on the fly.

The following is an example of a DDL statement which we use to create a new table with CustomerID as its primary key and two text fields for storing the customer's first and last name.

```
CREATE TABLE TempCustomer
(
CustomerID int Identity(1,1) Primary key,
LastName varchar(50),
FirstName varchar(50)
)
```

The following SQL DDL statement will alter the structure of the existing table "TempCustomer" and add one more field called "city". Notice how we can define the data type of the field we are adding as well as its length.

```
ALTER TABLE TempCustomer
ADD City varchar(25)
```

Finally, we can delete the table "TempCustomer" by using the DROP DDL statement:

```
DROP TABLE TempCustomer
```

Now, one might question the practicality of learning how to work with DDL statements since we can do all the above by using the design interface. The fact is we use DDL in many more circumstances than for basic database tasks. Specifically, we use DDL within server side pages in web servers like java server pages or active server pages.net or php to add, delete, and modify tables in the back-end database. The same is true for applications developed with hard-coded languages like C++, Java, or C#. In addition, we use SQL DDL a lot in extraction, transformation, and loading (ETL) packages to move data from one database to another or from a relational database to a data warehouse. Consequently, SQL DDL is a tool that must exist in the belt of any SQL professional.

an order is a transaction. Processing payment for an order is a transaction. All these transactions might aggregate to hundreds or thousands or even hundreds of thousands of transactions every day. That is, we have a lot of data generated every day in various parts of the corporation or more specifically in multiple functional areas such as accounting, sales, human resources, and others. This is the fragmented data we need to convert to information and direct it to the tactical and strategic levels for decision. This is exactly the place where SQL comes in to help us generate this data. We also, use SQL to aggregate, summarize, group by, add, update, and subtract data to generate information.

Figure 1: Organizational Hierarchical Levels

In Figure 2, we present a real life corporate transaction system. As you can see, this particular company has a functional design and is divided in four departments: Finance/Accounting, Sales/Marketing, Human Resources, and Production. We also notice that the transactional/operational system has two layers: an application layer and a data layer. The application layer consists of the actual front-end applications which corporate employees use to process transactions. A front-end application is usually made up by a number of forms that staff is using to enter, edit, delete, and update data. This front-end is also commonly called the user interface. Notice an additional couple of issues: The various applications do not communicate with each other among departments. Even within the department itself, the departmental units are using different applications. For instance, in the Finance/Accounting department, the accounts receivable, accounts payable, and investment management are all using different applications. This has as a result increased communication times among departments and units which in turn lead to higher cycle times for order processing, fulfillment, accounting debits/credits, and other corporate transactions.

These higher cycle times lead to increased transactional costs and thus in higher operating expenses and a corresponding decrease in our operating margin. Higher operating expenses result in increased risk for the corporation which means that in difficult times we will be the ones to have trouble first. To explain it further, the operational cost of a corporation is not directly related to production. This means that we will incur operational cost indirectly of the level of business turnover we have. In times of booming business this is not a problem because the added operational cost we experience becomes lower by unit of output. In times of recession however, that operational cost increases by unit of output and its weight shows in full.

It is exactly in these repressed business and economic conditions that managers make their biggest mistakes as well. Instead of trying to make the corporation more efficient, that is, look at cycle times, transactional cost, operating expenses, and risk, they look at the usual culprit: the employee of the corporation. This trend needs to stop at some point and one of the major ways to do it is for management to understand how data processing, analysis, and dissemination affect their businesses. That is why SQL represents an important technology for our business. We will see how this importance is exhibited when we discuss the data layer of the corporate transaction system.

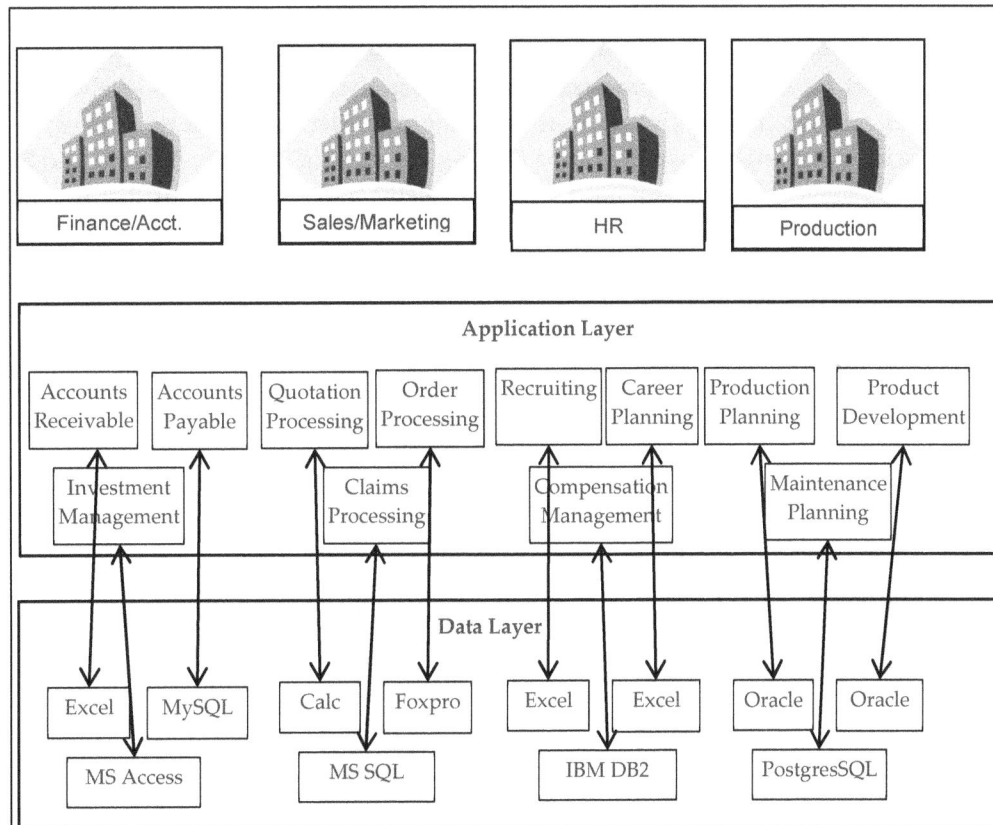

Figure 2: Corporate Transaction Processing System

The second layer we see in Figure 2 is the data layer of the corporation. In the vast majority of cases in the real business world, the corporate data layer consists of many heterogeneous data sources. In theory, in books, and in ERP (Enterprise Resource Planning) package pitches from marketing people an idealized solution is offered where the data layer consists of a single RDBMS (Relational Database Management System). This is very far from the truth and reality. What actually happens is what you see in Figure 2 where not only departments but also individual units within departments use different data sources. For instance, the Career Planning and Compensation Management units in Human Resources use different and separate data sources. Career Planning is using Excel to store and process its data while Compensation Management is using an IBM DB2 relational database and God help the one who will try to get data from the other or will try to integrate the applications or data sources from multiple departments. It is possible, but get ready for the ensuing political conflict that will lead to a quagmire and finally a compromise to a higher or lesser degree. The real situation for us at this point is that for the data layer of the corporate transaction system we have a suite of multiple and heterogeneous data sources. This of course leads to inefficient data exchange. However, what is inefficient? By inefficient we mean we need more time to exchange data and we are more prone to mistakes when we actually do the exchange. This practically means increased cycle times and increased transactional cost which will again lead to high operating costs for the corporation with direct reductions of the operating margin and net profits as well as an increase of perceived risk.

Now, the question is how can we use SQL in the corporation to help in the above situations? We will list specific situations here from the real world on how SQL is actually used throughout the hierarchical levels of the corporation. In addition, we will explore the possibilities of using SQL to get data from other entities in the external environment of the company like corporate customers, suppliers, partners, distributors, and the

the SQL developer will use calculated fields, concatenated fields, string and date functions, the group by clause, pivoting, union operators, aggregate functions, parameter queries, and other techniques to convert pieces of data to information that makes sense and is needed by the strategic and tactical levels of the corporation. This information is usually provided in the form of web based reports for larger corporations, or at least corporations that have the know-how to work with web servers. If not, usually a reporting capability is provided by the database software itself. No matter what the reporting platform is, the SQL professional has a central role in the provision of intelligence to the corporation and in many occasions this is a full time job with important responsibilities for the medium and long term planning of the company.

14. SQL for business processes – Stored Procedures

The most important reason to learn how to use stored procedures is because they represent the ultimate implementation of SQL statements. Corporate transaction processing systems process complex business transactions and for this purpose simple SELECT, INSERT, UPDATE, and DELETE SQL statements are not always enough. Often, we need to incorporate in the SQL code conditional processing (IF THEN statements) to process transactions according to the business rules given to us, use dynamic parameters within the SQL code, provide dynamic output according to the input data, automatically update history tables based on user interaction, send emails to administrators and managers, and communicate with other business databases within or outside the organization. The answer to the above are stored procedures, an essential piece in the knowledge portfolio of a SQL professional. Let us explore some examples:

Simple stored procedure

First of all, stored procedures can be simple SQL statements like the simple SELECT statement we see in this example. Some database administrators will use exclusively stored procedures to process select statements instead of views because they are compiled statements and run faster than a simple query. For this example, let us suppose we need a list of customers sorted by city. You see from the code that there is not much difference than writing SQL statements. Only the CREATE PROCEDURE in the beginning indicates that this is something different from a simple SELECT statement.

Code:
```
CREATE PROCEDURE sp_CustomersByCity
AS
SELECT FirstName, LastName, Address, City
FROM  Customers
ORDER BY City
```

Execute:
```
execute sp_CustomersByCity
```

Stored procedure with a parameter

Second, we said that stored procedures accept parameters. Parameters can be simple or complex according to our business logic and the way we want to process transactions (like checking credit, checking inventory quantities, etc.). Also, parameters can be passed around from other applications whether local or remote. Let's see how we pass the city as a parameter in the stored procedure we previously wrote:

Code:
```
CREATE PROCEDURE sp_CustomersByCityParam
@city varchar(30)
AS
SELECT FirstName, LastName, Address, City
```

FROM   Customers
WHERE City = @City

Execute:
execute sp_CustomersByCityParam @city = 'New York'

Please see chapter 31 where you can find multiple examples of stored procedures with control flow, error handling, and conditional processing.

15. SQL for automation – Triggers

Triggers are special types of stored procedures that execute automatically when UPDATE, INSERT, or DELETE statements are issued against a table or view. The main characteristic of triggers is that they fire automatically. That is, the SQL statement contained in the trigger will fire automatically when an insert, update, or delete is issued for the table. For example, when an order is deleted from the orders table, we can use triggers to manage this deleted data in many different ways. First, we can use a trigger to move this deleted data to an archive table. Second, we can use a trigger to notify via email a system administrator that an order has been deleted from the orders table. Third, we can use a trigger to beep the sales representative that the customer called in and canceled the order. The main advantage is that the process is automated. In addition, triggers can be setup to fire on inserts, or on updates, or on deletes, or on any combination of these statements. For instance, we can setup a trigger that runs only on updates and another that runs on updates and deletes but not on inserts. This fact gives us great flexibility to manipulate data and channel it to the most appropriate destination for processing.

We can also use triggers to enforce processing rules coming from business requirements. For example, a simple but important business requirement is that the shipping date should be greater than the order date because it is impossible to ship orders which we have not taken. To force this business rule, we can use a trigger that will fire on inserts and updates and which will check to make sure that the shipping date is greater than the order date. Consequently, triggers help us enforce the business logic of the corporation within our relational database. An example of this scenario is the trigger below:

Code:
```
CREATE TRIGGER trg_TestShippedDate
On orders
After insert, update
As
if update
(shippeddate)
begin
print 'test shippeddate'
If exists (select * from inserted where shippeddate < orderdate)
begin
raiserror ('shipping date should be greater than order date', 0, 1)
rollback transaction
return
end
end
GO
```

Consequently, a SQL professional who knows what triggers are and how to write them will definitely position himself or herself better in the market from someone who only knows how to create simple views.

16. SQL and its relation to web server side pages technologies

Another area in which you will work as a SQL professional is the web. Specifically, you might be asked to participate in a team for the development of server side web pages like active server pages (asp), asp.net, java server pages (jsp), and hypertext preprocessor (php) pages. These pages contain code in languages like java script, vb script, vb.net, c#, and others. They also contain HTML code. However, in many cases they also contain SQL code used to communicate with back-end databases. In these cases, you might be called to write the SQL part of the page since web developers might not have the depth required to write complex SQL statements.

In Figure 5, you can see a scenario of a web site that contains multiple php pages. Specifically, there are four php pages: SubmitOrder.php, UpdateOrder.php, ReviewOrder.php, and DeleteOrder.php. These four pages constitute an application to which customers connect through the web to place and manage orders. Notice that each customer uses a dissimilar browser as the client to connect to the web site on the web server. The beauty of server side pages is that they are browser independent. Consequently, we do not need to worry about the browser used by the customer. In addition, the php pages connect to a database on the back-end database server. Now, in most occasions, the web server and the database server are different machines but it might be the case that both the web server software and the relational database server software are installed on the same machine. For our purposes, the fundamental point is that php pages use SQL to connect to back-end databases. This in turn means that a SQL professional can find his or her way to the world of web development and this is of the essence for our discussion since it constitutes an additional career path.

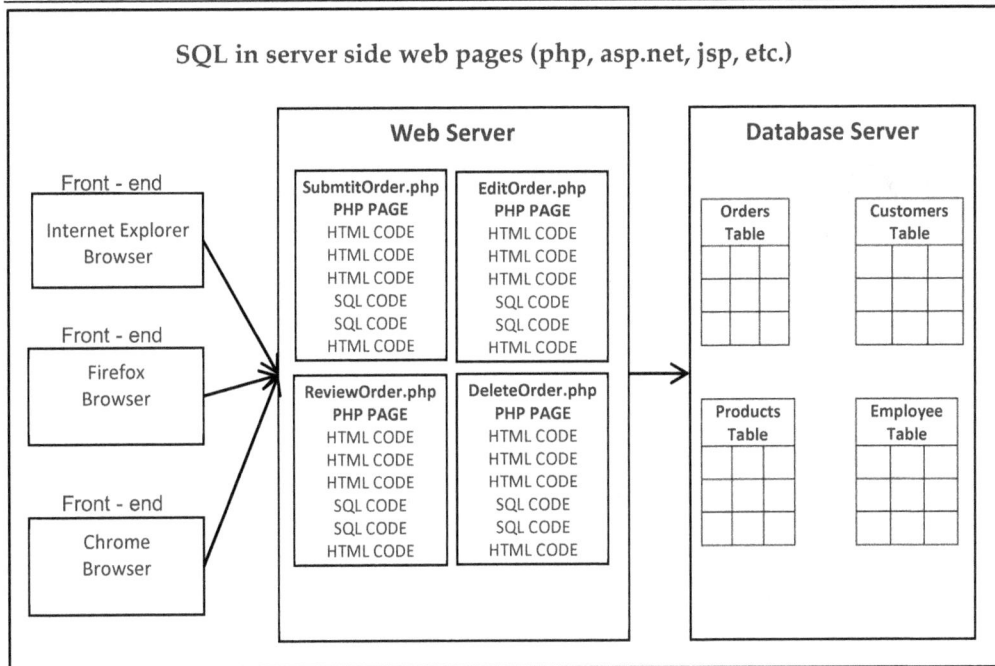

Figure 5: SQL in server side web pages

17. SQL to obtain data from entities in the external environment of the company

An additional area where you can work, shine, and show your true potential as a SQL professional is when connecting client databases like Access to server databases like MS SQL, Oracle, IBM DB2, and MySQL. Actually, you can connect desktop databases to any back-end database provided you can find and download the corresponding Open Database Connectivity Drivers (ODBC). Well, this is too technical already. Let us take a step back and first see why do we want to do this from a business point of view and second, what is in it for us, the SQL developers, so that our motivation stays high.

In today's business environment, when we do business with our customers, suppliers, distributors, and other entities, we practically buy or sell products or services. Those products or services have associated the so called "paperwork" which we need to process for every selling or purchasing transaction. This paperwork is what leads to the existence of the purchasing department, accounts payable, accounts receivable, and other places within the corporation where people go around with pieces of papers in their hands for the most part. Now, there are many ways to process this paperwork with direct consequences for the well-being of the company. For instance, let us consider the scenario in which we would like to re-order parts from our suppliers, a process we call replenishing. When we replenish our inventory we can communicate, i.e. transact with our supplier, in many different ways. First, we can call them and give our order on the phone. Second, we can send them a fax. Third, we can send them an email with an attached spreadsheet of what we need. Fourth, we can go to their online system and order the materials we need online, right away through the web. Fifth, we can have access to their databases through pre-defined queries so that we can look at the latest products, their descriptions, special pricing for us, and any other piece of information we might need. In this last case, we can also create reports for the tactical management of our company to look at before we make our purchase. We do not imply that the fifth method is always the best method to communicate with external entities but is the best from the four mentioned above. There are other methods to integrate corporate information systems well beyond the scope of this SQL book. However, the SQL developer can make a real difference in the efficiency of transaction processing if he or she has the knowledge to connect and manipulate external databases.

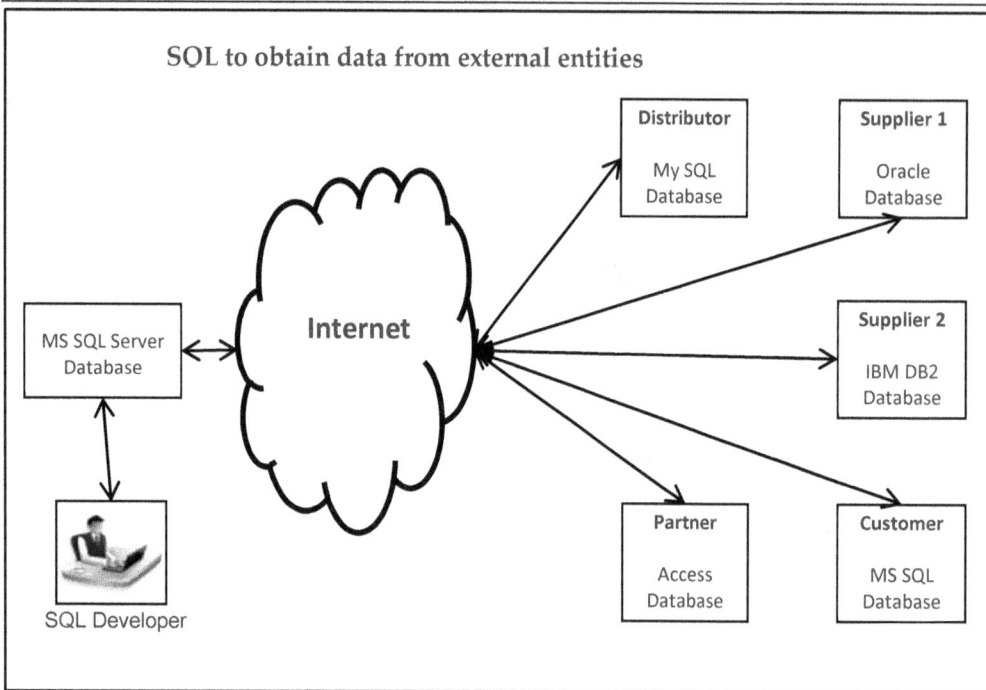

Figure 6: SQL to obtain data from external entities

What is the source of this corporate efficiency? The answer is reducing cycle times and transactional cost. It is one of the primary goals of every corporation to reduce transactional cost and cycle times. This is why banks went from tellers to ATMS and from ATMs to the web. The goal was to reduce transaction cost and they got it down to pennies per transaction. However, you need to have the know-how and the technology to do it. That is, you need to have access to database technology and know-how to work with it. Going back to our scenario, we would like to do replenishing directly from within the database and without involving any people who would call each other or exchange messages. Some problems might arise like if the sales person we try to reach is out on vacation, the fax machine is not working, the message went to the junk folder, there was a mistake in the order and a multitude of other things that can go wrong. All these situations lead to extended cycle times for replenishing that have multiple consequences all of which lead to increased costs. For example, we might need to keep more inventory which is costly, we lose a customer because we did not have the parts we needed on time, we re-ordered because someone typed in the wrong order amounts or wrong parts, and in general we make our corporation more expensive to operate.

By accessing our supplier databases and doing the work ourselves we avoid all the above and many more tricky situations. As we can see from Figure 6, we can use MS SQL Server to connect to the databases our customers, partners, and suppliers are using through the Internet. We can literally use the IP address of the database server of the external entity to connect through ODBC drivers or native data providers. ODBC is somewhat slower but nevertheless universal to use with any database and readily available for download through the web. Usually, the supplier or customer will not give us access to their whole database but have some views available for us to use with the appropriate security setup. From those basic views then, we can create our own queries and retrieve the data we need exactly the way we would like to retrieve it.

The requirement is that we know how to use ODBC and how above all to use SQL to retrieve the data we need and convert it to information that would be useful to our management. For these purposes a strong SQL developer is needed to work with multiple systems and since in this book we learn how to work with SQL which is the standard for all relational databases, it means that we will be able to write queries against any relational database management system without much difficulty. That is why it is imperative to know how to work with SQL and not just the design interface of MS SQL Server or any other database.

18. SQL and its relation to XML

The major business goal in this scenario is to outsource replenishing. That is, we want our suppliers to assume the cost of re-supplying us with inventory. Practically, we want to avoid devoting any human or financial resources to this process so that we can reduce our operational costs and decrease our replenishing cycles as well. At the same time the suppliers will be willing to do this since they will be selling more products. Incurring minimal cost for inventory replenishing sounds like an excellent idea but how can we achieve this in technical terms and what would be the role of the SQL developer in the process?

As you can see from figure 7, the developer is working with an MS SQL server database in which he will write queries that contain all the product related items for inventory purposes. Then, automation packages (ETL) will send the result of the SQL statements to XML files on the web server. For illustration purposes we named such a file Inventory.xml in figure 7. Today's database servers support the automated importing and exporting of XML data with easily set procedures. Then, the suppliers can access these XML files through the Internet. They check to see what we need from each product and they replenish our inventory without us getting involved in the process. The basic premise of this process is that it is repeatable. That is, every day, or every three days, or every week we replace the XML files on the web server so that the suppliers have access to all the latest data about the status of our inventory. Though the whole process can run manually once or twice a week we should strive to automate it given the flexibility we have by using today's advanced database software.

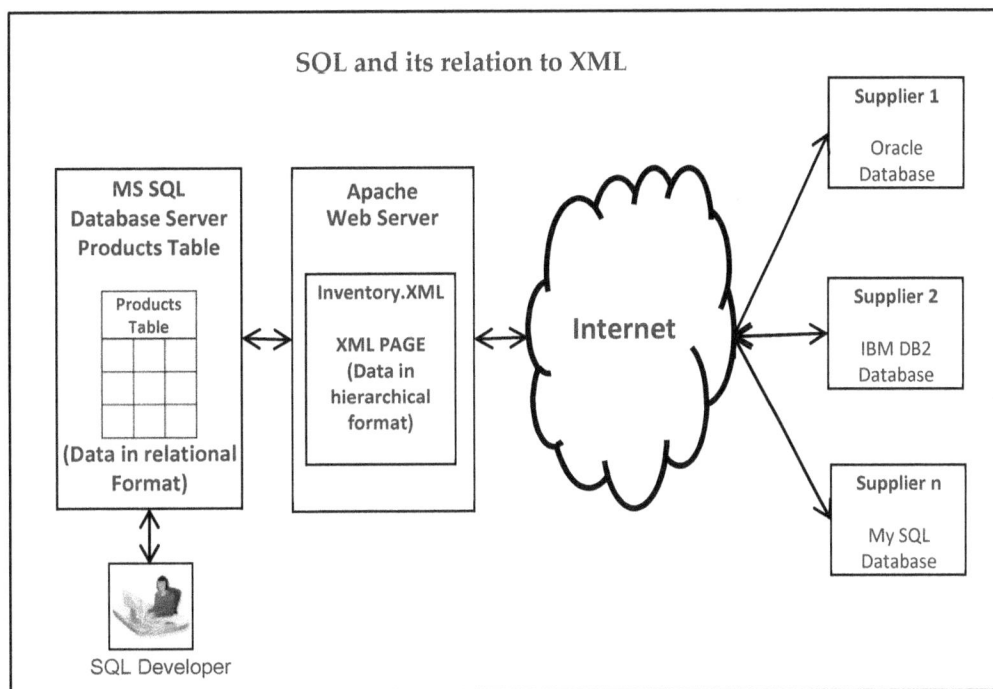

Figure 7: SQL and its relation to XML

On a more technical level, when we export data from a relational database to an XML file there are a couple of items we need to be aware of. First, databases follow the relational data model which means we have a set of related entities (tables) to store data. This for a business task of exchanging data is a problem since the data we need to send to our suppliers might be in four, five or even more related tables and there is no way to send those tables and their relationships across the web. Consequently, what we do is use SQL to get the data we need from those tables in a single view and then we export the result of this view to an XML file which follows the hierarchical data model. But what is an XML file? XML files are practically text documents containing elements. An element can be a book, an employee, a product etc. This single element contains sub-elements and these sub-elements contain additional elements down the hierarchy. Have you noticed the word hierarchy?

In figure 8, we see a simple XML file. Notice that this file contains information about two employees. In a relational database they would represent two records in the employee table. In this XML file we notice that we have a root element called <Employees> which contains two instances of the sub- element <Employee> or in other words information about two employees of ours. We also notice that in the sub-element <Employee> there are additional sub-elements like LastName, FirstName, Title, etc. We see that between the element tags we have the actual name, title, and address for each employee. Consequently, this single XML file contains both the data and the description of this data by means of its tags. When we receive a file like this, it is very easy to make sense of the data it contains. Consequently, when our suppliers connect to a file like this through the Internet, they can read it, they understand its meaning, import it into their database for processing, and finally send us the products we need to do our work with no or minimal cost to us.

```
<?xml version="1.0" encoding="UTF-8" ?>
<Employees>
  <Employee>
  <LastName>Smith</LastName>
  <FirstName>George</FirstName>
  <Title>Sales Representative</Title>
  <Address>507 - 20th Ave. E. Apt. 2A</Address>
  <City>Seattle</City>
  <Region>WA</Region>
  <PostalCode>98122</PostalCode>
  <Country>USA</Country>
</Employee>
  <Employee>
  <LastName>Fuller</LastName>
  <FirstName>Andrew</FirstName>
  <Title>Vice President, Sales</Title>
  <Address>908 W. Capital Way</Address>
  <City>Tacoma</City>
  <Region>WA</Region>
  <PostalCode>98401</PostalCode>
  <Country>USA</Country>
  </Employee>
</Employees>
```

Figure 8: Sample XML file

19. SQL and its relation to ETL

Another area with lots of opportunity and work potential for the SQL developer is the area of extraction, transformation, and loading of data (ETL). This area has a lot of potential for work or consulting since all corporations need to move data for transaction processing or for business intelligence. We can define ETL as the general process of extracting data from one or more data sources, transforming this data to appropriate formats and have the ability to load it in one or more data destinations. An ETL process might involve extracting data from a transaction processing system and load this data to a data warehouse (see figure 9). This is the most common scenario for which ETL is known but it is not the only one. ETL might involve the exchange of data between two transaction processing databases, an Excel file to an XML file, or an XML file to a data warehouse. The important point is that ETL is a process that needs careful consideration in any data transfer scenario.

One of the major differences between ad hoc data moves and rigorous ETL processes is the notion of the timing of data exchanges. A simple import of data from an Excel spreadsheet to a SQL Server database can hardly be described as an ETL process but rather as a data export procedure. However, when we have a process in place that takes data from ten heterogeneous data sources and processes any transformations automatically with workflow and error checking support, and it does this every week, every day, or even every hour, or based on a trigger event, then we can say we have an ETL process in place.

Data sources might be homogeneous or heterogeneous in nature. For example, let us suppose that we have an ETL process in place which takes data from ten data sources. These data sources are two Oracle databases, one Access database, one MySQL database, three XML files, an Excel spreadsheet, two text files, and an ODBC connection to our own DB2 database system. The two Oracle databases are considered to be homogeneous data sources but an XML file and the ODBC connection to IBM DB2 are considered to be heterogeneous data sources. In a data warehouse scenario we will usually have to work with a number of heterogeneous data sources so that we can have all the data needed for advanced business analytics.

Such a scenario is shown in figure 9, where we get data from multiple heterogeneous data sources from our suppliers, partners, and our own transaction processing system. The goal is to integrate all this data into a data warehouse which will function as the basis of our business intelligence system. A data warehouse is practically a historical data repository, or in other words, a repository of completed transactions. We will use this data to come up with information by using tools such as Data Mining, Online Analytical Processing (OLAP), and Multi-dimensional Expressions (MDX).

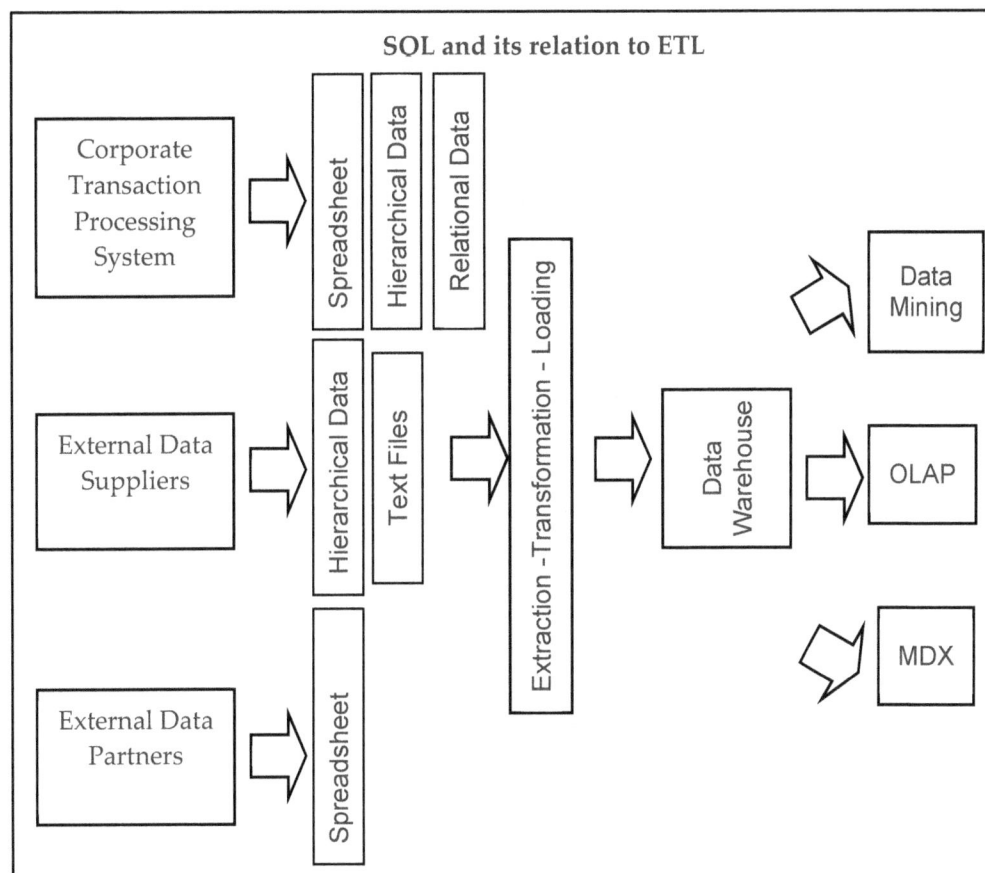

Figure 9: SQL and its relation to ETL

The job of the SQL developer is to provide his or her expertise in designing, developing and implementing the ETL packages. He or she needs to be able to connect to data sources (databases or others), write SQL code, develop queries, concatenate fields, write functions to alter existing data, convert data from text to numeric or other formats, write criteria, and a host of additional tasks that require real command of the SQL language. This is ongoing work as we might have tens or even hundreds of ETL packages setup. Moreover, ETL packages are repetitive and they need editing since business conditions change. For instance, we might need to include a new supplier, delete a partner, include one more data source, delete a field, change scrubbing rules, and a myriad of other tasks. We see at this point how important the role of the SQL developer becomes at any level of the company.

CHAPTER 1 DISCUSSION QUESTIONS

1. Is SQL a procedural or non-procedural language?
2. Is SQL working with relational or hierarchical databases?
3. What is the purpose of the SQL Data Definition Language?
4. Can you give some examples of DDL statements?
5. Why do we need to know how to work with DDL statements?
6. What is the purpose of the SQL Data Manipulation Language (DML)?
7. What are the main SQL DML statements?
8. Is SQL a language associated with a particular database product or vendor?
9. At what corporate level do we use SQL to insert, edit, and delete data?
10. Why do the strategic and tactical corporate levels need information?
11. What are some problems with the heterogeneous data layer in the corporate transaction processing system?
12. Can you give some specific examples of how we use SQL to generate information?
13. What are stored procedures and what is their role in a database?
14. What is the role of the SQL professional in web development?
15. What are triggers and what is their function in databases?
16. What is the difference between relational and hierarchical data?
17. Why do we want to export relational data in hierarchical (XML) format?
18. What is the role of extraction, transformation, and loading (ETL) packages in the corporation?
19. Can the SQL developer help with the development of ETL packages?
20. What is the role of SQL in the reduction of the overall transactional cost of the corporation?

CHAPTER 2
CREATE, EDIT, AND DELETE TABLES USING SQL

In this chapter, we will work with three DDL statements: CREATE TABLE, ALTER TABLE, and DROP TABLE. We use the CREATE statement to create new tables, the ALTER statement to modify existing ones, and the DROP statement to delete existing tables. The basic structures of the three statements appear below:

```
CREATE TABLE "tablename"
(
fieldname1 datatype (size),
fieldname2 datatype (size),
fieldname3 datatype (size)
)
```

```
ALTER TABLE "tablename"
[ADD] [ALTER] [DROP] COLUMN fieldname datatype(size)
```

```
DROP TABLE "tablename"
```

20. Create a table and define its primary key
Create a customer table, and assign CustomerID as the primary key
Discussion:
In this scenario, we create a table with a primary key of data type "int" and two simple text fields. Notice the primary key image on the left of the CustomerID field in the table design view in the picture below:

Code:
```
CREATE TABLE Customer1
(
CustomerID int Primary key,
LastName varchar(50),
FirstName varchar(50)
)
```

Result:

	Column Name	Data Type	Allow Nulls
🔑	CustomerID	int	☐
	LastName	varchar(50)	☑
	FirstName	varchar(50)	☑

21. Create a table defining the primary key as identity

Discussion:

Now, we create a table where the primary key value is entered automatically by the database, starts from the value one and increases by one. Check the image below to see the effects of the code on the properties of the table.

Code:

```
CREATE TABLE Customer2 (
[CustomerID] int  identity (1,1) Primary key ,
[LastName] varchar(50),
[FirstName] varchar(50))
```

Result:

Column Name	Data Type	Allow Nulls
CustomerID	int	☐
LastName	varchar(50)	☑
FirstName	varchar(50)	☑

Column Properties

Has Non-SQL Server Subscriber	No
Identity Specification	Yes
(Is Identity)	Yes
Identity Increment	1
Identity Seed	1

22. Create table with a field that does not accept nulls

Discussion:

On some occasions, we might want to create a table with a field that will not accept null values. Null values are different from zero-length strings or zeros (check chapter 23 for a full discussion of null values). To avoid nulls for a field, we simply make the field required. In other words, we force users to enter a value, or they will not be able to save the record in the database. We can do this with the following code, which makes the lastname field required.

Code:

```
CREATE TABLE Customer3 (
[CustomerID] int  identity (1,1) Primary key ,
[LastName] varchar(50) NOT NULL,
[FirstName] varchar(50),
[Address] varchar(50))
```

Result:

Column Name	Data Type	Allow Nulls
CustomerID	int	☐
LastName	varchar(50)	☐
FirstName	varchar(50)	☑
Address	varchar(50)	☑

23. Create a table using SQL, and populate it with data from another table

Discussion:

In some of our work tasks, we do not just need to create a table. We also need to put some data in it on the fly. Creating a table and populating it on the fly is possible using the SELECT INTO statement in SQL Server 2012. In this example, we create a table and we populate it with data from the customers table.

Code:

```
SELECT * INTO Customer4
FROM customers
```

Result:

The table customer4 has been created and populated with the records from the customers table. Of course, you can modify the SQL statement above to move specific fields and records as you can see in the next example.

24. Create a table using SQL, and populate it with a subset of data from another table

Discussion:

In this example, we create the table customer5 and we populate it with only three fields and 14 records from the customers table.

Code:

```
SELECT lastname, firstname, address INTO Customer5
FROM customers
WHERE city = 'Boston'
```

Result:

The table customer5 has been created and populated with fourteen records from the customers table.

25. ALTER table: add a field

Add a city field in the customer table

Discussion:

At some point we will need to modify the design of existing tables instead of creating new ones. We can modify table designs almost at will using pure SQL. In this example, we add the city field to the customer1 table. The field we add by default will allow null values.

Code:

```
ALTER TABLE Customer1
```

CREATE, EDIT, AND DELETE TABLES

ADD City varchar(50)

Result:

	Column Name	Data Type	Allow Nulls
🔑	CustomerID	int	☐
	LastName	varchar(50)	☑
	FirstName	varchar(50)	☑
	City	varchar(50)	☑

or if we would like to add a required field:

ALTER TABLE Customer1
ADD State char (2) NOT NULL

Result:

	Column Name	Data Type	Allow Nulls
🔑	CustomerID	int	☐
	LastName	varchar(50)	☑
	FirstName	varchar(50)	☑
	City	varchar(50)	☑
	State	char(2)	☐

26. ALTER table: add multiple fields
Add zip, phone, and fax fields in the customer table
Discussion:
In this example, we add three fields at once in the Customer1 table.

Code:
ALTER TABLE Customer1
ADD
Zip varchar (5),
Phone varchar (12),
Fax varchar (12)

Result:

Column Name	Data Type	Allow Nulls
🔑 CustomerID	int	☐
LastName	varchar(50)	☑
FirstName	varchar(50)	☑
City	varchar(50)	☑
State	char(2)	☐
Zip	varchar(5)	☑
Phone	varchar(12)	☑
Fax	varchar(12)	☑

27. ALTER table: delete a column

Delete the fax field from the customer table

Discussion:

We can easily delete a field from a table using the ALTER and DROP statements in combination. For instance, in this case, we delete the "city" field from the customer1 table.

Code:
```
ALTER TABLE Customer1
DROP COLUMN Fax
```

Result:

The column fax has been deleted from the table

28. ALTER table: delete multiple columns

Delete the zip and phone fields from the customer table

Discussion:

In this example we delete multiple fields at once.

Code:
```
ALTER TABLE Customer1
DROP COLUMN
Zip, Phone
```

Result:

The columns zip and phone have been deleted from the table

29. ALTER table: modify the size of an existing column

Change the size of the lastname field from 50 to 80 characters

Discussion:

In this example, we modify the size of the lastname field from 50 to 80 characters. Using the ALTER COLUMN statement we can also change the data type or the name of the field.

Code:

ALTER TABLE Customer1
ALTER COLUMN LastName varchar(80)

Result:

Column Name	Data Type	Allow Nulls
⚷ CustomerID	int	☐
LastName	varchar(80)	☑
FirstName	varchar(50)	☑
City	varchar(50)	☑
State	char(2)	☐

30. Delete Table

Delete the table customer1 from the database

Discussion:

We can use SQL to delete tables using the DROP statement. In this example, we delete the customer1 table. We must pay attention, however, when we delete tables using the DROP statement because there is no warning or undo action for it. The table will be deleted permanently from the database.

Code:

DROP TABLE Customer1

Result:

The table customer1 has been deleted from the database.

CHAPTER 2 DISCUSSION QUESTIONS

1. What type of SQL do we use when we create tables? DDL or DML?
2. What DDL keyword do we use to create a new table?
3. Can we use DDL to change the structure of an existing table? What is the keyword used?
4. Can we create and populate a table using a single statement? Which one is it?
5. What statement do we use to delete a table?
6. What keyword do we use to define a field as the primary key?
7. What keyword do we use to define a field as an auto increment?
8. For an auto increment field how do we define the seed value and the increment value in the DDL statement?
9. What is the keyword we use so that a field does not accept null values?
10. How do we use DDL to change the size of an existing field?

CHAPTER 2 HANDS-ON EXERCISES

Chapter 2 Case 1

Start SQL Server Management Studio. For each of the questions in this case you need to create a new query (Ctrl-N) and name it as per the instructions in each question. Submit your work to your instructor as one text file that contains all SQL statements or as per your instructor's directions.

1. Create a new table with the fields: ProductName varchar(30), ProductPrice (smallmoney), UnitsInStock (int), and ReorderLevel (int). Name the table Products21. Save the query you are using to create the table as Chapter02_Case1_Q1. Open the table in design view to see its structure.

   Your result should look like:

Column Name	Data Type	Allow Nulls
ProductName	varchar(30)	☑
ProductPrice	smallmoney	☑
UnitsInStock	int	☑
ReorderLevel	int	☑

2. Create a new table with the fields: ProductID (int) primary key, ProductName nvarchar(30), ProductPrice (smallmoney), UnitsInStock (int), and ReorderLevel (int). Name the table Products22. Save the query you are using to create the table as Chapter02_Case1_Q2. Open the table in design view to see its structure.

CREATE, EDIT, AND DELETE TABLES

Your result should look like:

Column Name	Data Type	Allow Nulls
🔑 ProductID	int	☐
ProductName	nvarchar(30)	☑
ProductPrice	smallmoney	☑
UnitsInStock	int	☑
ReorderLevel	int	☑

3. Create a new table with the fields: ProductID (primary key and identity with seed at 1 and increment at 1) ProductName nvarchar (30), ProductPrice (smallmoney), UnitsInStock (int), and ReorderLevel (int). Name the table Products23. Save the query you are using to create the table as Chapter02_Case1_Q3. Open the table in design view to see its structure.

Your result should look like:

Column Name	Data Type	Allow Nulls
🔑 ProductID	int	☐
ProductName	nvarchar(30)	☑
ProductPrice	smallmoney	☑
UnitsInStock	int	☑
ReorderLevel	int	☑

4. Create a new table that matches the structure of the products table. Populate the new table with all the data from the Products table in one step. Name the new table Products24. Save the query you are using to create the table as Chapter02_Case1_Q4. Open the table in design view to see its structure.

Your result should look like:

Column Name	Data Type	Allow Nulls
ProductID	int	☐
ProductName	varchar(100)	☑
SupplierID	int	☑
QuantityPerUnit	float	☑
ProductUnitPrice	money	☑
UnitsInStock	smallint	☑
UnitsOnOrder	smallint	☑
ReorderLevel	float	☑
SKU	nvarchar(255)	☑
Active	bit	☑

5. Delete the field UnitsOnOrder from the Products24 table. Save the query you are using as Chapter02_Case1_Q5. Open the table in design view to see its structure.

Your result should look like:

Column Name	Data Type	Allow Nulls
ProductID	int	☐
ProductName	varchar(100)	☑
SupplierID	int	☑
QuantityPerUnit	float	☑
ProductUnitPrice	money	☑
UnitsInStock	smallint	☑
ReorderLevel	float	☑
SKU	nvarchar(255)	☑
Active	bit	☑

Chapter 2 Case 2

Start SQL Server Management Studio. For each of the questions in this case you need to create a new query (Ctrl-N) and name it as per the instructions in each question. Submit your work to your instructor as one text file that contains all SQL statements or as per your instructor's directions.

1. Create a new table that matches the structure of the customers table. However, it should contain only customers from Florida. Name the table Customers22. Assign the CustomerID field as the PK of the table. Save the query as Chapter02_Case2_Q1. Open the table in design view to see its structure.

Your result should look like:

Column Name	Data Type	Allow Nulls
CustomerID	int	☐
FirstName	nvarchar(255)	☑
LastName	nvarchar(255)	☑
Address	nvarchar(255)	☑
City	nvarchar(255)	☑
State	nvarchar(255)	☑
Zip	nvarchar(255)	☑
Country	nvarchar(255)	☑

2. Add a new column named Address2 varchar (100) to the table Customers22. Save the query as Chapter02_Case2_Q2. Open the table in design view to see its structure.

Your result should look like:

Column Name	Data Type	Allow Nulls
CustomerID	int	☐
FirstName	nvarchar(255)	☑
LastName	nvarchar(255)	☑
Address	nvarchar(255)	☑
City	nvarchar(255)	☑
State	nvarchar(255)	☑
Zip	nvarchar(255)	☑
Country	nvarchar(255)	☑
Address2	varchar(100)	☑

3. Delete from the table Customers22 the column Country. Save the query as Chapter02_Case2_Q3. Open the table in design view to see its structure.

Your result should look like:

Column Name	Data Type	Allow Nulls
CustomerID	int	☐
FirstName	nvarchar(255)	☑
LastName	nvarchar(255)	☑
Address	nvarchar(255)	☑
City	nvarchar(255)	☑
State	nvarchar(255)	☑
Zip	nvarchar(255)	☑
Address2	varchar(100)	☑

4. In the table Customers22, modify the size of the column named Zip from 255 to 5 characters. Save the query as Chapter02_Case2_Q4. Open the table in design view to see its structure.

Your result should look like:

Column Name	Data Type	Allow Nulls
CustomerID	int	☐
FirstName	nvarchar(255)	☑
LastName	nvarchar(255)	☑
Address	nvarchar(255)	☑
City	nvarchar(255)	☑
State	nvarchar(255)	☑
Zip	varchar(5)	☑
Address2	varchar(100)	☑

5. Delete the table Customers22 from the database. Save the query as Chapter02_Case2_Q5.

    Result:

    The table has been deleted from the database

CHAPTER 3
CREATE, EDIT, AND DELETE INDEXES USING SQL

The use of indexes is another low-lighted topic in the world of databases. It is common knowledge that indexes are useful, but the guidelines to use them are obscure at best. In this chapter the goal is to highlight the importance of indexes in databases and as a result in business. First, indexes speed up search operations. They work great with the WHERE and ORDER BY clauses. However, they will slow down INSERT and UPDATE statements since every insert or update needs to be saved in both the table and the index. Third, they should be avoided in small tables with few records. They work better in large tables with thousands of records. Fourth, it is a good idea to create indexes for fields used a lot in search operations. If we have a web form that we use as the front-end in which we provide the users with the option to search customers by first and last name fields, then we need to index those two fields.

Clustered vs non clustered indexes
In SQL Server 2012 we distinguish between clustered and non-clustered indexes. We can have only one clustered index per table and this is usually the index on the primary key. The clustered index logically sorts the rows in the table according to their key values. Consequently, if we have primary key (PK) values 1, 2, 3, 4, etc. then the records in the table will be sorted based on those numeric values. Since records in the table can be sorted only in one order, in this case the primary key, this is why we have only one clustered index in the table.

I always like to compare database indexes to book indexes. In a book

Unique and non-unique indexes
In addition, indexes can be set up as unique or non-unique. In this case, the indexes accept unique or non-unique values and they can function as constraints disallowing duplicate values for the indexed field or fields. For example, if we set up a unique index on a last name field, all the last names in the table must have unique values. Primary key columns in SQL Server 2012 tables are automatically indexed when created, and these indexes are set up as unique.

Composite indexes
We can also create multi-field indexes that will index the combination of values of multiple fields instead of just indexing the values of each individual field. For example, we can create a multi-field unique index on both the last and first name fields that will accept duplicate values for the individual last and first name fields but will not accept duplicate values for their combinations. Let's go through some examples to demonstrate the points we mentioned above in practice.

31. Create a simple index

Add a non-unique, nonclustered index for the first name field in the customer table

Discussion:

Adding a non-unique index for the first name field means that the field will be indexed and we allow duplicate values for this field. In other words, we can have two "Johns" or two "Marys" in the table. As you can see from the figure below, the index "IndFirstName" is nonclustered since we already have a clustered index on the field CustomerID the primary key (PK) of the table.

Code:

CREATE INDEX indFirstName ON Customer3 (FirstName)

Result:

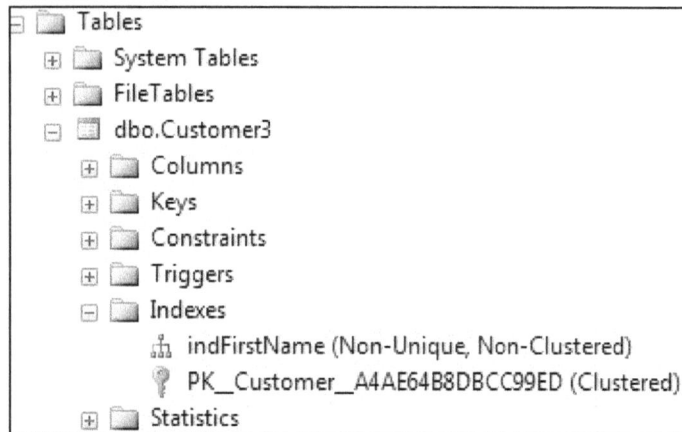

32. Create a unique index for the last name field

Add a unique index for the last name field in the existing customer table

Discussion:

We are creating a unique index on the LastName field which means we cannot have two customers in our table with the same last name. If we try to enter two customers with the same last name, the database will not allow their entry. Again, this is a nonclustered index since we already have a clustered index on the field CustomerID the primary key (PK) of the table.

Code:

CREATE UNIQUE INDEX indLastName ON Customer3 (LastName)

Result:

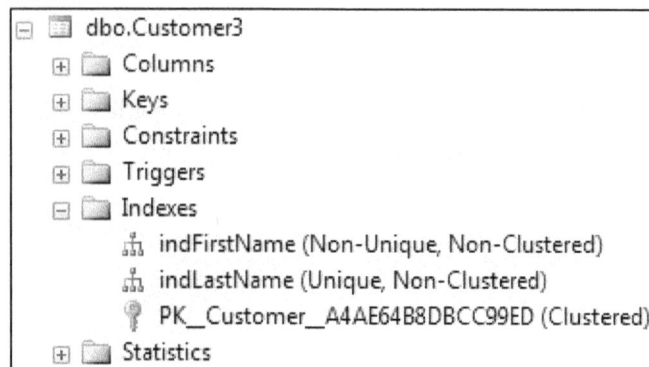

The above is not a desirable scenario since there might be multiple customers with the same last name. Let us see how we can delete an index and how we can we set up index constraints so that we allow multiple customers to have the same last name or the same first name, but disallow multiple customers to have the same last and first names at the same time.

33. Delete an index from a table

Delete the index Indlastname from the customer table

Discussion:

Since the unique IndLastName index does not make sense we use the code below to delete it from the table.

Code:

```
DROP INDEX indLastName ON Customer3
```

Result:

```
☐ 📁 Tables
    ⊞ 📁 System Tables
    ⊞ 📁 FileTables
    ☐ 🗐 dbo.Customer3
        ⊞ 📁 Columns
        ⊞ 📁 Keys
        ⊞ 📁 Constraints
        ⊞ 📁 Triggers
        ☐ 📁 Indexes
              🔓 indFirstName (Non-Unique, Non-Clustered)
              🔑 PK_Customer__A4AE64B8DBCC99ED (Clustered)
    ⊞ 📁 Statistics
```

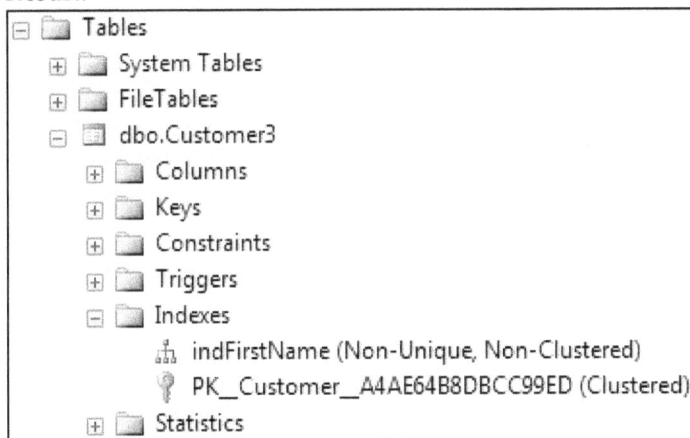

34. Create multiple-field (composite) indexes to avoid duplicates

Add a unique multi-field index for the last and first name fields

Discussion:

When working with customers, we would like to make sure that no duplicate customer records exist in our database. At the same time, it is logical that many customers might have the same last name, and many of them will have the same first name.

With a multi-field unique index, our database will accept values such as Smith John and Smith Tracy. However, if we try to enter another Smith John in the database, we will get a message that such an entry violates existing index rules and will not be accepted. Multi-field indexes are extremely useful to keep our data in good state.

Code:

```
CREATE UNIQUE INDEX indLastFirst ON Customer3 (LastName, FirstName)
```

Result:

```
☐ 🗔 dbo.Customer3
    ⊞ 🗀 Columns
    ⊞ 🗀 Keys
    ⊞ 🗀 Constraints
    ⊞ 🗀 Triggers
    ☐ 🗀 Indexes
            🔧 indFirstName (Non-Unique, Non-Clustered)
            🔧 indLastFirst (Unique, Non-Clustered)
            🔑 PK__Customer__A4AE64B8DBCC99ED (Clustered)
    ⊞ 🗀 Statistics
```

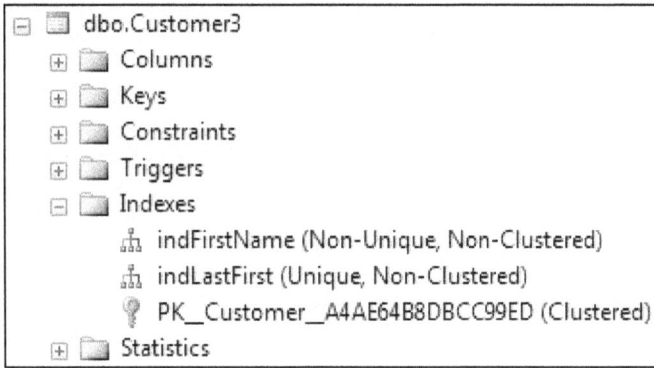

35. Create an index while creating the table

Create a table that contains a unique index as a constraint

Discussion:

We do not need to create a table first and then create its indexes. We can create a table and its indexes in one step. In this example, we create a suppliers table with a unique index on the company name field. We do this to avoid multiple instances of the same company name in the table.

Code:

```
CREATE TABLE Suppliers31 (
[SupplierID] int identity (1,1) Primary key,
[CompanyName] varchar(100),
[Address] varchar(100),
[City] varchar (100),
[State] char (2),
[Zip] char (5),
CONSTRAINT indCompanyName UNIQUE (CompanyName))
```

Result:

	Column Name	Data Type	Allow Nulls
🔑	SupplierID	int	☐
	CompanyName	varchar(100)	☑
	Address	varchar(100)	☑
	City	varchar(100)	☑
	State	char(2)	☑
	Zip	char(5)	☑

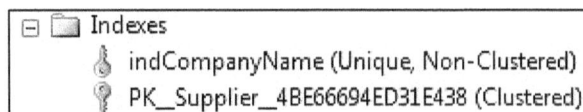

```
☐ 🗀 Indexes
        🔑 indCompanyName (Unique, Non-Clustered)
        🔑 PK__Supplier__4BE66694ED31E438 (Clustered)
```

36. Return index information for a specific table using T-SQL

Return index information of the Customer3 table

Discussion:

The best way to do this is to use the stored procedure supplied by SQL Server and not mess around with system tables.

Code:

exec sp_helpindex customer3

Result:

index_name	index_description	index_keys
indFirstName	nonclustered located on PRIMARY	FirstName
indLastFirst	nonclustered, unique located on PRIMARY	LastName, FirstName
PK__Customer__A4AE64B8DBCC99ED	clustered, unique, primary key located on PRIMARY	CustomerID

CHAPTER 3 DISCUSSION QUESTIONS

1. Why do we need to use indexes?
2. On what fields does it make sense to use indexes?
3. What does it mean to use indexes as constrains?
4. How can we use an index to disallow nulls in a field?
5. How can we avoid duplicate values in a field by using indexes?
6. What are the consequences of indexes on inserts and updates?
7. How can we avoid duplicate values in multiple fields by using indexes?
8. What are the consequences of indexes on WHERE and ORDER BY clauses?
9. Is it recommended to use indexes on small or large tables? Why?
10. Can we setup indexes to ignore null values in the field?

CHAPTER 3 HANDS-ON EXERCISES

Chapter 3 Case 1:
Start SQL Server Management Studio. For each of the questions in this case you need to create a new query (Ctrl-N) and name it as per the instructions in each question. Submit your work to your instructor as one text file that contains all SQL statements or as per your instructor's directions.

1. Create a new table with the fields: CustomerID Primary key, identity (seed 1, increment 1), unique index, Lastname (varchar, 50), FirstName (varchar 50), Address (varchar, 100), City (varchar, 50), State (char, 2), and Zip (char, 5). Name the table Customers31. Save the query you are using to create the table as Chapter03_Case1_Q1.

   Your result should look like:

	Column Name	Data Type	Allow Nulls
🔑	CustomerID	int	☐
	LastName	varchar(50)	☑
	FirstName	varchar(50)	☑
	Address	varchar(100)	☑
	City	varchar(50)	☑
	State	char(2)	☑
	Zip	char(5)	☑

2. Create a non-unique index on the FirstName field. Name the index "IndFirstName". Save the query you are using to create the index as Chapter03_Case1_Q2. Open the indexes folder for the table Customers31 and look at the new index you have just created.

Your result should look like:

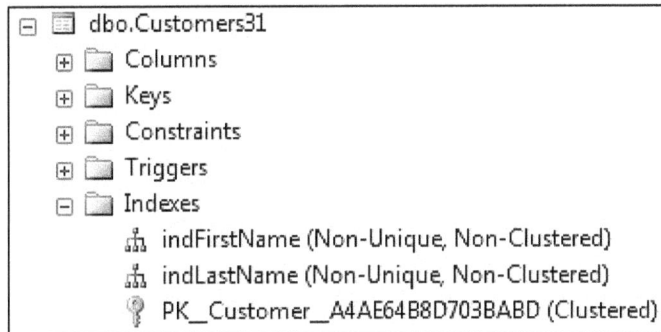

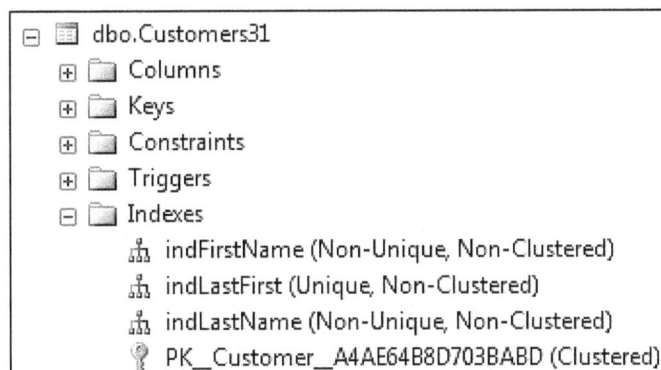

```
dbo.Customers31
   Columns
   Keys
   Constraints
   Triggers
   Indexes
      indFirstName (Non-Unique, Non-Clustered)
      PK_Customer__A4AE64B8D703BABD (Clustered)
```

3. Create a non-unique index on the LastName field. Name the index "IndLastName". Save the query you are using to create the index as Chapter03_Case1_Q3. Open the indexes folder for the table Customers31 and look at the new index you have just created.

Your result should look like:

```
dbo.Customers31
   Columns
   Keys
   Constraints
   Triggers
   Indexes
      indFirstName (Non-Unique, Non-Clustered)
      indLastName (Non-Unique, Non-Clustered)
      PK_Customer__A4AE64B8D703BABD (Clustered)
```

4. You have decided that you want to disallow entries of customers with the same first name and the same last name. You consider those entries as very probable duplicates. To achieve this goal create a unique multiple-field index on the first and last name fields. Save the query you are using to create the index as Chapter03_Case1_Q4. Open the indexes folder for the table Customers31 and look at the new index you have just created.

Your result should look like:

```
dbo.Customers31
   Columns
   Keys
   Constraints
   Triggers
   Indexes
      indFirstName (Non-Unique, Non-Clustered)
      indLastFirst (Unique, Non-Clustered)
      indLastName (Non-Unique, Non-Clustered)
      PK_Customer__A4AE64B8D703BABD (Clustered)
```

5. You have decided that you do not need an index on the firstname field since most user searches involve last name fields. Delete the indFirstName index from the table. Save the query you are using to delete the

index as Chapter03_Case1_Q5.

Your result should look like:

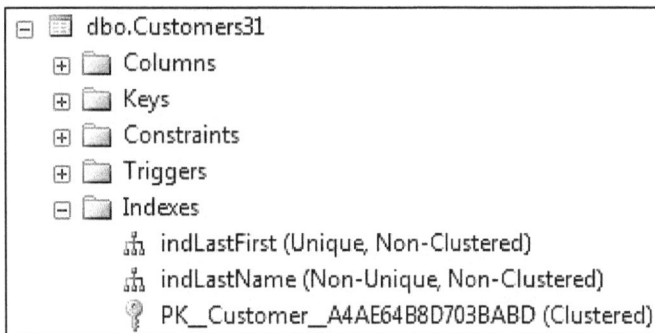

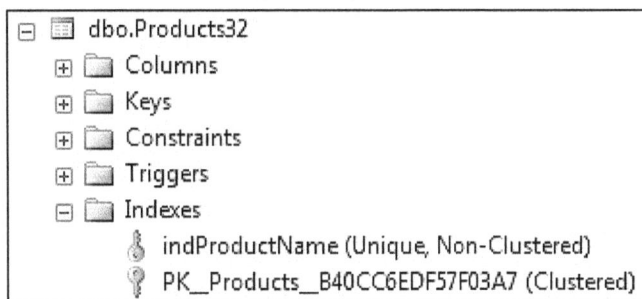

```
⊟  ▦ dbo.Customers31
   ⊞  📁 Columns
   ⊞  📁 Keys
   ⊞  📁 Constraints
   ⊞  📁 Triggers
   ⊟  📁 Indexes
          ⚏ indLastFirst (Unique, Non-Clustered)
          ⚏ indLastName (Non-Unique, Non-Clustered)
          🔑 PK_Customer__A4AE64B8D703BABD (Clustered)
```

Chapter 3 Case 2:

Start SQL Server Management Studio. For each of the questions in this case you need to create a new query (Ctrl-N) and name it as per the instructions in each question. Submit your work to your instructor as one text file that contains all SQL statements or as per your instructor's directions.

1. Create a new table with the fields: ProductID primary key, identity (seed 1, increment 1), ProductName (varchar 100), ProductDescription (varchar, 200), ProductPrice (smallmoney), UnitsInStock (int), and ReorderLevel (int). Name the table Products32. While creating the table, create a unique index on the field ProductName and name it IndProductName. Save the query you are using to create the table as Chapter03_Case2_Q1. Open the indexes folder for the table Products32 and look at the new index you have just created.

Your result should look like:

```
⊟  ▦ dbo.Products32
   ⊞  📁 Columns
   ⊞  📁 Keys
   ⊞  📁 Constraints
   ⊞  📁 Triggers
   ⊟  📁 Indexes
          ⚏ indProductName (Unique, Non-Clustered)
          🔑 PK_Products__B40CC6EDF57F03A7 (Clustered)
```

2. Create a non-unique index on the ProductDescription field since our customers search a lot on this field. Name the index IndProductDescription. Save the query you are using to create the index as Chapter03_Case2_Q2. Open the indexes folder for the table Products32 and look at the new index you have just created.

Your result should look like:

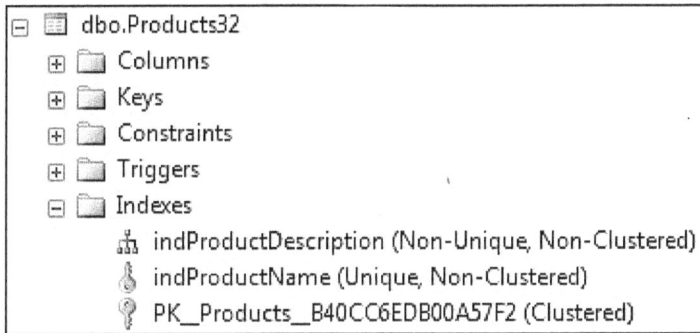

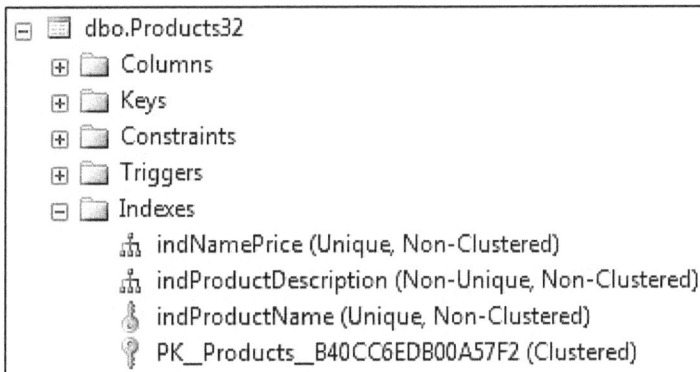

```
☐ ▦ dbo.Products32
   ⊞ ▢ Columns
   ⊞ ▢ Keys
   ⊞ ▢ Constraints
   ⊞ ▢ Triggers
   ☐ ▢ Indexes
        ⊹ indProductDescription (Non-Unique, Non-Clustered)
        ⌀ indProductName (Unique, Non-Clustered)
        ♥ PK_Products_B40CC6EDB00A57F2 (Clustered)
```

3. Create a unique index on the ProductName and ProductPrice fields. Name the index indNamePrice. Save the query you are using to create the index as Chapter03_Case2_Q3. Open the indexes folder for the table Products32 and look at the new index you have just created.

Your result should look like:

```
☐ ▦ dbo.Products32
   ⊞ ▢ Columns
   ⊞ ▢ Keys
   ⊞ ▢ Constraints
   ⊞ ▢ Triggers
   ☐ ▢ Indexes
        ⊹ indNamePrice (Unique, Non-Clustered)
        ⊹ indProductDescription (Non-Unique, Non-Clustered)
        ⌀ indProductName (Unique, Non-Clustered)
        ♥ PK_Products_B40CC6EDB00A57F2 (Clustered)
```

4. Generate a list of indexes for the products32 table using a stored procedure. Save the query you are using to execute the stored procedure as Chapter03_Case2_Q4.

Your result should look like:

	index_name	index_description	index_keys
1	indNamePrice	nonclustered, unique located on PRIMARY	ProductName, ProductPrice
2	indProductDescription	nonclustered located on PRIMARY	ProductDescription
3	indProductName	nonclustered, unique, unique key located on PRIMA...	ProductName
4	PK_Products_B40CC6EDB00A57F2	clustered, unique, primary key located on PRIMARY	ProductID

5. Delete the indProductDescription index from the table. Save the query you are using to delete the index as Chapter03_Case2_Q5. Open the indexes folder for the table Products32 and look at the remaining indexes.

Your result should look like:

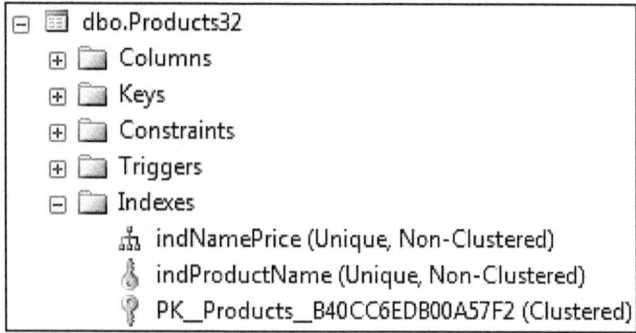

- dbo.Products32
  - Columns
  - Keys
  - Constraints
  - Triggers
  - Indexes
    - indNamePrice (Unique, Non-Clustered)
    - indProductName (Unique, Non-Clustered)
    - PK_Products__B40CC6EDB00A57F2 (Clustered)

CHAPTER 4
CREATE, EDIT, DELETE RELATIONSHIPS USING SQL

Our manager asked for a database to store information about our customers and their orders. One of our tasks will be to create relationships among tables. After almost 20 years of working with databases, I can say that this process is much more art than science. There are neither rigid rules to follow nor guidelines to cover all of the situational scenarios we might encounter.

To achieve this task, we first need to have a total and complete understanding of the meaning of relationships and their related topics like primary keys, foreign keys, referential integrity, cascade updates, cascade deletes, and join types. Second, we have to use our logic and experience to build an entity relationship diagram resulting in a solid database. The purpose of this chapter is to completely demystify relationships not only with respect to building them but, most importantly, with respect to their interpretation and usage.

37. Why and how to create a one-to-many relationship
Create a one-to-many relationship between customers and orders

Our task here is to create a relationship between the tbls_r_customers and tbls_r_orders tables. The logic is that each customer can have multiple orders while one order definitely belongs to one customer only. This is the rationale for a one-to-many relationship. This one-to-many relationship is depicted graphically in the figure below. I have included data values on purpose to actually show how records from one table relate to records in the other table. This is because when we talk about relationships among tables, we are actually talking about record relations. From a business point of view we see that Mary has two orders in the system, John and George one, and Stacy none.

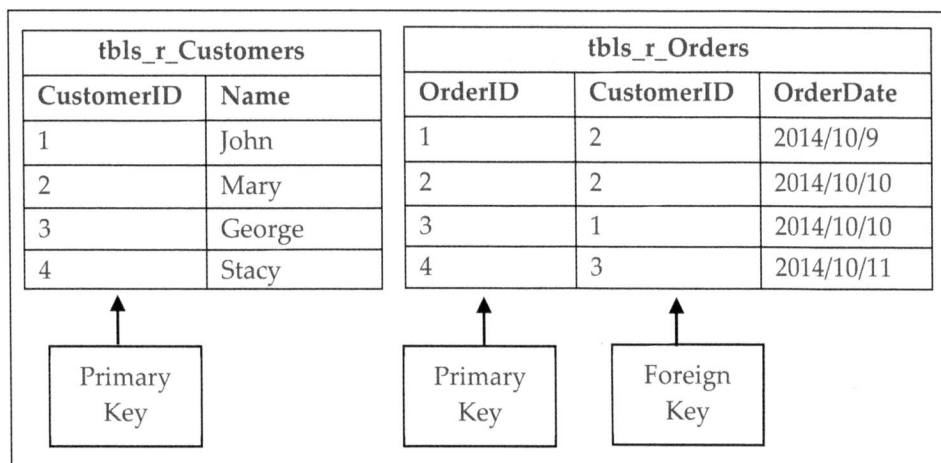

tbls_r_Customers		tbls_r_Orders		
CustomerID	Name	OrderID	CustomerID	OrderDate
1	John	1	2	2014/10/9
2	Mary	2	2	2014/10/10
3	George	3	1	2014/10/10
4	Stacy	4	3	2014/10/11

Primary Key   Primary Key   Foreign Key

The steps for creating a one-to-many relationship between two database tables (customers and orders in this case) are the following:

First let us create the tables:

Code:
```
CREATE TABLE tbls_r_Customers (
[CustomerID] int  identity (1,1) Primary key ,
[LastName] varchar(50))
```

Code:
```
CREATE TABLE tbls_r_Orders (
[OrderID] int  identity (1,1) Primary key ,
[CustomerID] int NOT NULL,
[OrderDate] date)
```

We assign a primary key to both tables and in this example, the primary key for the tbls_r_Customers table is "CustomerID", and the primary key for the tbls_r_Orders table is "OrderID".

Make sure your primary key is not a "natural" key like a social security number, or driver's license number. The data types for the primary keys in both tables should be of the "int" data type and have the identification specification property set to yes with an identity seed at 1 and an identity increment at 1. This means that the values for the PKs will be entered automatically by the database starting at value 1 and increasing by 1.

We have also created a field in the tbls_r_Orders table, which we named "CustomerID." The "CustomerID" field in the tbls_r_Orders table is the "foreign key" of the table. The data type of the "CustomerID" field in the tbls_r_Orders table should be of the "int" data type and it will be joined with the CustID in the tbls_r_Customers table.

At this point we are ready to populate the two tables with data:

Code:
```
INSERT INTO tbls_r_Customers(LastName)
VALUES ('John'), ('Mary'), ('John'), ('Stacy')
```

Code:
```
INSERT INTO tbls_r_Orders(CustomerID, OrderDate)
VALUES (2, '2014/10/9'), (2, '2014/10/10'), (1, '2014/10/10'), (3, '2014/10/11')
```

Now we are ready to establish the relationship between the two tables. In the second line of the code, the "FK_CustomerID" is the name we use for the relationship constraint and we can name it anything we like. In the third line we define the foreign key field in the tbls_r_Orders table. In the fourth and final line we reference the primary key field "CustomerID" in the tbls_r_Customers table.

Code:
```
ALTER TABLE tbls_r_Orders
ADD CONSTRAINT FK_CustomerID
FOREIGN KEY (CustomerID)
REFERENCES tbls_r_Customers (CustomerID)
```

Result:

As you can see from the entity relationship diagram below, the one-to-many relationship between the two tables has been established.

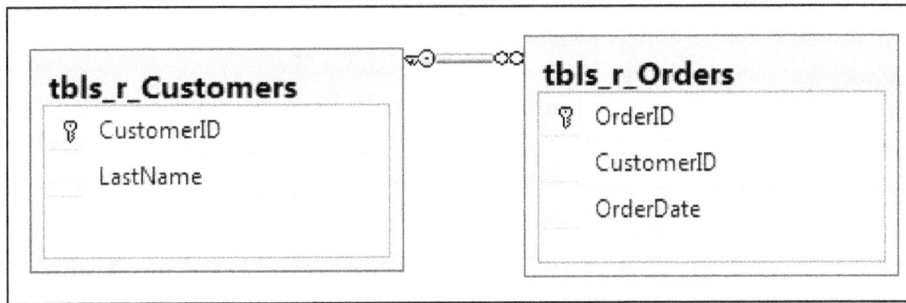

38. How to read, understand, and use one-to-many relationships
The meaning of one-to-many relationship between customers and orders

Learning how to create a one-to-many relationship is really a minimal goal in itself. The essential objective is to actually understand its meaning, be able to apply it, and take advantage of its many possibilities. In this respect, let us try to read what is happening in our two related tables of customers and orders.

First, when looking at the foreign key values in the tbls_r_orders table (the values of the CustomerID field), we notice that only John, Mary, and George have orders. Second, we see that John and George have one order each, while Mary has two orders. Third, we see that Stacy does not have any orders at all, so we might want to initiate a marketing effort for her. Fourth, when we look at the tbls_r_orders table and examine order number 3 (with OrderID = 3), we immediately understand that this order belongs to John because the corresponding foreign key (CustomerID) value is 1. If we look up this value in the tbls_r_customers table, we find that the corresponding customer name is John. This is the way relational databases work and are able to retrieve related records from two or more tables.

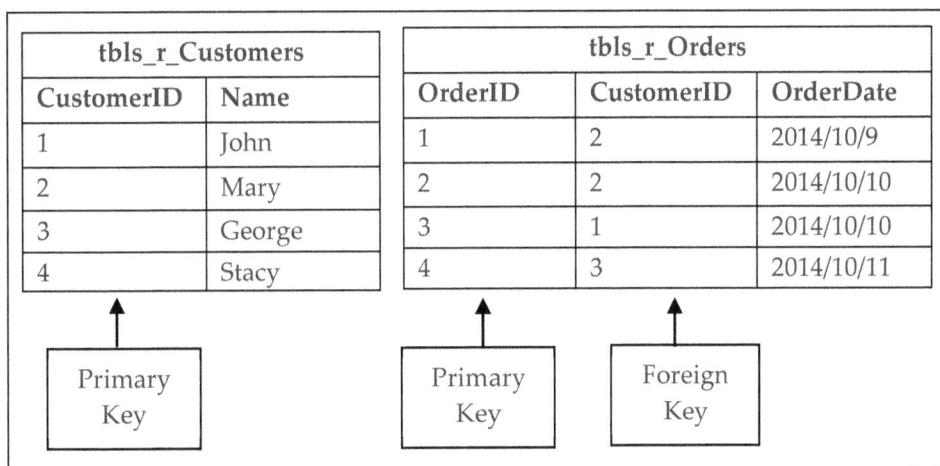

39. Why and how to create a many-to-many-relationship
Create a many-to-many relationship between orders and products

Our task this time is to create a database to keep track of customers, orders, and products. We already know how to create a one-to-many relationship between customers and orders. Now, we need to create a relationship between orders and products. Whenever we design a database, the setup of relationships is the cornerstone of the design process.

In this respect, we examine the relations among entities because this is how we refer to tables in database parlance. From the orders point of view, we conclude that each order can contain multiple products. It is only logical that a customer can order multiple products in one order. From the products point of view, we conclude that each product can participate in more than one order. It is logical that we can sell the same product to multiple customers through their orders. When this is the case, we need to establish a many-to-many relationship between Orders and Products.

In this example, to create a many-to-many relationship between the tbls_r_Orders and tbls_r_Products tables, we need to create a join table between them like the tbls_r_Products_Orders table. The primary key of the join table is the combination of the primary keys of the tables that we would like to join in a many-to-many relationship. In other words, the primary key of any join table in a many-to-many relationship is a composite key consisting of two fields. As we know already, the values of a primary key in a table must be unique, and this uniqueness is expressed in this case by the combination of the values of OrderID and ProductID. For example, in the figure below the value (1,2) of the first record in the tbls_r_Products_Orders table is different from the value (2,2) in the second record. This is how we obtain uniqueness of primary key values of join tables in many-to-many relationships.

tbls_r_Customers	
CustomerID	Name
1	John
2	Mary
3	George
4	Stacy

tbls_r_Orders		
OrderID	CustomerID	OrderDate
1	2	2014/10/9
2	2	2014/10/10
3	1	2014/10/10
4	3	2014/10/11

tbls_r_Products	
ProductID	ProductName
1	A
2	B
3	C
4	D

tbls_r_ProductsOrders		
OrderID	ProductID	Quantity
1	2	2
2	2	5
3	1	3
4	2	4

To create a many-to-many relationship between the tables tbls_r_Orders and tbls_r_Products, we follow these steps:

First we create the tbls_r_Products table and we populate it.

Code:
```
CREATE TABLE tbls_r_Products (
[ProductID] int identity (1,1) Primary key ,
[ProductName] varchar(50))
```

Code:
INSERT INTO tbls_r_Products(ProductName)
VALUES ('A'), ('B'), ('C'), ('D')

Now we create the table tbls_r_ProductsOrders whose name is the combination of the names of the two tables that you would like to join. You can follow any other naming convention you prefer as long as you can remember in the future that this is a join table between tbls_r_Orders and tbls_r_Products.

In the join table "tbls_r_ProductsOrders", create two fields whose names are: OrderID and ProductID. The data types of both OrderID and ProductID should be "int". This is because we need to join these fields with the corresponding keys in the tbls_r_Orders and tbls_r_Products tables, and we cannot join two fields with dissimilar data types.

We are not finished yet, however. Let us assume that a customer orders two units of product "A" and three units of product "B". This customer is ordering multiple quantities of the same product in the same order. In addition, we might want to give discounts on particular products in the same order while extending no discounts for other products. How do we accomplish this? The answer is to include additional fields in the tbls_r_Products_Orders table so that we can enter this information. Our final code will look like this: Please pay attention on how we define the combination of the OrderID and ProductID field as the primary key of the table.

Code:
```
CREATE TABLE tbls_r_ProductsOrders (
[OrderID] int  NOT NULL,
[ProductID] int  NOT NULL,
[Quantity] int
CONSTRAINT PrimaryKey_ProductsOrders PRIMARY KEY (OrderID, ProductID))
```

Result:

	Column Name	Data Type	Allow Nulls
🔑	OrderID	int	☐
🔑	ProductID	int	☐
	Quantity	int	☑

Next we populate the tbls_r_Products table:

Code:
INSERT INTO tbls_r_ProductsOrders(OrderID, ProductID, Quantity)
VALUES (1, 2, 2), (2, 2, 5), (3, 1, 3), (4, 2, 4)

Then, we join the tbls_r_Orders and tbls_r_Products tables to the tbls_r_ProductsOrders table. What we practically need to do is to create a one-to-many relationship between tbls_r_Orders and tbls_r_ProductsOrders and a one-to-many relationship between tbls_r_Products and tbls_r_ProductsOrders. Those two one-to-many relationships will result into a many-to-many relationship between the tbls_r_Orders and tbls_r_Products tables.

Let us create the one-to-many relationship between tbls_r_Orders and tbls_r_ProductsOrders:

Code:
```
ALTER TABLE tbls_r_ProductsOrders
ADD CONSTRAINT FK_OrderID
FOREIGN KEY (OrderID)
REFERENCES tbls_r_Orders (OrderID)
```

Now, let us create the one-to-many relationship between tbls_r_Products and tbls_r_ProductsOrders:

Code:
```
ALTER TABLE tbls_r_ProductsOrders
ADD CONSTRAINT FK_ProductID
FOREIGN KEY (ProductID)
REFERENCES tbls_r_Products (ProductID)
```

Result:
The relationships among the four tables will look like in the figure below. The many-to-many relationship between the tables tbls_r_Orders and tbls_r_Products is clearly seen.

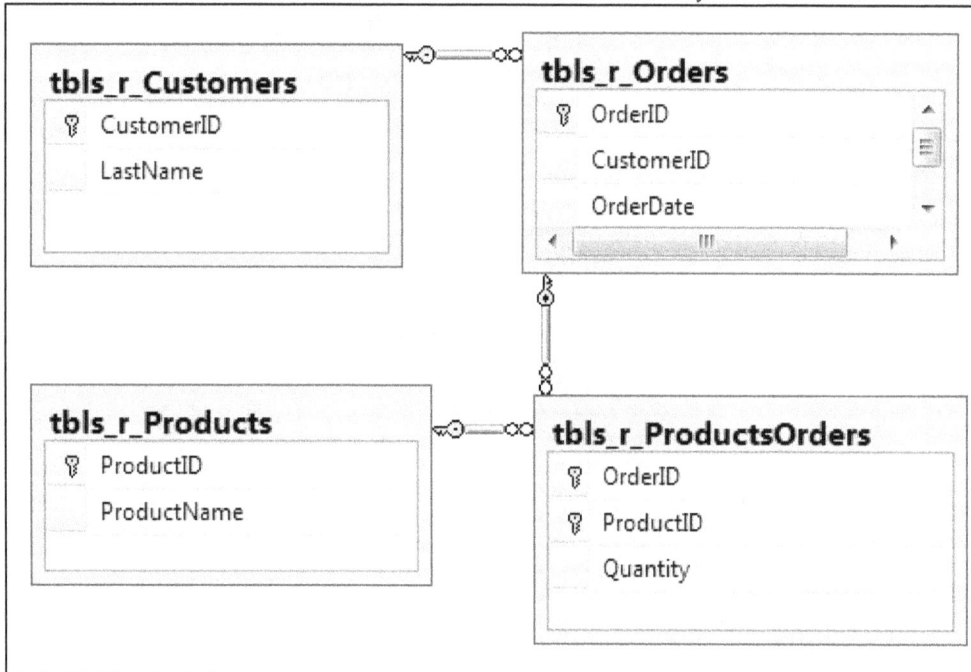

40. How to "read", understand, and use many-to-many relationships
The meaning of many-to-many relationship between orders and products

The important goal in any database work is to understand what we are doing and not so much the clicks on the user interface for doing it. If we do not remember the series of clicks to achieve a task, we can always resort to a handy reference. However, if we do not understand how many-to-many relationships work, we are reluctant to use them or, at the very least, cannot take full advantage of them.

Let us examine the meaning of a many-to-many relationship from A to Z. The figure below depicts a many-to-many relationship between the tbls_r_Orders and tbls_r_Products tables. Let us try to answer a couple of questions:

What specific products were included in John's order?

To answer this question, we should go to John's record in the tbls_r_customer table. There, we see that John's primary key value is 1 (PK=1). Then, we proceed to the tbls_r_Orders table, which is joined with the customer table through a one-to-many relationship. There, we see that John appears in the third record of the table where CustomerID = 1. In database parlance, this translates to foreign key value = 1 or FK=1. Next, we see that the corresponding OrderID value for FK=1 is 3 (OrderID =3). From there, we are looking for OrderID = 3 in the tbls_r_ProductsOrders table. We see that we have one OrderID with the value of 3 in the tbls_r_ProductsOrders table. The corresponding ProductID value is 1. Next, we go to the tbls_r_Products table and see that ProductID = 1 corresponds to product A. Since the quantity for the pair (3,1) in the tbls_r_Products_Orders table is 3, we can finally answer that John ordered three units of product (A). This is exactly how relational databases use associations (relationships) to store and retrieve information.

tbls_r_Customers	
CustomerID	Name
1	John
2	Mary
3	George
4	Stacy

tbls_r_Orders		
OrderID	CustomerID	OrderDate
1	2	2014/10/9
2	2	2014/10/10
3	1	2014/10/10
4	3	2014/10/11

tbls_r_Products	
ProductID	ProductName
1	A
2	B
3	C
4	D

tbls_r_ProductsOrders		
OrderID	ProductID	Quantity
1	2	2
2	2	5
3	1	3
4	2	4

What specific products were included in Mary's orders?

Mary's PK in the tbls_r_Customer table is 2. For FK=2 in the tbls_r_Orders table, the corresponding PK values are 1 and 2. We now know that Mary placed two orders. For OrderID 1 and 2 in the tbls_r_ProductsOrders table, the corresponding ProductIDs are 2 and 2. The quantities are 2 and 5. Therefore, we know right away that Mary ordered seven product Bs in two separate orders. We also note that Mary has a pattern of ordering only product Bs, which allows us to direct our marketing efforts.

41. What is referential integrity, how to apply it, and what it means

The meaning and implications of referential integrity in table relationships

Referential Integrity is a concept misunderstood and underused in the database professional world. Some developers will turn this option on because it is a good "thing" to do even though they do not fully understand its implications. Referential integrity in relational databases means that relationships among joined tables remain consistent. Of course, as is the case with all definitions, we do not understand much from them. Let us try to approach it from a more practical perspective using the tables tbls_r_Customers and tbls_r_Orders . There are two major consequences of referential integrity in the relationship between these two tables:

First, the database will not allow us to enter an order without a corresponding customer. That is, a customer must exist before we can enter an order for that customer. That is, if we enter an FK value (CustomerID) in the tbls_r_Orders table, a corresponding PK value for the CustomerID field must exist in the tbls_r_Customers table. Without referential integrity on, we would be able to enter an order without a corresponding customer which means we will have orphaned records in the tbls_r_Orders table. Orders without any associated customers constitute a very undesirable outcome for the database and compromise its integrity.

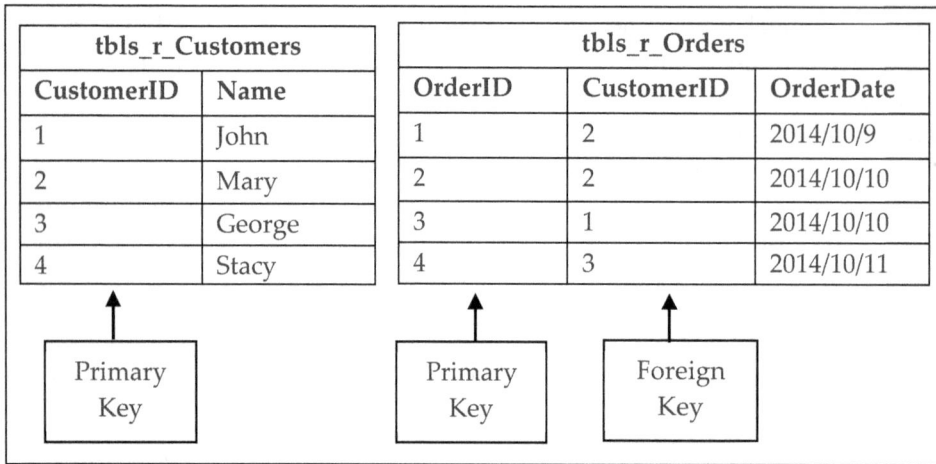

tbls_r_Customers		tbls_r_Orders		
CustomerID	Name	OrderID	CustomerID	OrderDate
1	John	1	2	2014/10/9
2	Mary	2	2	2014/10/10
3	George	3	1	2014/10/10
4	Stacy	4	3	2014/10/11

Primary Key   Primary Key   Foreign Key

Let's see how we can technically enforce referential integrity for the relationship between the two tables below.

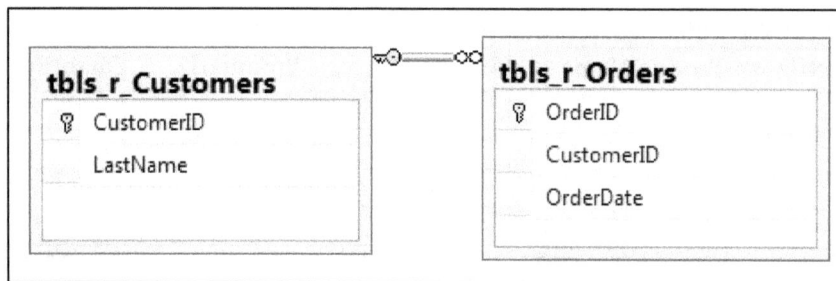

tbls_r_Customers
- CustomerID
- LastName

tbls_r_Orders
- OrderID
- CustomerID
- OrderDate

In the database diagram, if we click on the relationship line between the two tables, the following properties appear in the property window. Referential integrity is set through the entry "Enforce Foreign Key Constraint". By default in SQL server referential integrity is set on when the relationship is created. You can change the entry to "No" to remove the enforcement of referential integrity for the relationship, which is not recommended.

Properties

[Rel] FK_CustomerID

▲ (General)
Check Existing Data On Creation Or Re· Yes
▷ Tables And Columns Specification
▲ Database Designer
Enforce For Replication   Yes
Enforce Foreign Key Constraint   Yes
▷ INSERT And UPDATE Specification
▲ Identity
(Name)   FK_Custome
Description

Now, let us see how we can enforce referential integrity using pure T-SQL code. For the relationship between the tables tbls_r_Customers and tbls_r_Orders referential integrity is on. This means that the property "Enforce Foreign Key Constraint" is set to yes. We can disable it using the following code.

Code: disable foreign key constraint
```
ALTER TABLE tbls_r_Orders
NOCHECK CONSTRAINT FK_CustomerID
```

Result:

Properties

[Rel] FK_CustomerID

▲ (General)
Check Existing Data On C No
▷ Tables And Columns Spe
▲ Database Designer
Enforce For Replication   Yes
Enforce Foreign Key Con: No
▷ INSERT And UPDATE Spe
▲ Identity
(Name)   FK_CustomerID
Description

To enable the foreign key constraint we use the code below:

Code: enable foreign key constraint
```
ALTER TABLE tbls_r_Orders
CHECK CONSTRAINT FK_CustomerID
```

The above code is equivalent to the code below. The NOCHECK option means that we apply the foreign key constraint without first checking for orphaned records in the tbls_r_Orders table. This is the default behavior in

73

SQL Server 2012 when we re-enable a foreign key constraint. This means that we might have orders with CustomerID (FK) values without corresponding CustomerID (PK) values in the tbls_r_customers table. In short, we might have orders without corresponding customers which violates the referential integrity of the database.

Code: enable foreign key constraint
ALTER TABLE tbls_r_Orders
WITH NOCHECK CHECK CONSTRAINT FK_CustomerID

Result:

Properties	▾ ⊣ ×
[Rel] FK_CustomerID	▾

▲ (General)
  Check Existing Data On Creation Or Re·   Yes
  ▷ Tables And Columns Specification
▲ Database Designer
  Enforce For Replication   Yes
  Enforce Foreign Key Constraint   Yes
  ▷ INSERT And UPDATE Specification
▲ Identity
  (Name)   FK_Custome
  Description

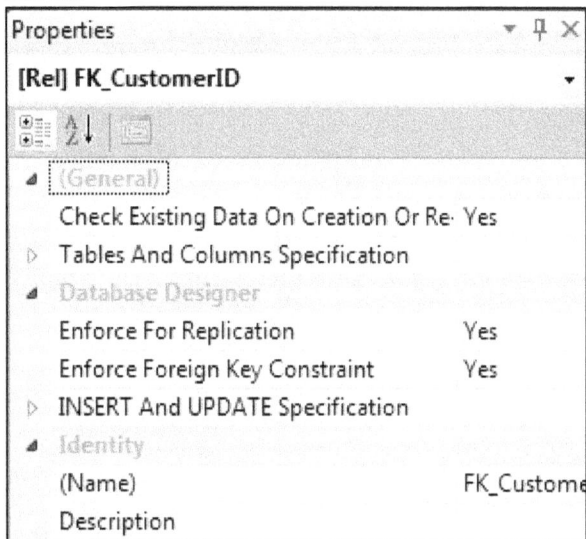

To check for orphaned records before we set the foreign key constraint we can use the WITH CHECK option as in the code below:

Code: enable foreign key constraint
ALTER TABLE tbls_r_Orders
WITH CHECK CHECK CONSTRAINT FK_CustomerID

If the database does not allow you to apply referential integrity, then you should immediately look for orphaned records in the tbls_r_Orders table. How do we find orphaned records? Please see chapter 22 for numerous examples.

The next major consequence of referential integrity is that the database will not allow us to delete a customer for whom we have orders in the database. First, we need to delete all the orders for that customer and then try to delete the customer.

If we want to delete a customer and all her existing orders in one step, we need to enable "Cascade Deletes". This option enables us to delete all related information about a customer in the database, but it is very dangerous to leave on since end users might delete customers and their related information by mistake. Check chapters 27 and 28 on "Cascade Updates" and "Cascade Deletes" for full details on their use since they are an important productivity tool.

CHAPTER 4 DISCUSSION QUESTIONS

1. What scenario are we in if we have customers without orders in our database?
2. What scenario are we in if we have orders without customers in our database?
3. How do we establish a many-to-many relationship between two tables, for example, orders and products?
4. Why do we have to establish a many-to-many relationship between singers and songs?
5. Why do we have to establish a one-to-many relationship between customers and orders?
6. How do we setup a one-to-many relationship between customers and orders? How many primary keys we need? How many foreign keys?
7. If referential integrity is on, can we enter orders without customers in the database?
8. If referential integrity is on, can we enter customers without orders in the database?
9. What scenario are we in if we try to apply referential integrity for a relationship but the database does not allow us to do so?
10. If referential integrity is on, can we delete a customer with existing orders in the database?

CHAPTER 4 HANDS-ON EXERCISES

Chapter 4 Case 1:

Start SQL Server Management Studio. For each of the questions in this case you need to create a new query (Ctrl-N) and name it as per the instructions in each question. Submit your work to your instructor as one text file that contains all SQL statements or as per your instructor's directions.

1. Create a new table and name it "Actors41". Setup three fields: ActorID as the primary key and auto increment with seed 1 and increment at 1, ActorFirstName varchar (50) and ActorLastName varchar (50). Create the table using pure T-SQL code. Save the query you are using to create the table as Chapter04_Case1_Q1.

   Result:

	Column Name	Data Type	Allow Nulls
🔑	ActorID	int	☐
	ActorFirstName	varchar(50)	☑
	ActorLastName	varchar(50)	☑

2. Create a new table and name it "Films41". Setup three fields: FilmID, FilmTitle, and FilmDate. Assign FilmID as as the primary key and auto increment with seed 1 and increment at 1, FilmTitle as varchar (200), and FilmDate as date. Create the table using SQL code. Save the query you are using to create the table as Chapter04_Case1_Q2

Result:

	Column Name	Data Type	Allow Nulls
🔑	FilmID	int	☐
	FilmTitle	varchar(200)	☑
	FilmDate	date	☑

3. Create a new table and name it FilmsActors. This table will serve as the middle table for the many-to-many relationship between the tables Actors41 and Films41. Setup the primary key and data types of its fields using pure T-SQL. Save the query you are using to create the table as Chapter04_Case1_Q3.

Result:

	Column Name	Data Type	Allow Nulls
🔑	ActorID	int	☐
🔑	FilmID	int	☐

4. Setup a one-to-many relationship between the tables Actors41 and FilmsActors. Save the query you are using to create the relationship as Chapter04_Case1_Q4.

5. Setup a one-to-many relationship between the tables Films41 and FilmsActors. Save the query you are using to create the relationship as Chapter04_Case1_Q5.

Result: Create a new database diagram and include the tables Actors41, FilmsActors, and Films41. The many-to-many relationship between Actors41 and Films41 should be shown as in the following image:

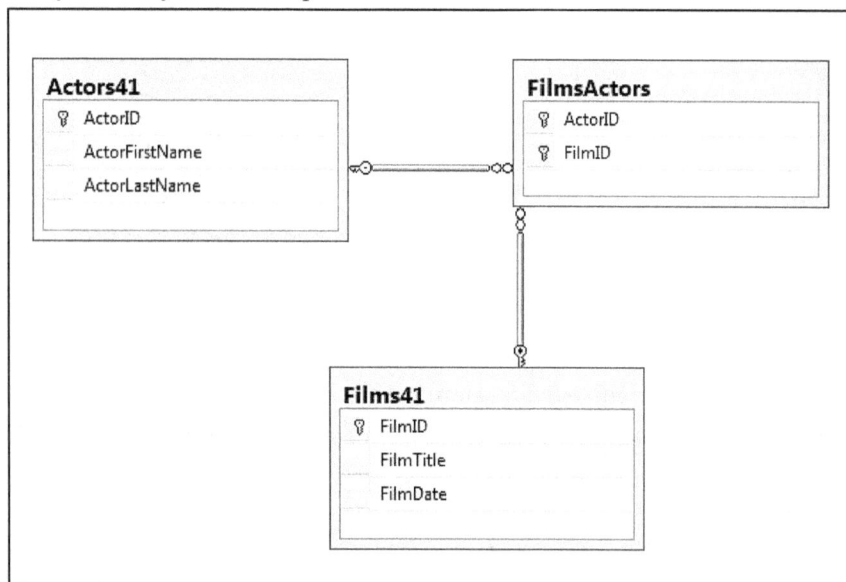

Actors41
- 🔑 ActorID
- ActorFirstName
- ActorLastName

FilmsActors
- 🔑 ActorID
- 🔑 FilmID

Films41
- 🔑 FilmID
- FilmTitle
- FilmDate

Chapter 4 Case 2:

Start SQL Server Management Studio. For each of the questions in this case you need to create a new query (Ctrl-N) and name it as per the instructions in each question. Submit your work to your instructor as one text file that contains all SQL statements or as per your instructor's directions.

1. Create a new table and name it "Patrons42". Setup three fields: PatronID as the primary key and auto increment with seed 1 and increment at 1, PatronFirstName varchar (30), and PatronLastName varchar (50). Create the table using pure T-SQL code. Save the query you are using to create the table as Chapter04_Case2_Q1.

   Result:

Column Name	Data Type	Allow Nulls
⚷ PatronID	int	☐
PatronFirstName	varchar(30)	☑
PatronLastName	varchar(50)	☑

2. Create a new table and name it "Events42". Setup three fields: EventID as the primary key and auto increment with seed 1 and increment at 1, EventTitle varchar (200), and EventDate as date. Create the table using pure T-SQL code. Save the query you are using to create the table as Chapter04_Case2_Q2.

   Result:

Column Name	Data Type	Allow Nulls
⚷ EventID	int	☐
EventTitle	varchar(200)	☑
EventDate	date	☑

3. Create a new table and name it PatronsEvents. This table will serve as the middle table for the many-to-many relationship between the tables Patrons42 and Events42. Setup the primary key and data types of its fields using pure T-SQL. Save the query you are using to create the table as Chapter04_Case2_Q3.

   Result:

Column Name	Data Type	Allow Nulls
⚷ PatronID	int	☐
⚷ EventID	int	☐

4. Setup a one-to-many relationship between the tables Patrons42 and PatronsEvents. Save the query you are using to create the relationship as Chapter04_Case2_Q4.

5. Setup a one-to-many relationship between the tables Events42 and PatronsEvents. Save the query you are using to create the relationship as Chapter04_Case2_Q5.

Result:

Create a new database diagram and include the tables Patrons42, PatronsEvents, and Events42. The many-to-many relationship between Patrons42 and Events42 should be shown as in the following image:

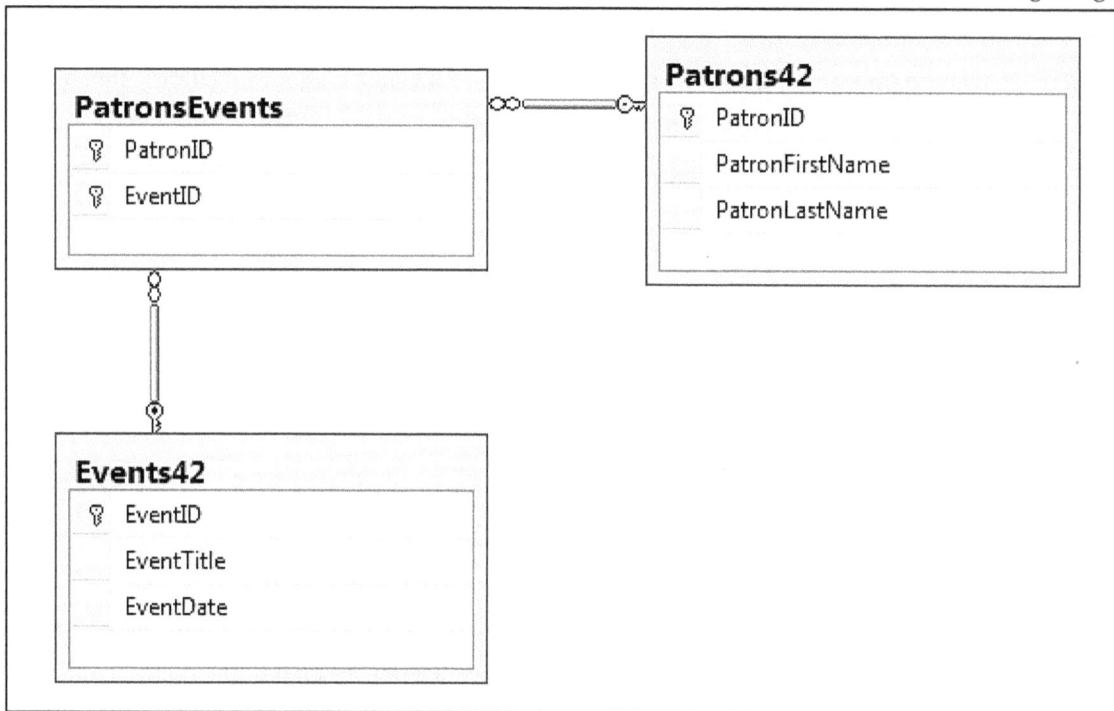

CHAPTER 5
THE SELECT STATEMENT

The SELECT statement is the most widely used keyword in any relational database, and it constitutes the basis for a multitude of Structured Query Language (SQL) code statements. We will go through examples of how to use the SELECT statement alone or in combination with its various clauses like WHERE, GROUP BY, HAVING, and ORDER BY. We will devote whole chapters to some of its clauses since there are many ways and tricks in using them to achieve the intricate results we need in our daily business tasks. In this chapter, we will focus on the SELECT statement in detail, and you will be surprised to see that SELECT can be used in many more ways than simply selecting records. The general structure of the SELECT statement in SQL Server 2012 appears below:

```
SELECT field1, field2, field3
FROM table
[WHERE]
[GROUP BY]
[HAVING]
[ORDER BY]
```

42. SELECT with * to retrieve all columns and rows from a table
Create a quick report selecting all columns and rows from the customer table
Discussion:
We can use the * wildcard character to quickly retrieve all of the columns and records from a table. Note that a SELECT statement used this way will retrieve records in the order they are stored in the table.

Code:
```
SELECT *
FROM Customers
```

Result:

	CustomerID	First Name	Last Name	Address	City	State	Zip	
1	1	John	Demarco	11 Lark Street	New York	NY	12189	
2	2	Mary	Demania	12 Madison Ave	New York	NY	12189	
3	3	George	Demers	23 New Scotland Ave	New York	NY	12189	
4	4	Phillip	Demetriou	22 Academy Road	New York	NY	12189	

(201 row(s) returned)

43. SELECT to retrieve only field names
Provide documentation for the Orders table by retrieving a list of its fields
Discussion:
There are occasions when we want to retrieve only field names and not any records. This is usually for documentation purposes or for just having a look at the field names before we write a query. We can easily do this by using the following code, which will result in no records because there is no way for 0 to equal 1.

79

Code:
```
SELECT *
FROM Orders
WHERE 0=1;
```

Result:

OrderID	CustomerID	SalesRepID	ShipperID	OrderDate	RequiredDate	ShippedDate

44. SELECT to retrieve specific columns from a table

Create a quick customer list for mailing labels

Discussion:

Experience indicates that in the vast majority of cases, we need to retrieve only a subset of columns from a table. We can define exactly what columns to get using the SELECT statement. In this particular example, we need to send out letters to our customers, and we only need to retrieve address related fields.

Code:
```
SELECT lastname, firstname, address, city, state, zip
FROM Customers
```

Result:

	lastname	firstname	address	city	state	zip
1	Demarco	John	11 Lark Street	New York	NY	12189
2	Demania	Mary	12 Madison Ave	New York	NY	12189
3	Demers	George	23 New Scotl...	New York	NY	12189
4	Demetriou	Phillip	22 Academy ...	New York	NY	12189

```
(201 row(s) returned)
```

45. SELECT to retrieve columns in the order you prefer

Retrieve a customer list arranging the columns in a specific order

Discussion:

We can specify the order in which we would like to see columns in the query output. In this case, we would like to see the state field first, followed by the last and first names of our customers. When rearranging columns in SQL statements, pay attention to your commas. It is prohibited to have a comma after the last field before the FROM clause.

Code:
```
SELECT state, city, lastname, firstname
FROM Customers
```

Result:

	state	city	lastname	firstname	▲
1	NY	New York	Demarco	John	
2	NY	New York	Demania	Mary	
3	NY	New York	Demers	George	
4	NY	New York	Demetriou	Phillip	

```
(201 row(s) returned)
```

46. SELECT to retrieve specific records from a table

Create a report of customers in Boston

Discussion:

SQL statements provide great flexibility for retrieving records. For instance, we can retrieve all columns from a table, all rows, some columns and all rows, some rows and all columns, or some rows and some columns. In this example, we are retrieving all of the columns from the customer table but limiting the rows by selecting customers who reside in Boston. Notice from the result set that the database returned only 14 customers.

Code:

```
SELECT *
FROM Customers
WHERE city = 'Boston'
```

Result:

CustomerID	FirstName	LastName	Address	City	State	Zip	Country	▲
163	Arnold	Cormack	31 2nd Street	Boston	MA	22459	USA	
164	Carolyn	Currier	58 Holmes CT	Boston	MA	22459	USA	
165	Catherine	Davis	87 Coral Street	Boston	MA	22459	USA	
166	Cristopher	Geisler	93 Kate Street	Boston	MA	22459	USA	▼

```
(14 row(s) returned)
```

47. SELECT to retrieve specific columns and specific rows

Create a list of suppliers from NY but do not display the state

Discussion:

Sometimes, we need to retrieve specific columns and specific rows from a table. When in this situation, always work with the process of getting the columns first and then, apply the appropriate clauses (WHERE) and criteria ('Houston', 'Texas') to get the rows that you need. In this example, we are retrieving only the company name and the contact name of suppliers who operate in New York. In addition, notice that although we use the state as a criterion field, the state itself will not appear in the result set.

Code:

```
SELECT companyname, contactname
FROM suppliers
WHERE state = 'NY'
```

Result:

	companyname	contactname
1	America's Greatest Snacks, Inc.	Andrew Daves
2	Berkley Bakery Co.	Frank Baker
3	Mediterranean Foods, LLC.	Nick Papadopoulos
4	BayLine Farms Co.	Lisa Anderson

```
(5 row(s) returned)
```

48. SELECT AS: column aliases

Retrieve data from the suppliers table but change the column titles

Discussion:

In many cases, table fields have names that make sense to the database developer but not the end user. For example, Cust_LN and Cust_FN might make sense to the database developer because they represent naming conventions for the customer last name and customer first name fields. However, if we use them as titles for queries or reports, no one will be able to discern their meaning.

In these cases, we use the SELECT AS statement to assign field aliases or column titles that make sense for all of us. We can do this on the fly in a SELECT statement. In the example below, we change the titles of the fields for two columns in the suppliers table. Notice we enclose the second alias [Supplier Contact] in brackets because we have a space between the two words. If we forget the brackets, the SQL statement will not run.

Code:

```
SELECT companyname AS Company, contactname AS [Supplier Contact]
FROM suppliers
```

Result:

	Company	Supplier Contact
1	Home of Snacks	Pedro Adkins
2	American Foods, LLC.	John Marrey
3	American Imports Inc.	Maria Hopkins
4	America's Greatest Snacks, Inc.	Andrew Daves

```
(10 row(s) returned)
```

49. SELECT combined with plain text

Create a quick letter to customers

Discussion:

SQL allows us to mingle field data with plain text, which results in the creation of some interesting results. In this example, we are writing a quick letter to customers. Notice that we enclose plain text in single quotes (' '). In addition, note that the characters (+ ' ' +) add spaces between fields and plain text. Finally, the whole statement in the code below is just one concatenated field named "CustomerLetter." For a full understanding of concatenated fields, refer to chapter 16 where you will find many tips and tricks working with them.

Code:

```
SELECT 'Dear' + ' ' + [firstname] + ' ' + 'We would like you to know that our full product catalog is on
sale in the city of' + ' ' +[city] + ' ' + 'Please visit our website at: http://www.company.com' As
CustomerLetter
FROM customers
```

Result:

	CustomerLetter
1	Dear John We would like you to know that our full product catalog is on sale in the city of New Y...
2	Dear Mary We would like you to know that our full product catalog is on sale in the city of New Y...
3	Dear George We would like you to know that our full product catalog is on sale in the city of New..
4	Dear Phillip We would like you to know that our full product catalog is on sale in the city of New ...

```
(201 row(s) returned)
```

50. SELECT with ORDER BY

Sort a customer list by last name

Discussion:

In this example, we use the * wildcard character to retrieve all of the columns and rows in the customers table and then, sort the data on last name. To sort data in SQL, we use the ORDER BY clause. Specifically, to sort in ascending order, we use ORDER BY ASC, and to sort in descending order, we use ORDER BY DESC. In this example, the ORDER BY clause is not followed by the ASC or DESC keywords. This is fine since it will sort in ascending order by default.

Code:

```
SELECT *
FROM Customers
ORDER BY lastname
```

Result:

	CustomerID	FirstName	LastName	Address	City	State	Zip
1	93	Nicholas	Ackerman	5 Buckingham Dr	Dallas	TX	52347
2	141	Alfred	Allen	29 Water Street	New York	NY	12189
3	15	Pindar	Ames	23 Cornell Dr	New York	NY	45357
4	50	Thomas	Andersen	52 Betwood Street	Orlando	FL	89754

```
(201 row(s) returned)
```

51. SELECT with WHERE and ORDER BY

Retrieve all customers except those in Boston and sort by last name

Discussion:

In this example, we use the * wildcard character to retrieve all columns in the customers table. For rows, we filter the result set by using the WHERE clause with the inequality predicate "<>" to select all customers except those in the city of Boston. Then, we sort ascending on lastname.

Code:

```
SELECT *
FROM Customers
WHERE city <> 'Boston'
ORDER BY lastname
```

Result:

CustomerID	First Name	Last Name	Address	City	State	Zip
93	Nicholas	Ackerman	5 Buckingham Dr	Dallas	TX	52347
141	Alfred	Allen	29 Water Street	New York	NY	12189
15	Pindar	Ames	23 Cornell Dr	New York	NY	45357
50	Thomas	Andersen	52 Betwood Street	Orlando	FL	89754

(187 row(s) returned)

52. SELECT with WHERE, GROUP BY, HAVING and ORDER BY

Calculate the number of customers in all states except NY and show states with more than ten customers

Discussion:

Our business manager asked us to calculate the number of customers in each state. In addition, she asked us to exclude New York State from the results. From the remaining states, she also asked us to exclude states with less than ten customers. Finally, states with bigger numbers of customers should appear first in the result set.

To comply with the above requirements, we need to use SELECT, WHERE, GROUP BY, HAVING, and ORDER BY in combination. Let us examine the purpose of each statement: First, we use the SELECT statement to select two fields from the customers table. Specifically, we select the state field as it is and the CustomerID field on which we apply the Count() function to calculate the number of occurrences of CustomerID in the table. Since CustomerID is the primary key of the table, we know that Count() will produce reliable results because there is no way to have null values in a primary key field.

Then, we use the WHERE clause with the inequality operator "<>" to exclude from the calculations customers in New York State. Practically, "<>" means retrieve everything else except 'NY'. Next, we use the GROUP BY clause to aggregate calculations by state. The database will calculate the number of customers and produce results by state since we group on that field.

The next point is a bit tricky if not understood well. The WHERE and HAVING clauses are both filtering statements. We use them both to obtain a subset of records. They do, however, have their specific roles in SQL statements, and they can be used individually or in combination. In this specific example, we use the WHERE clause to exclude customers from the state of New York from the result set. The WHERE clause will run before any groupings and calculations by the GROUP BY clause. In this particular example, the WHERE clause will exclude customers from NY, and the GROUP BY clause will produce groups and count customers for the remaining records. After the groups of customers by state are generated from the GROUP BY clause, and the customer numbers are calculated by the count() function, the HAVING clause takes effect. It will exclude from the final result any states with less than ten customers. Therefore, the HAVING clause will wait until the groupings and calculations are complete before it takes effect. This is logical since the numbers produced by the count() function are not known in advance.

Finally, the ORDER BY clause takes effect, and it will sort results by the highest number of customers. What you need to remember in one sentence is that when using the WHERE and HAVING clauses in combination, the WHERE clause always takes effect first, while the HAVING clause takes effect after the groups by the GROUP BY clause have been established. The ORDER BY clause will take effect last.

Code:
SELECT State, Count(CustomerID) As NumberOfCustomers
FROM Customers
WHERE State <> 'NY'
GROUP BY State
HAVING Count(CustomerID) >10
ORDER BY Count(CustomerID) DESC

Result:

	State	NumberOfCustomers
1	CA	48
2	TX	25
3	FL	21
4	MA	14

(8 row(s) returned)

53. SELECT with INSERT INTO to append records in an existing table
Append records from the customer table to a historical customer table
Discussion:
Our goal in this example is to copy (append) a number of records from our customer table to another table in which we keep historical customer data. This scenario applies in situations where we no longer do business with some customers, but we do not want to delete them from the database. At the same time, we do not want these old customers to clutter our operational customer table, slow it down, or interfere with our calculations. We can easily copy them to a historical table by using the INSERT INTO statement. The general structure of the INSERT INTO statement appears below:

INSERT INTO TargetTable (field1, field2, field3...)
SELECT (field1, field2, field3...)
FROM SourceTable

In this particular example, we copy records from the customers table to the customer2 table. Since customer2 does not exist, we create it with the CREATE statement below. Then, we use the INSERT INTO statement to append three fields with 201 records (all records in the customer table) in the customer2 table.

Code:
CREATE TABLE Customer2 (
[CustomerID] int identity (1,1) Primary key not null,
[LastName] nvarchar(50),
[FirstName] nvarchar(50),
[Address] nvarchar(100),
[City] nvarchar(50))

Result:
The table Customer2 has been created in the database

CHAPTER 5

Code:
INSERT INTO Customer2 (firstname, lastname, address, city)
SELECT firstname, lastname, address, city
FROM customers

Result:
```
(201 row(s) affected)
```

54. SELECT with INSERT INTO to append specific records in a table

Append selected customer records to a historical table

Discussion:

In some occasions, we might want to copy only a subset of records in one table into another table. We can easily achieve this by using the INSERT TO statement and the WHERE clause in combination. In this specific example, we append customer records from NY only.

Code:
INSERT INTO Customer2 (firstname, lastname, address, city)
SELECT firstname, lastname, address, city
FROM customers
WHERE State = 'NY'

Result:
```
(31 row(s) affected)
```

55. SELECT INTO to create a backup or temp table

Create a quick backup copy of the products table

Discussion:

The SELECT INTO statement accomplishes two tasks simultaneously. First, it can create a new table, and second, it can populate this table with records from another table. We do not need to use the CREATE statement to create a new table and then the INSERT INTO to copy records from one table to another. The SELECT INTO statement can accomplish both tasks at once.

We can use the SELECT INTO statement to create quick backup copies of tables, or we can create temporary tables and work on their data leaving the original tables untouched. For instance, we might want to manipulate data in the products table, but we would like to see the results of the edits first before we apply them in the operational products table. In this particular example, we create a backup copy of the products table, and we name it Products_Backup.

Code:
SELECT *
INTO Products_Backup
FROM Products

Result:
```
(70 row(s) affected)
```

56. SELECT INTO to create a backup table with a subset of data from the original table
Create a temporary table that contains a subset of data from the products table
Discussion:
We can use the SELECT INTO statement and the WHERE clause in combination to create a new table that will contain a subset of data from the original table. In fact, using the SELECT INTO statement in combination with the WHERE clause, we can transfer any fields and records we wish. In this particular example, we create a new table named "Products_Subset" which will contain only three fields and product records from suppliers with supplier ID 1, 2, 3, and 4 only.

Code:
SELECT ProductName, UnitsInStock, UnitsOnOrder
INTO Products_Subset
FROM Products
WHERE SupplierID IN (1,2,3,4)

Result:
```
(32 row(s) affected)
```

57. SELECT INTO to create a new table with a subset of data from three joined tables
Create a new table that contains data from the three joined tables
Discussion:
The SELECT INTO statement can create a new table that contains data from multiple joined tables. In this example, we create a new table that contains fields from the customers, orders, and productsorders tables. In addition, we restrict the number of records it will contain by using the WHERE clause for customers in NY only. Why do we need to create a new table since we can easily retrieve the same records using a view? Actually, a move like this one serves multiple purposes. First, we might want to give access to this data to other people and not worry if they edit or change it any way they want. If we provide them with a query, they could affect the data in the underlying tables. Another scenario might be that we would like to hide the complexities of the joins to the people working with this data. It is much easier to work with one table than with two inner joins from three tables. Finally, we might be in a business scenario in which this table is the data source for XML or PHP or ASP.Net or other server side pages on our website, and we generate this table every week. Those pages will return results much faster working out of a table data source instead of multiple joins and WHERE clauses.

Code:
SELECT customers.lastname, customers.firstName, Orders.OrderDate, ProductsOrders.UnitPrice, ProductsOrders.Quantity
INTO TempCustomersOrders
FROM (customers INNER JOIN Orders ON customers.CustomerID = Orders.CustomerID) INNER JOIN ProductsOrders ON Orders.OrderID = ProductsOrders.OrderID
WHERE customers.State='NY'

Result:
```
(375 row(s) affected)
```

58. SELECT INTO to create a new table with the structure of an existing table but without the data

Discussion:

Using the code below, we will create a new table named "Products1" which will be identical to the Products table but without any data. Field names and corresponding data types transfer wonderfully but remember to define the primary key and any indexes in your new table.

Code:

```
SELECT * INTO Products1
FROM Products
WHERE 1=2
```

Result:

```
(0 row(s) affected)
```

59. SELECT INTO to create a new table with part of the structure of an existing table

Discussion:

As a continuation from the previous example, you can transfer part of the structure of an existing table to a new one as in the code below. Remember, no data will be moved to the new table.

Code:

```
SELECT ProductID, ProductName, QuantityPerUnit, ProductUnitPrice INTO Products2
FROM Products
WHERE 1=2
```

Result:

```
(0 row(s) affected)
```

60. SELECT to retrieve a list of user tables in the database

Discussion:

Sometimes, we might want to obtain a simple list of the user tables in our database. We can achieve this goal using the code below.

Code:

```
SELECT Name, Type
FROM SysObjects
WHERE Type = 'U'
```

Result:

	Name	Type
1	tbls_Customers_UN	U
2	tempTable_UN	U
3	tblS_Products_Lo...	U
4	tble_CustomersN	U

```
(39 row(s) returned)
```

61. SELECT to retrieve a list of system tables in the database

Discussion:

If we want to obtain a list of the system tables in our database we write:

Code:

SELECT Name, Type
FROM SysObjects
WHERE Type = 'S'

Result:

	Name	Type
1	sysrscols	S
2	sysrowsets	S
3	sysclones	S
4	sysallocunits	S

(39 row(s) returned)

CHAPTER 5 DISCUSSION QUESTIONS

1. What is the primary purpose of the SELECT statement? Retrieve a subset of rows from a table, a subset of columns, or both?
2. What is the purpose of using column aliases in SELECT statements?
3. Can we insert plain text in SELECT statements? How can this help us in our business communications?
4. What is the purpose of the WHERE clause in the SELECT statement?
5. What is the purpose of the ORDER BY clause in the SELECT statement?
6. What is the purpose of using the GROUP BY clause with SELECT?
7. Is HAVING a clause we can use with SELECT? What is its purpose?
8. What is the difference between the WHERE and HAVING clauses?
9. What statement can we use with SELECT to append records to an existing table?
10. What keyword we can use to create a new table using a single SELECT statement?

CHAPTER 5 HANDS-ON EXERCISES

Chapter 5 Case 1:

Start SQL Server Management Studio. For each of the questions in this case you need to create a new query (Ctrl-N) and name it as per the instructions in each question. Submit your work to your instructor as one text file that contains all SQL statements or as per your instructor's directions.

1. Create a query to select all columns and rows from the products table. Save the query as Chapter05_Case1_Q1.

Your result should look like:

ProductID	ProductName	SupplierID	QuantityPerUnit	ProductUnitPrice	UnitsInStock
1	Almonds, Hickory Smoked - 12 oz. Bag	1	12	35.00	40
2	Almonds, Roasted and Salted - 18 oz. Bag	1	12	22.00	32
3	Banana Chips - 20 oz. Bag	1	12	27.00	25
4	Berry Cherry in 8 oz. Bag	1	15	30.00	50
5	California Original Pistachios - 1 lb. Bag	1	15	29.00	35

(70 row(s) returned)

2. Retrieve all records from the products table but only include the following fields: ProductName, ProductUnitPrice, UnitsInStock, and UnitsOnOrder. Save the query as Chapter05_Case1_Q2.

Your result should look like:

	ProductName	ProductUnitPrice	UnitsInStock	UnitsOnOrder
1	Almonds, Hickory Smoked - 12 oz. Bag	35.00	40	5
2	Almonds, Roasted and Salted - 18 oz. Bag	22.00	32	0
3	Banana Chips - 20 oz. Bag	27.00	25	0
4	Berry Cherry in 8 oz. Bag	30.00	50	0

(70 row(s) returned)

3. Create a view to retrieve all products for which the UnitsOnOrder quantity is zero. Save the query as Chapter05_Case1_Q3.

Your result should look like:

ProductID	ProductName	SupplierID	QuantityPerUnit	ProductUnitPrice
2	Almonds, Roasted and Salted - 18 oz. Bag	1	12	22.00
3	Banana Chips - 20 oz. Bag	1	12	27.00
4	Berry Cherry in 8 oz. Bag	1	15	30.00
5	California Original Pistachios - 1 lb. Bag	1	15	29.00

(46 row(s) returned)

4. Create a query that includes the fields ProductName, ProductUnitPrice, UnitsInStock, and UnitsOnOrder. The query should include all the records in the table. However, in the result set the field names should appear as: Product Name, Price, Units In Stock, and Units On Order. Save the query as Chapter05_Case1_Q4.

Your result should look like:

Product Name	Price	Units In Stock	Units on Order
Almonds, Hickory Smoked - 12 oz. Bag	35.00	40	5
Almonds, Roasted and Salted - 18 oz. Bag	22.00	32	0
Banana Chips - 20 oz. Bag	27.00	25	0
Berry Cherry in 8 oz. Bag	30.00	50	0

(70 row(s) returned)

5. Create a query to retrieve all columns and rows in the products table. The result set should be sorted ascending on the ProductUnitPrice field. Save the query as Chapter05_Case1_Q5.

Your result should look like:

ProductID	ProductName	SupplierID	QuantityPerUnit	ProductUnitPrice
49	Chunky Chocolate Cookies	7	30	15.00
70	Fried Jalapeños	10	30	15.00
62	Dried Red Tart Cherries - 1lb.	9	20	16.00
63	Dried Cranberries - 6oz.	9	30	16.00

(70 row(s) returned)

Chapter 5 Case 2:

Start SQL Server Management Studio. For each of the questions in this case you need to create a new query (Ctrl-N) and name it as per the instructions in each question. Submit your work to your instructor as one text file that contains all SQL statements or as per your instructor's directions.

1. Create a backup copy of the entire products table. Name the backup products table Products52_Backup. Save the query as Chapter05_Case2_Q1.

Result: A new table has been created as shown in the image below. Notice how the field data types moved intact. The ProductID primary key property however is not transferred. We need to set it ourselves. Also, if you check, no indexes are transferred although we have three in the products table.

Column Name	Data Type	Allow Nulls
ProductID	int	☐
ProductName	varchar(100)	☑
SupplierID	int	☑
QuantityPerUnit	float	☑
ProductUnitPrice	money	☑
UnitsInStock	smallint	☑
UnitsOnOrder	smallint	☑
ReorderLevel	float	☑
SKU	nvarchar(255)	☑
Active	bit	☑

```
The new table should have 70 rows.
```

2. Create a backup table for the products table. However, only include the ProductName, QuantityPerUnit, ProductUnitPrice, and UnitsInStock fields. Also, the backup table should include products from suppliers 5,6,7,8, and 9. Name the backup products table Products53_Backup. Save the query as Chapter05_Case2_Q2.

Result: A new table has been created as shown in the image below.

Column Name	Data Type	Allow Nulls
ProductName	varchar(100)	☑
QuantityPerUnit	float	☑
ProductUnitPrice	money	☑
UnitsInStock	smallint	☑

```
The new table should have 34 rows.
```

3. Create a new table and name it Products54. This table should have the following fields: ProductID primary key and auto increment with seed 1 and increment at 1, Product varchar(100), Quantity (int), Price (smallmoney), Stock (int), and OnOrder (int). Then, insert all records from the Products table into the Products54 table. Save the query as Chapter05_Case2_Q3.

Result1:

Column Name	Data Type	Allow Nulls
⚷ ProductID	int	☐
Product	varchar(100)	☑
Quantity	int	☑
Price	smallmoney	☑
Stock	int	☑
OnOrder	int	☑

Result2:

```
70 rows have been transferred to the products54 table.
```

4. Now, insert into the Products54 table only those products from the Products table whose price is more than $25. Save the query as Chapter05_Case2_Q4.

Result:

```
45 rows have been transferred to the products54 table.
```

5. Create a query to select all fields from the Products table for those products whose price is above $30 and sort ascending by productname. Save the query as Chapter05_Case2_Q5.

Result:

ProductID	Product Name	SupplierID	QuantityPerUnit	Product Unit Price
67	All-Purpose Marinade II	10	30	39.00
1	Almonds, Hickory Smoked - 12 oz. Bag	1	12	35.00
41	Banana Bisquits	6	30	38.00
59	Buttermilk Muffins	8	34	46.00
11	Cappuccino Almonds in 8oz. Bag	2	30	35.00

(31 row(s) returned)

CHAPTER 6
THE OR AND AND OPERATORS

There are four points you need to remember about the OR and AND operators: First, their task is to produce a subset of records from the total records in a table or query. Second, they have no effect on the columns we retrieve from that table or query. Third, they are always used with other operators such as LIKE, equality and inequality predicates, and wildcard characters. Fourth, the OR and AND operators can be used individually or in combination with varying results as we shall see in the following examples.

The OR operator is inclusive which means that records will be returned for every OR condition satisfied in our query. The AND operator is exclusive, and it will produce results only when all of the AND conditions are met.

62. Using OR on the same column
Create a quick report with customers in New York or Houston
Discussion:
Let us suppose we have a request to create a list of all customers who reside in New York or Houston. In this case, we need to use the OR operator on the city field with two equality predicates. Note that since we use the SELECT statement with *, the database will return all columns in the table. However, when it comes to records, only 39 out of 201 will be returned. This is because we filtered the recordset to include customers in the cities of New York or Houston only.

We can use the OR operator on the same column multiple times as in this example to retrieve customers from multiple cities. However, we cannot use the AND operator multiple times on the same column because we would ask the impossible: that is, having a customer who resides in many cities simultaneously.

Code:
SELECT *
FROM customers
WHERE city = 'New York' OR city = 'Houston'

Result:

	CustomerID	FirstName	LastName	Address	City	State	Zip	Country
1	1	John	Demarco	11 Lark Street	New York	NY	12189	USA
2	2	Mary	Demania	12 Madison Ave	New York	NY	12189	USA
3	3	George	Demers	23 New Scotland Ave	New York	NY	12189	USA
4	4	Phillip	Demetriou	22 Academy Road	New York	NY	12189	USA

(39 row(s) returned)

63. Use the IN operator to replace multiple OR operators
Produce a report of customers from four cities
Discussion:

The OR operator works fine with two cities as we have seen in the previous example. What if we need to use OR with five or six cities as criteria? We have two problems in this case: First, we need to write a long SQL statement using multiple OR operators. Second, if we have a big number of records in the table, the query will be slow to return results. In cases like this one, we can use the IN operator that produces much cleaner code. It is easy to modify and maintain as you can see below:

Code:
```
SELECT lastname, firstname, city, state
FROM customers
WHERE city IN ('Albany', 'Denver', 'Houston', 'Phoenix')
ORDER BY lastname ASC
```

Result:

	lastname	firstname	city	state
1	Bink	Jim	Houston	TX
2	Bittel	David	Houston	TX
3	Clark	Allen	Houston	TX
4	Clarson	Erin	Houston	TX

(42 row(s) returned)

64. Using OR on multiple columns
Create an inventory report listing product quantities for units in stock and units on order
Discussion:

A very efficient way to use the OR operator is to apply it on multiple columns. For instance, we might have a business request to create an inventory report that lists products for which we have more than 10 units in stock or products for which we have more than 10 units on order. The result set returned 70 products. This means that 70 records satisfied at least one condition. This is because any record that satisfies at least one of the conditions will appear in the result set.

In addition, this is why the second record in the result set with 32 units in stock and 0 on order appears as well. We asked for units in stock >10 or units on order >10. This particular record satisfies only the first condition, and this is enough to appear in the result set. The outcome will be very different when we use the AND operator as we will see presently.

Code:
```
SELECT productname, unitsinstock, unitsonorder
FROM products
WHERE UnitsInStock > 10 OR UnitsOnOrder > 10
```

Result:

	productname	unitsinstock	unitsonorder
1	Almonds, Hickory Smoked - 12 oz. Bag	40	5
2	Almonds, Roasted and Salted - 18 oz. Bag	32	0
3	Banana Chips - 20 oz. Bag	25	0
4	Berry Cherry in 8 oz. Bag	50	0

```
(70 row(s) returned)
```

65. Use UNION instead of OR to speed up results

Create an inventory report using UNION instead of OR operators

Discussion:

We can use the UNION statement instead of multiple OR operators to speed up the response time of the database engine. This is a trick and the difference in response time is enormous. The SQL statement below with the UNION operation achieves the exact same results as the SQL code in the previous example. However, the response is instant using UNION, while it takes quite a few seconds using the OR operators.

Response times deteriorate as the number of records or the number of OR operators increase. Consequently, if you have statements with multiple OR operators that you use often, you might consider replacing them with UNION statements. The only difference is the order in which the retrieved records appear since in this case, the results of the first SELECT statement in the UNION operation will appear first. The results of the second SELECT will follow and so on. You can easily reorder the recordset using the ORDER BY clause with a UNION statement. For a full understanding of UNION operations, plus related tips and tricks refer to chapter 21.

Code:

```
SELECT productname, unitsinstock, unitsonorder
FROM products
WHERE UnitsInStock > 10
UNION
SELECT productname, unitsinstock, unitsonorder
FROM products
WHERE UnitsOnOrder > 10
```

Result:

	productname	unitsinstock	unitsonorder
1	All-Purpose Marinade I	27	15
2	All-Purpose Marinade II	26	15
3	Almonds, Hickory Smoked - 12 oz. Bag	40	5
4	Almonds, Roasted and Salted - 18 oz. Bag	32	0

```
(70 row(s) returned)
```

66. Using AND on multiple columns

Produce a report of customers from a specific state and a specific city

Discussion:

This time, we need to produce a report of customers who reside in the state of NY and, in particular, the city of Albany. In this case, we need to use the AND operator to isolate records which satisfy both criteria at the same time. Note that if we use only the city as a criterion it will be a problem since there are 28 cities in the U.S. named Albany! If we do business worldwide, there are six additional cities named Albany. An experienced database user will always use AND to isolate the customers only for Albany, New York. As you can see from the result set, we have only four customers that satisfy both criteria.

Code:
SELECT lastname, firstname, city, state
FROM customers
WHERE state = 'NY' AND city = 'Albany'

Result:

	lastname	firstname	city	state
1	Vanton	Kenneth	Albany	NY
2	Trindan	Luis	Albany	NY
3	Riegert	Joanne	Albany	NY
4	Miller	Anthony	Albany	NY

(4 row(s) returned)

67. Using OR and AND in combination
Produce a report of customers from one state and two cities
Discussion:
Our objective in this scenario is to produce a report that will list customers from the cities of Albany and New York in NY State. In this case, we need to use the AND operator twice and the OR operator once as it appears in the code below:

Code:
SELECT lastname, firstname, city, state
FROM customers
WHERE
state = 'NY' AND city = 'Albany'
OR
state = 'NY' AND city = 'New York'
ORDER BY lastname

Result:

	lastname	firstname	city	state
1	Allen	Alfred	New York	NY
2	Ames	Pindar	New York	NY
3	Anderson	Peter	New York	NY
4	Anthopolis	Ricky	New York	NY
5	Aversa	Scott	New York	NY

(31 row(s) returned)

68. Using multiple OR and multiple AND operators in combination
Produce a report of customers from three states and three cities
Discussion:
This time, we have a request to create a customer report that will list customers in the cities of Houston, Albany, and Phoenix from the states of Texas, New York, and Arizona respectively. In this case, we need to use the AND operator three times and the OR operator twice as it appears in the code below.

Code:
SELECT lastname, firstname, city, state
FROM customers
WHERE
state = 'NY' AND city = 'Albany'
OR
state = 'TX' AND city = 'Houston'
OR
state = 'AZ' AND city = 'Phoenix'
ORDER BY lastname

Result:

	lastname	firstname	city	state
1	Bink	Jim	Houston	TX
2	Bittel	David	Houston	TX
3	Clark	Allen	Houston	TX
4	Clarson	Erin	Houston	TX
5	Clinton	Charles	Houston	TX

```
(29 row(s) returned)
```

CHAPTER 6 DISCUSSION QUESTIONS
1. What is the primary purpose of the OR and AND operators in a query?
2. Is the OR operator inclusive or exclusive? What is the implication of this?
3. Is the AND operator inclusive or exclusive? What is the implication of this?
4. When using the OR and AND operators, can we control what columns (fields) will appear in the result set?
5. Can we use the OR and AND operators alone or in conjunction with other operators and predicates?
6. Can we use the OR operator multiple times on the same column? What is the meaning of doing this?
7. Can we use the OR operator on multiple columns? How many conditions need to be true to obtain results?
8. What operator can we use to replace multiple OR operators?
9. Can we use the AND operator multiple times on the same column? Why it does not make sense to use the AND operator on the same column?
10. What will the result be if we use the AND operator on multiple columns? How many conditions need to be true to obtain results?

CHAPTER 6 HANDS-ON EXERCISES

Chapter 6 Case 1:
Start SQL Server Management Studio. For each of the questions in this case you need to create a new query (Ctrl-N) and name it as per the instructions in each question. Submit your work to your instructor as one text file that contains all SQL statements or as per your instructor's directions.

1. Create a query to select all customers from the states of New York and Massachusetts. Save the query as Chapter06_Case1_Q1.

   Result:

CustomerID	FirstName	LastName	Address	City
1	John	Demarco	11 Lark Street	New York
2	Mary	Demania	12 Madison Ave	New York
3	George	Demers	23 New Scotland Ave	New York
4	Phillip	Demetriou	22 Academy Road	New York
5	Andrew	Demichele	14 Glandel Ave	New York

   (45 row(s) returned)

2. Create a query to select all customers from the states of New York, Massachusetts, Ohio, Texas, and Colorado. Hint: Use the IN operator. Save the query as Chapter06_Case1_Q2.

   Result:

CustomerID	FirstName	LastName	Address	City
1	John	Demarco	11 Lark Street	New York
2	Mary	Demania	12 Madison Ave	New York
3	George	Demers	23 New Scotland Ave	New York
4	Phillip	Demetriou	22 Academy Road	New York
5	Andrew	Demichele	14 Glandel Ave	New York

(97 row(s) returned)

3. Create a query to select all customers from the city of Boston and the State of California. Save the query as Chapter06_Case1_Q3.

Result:

CustomerID	FirstName	LastName	Address	City
16	Joseph	Anderson	34 Cortland Ave	Los Angeles
17	Allen	Restad	72 Providence Dr	Los Angeles
18	Charles	Zensons	23 Tampa Ave	Los Angeles
19	Erin	Erin	28 Karrie Terrace	Los Angeles
20	Lisa	Zartons	34 Home Ave	Los Angeles

(62 row(s) returned)

4. Create a query to select all customers from the city of Albany in the state of New York and the city of San Jose in the state of California. Name the query Chapter06_Case1_Q4.

Result:

CustomerID	FirstName	LastName	Address	City	State
14	Kenneth	Vanton	855 Hackett Blvd	Albany	NY
35	Luis	Trindan	37 Greenbush Ave	Albany	NY
109	Roy	Cutillo	22 Woodville Ave	San Jose	CA
110	Diane	Darek	9 North Bridge Dr	San Jose	CA
111	Julia	Datek	3 Woodscape Dr	San Jose	CA

(12 row(s) returned)

5. Create a query to select all customers form the cities of San Jose, Phoenix, and Boston, for the states of California, Arizona, and Massachusetts respectively. Save the query as Chapter06_Case1_Q5.

Result:

CustomerID	FirstName	LastName	Address	City
109	Roy	Cutillo	22 Woodville Ave	San Jose
110	Diane	Darek	9 North Bridge Dr	San Jose
111	Julia	Datek	3 Woodscape Dr	San Jose
112	Gerald	Edwards	2 Norfok Street	San Jose
113	Colin	Ellison	123 Front Ave	San Jose

(35 row(s) returned)

Chapter 6 Case 2:

Start SQL Server Management Studio. For each of the questions in this case you need to create a new query (Ctrl-N) and name it as per the instructions in each question. Submit your work to your instructor as one text file that contains all SQL statements or as per your instructor's directions.

1. Create a query to select all customers from the states of New York, Massachusetts, Arizona, and Texas. Use the OR operator to achieve your result. Save the query as Chapter06_Case2_Q1.

   Result:

CustomerID	FirstName	LastName	Address	City
1	John	Demarco	11 Lark Street	New York
2	Mary	Demania	12 Madison Ave	New York
3	George	Demers	23 New Scotland Ave	New York
4	Phillip	Demetriou	22 Academy Road	New York
5	Andrew	Demichele	14 Glandel Ave	New York

   (83 row(s) returned)

2. Create the same query as in step 1 but this time use the IN operator to achieve your result. Name the query Chapter06_Case2_Q2.

   Result:

CustomerID	FirstName	LastName	Address	City
1	John	Demarco	11 Lark Street	New York
2	Mary	Demania	12 Madison Ave	New York
3	George	Demers	23 New Scotland Ave	New York
4	Phillip	Demetriou	22 Academy Road	New York
5	Andrew	Demichele	14 Glandel Ave	New York

   (83 row(s) returned)

3. Create the same query as in step 1 but this time use the UNION operator to achieve your result. Name the query Chapter06_Case2_Q3.

   Result:

CustomerID	FirstName	LastName	Address	City
1	John	Demarco	11 Lark Street	New York
2	Mary	Demania	12 Madison Ave	New York
3	George	Demers	23 New Scotland Ave	New York
4	Phillip	Demetriou	22 Academy Road	New York
5	Andrew	Demichele	14 Glandel Ave	New York

   (83 row(s) returned)

4. Create a query to select all customers except those in the states of California, Arizona, and Massachusetts. Save the query as Chapter06_Case2_Q4.

Result:

CustomerID	FirstName	LastName	Address	City
1	John	Demarco	11 Lark Street	New York
2	Mary	Demania	12 Madison Ave	New York
3	George	Demers	23 New Scotland Ave	New York
4	Phillip	Demetriou	22 Academy Road	New York
5	Andrew	Demichele	14 Glandel Ave	New York

```
(126 row(s) returned)
```

5. Create a query to select all customers except those in area code 22459. Save the query as Chapter06_Case2_Q5.

Result:

CustomerID	FirstName	LastName	Address	City
1	John	Demarco	11 Lark Street	New York
2	Mary	Demania	12 Madison Ave	New York
3	George	Demers	23 New Scotland Ave	New York
4	Phillip	Demetriou	22 Academy Road	New York
5	Andrew	Demichele	14 Glandel Ave	New York

```
(187 row(s) returned)
```

CHAPTER 7
SORTING RECORDS: THE ORDER BY CLAUSE

The ORDER BY clause, with the ASC or DESC keywords, allows the sorting of records in ascending or descending order respectively. The ORDER BY clause is much stronger than what is generally assumed and it allows for some cool tricks with our data.

69. Sorting ascending on one column

Create a list of customers sorting by last name in ascending order

Discussion:

This is a basic example of how to sort our customers by last name and in ascending order. Customers whose last names start with an "A" will appear first. The keyword "ASC" is not required to sort records in ascending order. If we leave the keyword "ASC" out, the ORDER BY clause will sort ascending by default.

Code:

```
SELECT *
FROM Customers
ORDER BY lastname ASC
```

Result:

CustomerID	First Name	Last Name	Address	City	State
93	Nicholas	Ackerman	5 Buckingham Dr	Dallas	TX
141	Alfred	Allen	29 Water Street	New York	NY
15	Pindar	Ames	23 Cornell Dr	New York	NY
50	Thomas	Andersen	52 Betwood Street	Orlando	FL
16	Joseph	Anderson	34 Cortland Ave	Los Angeles	CA

(201 row(s) returned)

70. Sorting descending on one column

Create a list of customers sorting by last name in descending order

Discussion:

Sometimes, we want to see names in reverse alphabetical order—names that start with Z, Y, or X first. In this case, we add the DESC keyword to our SQL statement. Note that if we want to sort descending, the DESC keyword is required.

Code:

```
SELECT *
FROM Customers
ORDER BY lastname DESC
```

Result:

CustomerID	FirstName	LastName	Address	City	State
48	Stephen	Zinter	110 Johnson Ave	Philadelphia	PA
21	Lauren	Zentons	23 Crescent Dr	Los Angeles	CA
18	Charles	Zensons	23 Tampa Ave	Los Angeles	CA
20	Lisa	Zartons	34 Home Ave	Los Angeles	CA
49	Chris	Youkon	11 Rose CT	Orlando	FL

```
(201 row(s) returned)
```

71. Sorting on multiple columns

Create a customer list sorting by city and last name simultaneously

Discussion:

We can sort records on the values of multiple columns. For example, we might want to obtain a report which will include a list of customers sorted first by city and then, by last name.

Let's say we have some customers in Albany and some customers in Boston. Sorting ascending on both city and last name fields will create the following result: The records with the city of Albany will appear first in the result set, followed by the records with the city of Boston. Now, within the Albany records, customers will be sorted alphabetically and in ascending order. Within the city of Boston records, customers will again be sorted alphabetically and in ascending order. We should not be surprised to see a customer from Boston whose last name starts with an "A" being listed after a customer in Albany whose last name starts with a "Z".

Code:

```
SELECT city, lastname, firstname
FROM Customers
ORDER BY city, lastname ASC
```

Result:

	city	lastname	firstname
1	Albany	Miller	Anthony
2	Albany	Riegert	Joanne
3	Albany	Trindan	Luis
4	Albany	Vanton	Kenneth
5	Boston	Cormack	Arnold

```
(201 row(s) returned)
```

72. Use the ORDER BY clause to sort multiple columns with different sorting directions

Create a customer list sorting by city ascending and customer name descending

Discussion:

We also have the ability to sort on multiple columns forcing a different sorting direction for each column. In this example we sort ascending on the city and then for each city we sort descending on the last name.

Code:

```
SELECT city, lastname, firstname
FROM Customers
ORDER BY city ASC, lastname DESC
```

Result:

	city	lastname	firstname
1	Albany	Vanton	Kenneth
2	Albany	Trindan	Luis
3	Albany	Riegert	Joanne
4	Albany	Miller	Anthony
5	Boston	Strack	Joanne

```
(201 row(s) returned)
```

73. Use the ORDER BY clause with null values

Find customers who do not have a first name registered in the database

Discussion:

Let us suppose that we have a suspicion that some first name values are missing from our records. How can we quickly find out which ones they are? We can simply create a view that includes the fields we would like to check and sort ascending on the field we suspect includes blank entries. In this instance, we sort ascending on the first name field from our customers table. As you can see from the result set, we immediately found one customer without a first name.

Code:

```
SELECT lastname, firstname
FROM Customers
ORDER BY firstname ASC
```

Result:

	lastname	firstname
1	Corelli	NULL
2	Allen	Alfred
3	Kashisnky	Alfred
4	Tranton	Alfred

```
(201 row(s) returned)
```

74. Use the ORDER BY clause with numbers

Create an inventory report listing products with biggest quantities first

Discussion:

In this scenario, we list products from our inventory with the biggest quantities on hand at the top. We can easily achieve this task using the DESC keyword with numbers. When sorting numbers, the DESC keyword will cause the biggest ones to show first, while the ASC keyword will cause the smallest numbers to show first.

Code:

```
SELECT productname, unitsinstock
FROM products
ORDER BY unitsinstock DESC
```

Result:

	productname	unitsinstock
1	Berry Cherry in 8 oz. Bag	50
2	Artichokes in white sauce	50
3	Chocolate Chip Cookies	50
4	Biscuits with cream	49

```
(70 row(s) returned)
```

75. The ORDER BY clause with dates

Create a list with the latest orders on top

Discussion:

The ORDER BY clause works with dates the same way it works with numbers. So, to list the latest dates first, we use the DESC keyword. If we would like to show the oldest dates first, we use the ASC keyword.

Code:

```
SELECT orderid, orderdate, shippeddate
FROM ORDERS
ORDER BY orderdate DESC
```

Result:

	orderid	orderdate	shippeddate
1	4	2014-12-19	2014-12-24
2	874	2014-12-16	2014-12-21
3	165	2014-12-14	2014-12-19
4	881	2014-12-12	2014-12-17

```
(1000 row(s) returned)
```

76. TIP: Combine the ORDER BY and TOP clauses to control the result set

List the top five products in the inventory with the biggest quantities on hand

Discussion:

The ORDER BY clause produces very meaningful results when used in combination with the TOP clause. For instance, what if we want to list the top five products in our inventory with the biggest quantities on hand? We can achieve this task by combining the ORDER BY and TOP clauses. Notice the number of records in the result set. Only five products appear, and these five products have the largest unit quantities in stock in our inventory.

Code:

```
SELECT TOP 5 unitsinstock, productname
FROM products
ORDER BY unitsinstock DESC
```

Result:

	unitsinstock	productname
1	50	Berry Cherry in 8 oz. Bag
2	50	Artichokes in white sauce
3	50	Chocolate Chip Cookies
4	49	Biscuits with cream

```
(5 row(s) returned)
```

You need to pay attention to the results of the TOP clause however. It will provide consistent results as soon as there are distinct values in the field on which we are using it. If there are identical values, then all of them will appear in the result set if the first one appears. For example, let us say we have four products with quantity per unit at 50 units and ten products with quantity per unit at 49 units. If we use TOP 5 to get the top five quantities per unit, we will actually get fourteen records.

77. Determine your own sort order using the CASE function

Discussion:

Now, we have an odd request from the marketing department. They want a list of customers sorted by state but they want to determine the sort order themselves, that is, which state will appear first, which second, etc. In this case, they want the customers from New York to appear first, those from California next, and those from Texas last. This is impossible to achieve by using the simple ascending and descending qualifiers of the ORDER BY clause. However, it is possible using the CASE function as in the code below. This is a very flexible way to order records in any way we like. Notice also that we exclude other states from the result set for simplicity.

Code:
```
SELECT *
FROM View_Conditions
WHERE STATE in ('NY','CA','TX')
ORDER BY
CASE State
When 'NY' THEN 1
When 'CA' THEN 2
When 'TX' THEN 3
Else 4
End
```

Result:

	OrderID	LastName	FirstName	City	State	OrderDate	ShippedDate
1	10	Demaria	Matthew	New York	NY	2013-12-13	2013-12-18
2	11	Demers	George	New York	NY	2013-06-07	2013-06-12
3	1	Riegert	Joanne	Albany	NY	2013-11-11	2013-11-16
4	23	Dube	Jean	New York	NY	2012-01-18	2012-01-23

```
(512 row(s) returned)
```

107

CHAPTER 7 DISCUSSION QUESTIONS

1. What is the difference between sorting ascending and sorting descending?
2. Is the keyword "ASC" ascending optional or required in the ORDER BY clause?
3. Is the keyword "DESC" optional or required in the ORDER BY clause?
4. Can we use the ORDER BY clause to sort multiple fields? In what order are multiple fields sorted?
5. If we sort ascending on a field that contains null values, do those values appear at the top or the bottom of the sorted column?
6. If we sort descending on a number field, do big numbers appear at the top or the bottom of the sorted column?
7. We want to sort a date field so that the most recent dates appear first. Shall we use ASC or DESC?
8. You need to obtain the five most recent orders. Shall you combine TOP with ORDER BY and DESC or TOP with ORDER BY and ASC on the date field?
9. You need to obtain the top five most expensive products. Shall you combine TOP with ORDER BY and DESC or TOP with ORDER BY and ASC on the price field?
10. What function can we use to implement our own custom sort order in SQL Server?

CHAPTER 7 HANDS-ON EXERCISES

Chapter 7 Case 1:
Start SQL Server Management Studio. For each of the questions in this case you need to create a new query (Ctrl-N) and name it as per the instructions in each question. Submit your work to your instructor as one text file that contains all SQL statements or as per your instructor's directions.

1. Create a query that includes the fields ProductName, ProductUnitPrice, UnitsInStock, UnitsOnOrder, ReorderLevel, SKU, and Active from the Products table. Your supervisor wants the records sorted in a way so that products with no UnitsOnOrder show first in the result set. Save the query as Chapter07_Case1_Q1.

   Result:

ProductName	ProductUnitPrice	UnitsInStock	UnitsOnOrder
Almonds, Roasted and Salted - 18 oz. Bag	22.00	32	0
Banana Chips - 20 oz. Bag	27.00	25	0
Berry Cherry in 8 oz. Bag	30.00	50	0
California Original Pistachios - 1 lb. Bag	29.00	35	0
Choice Apricots - 16 oz. Bag	32.00	22	0

   (70 row(s) returned)

2. Create a query that includes all the fields from the Products table. Your supervisor wants the records sorted in a way so that products with the most UnitsInStock show first in the result set. Save the query as Chapter07_Case1_Q2.

   Result:

ProductID	ProductName	SupplierID	QuantityPerUnit	ProductUnitPrice	UnitsInStock
4	Berry Cherry in 8 oz. Bag	1	15	30.00	50
46	Artichokes in white sauce	6	20	22.00	50
47	Chocolate Chip Cookies	6	25	49.00	50
40	Biscuits with cream	5	25	27.00	49
69	Salsa Verde	10	31	35.00	49

(70 row(s) returned)

3. Create a query that includes the fields ProductName, ProductUnitPrice, and UnitsInStock from the Products table. Your supervisor needs a list of the ten products with the highest number of units in stock. Save the query as Chapter07_Case1_Q3.

Result:

UnitsInStock	ProductName	ProductUnitPrice
50	Berry Cherry in 8 oz. Bag	30.00
50	Artichokes in white sauce	22.00
50	Chocolate Chip Cookies	49.00
49	Biscuits with cream	27.00
49	Salsa Verde	35.00

(10 row(s) returned)

4. Create a query that includes the fields ProductName, ProductUnitPrice, and UnitsOnOrder from the Products table. Your supervisor wants a list of the five products with the highest number of units on order. Save the query as Chapter07_Case1_Q4.

Result:

UnitsOnOrder	ProductName	ProductUnitPrice
25	Nacho Chips Bag	25.00
20	Chocolate Chunk Cookies, 9.5 oz.	48.00
20	Oatmeal Raisin Walnut Cookies	43.00
20	Chunky Chocolate Cookies	15.00
20	Apple Cinnamon Raisin Cookies	27.00

(5 row(s) returned)

5. Create a query that includes the fields ProductName, ProductUnitPrice, UnitsInStock, and ReorderLevel from the Products table. Your supervisor wants a list of the ten products with the lowest reorder level. Save the query as Chapter07_Case1_Q5. You see that you get 26 records in the result set and not ten.

Result:

Product Name	Product Unit Price	Units In Stock	Reorder Level
Banana Chips - 20 oz. Bag	27.00	25	20
Almonds, Roasted and Salted - 18 oz. Bag	22.00	32	20
Raw Sunflower Seeds in 19 oz. Bag	25.00	12	20
Dried Cranberries - 34 oz.	35.00	15	20
Water Crackers 4.4 oz.	24.00	44	20

```
(10 row(s) returned)
```

Chapter 7 Case 2:

Start SQL Server Management Studio. For each of the questions in this case you need to create a new query (Ctrl-N) and name it as per the instructions in each question. Submit your work to your instructor as one text file that contains all SQL statements or as per your instructor's directions.

1. Create a query that includes the fields State, City, LastName, and FirstName from the Customers table. Your supervisor wants the records sorted simultaneously by State and then City in ascending order. Save the query as Chapter07_Case2_Q1.

Result:

State	City	Last Name	First Name
AZ	Phoenix	Lanci	Christine
AZ	Phoenix	Latta	Lloyd
AZ	Phoenix	Lareous	Angelo
AZ	Phoenix	Papadopoulos	Cynthia
AZ	Phoenix	Mahoney	Dolores

```
(201 row(s) returned)
```

2. Create a query that includes the fields State, City, LastName, and FirstName from the Customers table. Your supervisor wants the records sorted simultaneously by State ascending and then City in descending order. Save the query as Chapter07_Case2_Q2.

Result:

State	City	Last Name	First Name
AZ	Phoenix	Lanci	Christine
AZ	Phoenix	Latta	Lloyd
AZ	Phoenix	Lareous	Angelo
AZ	Phoenix	Papadopoulos	Cynthia
AZ	Phoenix	Mahoney	Dolores

```
(201 row(s) returned)
```

3. Create a query that includes the fields OrderID, CustomerID, OrderDate, ShippedDate, and ShippingCost from the Orders table. Provide a list with the ten most recent shipped orders. Save the query as Chapter07_Case2_Q3.

Result:

OrderID	CustomerID	OrderDate	ShippedDate	ShippingCost
4	165	2014-12-19	2014-12-24	48
874	159	2014-12-16	2014-12-21	39
165	120	2014-12-14	2014-12-19	52
881	167	2014-12-12	2014-12-17	44
628	157	2014-12-11	2014-12-16	47

(10 row(s) returned)

4. Create a query that includes the fields OrderID, CustomerID, OrderDate, ShippedDate, and ShippingCost from the Orders table. Provide a list with the ten orders with the most expensive shipping cost. Save the query as Chapter07_Case2_Q4.

Result:

OrderID	CustomerID	OrderDate	ShippedDate	ShippingCost
13	53	2012-02-10	2012-02-15	52
49	17	2013-07-07	2013-07-12	52
68	35	2012-09-03	2012-09-08	52
69	125	2012-02-24	2012-02-29	52
85	147	2012-04-30	2012-05-05	52

(10 row(s) returned)

5. Create a query that includes the fields OrderID, CustomerID, OrderDate, ShippedDate, and ShippingCost from the Orders table. Provide a list with 5% of the orders with the most expensive shipping cost. Save the query as Chapter07_Case2_Q5. Why the query returns 101 records?

Result:

OrderID	CustomerID	OrderDate	ShippedDate	ShippingCost
13	53	2012-02-10	2012-02-15	52
49	17	2013-07-07	2013-07-12	52
68	35	2012-09-03	2012-09-08	52
69	125	2012-02-24	2012-02-29	52
85	147	2012-04-30	2012-05-05	52

(100 row(s) returned)

CHAPTER 8
WORKING WITH WILDCARD CHARACTERS

Wildcard characters like (%, _ , ^ , [], -) provide essential functionality and power in databases. They are used in combination with operators such as (LIKE, OR, AND, BETWEEN, IN, etc.) and predicates like (<, >, <>, =, >=). They allow for the formulation of very sophisticated search criteria on text and number data.

78. The % wildcard character
Create a list of customers whose last name starts with D
Discussion:

The % is the wildest of the wildcard characters, and it will match any number and type (letters or numbers) of characters whether we put it in the beginning, middle, or end of a search condition. For example, we can search for all of the customer last names that start with the letter D. As we can see in this example, every customer whose last name starts with a D will appear in the result set. Notice in the code the % is positioned after the letter D. This means that entries such as Dem, D1a, d123, or Dzo will appear in the result set.

Code:
```
SELECT *
FROM customers
WHERE lastname Like 'D%'
```

Result:

	CustomerID	First Name	Last Name	Address	City	State
1	1	John	Demarco	11 Lark Street	New York	NY
2	2	Mary	Demania	12 Madison Ave	New York	NY
3	3	George	Demers	23 New Scotland Ave	New York	NY
4	4	Phillip	Demetriou	22 Academy Road	New York	NY

```
(21 row(s) returned)
```

79. The _ wildcard character in combination with %
Create a customer list using _ and % to create intricate search patterns
Discussion:

The _ character matches any single character. Though not used as much as the %, it can still make the difference and enable us to get exactly the results we want in certain cases. Usually, we use it in combination with other wildcard characters. For instance, let's say we want to find names starting with "Da", have any character after the "Da" pattern, and the next letter is "e" followed by any number of characters—'Da_e%'. This will give us results such as Darec, Datek, Dale, and Daleney.

Code:
SELECT *
FROM customers
WHERE lastname Like 'Da_e%'

Result:

CustomerID	FirstName	LastName	Address	City	State
110	Diane	Darek	9 North Bridge Dr	San Jose	CA
111	Julia	Datek	3 Woodscape Dr	San Jose	CA
196	Matthew	Darek	78 Unity Street	Denver	CO
197	Jason	Datek	19 Paul Street	Denver	CO

(4 row(s) returned)

80. Create multi-character search strings with [ ]
Create a customer list using multi-character search patterns
Discussion:
Let us assume we would like to search for a number of specific characters within a character string such as a name field. We can do this by using the brackets [ ]. Any character or characters that we include within the brackets will be included in our search. For example, C[ru]% will find Croney, Culey, but not Colonie. Note that we use the % in this example to allow any characters to be included after the brackets.

Code:
SELECT *
FROM customers
WHERE lastname Like 'C[ru]%'

Result:

CustomerID	FirstName	LastName	Address	City	State
99	Kenneth	Crondos	158 West Lawrence Ave	Houston	TX
100	Pindar	Crooney	16 Warren Street	Houston	TX
101	Joseph	Crandil	192 Tampa Ave	Houston	TX
107	Mary	Crawford	21 Aegean Dr	Houston	TX

(8 row(s) returned)

81. Use the ^ and [ ] wildcard characters to create exclusion patterns
Create a customer list using specific characters as exclusion search patterns
Discussion:
Sometimes, we need to exclude a set of characters to obtain the results we need. For example, we might want to retrieve all of our customers from the customers table except those whose names start with an A, B, C, D, or E. How about using the ^ wildcard to get the results we want? Note that the returned recordset is sorted by last name, and the first customer record to appear has a last name value starting with "F". All of the customers whose names start with a letter before that have been excluded from the recordset.

Code:
```
SELECT *
FROM customers
WHERE lastname Like '[^abcde]%'
ORDER BY lastname
```

Result:

CustomerID	First Name	Last Name	Address	City	State
115	Sonya	Ford	5 Beach Ave	San Jose	CA
166	Cristopher	Geisler	93 Kate Street	Boston	MA
116	William	Gibson	17 Grove Street	San Jose	CA
117	Kathy	Giordano	21 Garden Ave	San Diego	CA

```
(130 row(s) returned)
```

82. Use the ^ and [ ] and - wildcards to create exclusion ranges

Create a customer list using sets of characters as exclusion ranges

Discussion:

What if we continue from the previous example using ^ and [], but instead of typing in all of the characters, we use ranges? For example, we might want to obtain a recordset of customers whose names do not start with a letter in the range A-P. We can do this by using the '[^a-p]%' exclusion pattern. As you can see from the figure below, the customers who appear in the list have names starting with an "R", which is the one immediately following "P" that was included in our exclusion range.

Code:
```
SELECT *
FROM customers
WHERE lastname Like '[^a-p]%'
ORDER BY lastname
```

Result:

CustomerID	First Name	Last Name	Address	City	State
61	Richard	Ramirez	48 Mereline Ave	Miami	FL
184	Lisa	Read	12 Madison Ave	Washington	DC
17	Allen	Restad	72 Providence Dr	Los Angeles	CA

```
(59 row(s) returned)
```

83. Use the - and [ ] wildcards to create inclusion ranges

Create a customer list using sets of characters as inclusion ranges

Discussion:

We can continue from the previous example and use [ ] and - to obtain a recordset of customers whose names start with a letter between A and P.

Code:
SELECT *
FROM customers
WHERE lastname Like '[a-p]%'
ORDER BY lastname

Result:

CustomerID	FirstName	LastName	Address	City	State
93	Nicholas	Ackerman	5 Buckingham Dr	Dallas	TX
141	Alfred	Allen	29 Water Street	New York	NY
15	Pindar	Ames	23 Cornell Dr	New York	NY
50	Thomas	Andersen	52 Betwood Street	Orlando	FL

(142 row(s) returned)

CHAPTER 8 DISCUSSION QUESTIONS

1. What is the role of the % wildcard character?
2. How is the _ wildcard character different from the % one?
3. What is the role of the ^ wildcard character?
4. Can the % wildcard character find only letters, only numbers, or both?
5. What is the function of the [] wildcard character?
6. What is the difference between a range and a pattern?
7. What wildcard character can we use if we want to look for ranges?
8. What wildcard character can we use if we want to look for patterns?
9. How can we define exclusion ranges using wildcard characters?
10. How can we define inclusion ranges using wildcard characters?

CHAPTER 8 HANDS-ON EXERCISES

Chapter 8 Case 1:

Start SQL Server Management Studio. For each of the questions in this case you need to create a new query (Ctrl-N) and name it as per the instructions in each question. Submit your work to your instructor as one text file that contains all SQL statements or as per your instructor's directions.

1. Create a query that includes all fields from the Products table. The query should return all records having a product name that starts with "ch". Save the query as Chapter08_Case1_Q1.

Result:

ProductID	ProductName	SupplierID	QuantityPerUnit	ProductUnitPrice
6	Choice Apricots - 16 oz. Bag	1	25	32.00
12	Chocolate Covered Cherries in 8...	2	35	37.00
13	Chocolate Blueberries in 10 oz. ...	2	25	29.00
14	Chocolate Fudge	2	28	41.00
15	Chocolate Blueberries in 10 oz. ...	2	28	24.00

```
(16 row(s) returned)
```

2. Create a query that includes the fields ProductName, ProductUnitPrice, UnitsInStock, and ReorderLevel from the Products table. The inventory department needs a list of all the products whose name starts with a "C", the second character is any character, the third character is a "C", followed by any characters after that. Save the query as Chapter08_Case1_Q2.

Result:

ProductName	ProductUnitPrice	UnitsInStock	ReorderLevel
Coconut Flavour Cream Wafers 10 oz.	38.00	27	30
Cocoa and Hazelnut Biscuits	35.00	42	35
Cocoa and Hazelnut Biscuits	28.00	23	40
Coconut Chocolate Chip Cookies	25.00	28	25

`(4 row(s) returned)`

3. Create a query that includes the fields ProductName, ProductUnitPrice, UnitsInStock, and SKU from the Products table. This time, the inventory department needs a list of all the products whose SKU starts with "ASD", followed by any of the characters T,D,L, followed by any character or number. Save the query as Chapter08_Case1_Q3.

Result:

ProductName	ProductUnitPrice	UnitsInStock	SKU
Chocolate Chunk Cookies, 9.5 oz.	48.00	15	ASDT-3456
Peanut Butter Creme Cookies, 9.6 oz.	18.00	37	ASDT-3456
Cinnamon Flavor Cookies 27 oz.	24.00	41	ASDT-3456
Coconut Flavour Cream Wafers 10 oz.	38.00	27	ASDT-3456
Coffee biscuits	50.00	24	ASDT-3456

`(10 row(s) returned)`

4. Create a query that includes the fields ProductName, ProductUnitPrice, UnitsInStock, and SKU from the Products table. The inventory department needs a list of all the products whose SKU does not start with "ASD". Save the query as Chapter08_Case1_Q4.

Result:

ProductName	ProductUnitPrice	UnitsInStock	SKU
Almonds, Hickory Smoked - 12 oz. B...	35.00	40	PDKLS-2332
Almonds, Roasted and Salted - 18 o...	22.00	32	PDKLSD-2344
Banana Chips - 20 oz. Bag	27.00	25	PDKLSD-2347
Berry Cherry in 8 oz. Bag	30.00	50	PDK-2589
California Original Pistachios - 1 lb. B...	29.00	35	PDK-2347

`(48 row(s) returned)`

5. Create a query that includes the fields ProductName, ProductUnitPrice, UnitsInStock, and SKU from the Products table. Your manager needs to send to the inventory department a list of all the products whose SKU does not start with the letters A,B,C,D, and E . Save the query as Chapter08_Case1_Q5.

Result:

You will notice in the result set that the SKU field for records 24 and 25 starts with an A. These two records are retrieved because there is a space in the beginning of the SKU field that messes up the results on purpose. Please read chapter 25 to see how you can use string functions to eliminate this problem.

Product Name	Product Unit Price	Units In Stock	SKU
Almonds, Hickory Smoked - 12 oz. Bag	35.00	40	PDKLS-2332
Almonds, Roasted and Salted - 18 oz. Bag	22.00	32	PDKLSD-2344
Banana Chips - 20 oz. Bag	27.00	25	PDKLSD-2347
Berry Cherry in 8 oz. Bag	30.00	50	PDK-2589
California Original Pistachios - 1 lb. Bag	29.00	35	PDK-2347

(38 row(s) returned)

Chapter 8 Case 2:

Start SQL Server Management Studio. For each of the questions in this case you need to create a new query (Ctrl-N) and name it as per the instructions in each question. Submit your work to your instructor as one text file that contains all SQL statements or as per your instructor's directions.

1. Create a query that includes all fields from the Products table. The query should return all products having a product name starting with the letters a through e. Save the query as Chapter08_Case2_Q1.

Result:

ProductID	Product Name	SupplierID	Quantity PerUnit
1	Almonds, Hickory Smoked - 12 oz. Bag	1	12
2	Almonds, Roasted and Salted - 18 oz. Bag	1	12
3	Banana Chips - 20 oz. Bag	1	12
4	Berry Cherry in 8 oz. Bag	1	15
5	California Original Pistachios - 1 lb. Bag	1	15

(49 row(s) returned)

2. Create a query that includes all fields from the Products table. The query should return all products with a product name starting with the letters a,d,e,k, and l. Save the query as Chapter08_Case2_Q2.

Result:

ProductID	Product Name	SupplierID	Quantity PerUnit
1	Almonds, Hickory Smoked - 12 oz. Bag	1	12
2	Almonds, Roasted and Salted - 18 oz. Bag	1	12
8	Dried Blueberries - 1 lb. Bag	1	10
9	Dried Cranberries - 34 oz.	1	15
17	Dark Chocolate Apricots in 20 oz. Bag	2	35

(15 row(s) returned)

3. Create a query that includes the ProductName, ProductUnitPrice, and SKU fields from the products table. The query should return all products having an SKU starting with the letters PD, having any characters after PD, followed by a dash and ending with exactly four digits. Save the query as Chapter08_Case2_Q3.

Result:

Product Name	Product Unit Price	SKU
Almonds, Hickory Smoked - 12 oz. Bag	35.00	PDKLS-2332
Almonds, Roasted and Salted - 18 oz. Bag	22.00	PDKLSD-2344
Banana Chips - 20 oz. Bag	27.00	PDKLSD-2347
Berry Cherry in 8 oz. Bag	30.00	PDK-2589
California Original Pistachios - 1 lb. Bag	29.00	PDK-2347

(23 row(s) returned)

4. Create a query that includes the ProductName, ProductUnitPrice, and SKU fields from the products table having an SKU starting with any letters between A and P, any characters after those letters, followed by a dash, and ending with exactly four digits. The first two digits should be any digits and the last two 89. Save the query as Chapter08_Case2_Q4.

Result:

Product Name	Product Unit Price	SKU
Berry Cherry in 8 oz. Bag	30.00	PDK-2589
Chocolate Coconut Bar	26.00	PDKL-2389
Roasted & Salted Almonds	19.00	PDKL-2389
Roasted & Salted Cashews	30.00	PDKL-2389
Roasted No-Salt Almonds	39.00	PDKL-2389

(21 row(s) returned)

5. Create a query that includes the ProductName, ProductUnitPrice, and SKU fields from the products table. The query should return all products having an SKU starting with any character, followed by a dash, and ending in 2345. Save the query as Chapter08_Case2_Q5.

Result:

Product Name	Product Unit Price	SKU
Oatmeal Raisin Walnut Cookies	43.00	KDRT-2345
Chunky Chocolate Cookies	15.00	KDRT-2345
Fudge Nut Brownie Cookies	44.00	KDRT-2345
Dried Red Tart Cherries Gift Box - 6 oz.	43.00	EPDA-2345
Dried Red Tart Cherries - 1lb.	16.00	EPDA-2345

(13 row(s) returned)

CHAPTER 9
THE LIKE OPERATOR

The major aspect of the LIKE operator is its flexibility in creating search expressions. In other words, it has the flexibility to work on text, number, and date data types using intricate expressions to produce results. We use the LIKE operator mainly with text data to identify patterns. The LIKE operator needs to be used in combination with wildcard characters such as (%, _, ^, [], -) to produce elaborate results.

We need to remember two points when using the LIKE operator. First, to supply this flexibility and functionality, it consumes resources, so it should not be the first operator that we resort to for all of our search expressions. Second, we should really know how to use it to get the results we need since it might not always return the expected results.

In this chapter, we approach the usage of the LIKE operator from all perspectives, and we point out tips for using it optimally. To demonstrate the cool functionality of the LIKE operator, all of the examples in this chapter use the table called tbls_CustomerOrders. The records of this table are edited with special values to show how LIKE applies to various circumstances in our working environment.

84. The LIKE operator with the % wildcard character
Create a list of customers whose last name starts with M
Discussion:
This simple example uses the LIKE operator to find customers whose last names start with an "M". The LIKE operator is used within the WHERE clause, and we enclose the search expression in single quotes. In addition, we use the % wildcard to obtain the result we need.

Code:
```
SELECT *
FROM tbls_CustomerOrders
WHERE lastname like 'M%'
```

Result:

OrderID	lastname	firstname	city	state	OrderDate
3	Moore	Gerald	Phoenix	AZ	2013-06-29
32	Madsen	Patricia	Boston	MA	2013-01-01
37	Millman	Arnold	Los Angeles	CA	2013-11-17

(79 row(s) returned)

85. The LIKE operator with [ ] and % to search for ranges

Find customers whose zip code starts with a number between 1 and 4

Discussion:

This time, we have a request to prepare a customer report showing customers whose zip codes start with numbers between 1 and 4, such as 12189, 26890, 34123, or 41289 (as opposed to 58659, which would not be included). To obtain the report, we use the LIKE operator with the [ ] and % wildcard characters. The [ ] wildcard will identify all zip codes starting with 1, 2, 3, and 4. The % will then allow for the retrieval of any number of characters after 1, 2, 3, and 4. So, even if we had to work with zip codes comprising of ten characters like 23546-1295, the SQL code in this example would work the same. Of course, we could modify the search condition as "[1-4]____" to only look for five digit zip codes.

Code:

SELECT lastname, firstname, city, zip
FROM tbls_CustomerOrders
WHERE zip like '[1-4]%'

Result:

lastname	firstname	city	zip
Riegert	Joanne	New York	12189
Read	Lisa	Washington	11882
Moore	Gerald	Phoenix	44895
Davis	Catherine	Boston	22459

(492 row(s) returned)

86. The LIKE operator with date fields

Create a report of orders for the month of April for all years

Discussion:

The LIKE operator can produce very useful pieces of information when used with date fields. In this particular example, we look for orders in the month of April irrespective of the day or year they were placed. To achieve what we need, we use the LIKE operator with the % wildcard character. Notice how we use the % twice for days and years, while we fix the month at 4 (April). I know from experience that in your own working environment, dates might not be in the format of "Month number/Day number/Year" (1/1/2012), but perhaps like January 12 2012, for example. This is not a problem at all since we can manipulate dates and change their format on the fly any way we need. I have devoted chapter 26 on date manipulation for your reference. In addition, using LIKE, we can fix the day, the year, or any combination of month, day, and year and retrieve the corresponding results.

Code:

SELECT lastname, firstname, orderdate
FROM tbls_CustomerOrders
WHERE OrderDate Like '%-04-%'

Result:

lastname	firstname	orderdate
Cambell	Veronica	2014-04-01
Stoll	Nicholas	2014-04-14
Stoll	Nicholas	2014-04-09
Stoll	Nicholas	2014-04-14

```
(919 row(s) returned)
```

87. The LIKE operator with number fields

Create a report of customer orders with order totals of $200

Discussion:

The LIKE operator can as easily be used with number fields as it can with text and date data. In this example, we have a request to find all customer orders with a total of $200. When we use LIKE with numbers, we do not enclose the numbers in quotes.

Code:

SELECT lastname, firstname, orderdate, OrderTotal

FROM tbls_CustomerOrders

WHERE OrderTotal Like 200

Result:

lastname	firstname	orderdate	OrderTotal
Tinons	Matthew	2012-04-18	200
Demaico	Nicholas	2014-05-08	200
Martini	Stephen	2014-04-29	200
Trindan	Luis	2013-04-12	200

```
(5 row(s) returned)
```

Although we can use LIKE to search for numbers, it is a much better practice to use equality and inequality predicates such as (<, >, <>, =, >=). The above example could be written with the equality predicate "=", and it will produce the same results.

Code:

SELECT lastname, firstname, orderdate, OrderTotal

FROM tbls_CustomerOrders

WHERE OrderTotal = 200

Result:

lastname	firstname	orderdate	OrderTotal
Tinons	Matthew	2012-04-18	200
Demaico	Nicholas	2014-05-08	200
Martini	Stephen	2014-04-29	200
Trindan	Luis	2013-04-12	200

```
(5 row(s) returned)
```

88. Compare LIKE, BETWEEN, and "<=" "=>" for number ranges

Create a report of customer orders with order totals between $200 and $400

Discussion:

In this scenario, we have a request from management to prepare a report showing customer orders with order totals between $200 and $400. To achieve this goal, we have three alternatives: We can use the LIKE operator, the BETWEEN operator, or the "<=" "=>" predicates. Which one is the best solution? Let us explore the three cases before we make a decision. In the first case, we use the LIKE operator with the [ ] wildcard for ranges and the "_" character to establish the number of characters to be returned at 3. In other words, we are looking for numbers such as 234, 345, or 385. If we have used % after the [ ], we will also get numbers such as 26, 30, and 35, which is not what we want. The result set includes 230 records starting with order totals at $200 and going all the way up to the order total of $393. Attention, here. The LIKE operator is not able to include order totals that are exactly $400. It can go as far up as $399. Consequently, if we have any order totals at exactly $400 they will not be included.

Pay attention to the code below: The line after '[2-3] is actually two underscores. If you leave a space between them, the code will not work.

Code:
```
SELECT lastname, firstname, orderdate, OrderTotal
FROM tbls_CustomerOrders
WHERE OrderTotal LIKE '[2-3]__'
ORDER BY OrderTotal
```

Result:

lastname	firstname	orderdate	OrderTotal
Tinons	Matthew	2012-04-18	200
Demaico	Nicholas	2014-05-08	200
Martini	Stephen	2014-04-29	200
Trindan	Luis	2013-04-12	200

```
(230 row(s) returned)
```

Discussion:
No we will use the BETWEEN operator to achieve the same task. We know the BETWEEN operator is inclusive, that is boundaries will be included in the result set. For ranges of order totals between $200 and $400, it will include the order totals of exactly $200 and exactly $400 if they are available.

Code:
```
SELECT lastname, firstname, orderdate, OrderTotal
FROM tbls_CustomerOrders
WHERE OrderTotal BETWEEN 200 AND 400
ORDER BY OrderTotal
```

Result:

lastname	firstname	orderdate	OrderTotal
Tinons	Matthew	2012-04-18	200
Demaico	Nicholas	2014-05-08	200
Martini	Stephen	2014-04-29	200
Trindan	Luis	2013-04-12	200

```
(230 row(s) returned)
```

Discussion:
In this case, we are using the "<=" "=>" predicates to achieve the same goal of finding orders between $200 and $400. When it comes to numbers, the "<=" "=>" predicates are the most flexible and trusted to work with. In addition, predicates will produce consistent results, while operators have issues with result accuracy and performance.

Code:

```
SELECT lastname, firstname, orderdate, OrderTotal
FROM tbls_CustomerOrders
WHERE OrderTotal >= 200 AND OrderTotal <= 400
ORDER BY OrderTotal
```

Result:

lastname	firstname	orderdate	OrderTotal
Tinons	Matthew	2012-04-18	200
Demaico	Nicholas	2014-05-08	200
Martini	Stephen	2014-04-29	200
Trindan	Luis	2013-04-12	200

```
(230 row(s) returned)
```

89. The NOT LIKE operator

Find customer orders with order totals different than $200

Discussion:

We can use the negation keyword "NOT" to completely change the result set of an operation using LIKE. In this particular example, we are looking for order totals different from $200. Though we can use LIKE to achieve this, we will be better off using the inequality predicates "!=" or "<>". All three pieces of code will produce the same result but prefer to use the "<>" predicate instead because it is ANSI compliant and more reliable than LIKE.

Code1:

```
SELECT lastname, firstname, orderdate, OrderTotal
FROM tbls_CustomerOrders
WHERE OrderTotal NOT Like 200
```

Code1:

```
SELECT lastname, firstname, orderdate, OrderTotal
FROM tbls_CustomerOrders
WHERE OrderTotal != 200
```

Code2:

```
SELECT lastname, firstname, orderdate, OrderTotal
FROM tbls_CustomerOrders
WHERE OrderTotal <> 200
```

Result:

lastname	firstname	orderdate	OrderTotal
Riegert	Joanne	2013-11-06	30
Read	Lisa	2013-07-25	210
Moore	Gerald	2013-06-29	231
Davis	Catherine	2014-12-14	45

```
(914 row(s) returned)
```

90. TIP: Use LIKE with the ltrim() function to get the right results

Filter customer names effectively by eliminating blank spaces

Discussion:

We have a request from our manager to find all orders for which the first name is Mary so that she can have a look and send them a card for their name day. We know how to use the LIKE operator, so we write a statement like the one below and get 20 records. We provide the report to our manager, and two weeks later, she comes back and says we missed three customers. What happened? Well, for three Marys, there were spaces in front of their first names and the LIKE operator did not pick them up. When it comes to LIKE, the statement (LIKE ' Mary') is different from (LIKE 'Mary'). Consequently, if there are any spaces, the two LIKE statements above will produce different results. What can we do about it? We can use the ltrim() function to trim any spaces in front of the customer's first name and obtain exactly the results we want:

Code:

SELECT lastname, firstname, orderdate, OrderTotal
FROM tbls_CustomerOrders
WHERE firstname LIKE 'Mary'

Result:

lastname	firstname	orderdate	OrderTotal
Stewart	Mary	2014-03-09	196
Simmons	Mary	2012-06-24	253
Simmons	Mary	2013-02-26	105
Simmons	Mary	2014-09-16	115

(20 row(s) returned)

Discussion:

The ltrim() function will eliminate any spaces before a string in a field, and this will allow the LIKE operator to function properly. We can use the ltrim() function together with the LIKE operator in the WHERE clause as you can see in the code below. Notice that this time, the database returned 23 records instead of 20. For a full understanding of string functions and their cool functionality, please refer to chapter 25 where we list multiple examples.

Code:

SELECT lastname, firstname, orderdate, OrderTotal
FROM tbls_CustomerOrders
WHERE ltrim(firstname) LIKE 'Mary'

Result:

lastname	firstname	orderdate	OrderTotal
Stewart	Mary	2014-03-09	196
Simmons	Mary	2012-06-24	253
Simmons	Mary	2013-02-26	105
Simmons	Mary	2014-09-16	115

(23 row(s) returned)

91. TIP: Use LIKE to test a field for the presence of spaces
Check for the presence of blank spaces in a city field
Discussion:

The same supervisor comes back and says she needs a report of customers from certain cities. This time, we are wise enough to know that to get the right results, we need to check for spaces first. Then, however, we reason that some city names do contain spaces. For example, New York contains a space, and Los Angeles contains a space. In addition, we realize that the ltrim() and rtrim() functions are good for leading and trailing spaces. What if we have a space right in the middle of the word, however? We can actually look for spaces using the LIKE operator with the % wildcard character. In this example, we are looking for two spaces in any part of the field value. To achieve this, we use the % three times. We can test for one space using two percent signs ('% %'). The cool thing is that we have found two city names with two blank spaces as you can see in the figure below:

Code:
```
SELECT lastname, firstname, city, orderdate
FROM tbls_CustomerOrders
WHERE city LIKE '% % %'
```

Result:

lastname	firstname	city	orderdate
Simmons	Mary	Los Angele s	2014-07-19
Demania	Mary	New Yor k	2012-06-16

(2 row(s) returned)

92. TIP: Use LIKE to test a field for the presence of numbers
Check for the presence of numbers in a city field
Discussion:

Now, what if someone entered some city names and did not pay attention, and as he was typing, he mingled some numbers with the name of the city? For example, he might have entered "New 9York". How can we check a field for the presence of numbers within text strings? The answer is by using the LIKE operator, the [ ] wildcard character for ranges, and the % wildcard character as in the code below. Notice we use the [ ] to check for any number between 0 and 9. In addition, we use the % twice to look for the presence of a number at any part of the field, including the end and the beginning of its value. We actually caught two records with numbers mistyped in them.

Code:
```
SELECT lastname, firstname, city, orderdate
FROM tbls_CustomerOrders
WHERE city LIKE '%[0-9]%'
```

Result:

lastname	firstname	city	orderdate
Cindon	Barbara	New York9	2014-08-24
Demarist	Paul	New 9York	2013-09-28

(2 row(s) returned)

93. TIP: Create an index on a field used often with the LIKE operator

Create an index on the city field

Discussion:

In chapter two, we discussed indexing in detail. Specifically, we mentioned that if a field is often used in searches, we need to create an index on it. We can easily create an index on the city field using the code below. This SQL statement will create a non-unique index because we want to be able to store two cities with the same name in the field "city".

Code:

CREATE INDEX indCity ON tbls_CustomerOrders (city)

Result:
```
Command(s) completed successfully.
```

CHAPTER 9 DISCUSSION QUESTIONS

1. On what kind of data can we use the LIKE operator?
2. Do we use LIKE mostly on string or numeric data?
3. Can we use the LIKE operator by itself in a query?
4. What special characters are necessary for the LIKE operator to produce meaningful results?
5. What is the tradeoff for the LIKE operator's flexibility?
6. How can we use the LIKE operator to test for the presence of spaces?
7. What wildcard character can we use with LIKE to search for ranges?
8. How do we search for patterns using the LIKE operator?
9. How can we use the LIKE operator to test field values for the presence of numbers?
10. Why do we need to create indexes on fields on which the LIKE operator is often used?

CHAPTER 9 HANDS-ON EXERCISES

Chapter 9 Case 1:
Start SQL Server Management Studio. For each of the questions in this case you need to create a new query (Ctrl-N) and name it as per the instructions in each question. Submit your work to your instructor as one text file that contains all SQL statements or as per your instructor's directions.

1. Create a query that includes all fields from the tbls_CustomerOrders table. Your manager wants to see all customers whose first name starts with the letter K. Save the query as Chapter09_Case1_Q1.

   Your result should look like:

OrderID	lastname	firstname	city	state	OrderDate	ShippedDate
35	Crondos	Kenneth	Huston	TX	2014-01-27	2014-02-01
69	Knortz	Kelly	San Diego	CA	2012-02-19	2012-02-24
95	Knortz	Kelly	San Diego	CA	2012-02-25	2012-03-01
132	Vanton	Kenneth	New York	NY	2014-11-13	2014-11-18
141	Giordano	Kathy	San Diego	CA	2014-07-09	2014-07-14

   (38 row(s) returned)

2. Create a query that includes the lastname, firstname, city, state, and ordertotal fields from the tbls_CustomerOrders table. Your supervisor wants to see all customers whose total order amount is between $60 and a $100. Sort results by OrderTotal ascending. Save the query as Chapter09_Case1_Q2.

Your result should look like:

lastname	firstname	city	state	ordertotal
Cendemic	Linda	Philadelphia	PA	60
Millman	Amold	Los Angeles	CA	60
Ackerman	Nicholas	Dallas	TX	60
Read	Lisa	Washington	DC	60
Mahoney	Scott	Orlando	FL	60

(183 row(s) returned)

3. The finance department ordered a report to include all orders for the month of November 2014. Create a new query that will include all fields from the tbls_CustomerOrders table, satisfy the demand of the finance department, and name it Chapter09_Case1_Q3.

Your result should look like:

OrderID	lastname	firstname	city	state	OrderDate
52	Read	Lisa	Washington	DC	2014-11-16
54	Read	Lisa	Washington	DC	2014-11-11
55	Zartons	Lisa	Los Angeles	CA	2014-11-09
58	Karter	Janet	Chicago	OH	2014-11-30
59	Read	Lisa	Washington	DC	2014-11-20

(25 row(s) returned)

4. The inventory department asked for a report of all products whose quantity per unit is 35. This is because they need to plan for the handling of heavy packages. Create a new query that will include all the fields from the Products table, satisfy the request of the inventory people, and name it Chapter09_Case1_Q4.

Your result should look like:

ProductID	ProductName	SupplierID	QuantityPerUnit
12	Chocolate Covered Cherries in 8 oz. Bag	2	35
17	Dark Chocolate Apricots in 20 oz. Bag	2	35
22	Roasted & Salted Almonds	3	35
34	Coconut Flavour Cream Wafers 10 oz.	5	35
51	Coconut Chocolate Chip Cookies	7	35

(7 row(s) returned)

5. The marketing department asked for a report that will include all products with prices between 30 and 40 dollars. Create a new query that includes the productname, quantityperunit, productunitprice, and unitsinstock fields from the products table and satisfies the request of the marketing department. Sort results by ProductUnitPrice ASC. Name the query as Chapter09_Case1_Q5.

Your result should look like:

productname	quantityperunit	productunitprice	unitsinstock
Berry Cherry in 8 oz. Bag	15	30.00	50
Roasted & Salted Cashews	26	30.00	22
Chocolate Chip Brownie	35	30.00	47
Cran Raisin Mix in 17 oz. Bag	12	31.00	24
Choice Apricots - 16 oz. Bag	25	32.00	22

`(19 row(s) returned)`

Chapter 9 Case 2:

Start SQL Server Management Studio. For each of the questions in this case you need to create a new query (Ctrl-N) and name it as per the instructions in each question. Submit your work to your instructor as one text file that contains all SQL statements or as per your instructor's directions.

1. You need to test the ProductName field for the existence of spaces before the name of the product. This is necessary so that the LIKE operator returns the right results. Create a new query that includes the ProductName, ProductUnitPrice, and SKU fields from the Products table and remove from the ProductName field any blank spaces from the beginning the field. Name the query Chapter09_Case2_Q1.

Your result should look like:

ProductName1	ProductUnitPrice	SKU
Almonds, Hickory Smoked - 12 oz. Bag	35.00	PDKLS-2332
Almonds, Roasted and Salted - 18 oz. Bag	22.00	PDKLSD-2344
Banana Chips - 20 oz. Bag	27.00	PDKLSD-2347
Berry Cherry in 8 oz. Bag	30.00	PDK-2589
California Original Pistachios - 1 lb. Bag	29.00	PDK-2347

`(70 row(s) returned)`

2. The inventory people need a report that will list the weight of the various products in the inventory. However, you do not have a weight field in your products table. On the other hand, you do have weights within the product name field. Create a new query that will include all the fields from the products table and will retrieve all the products for which there is a weight entry in the product name field. Name the query Chapter09_Case2_Q2.

Your result should look like:

ProductID	ProductName	SupplierID	QuantityPerUnit
1	Almonds, Hickory Smoked - 12 oz. Bag	1	12
2	Almonds, Roasted and Salted - 18 oz. Bag	1	12
3	Banana Chips - 20 oz. Bag	1	12
4	Berry Cherry in 8 oz. Bag	1	15
5	California Original Pistachios - 1 lb. Bag	1	15

`(30 row(s) returned)`

3. It is the corporate business rule that all SKUs start with a three letter code, followed by a dash, followed by a four digit numeric code. Create a new query that will include the product name and SKU fields. This

query should list all products which have a blank space anywhere in the SKU field. Name the query Chapter09_Case2_Q3.

Your result should look like:

productname	SKU
Banana Bisquits	ADSE 2345
Chocolate Bisquits	ADST 2345
Cocoa and Hazelnut Biscuits	ADSD 2345
Cream and honey biscuits	ADSL 2345
Mushrooms Sauce	ADST 2345

(7 row(s) returned)

4. Since many staff members query the products table creating searches on the product name field, your supervisor has asked you to create an index on the ProductName field. Name the index IndProductName and the query you used to create this index Chapter09_Case2_Q4. Look in the indexes folder of the product table to find your newly created index.

Your result should look like:
Command(s) completed successfully.

5. Your marketing department is reviewing pricing to initiate a new marketing campaign. They think that pricing is skewed at the extremes. That is, products in the $10 price range are priced too low and products in the upper range of fifties are priced too high. They need a report that includes products priced at the $10 price range and those at the $50 range to adjust prices. Create a query that will list all fields from the Products table and will include products in the 10 and 50 ranges. That is, if a product is priced at 11,12, 13, ... 19 or 51, 52, 53, ... 59 should appear in the result set. You must use the LIKE operator to achieve your results. Sort results by ProductUnitPrice ascending. Name the query Chapter09_Case2_Q5.

Result:

ProductID	ProductName	SupplierID	QuantityPerUnit	ProductUnitPrice
49	Chunky Chocolate Cookies	7	30	15.00
70	Fried Jalapeños	10	30	15.00
55	Caramel Brownie	8	26	16.00
62	Dried Red Tart Cherries - 1lb.	9	20	16.00
63	Dried Cranberries - 6oz.	9	30	16.00

(10 row(s) returned)

CHAPTER 10
EQUALITY AND INEQUALITY PREDICATES

The primary goal of equality and inequality predicates in search expressions is to find absolute matches. They are more flexible than using the LIKE operator, and their results are solid and unquestionable. They are used in the WHERE clause of a SQL statement, and they can be used by themselves to construct a search condition without the need of any wildcard characters. For instance, the statement (WHERE lastname = 'Smith') is valid. They should be given preference over operators such as LIKE, BETWEEN, and TOP.

The equality and inequality predicates in SQL Server 2012 are the following:

Meaning	Predicate
Equal to	=
Not equal to	<>
Less than	<
Less than or equal to	<=
Greater than	>
Greater than or equal to	>=

94. The equality predicate "=" for absolute searches in text data

Find a specific customer record searching on last name

Discussion:

In this example, we use the equality predicate to retrieve the record of a particular customer. What we need to know about the equality predicate is that we search for a known value. In other words, we know the last name of the customer we are looking for in advance. Then, we use the equality predicate to find that customer. This is very different when we conduct approximate searches using the LIKE operator where we might know the customer last name starts with "Ma", but we are not certain about the rest of it. That is why we use the expression (LIKE "Ma%") to find all of the customers whose last names start with "Ma" and then, select the one we need to work with. The point to remember is that whenever we can, we should give preference to the equality predicate over the LIKE operator because it will retrieve exactly what we need, faster, with less overhead for the database, and less clutter in the results.

Code:
```
SELECT *
FROM Customers
WHERE lastname = 'Delaney'
```

Result:

CustomerID	FirstName	LastName	Address	City	State
11	Jason	Delaney	92 Madison Ave	New York	NY
45	Dolores	Delaney	25 Marwood Street	Philadelphia	PA

(2 row(s) returned)

95. The equality predicate "=" for absolute searches in number data

Find a specific customer record searching on CustomerID

Discussion:

The equality predicate is very efficient with numbers as well. Actually, it should be preferred and used in working scenarios involving numbers and especially primary keys. For example, let us assume we need to use an UPDATE statement to change the record of a customer. We should unequivocally identify the customer using the equality predicate on the primary key of the table so that we are certain we are updating the right customer. The same logic is valid with DELETE statements where we should use the equality predicate to identify the correct customer for deletion. Another scenario is for those who work with server side pages like ASP.Net, PHP, ASP, JSP, etc. and who need to connect back to the database server to get customer records. Obviously, they would want to transfer as little data as possible between the database server and web server, so the equality predicate is the one of choice. In this example, we retrieve all of the information on a particular order searching on the OrderID, which is the primary key of the Orders table.

Code:
```
SELECT *
FROM Orders
WHERE OrderID = 972
```

Result:

OrderID	CustomerID	SalesRepID	ShipperID	OrderDate	RequiredDate
972	199	10	3	2012-08-24	2012-09-03

(1 row(s) returned)

96. The ">" inequality predicate with date data

Retrieve orders placed after a certain date

Discussion:

The ">" inequality predicate means "greater than", and we can freely use it with numbers and dates. For instance, we might want to find orders placed after June 2013. We can easily achieve this using the code below. The last day of June will not be included in the result set because we are using a "greater than" argument. In the next example, we will see how we can include the last day of June as well. In addition, we sort by orderdate ascending so that older orders appear first. We can sort descending (DESC) to get the latest orders. When sorting ascending, the ASC keyword is not needed in SQL Server. Finally, before creating a date query in SQL Server check the back-end table or view to see how the date field is formatted. Here we query against a date field with a date datatype.

Code:
```
SELECT OrderID, OrderDate, ShippedDate, ShippingCost
FROM Orders
WHERE OrderDate > '2013-06-30'
ORDER BY OrderDate
```

Result:

OrderID	OrderDate	ShippedDate	ShippingCost
479	2013-07-01	2013-07-06	52
99	2013-07-02	2013-07-07	36
3	2013-07-04	2013-07-09	34
577	2013-07-04	2013-07-09	46

(543 row(s) returned)

97. The "=>" inequality predicate with date data

Retrieve orders placed after a certain date including the date specified

Discussion:

The ">=" inequality predicate means "greater than or equal to", and we can use it with numbers and dates as well. In this example, we want to find orders placed after June 2013 including the last day of June. In addition, we sort by orderdate ascending so that older orders appear first.

Code:

SELECT OrderID, OrderDate, ShippedDate, ShippingCost
FROM Orders
WHERE OrderDate >= '2013/6/30'
ORDER BY OrderDate

Result:

OrderID	OrderDate	ShippedDate	ShippingCost
661	2013-06-30	2013-07-05	50
479	2013-07-01	2013-07-06	52
99	2013-07-02	2013-07-07	36
3	2013-07-04	2013-07-09	34

(544 row(s) returned)

98. The "<" inequality predicate with number data

Find orders for which the shipping cost was less than $35

Discussion:

The "<" inequality predicate means "less than", and, in this example, we use it to find shipping costs lower than $35 per order regardless of the date placed. Notice that we do not use quotes or other symbols to enclose numerical data in criteria expressions. We simply type the number. In addition, the first number appearing in the result set is 34 because we specifically asked for "less than 35".

Code:

SELECT OrderID, OrderDate, ShippedDate, ShippingCost
FROM Orders
WHERE ShippingCost < 35
ORDER BY ShippingCost DESC

Result:

OrderID	OrderDate	ShippedDate	ShippingCost
3	2013-07-04	2013-07-09	34
33	2014-03-06	2014-03-11	34
73	2013-05-19	2013-05-24	34

(180 row(s) returned)

99. The "<=" inequality predicate with number data

Find orders for which the shipping cost was less than or equal to $35

Discussion:

The "<=" inequality predicate means "less than or equal to", and we can use it with numbers and dates. In this example, we want to find shipping costs of less than 35 per order, including those orders with a shipping cost of exactly 35.

Code:

```
SELECT OrderID, OrderDate, ShippedDate, ShippingCost
FROM Orders
WHERE ShippingCost <= 35
ORDER BY ShippingCost DESC
```

Result:

OrderID	OrderDate	ShippedDate	ShippingCost
10	2013-12-13	2013-12-18	35
12	2013-12-29	2014-01-03	35
16	2013-10-22	2013-10-27	35

(219 row(s) returned)

100.   The "<>" inequality predicate with number data

Find orders for which the shipping cost is not equal to $35

Discussion:

The "<>" inequality predicate means "not equal to". This time, we want to find shipping costs different from the amount of $35 per order. Notice that we do not use quotes or other symbols to enclose numerical data as criteria. In addition, we can use the inequality predicate efficiently with date and text data.

Code:

```
SELECT OrderID,  OrderDate, ShippedDate, ShippingCost
FROM Orders
WHERE ShippingCost <> 35
ORDER BY ShippingCost DESC
```

Result:

OrderID	OrderDate	ShippedDate	ShippingCost
13	2012-02-10	2012-02-15	52
49	2013-07-07	2013-07-12	52
68	2012-09-03	2012-09-08	52

(960 row(s) returned)

101.   The ">" predicate with number and date data concurrently

Find orders placed after a certain date and with shipping cost less than $35

Discussion:

In this example, we are looking for orders placed after June 2013, which also have shipping costs of less than $35.

Code:

SELECT OrderID, OrderDate, ShippedDate, ShippingCost
FROM Orders
WHERE OrderDate > '2013-06-30'
AND ShippingCost < 35
ORDER BY ShippingCost DESC

Result:

OrderID	OrderDate	ShippedDate	ShippingCost
3	2013-07-04	2013-07-09	34
33	2014-03-06	2014-03-11	34
219	2013-11-22	2013-11-27	34

(89 row(s) returned)

CHAPTER 10 DISCUSSION QUESTIONS

1. What is the difference between absolute and approximate searches?
2. What SQL operator do we use to conduct approximate data searches?
3. What is the rationale behind absolute data searches?
4. Why inequality and equality predicates are the first choice for number searches?
5. Do we have to use wildcard characters with equality and inequality predicates?
6. On what data types can we use equality and inequality predicates?
7. Why is it a very good idea to use the equality predicate "=" in delete and update statements?
8. What is the difference between the "=>" and ">" inequality predicates?
9. How does the BETWEEN operator compare with the "=>" and ">" inequality predicates?
10. Why do we prefer equality and inequality predicates over operators such as BETWEEN and LIKE which can achieve the same results?

CHAPTER 10 HANDS-ON EXERCISES

Chapter 10 Case 1:
Start SQL Server Management Studio. For each of the questions in this case you need to create a new query (Ctrl-N) and name it as per the instructions in each question. Submit your work to your instructor as one text file that contains all SQL statements or as per your instructor's directions.

1. The marketing department is about to initiate a new promotion in New York State. They are asking for a list of customers in the state of New York. Create a new query that includes all fields from the Customers table for customers in New York state. Save the query as Chapter10_Case1_Q1.

    Your result should look like:

CustomerID	FirstName	LastName	Address	City
1	John	Demarco	11 Lark Street	New York
2	Mary	Demania	12 Madison Ave	New York
3	George	Demers	23 New Scotland Ave	New York
4	Phillip	Demetriou	22 Academy Road	New York
5	Andrew	Demichele	14 Glandel Ave	New York

    (31 row(s) returned)

2. The accounting people are calling for help because a customer has complained about the number of invoices she received to pay. In particular, they need to know what is happening with the orders of customer with customer id 199. Create a new query that includes all fields from the orders table. This query should list all the orders for the customer with customerID 199. Save the query as Chapter10_Case1_Q2.

    Your result should look like:

OrderID	CustomerID	SalesRepID	ShipperID	OrderDate	RequiredDate	ShippedDate
113	199	1	3	2013-06-14	2013-06-24	2013-06-19
668	199	7	1	2012-10-26	2012-11-05	2012-10-31
719	199	7	3	2013-01-07	2013-01-17	2013-01-12
743	199	7	1	2012-02-08	2012-02-18	2012-02-13
748	199	8	1	2013-09-01	2013-09-11	2013-09-06

(9 row(s) returned)

3. The inventory people want to plan stock replenishment and are asking for a list of products with a reorder level higher than 35 units. Create a new query that includes the ProductName, UnitsInStock, UnitsOnOrder, and Reorder Level fields and which query satisfies the inventory department requirements. Save the query as Chapter10_Case1_Q3.

    Your result should look like:

ProductName	UnitsInStock	UnitsOnOrder	ReorderLevel
Almonds, Hickory Smoked - 12 oz. Bag	40	5	45
Chocolate Covered Cherries in 8 oz. Bag	42	0	40
Chunky Pretzels	43	0	45
Chocolate Coconut Bar	37	0	45
Roasted & Salted Almonds	35	0	45

(14 row(s) returned)

4. A few weeks later the inventory department complains heavily to your supervisor. Apparently, many products were left out from the report you gave them. Create a new query that includes the ProductName, UnitsInStock, UnitsOnOrder, and Reorder Level fields and which query also includes the products that have a reorder level at exactly 35 units. Save the query as Chapter10_Case1_Q4.

    Your result should look like:

ProductName	UnitsInStock	UnitsOnOrder	ReorderLevel
Almonds, Hickory Smoked - 12 oz. Bag	40	5	45
Chocolate Covered Cherries in 8 oz. Bag	42	0	40
Sesame Crackers in 20 oz. Pack	43	0	35
Crispy Pears	31	0	35
Chunky Pretzels	43	0	45

(26 row(s) returned)

5. Finally, for replenishing purposes again, the Inventory department asks for a report of products with current units on order levels at 0. Create a new query that includes the ProductName, UnitsInStock, UnitsOnOrder, and Reorder Level fields having a quantity of units on order at 0. Save the query as Chapter10_Case1_Q5.

    Your result should look like:

ProductName	UnitsInStock	UnitsOnOrder	ReorderLevel
Almonds, Roasted and Salted - 18 oz. Bag	32	0	20
Banana Chips - 20 oz. Bag	25	0	20
Berry Cherry in 8 oz. Bag	50	0	30
California Original Pistachios - 1 lb. Bag	35	0	30
Choice Apricots - 16 oz. Bag	22	0	25

(46 row(s) returned)

Chapter 10 Case 2:

Start SQL Server Management Studio. For each of the questions in this case you need to create a new query (Ctrl-N) and name it as per the instructions in each question. Submit your work to your instructor as one text file that contains all SQL statements or as per your instructor's directions.

1. The marketing department needs to understand the seasonality effects on sales. For this reason they asked for a preliminary report of sales for the months of March and April for the whole country and for all years. Create a new query that includes the fields OrderID, CustomerID, and OrderDate from the Orders table and satisfies the above criteria. Save the query as Chapter10_Case2_Q1.

Your result should look like:

OrderID	CustomerID	OrderDate
8	71	2014-04-06
9	194	2014-04-19
24	127	2012-03-12
31	194	2014-04-14
34	39	2013-03-17

(138 row(s) returned)

2. Achieve the same result you have achieved in step 1 but using a different criterion in your WHERE clause. Save the query as Chapter10_Case2_Q2.

Your result should look like:

OrderID	CustomerID	OrderDate
8	71	2014-04-06
9	194	2014-04-19
24	127	2012-03-12
31	194	2014-04-14
34	39	2013-03-17

(138 row(s) returned)

3. Accounting is asking for a report that lists the orders with a shipping cost between $30 and $40, boundaries included. Create a new query that includes the fields OrderID, CustomerID, OrderDate, and ShippingCost from the Orders table and satisfies the above criteria. Sort results by shipping cost ascending. Save the query as Chapter10_Case2_Q3.

Your result should look like:

OrderID	CustomerID	OrderDate	ShippingCost
34	39	2013-03-17	31
74	98	2012-08-10	31
124	182	2013-01-30	31
114	51	2014-08-30	31
148	117	2013-10-07	31

(440 row(s) returned)

4. Your supervisor is asking for a report that includes the fields OrderID, OrderDate, and ShippingCost from the Orders table. It should list all orders except those with a shipping cost equal to 35. Save the query as Chapter10_Case2_Q4.

Your result should look like:

OrderID	OrderDate	ShippingCost
1	2013-11-11	36
2	2013-07-30	39
3	2013-07-04	34
4	2014-12-19	48
5	2012-11-19	40

(960 row(s) returned)

5. The six sigma team is evaluating new shipment processes. They need a report that will list all orders from the United Postal Service. Create a new query that includes the fields OrderID, CustomerID, OrderDate, and ShippingCost from the Orders table and satisfies the above criteria. Save the query as Chapter10_Case2_Q5.

Your result should look like:

OrderID	CustomerID	OrderDate	ShippingCost
12	68	2013-12-29	35
13	53	2012-02-10	52
18	94	2013-07-29	42
27	186	2014-03-14	38
31	194	2014-04-14	38

(196 row(s) returned)

CHAPTER 11
THE BETWEEN OPERATOR

The BETWEEN … AND operator is designed to retrieve subsets or ranges from a data set. It works primarily with number and date data. In this sense, it can be used to retrieve records that exist between two values acting as boundaries. Those two boundary values can be numbers or dates. In addition, while we cannot use BETWEEN with wildcard characters or predicates, we can still use functions to augment its range of applicability. It is important to know that BETWEEN is inclusive such that the values acting as boundaries will be included in the recordset. For example, if we use BETWEEN with two date values, the records containing those date values will be included in the result set.

102.   The BETWEEN operator with numbers
Find products with prices between $15 and $18
Discussion:
In this example, we are looking for product prices between the $15 and $18 values. The BETWEEN operator is inclusive, so the products with unit prices of 15 and 18 are included in the result set.

Code:
SELECT productname, productunitprice
FROM products
WHERE productunitprice BETWEEN 15 AND 18
ORDER BY productunitprice

Result:

productname	productunitprice
Chunky Chocolate Cookies	15.00
Fried Jalapeños	15.00
Caramel Brownie	16.00
Dried Red Tart Cherries - 1lb.	16.00

(6 row(s) returned)

103.   The BETWEEN operator with dates
Find orders placed within a date range
Discussion:
In this example, we would like to retrieve order dates that fall between 6/15/2012 and 6/15/2013. The BETWEEN operator is inclusive, and it will include orders placed on 6/15/2012 and 6/15/2013 as it is shown in the result set. Notice how we enclose the date values in quotes in SQL Server.

Code:

```
SELECT OrderID, orderdate, shippeddate
FROM orders
WHERE orderdate BETWEEN '2012-06-15' AND '2013-06-15'
ORDER BY orderdate DESC
```

Result:

OrderID	orderdate	shippeddate
136	2013-06-15	2013-06-20
250	2013-06-15	2013-06-20
113	2013-06-14	2013-06-19

```
(296 row(s) returned)
```

104.   The BETWEEN operator with the year() function

Find orders placed within a year range

Discussion:

In this example, we use the year() function to extract the year out of the orderdate field so that we can use year values as the lower and upper boundaries. All orders from 2013 and 2014 will be included in the result set due to the inclusivity characteristic of the BETWEEN operator.

Code:

```
SELECT OrderID, orderdate, shippeddate
FROM orders
WHERE year(orderdate) BETWEEN 2013 AND 2014
ORDER BY orderdate DESC
```

Result:

OrderID	orderdate	shippeddate
4	2014-12-19	2014-12-24
874	2014-12-16	2014-12-21
165	2014-12-14	2014-12-19
881	2014-12-12	2014-12-17

```
(687 row(s) returned)
```

105.   The NOT BETWEEN operator with numbers

Find products with prices outside a price range

Discussion:

In this instance, we are looking for products with prices outside the $10 to $40 range, so we are asking the database to give us all products whose prices do not fall between $10 and $40. In practical terms, when we use the BETWEEN operator with NOT, we are usually looking for extreme values or outliers. The products with prices of exactly $10 or $40 will not be included in the result set.

Code:

SELECT productname, productunitprice
FROM products
WHERE productunitprice NOT BETWEEN 10 AND 40
ORDER BY productunitprice ASC

Result:

productname	productunitprice
Chocolate Fudge	41.00
Oatmeal Raisin Walnut Cookies	43.00
Dried Red Tart Cherries Gift Box - 6 oz.	43.00
Fudge Nut Brownie Cookies	44.00

```
(15 row(s) returned)
```

106.   Comparison of BETWEEN with "<=" or "=>"

Find products with prices within a price range

Discussion:

In this paradigm, we show that using the BETWEEN operator is the same as using the two inequality predicates "<=" and "=>".   Both SQL statements below will produce the same result.   However, we should always give preference to equality and inequality predicates since they produce faster results with less overhead for the database engine.

Code:

SELECT productname, productunitprice
FROM products
WHERE productunitprice BETWEEN 15 AND 18
ORDER BY productunitprice ASC

Or

Code:

SELECT productname, productunitprice
FROM products
WHERE productunitprice >=15 AND productunitprice <=18
ORDER BY productunitprice ASC

Result:

productname	productunitprice
Chunky Chocolate Cookies	15.00
Fried Jalapeños	15.00
Caramel Brownie	16.00
Dried Red Tart Cherries - 1lb.	16.00

```
(6 row(s) returned)
```

CHAPTER 11 DISCUSSION QUESTIONS

1. What is the primary goal of the BETWEEN operator?
2. What equality/inequality predicates can we use to simulate the function of the BETWEEN operator?
3. Are boundary values included in the result set when we use the BETWEEN operator?
4. Can we use the BETWEEN operator with wildcard characters or predicates for more intricate searches?
5. With what data types do we primarily use the BETWEEN operator?
6. How can we use the BETWEEN operator with functions to augment its functionality?
7. Can we use the BETWEEN operator with dates?
8. Why would someone prefer to use equality and inequality predicates instead of the BETWEEN operator?
9. What do we need to do if we do not want to include the boundaries of a range in our searches?
10. The BETWEEN operator allows us to get the range within two numbers. What keyword can we use to retrieve the respective outside ranges?

CHAPTER 11 HANDS-ON EXERCISES

Chapter 11 Case 1:

Start SQL Server Management Studio. For each of the questions in this case you need to create a new query (Ctrl-N) and name it as per the instructions in each question. Submit your work to your instructor as one text file that contains all SQL statements or as per your instructor's directions.

1. The marketing department needs a list of customers with orders between $100 and $200 for customer segmentation purposes. Create a new query that includes all fields from the tbls_CustomerOrders table satisfying the marketing request. Order results by OrderTotal ascending. Save the query as Chapter11_Case1_Q1.

    Your result should look like:

OrderID	lastname	firstname	city	state	OrderDate
35	Crondos	Kenneth	Huston	TX	2014-01-27
112	Lareous	Angelo	Phoenix	AZ	2013-04-27
181	Balfur	Carolyn	Miami	FL	2012-04-22
212	Datek	Jason	Denver	CO	2013-06-05
364	Zensons	Charles	Los Angeles	CA	2014-09-18

    (343 row(s) returned)

2. The inventory people need a quick list of all orders placed in May and June 2014 to compare it against their shipments for accuracy. Create a new query that includes all fields from the tbls_CustomerOrders table satisfying the inventory department's request. Order results by OrderDate ascending. Save the query as Chapter11_Case1_Q2.

    Your result should look like:

OrderID	lastname	firstname	city	state	OrderDate
150	Demarist	Paul	New York	NY	2014-05-04
609	Demania	Mary	New York	NY	2014-05-04
280	Demaico	Nicholas	New York	NY	2014-05-08
186	Wilkinson	Pamela	Philadelphia	PA	2014-05-09
531	Mahoney	Scott	Orlando	FL	2014-05-13

(35 row(s) returned)

3. The management of the corporation asked for a report that will include all orders in the years 2012 and 2013. They need this data for a historical assessment of orders. Create a new query that includes the OrderID, OrderDate, ShippedDate, and OrderTotal fields as well as a field that shows only the year out of the OrderDate date. The query should include all orders for the years 2012 and 2013. Order the results by year, ascending. Save the query as Chapter11_Case1_Q3.

    Your result should look like:

OrderID	OrderDate	ShippedDate	OrderTotal	Year
5	2012-11-14	2012-11-19	253	2012
6	2012-06-10	2012-06-15	378	2012
13	2012-02-05	2012-02-10	328	2012
15	2012-10-18	2012-10-23	205	2012
21	2012-10-02	2012-10-07	167	2012

(616 row(s) returned)

4. Management is asking for a report of orders shipped within 2014 but outside the period between June 2014 and August 2014 for reviewing performance outside the summer months. Create a new query that includes the OrderID, OrderDate, ShippedDate, and OrderTotal fields and satisfies the managerial request. Sort the result set by ShippedDate ascending. Save the query as Chapter11_Case1_Q4.

    Your result should look like:

OrderID	OrderDate	ShippedDate	OrderTotal
581	2013-12-28	2014-01-02	60
431	2013-12-29	2014-01-03	100
473	2013-12-30	2014-01-04	415
146	2013-12-30	2014-01-04	120
402	2013-12-31	2014-01-05	75

(232 row(s) returned)

5. The sales people need a list of customers with order totals between $400 and $500. However, they do not want the customers with exactly $400 or $500 in order totals to appear in the result set. Create a new query that includes the OrderID, LastName, FirstName, OrderDate, and OrderTotal fields from the tbls_CustomerOrders table and satisfies the sales people request. Order the results by OrderTotal descending. Save the query as Chapter11_Case1_Q5.

    Your result should look like:

OrderID	Last Name	First Name	OrderDate	OrderTotal
353	Demania	Mary	2012-05-06	490
169	Anderson	Joseph	2014-06-11	477
547	Hudson	Allan	2013-07-13	462
932	Weinberger	Fred	2013-05-23	455
433	Elser	Stephanie	2013-08-14	441

(20 row(s) returned)

Chapter 11 Case 2:

Start SQL Server Management Studio. For each of the questions in this case you need to create a new query (Ctrl-N) and name it as per the instructions in each question. Submit your work to your instructor as one text file that contains all SQL statements or as per your instructor's directions.

1. The management of the company needs to review shipped orders within the year 2014 but outside the months January through March. Create a new query that includes the fields OrderID, State, City, ShippedDate, and OrderTotal from the tbls_CustomerOrders table and satisfies the above criteria. Order the result set by ShippedDate descending. Save the query as Chapter11_Case2_Q1.

    Your result should look like:

OrderID	State	City	ShippedDate	OrderTotal
4	MA	Boston	2014-12-19	45
874	CA	Los Angeles	2014-12-16	282
165	CA	San Diego	2014-12-14	60
881	MA	Boston	2014-12-12	30
628	CA	Los Angeles	2014-12-11	134

(226 row(s) returned)

2. The marketing people need a list of all orders within the period June 2014 to December 2014 which also have order total amounts between $200 and $300. Create a new query that includes the fields OrderID, State, City, OrderDate, and OrderTotal from the tbls_CustomerOrders table and satisfies the above criteria. Sort results by OrderTotal so that bigger orders show on top. Save the query as Chapter11_Case2_Q2.

    Your result should look like:

OrderID	State	City	OrderDate	OrderTotal
830	NY	New York	2014-10-25	296
375	CA	Los Angeles	2014-08-30	294
71	FL	Orlando	2014-10-05	288
874	CA	Los Angeles	2014-12-11	282
81	NY	New York	2014-08-15	276

(30 row(s) returned)

3. The inventory people need a report of all orders shipped within the month of June 2014. They had a breakdown with their trucks and they need to compare their shipment slips with your report data to see if they missed to report a shipment. Create a new query that includes all fields from the tbls_CustomerOrders table and satisfies the above criteria. Save the query as Chapter11_Case2_Q3.

Your result should look like:

OrderID	lastname	firstname	city	state	OrderDate	ShippedDate
40	Cutillo	Roy	San Jose	CA	2014-05-27	2014-06-01
60	Sterling	Fred	Boston	MA	2014-05-29	2014-06-03
89	Vincent	Lloyd	Philadelphia	PA	2014-06-22	2014-06-27
94	Steiner	James	Los Angeles	CA	2014-06-04	2014-06-09
130	Elser	Stephanie	San Jose	CA	2014-06-01	2014-06-06

(21 row(s) returned)

4. The accounting department asks for a report of customer orders with OrderTotals between $0 and $50. There have been discrepancies in the billing of small orders which need to be checked. Create a new query that includes the fields OrderID, State, City, OrderDate, and OrderTotal from the tbls_CustomerOrders table and satisfies the above criteria. Sort results so that smaller order totals appear first. Save the query as Chapter11_Case2_Q4.

Your result should look like:

OrderID	State	City	OrderDate	OrderTotal
88	CA	Los Angeles	2013-11-02	5
282	CA	Los Angeles	2014-06-18	8
487	MA	Boston	2012-10-04	8
925	CA	San Diego	2014-04-10	8
479	FL	Miami	2013-06-26	10

(138 row(s) returned)

5. The senior management of the company wants a report that lists all the orders placed in the months of September and December 2014. It has been reported to them that orders in that period experience higher processing cycles because of the holiday volume. Consequently they want to compare the intervals between the order dates and shipped dates, especially for large orders such as those between $300 and $500. Create a new query that includes the fields OrderID, OrderDate, ShippedDate, and OrderTotal from the tbls_CustomerOrders table and satisfies the above criteria. Sort the results so that bigger orders appear first. Save the query as Chapter11_Case2_Q5.

Your result should look like:

OrderID	OrderDate	ShippedDate	OrderTotal
857	2014-09-22	2014-09-27	406
860	2014-10-24	2014-10-29	349
765	2014-10-13	2014-10-18	340
228	2014-11-04	2014-11-09	328
622	2014-09-18	2014-09-23	304

(6 row(s) returned)

CHAPTER 12
THE IN OPERATOR

The major role of the IN operator is to participate in search conditions for filtering records. It is always used within the WHERE clause of a SQL statement and usually takes the place of multiple OR operators. It is an extremely useful search operator, and it will check the existence of a value against a list of values provided or constructed dynamically. Moreover, the IN operator can be used with text, number, and date data, making it suitable for a wide range of applications. Finally, it is really indispensable when used with subqueries as it will be shown in this chapter and in chapter 30. Using IN with subqueries allows the database professional to obtain results that would have been very difficult or impossible to obtain otherwise. The IN operator should be well understood and at the top of the toolbox of a database user or developer.

107.   The IN operator with text data
Create a report of customers from multiple cities
Discussion:
Our supervisor is requesting a report that lists all customers from the cities of New York, Boston, Chicago, Los Angeles, and Dallas. Of course, we could use the OR operator to produce this report:

Code:
```
SELECT LastName, FirstName, City
FROM customers
WHERE (city = 'New York')
OR (city = 'Boston')
OR (city = 'Chicago')
OR (city = 'Los Angeles')
OR (city = 'Dallas')
```

Using multiple OR operators to obtain a solution is rather tedious in both time and effort. Then, as soon as we provide the report to the supervisor, she comes back and says: "This is excellent; can I please have another report with our customers in the rest of the cities in the country?" To produce the second report, we will need to create an additional multitude of OR statements with the remaining cities.

The IN operator solves these problems quickly and efficiently. In addition, since the ORDER BY clause is not used, the records will appear in the order they are stored in the table.

Code:
```
SELECT lastname, firstname, City
FROM customers
WHERE city in ('New York', 'Boston', 'Chicago', 'Los Angeles', 'Dallas')
```

Result:

lastname	firstname	city
Demarco	John	New York
Demania	Mary	New York
Demers	George	New York
Demetriou	Phillip	New York

(99 row(s) returned)

108. The NOT IN operator with text data

Create a report of customers excluding several cities

Discussion:

This time, our supervisor reverses the request and asks for a report of customers from all cities not included in our previous report—every city except New York, Boston, Chicago, Los Angeles, and Dallas. Since we have the code using the IN operator from the previous example, the only thing we need to do is put the keyword "NOT" in front of the IN operator!

Code:

SELECT lastname, firstname, city
FROM customers
WHERE city NOT IN ('New York', 'Boston', 'Chicago', 'Los Angeles', 'Dallas')

Result:

lastname	firstname	city
Vanton	Kenneth	Albany
Trindan	Luis	Albany
Cendemic	Linda	Philadelphia
Costa	Kelly	Philadelphia

(102 row(s) returned)

109. The IN operator with numeric data

Create a report of products based on their prices

Discussion:

In this scenario, we need to produce a report that lists products from our product catalog with the following prices: 15, 19, 22, 23, and 42. Since the numbers are not sequential, we cannot use the BETWEEN operator to get our results. We can, however, use the IN operator to produce the report almost as fast. When we employ IN with numbers, we do not use quotes.

Code:

SELECT productname, quantityperunit, productunitprice
FROM products
WHERE productunitprice in (15, 19, 22, 23, 42)

Result:

productname	quantityperunit	productunitprice
Almonds, Roasted and Salted - 18 oz. Bag	12	22.00
Chunky Pretzels	30	22.00
Roasted & Salted Almonds	35	19.00
Cream and honey biscuits	28	22.00

```
(11 row(s) returned)
```

110.   The IN operator with date data

Create a report of products based on prices

Discussion:

We have a request from the sales department to have a look at the orders in the first day of the three summer months because they are missing an order. They want to know what happened so that they can communicate to the customer. We can absolutely use IN with date fields as can be seen in the code below. Pay attention that the dates provided are all actual date values and not ranges. We cannot use date ranges with the IN operator. Still, the worth of the IN operator with dates is highly desirable.

Code:

```
SELECT OrderID, OrderDate, ShippedDate, ShippingCost
FROM Orders
WHERE
OrderDate IN ('2012-6-1', '2012-7-1', '2012-8-1')
```

Result:

OrderID	OrderDate	ShippedDate	ShippingCost
170	2012-06-01	2012-06-06	40
201	2012-07-01	2012-07-06	41
905	2012-07-01	2012-07-06	51
959	2012-06-01	2012-06-06	32

```
(4 row(s) returned)
```

111.   Search for the same value in multiple fields

Discussion:

Let us suppose we inherited an un-normalized database and we need to search for the same value in multiple fields. For instance, the previous database administrator might have used four "supplier" fields in the products table to keep track of available suppliers for the same product. This is unacceptable under database normalization rules and our first step should be to normalize our database which means creating a separate supplier table. However, if we must do the search now, the IN operator can solve our problem if we use it upside down!

For instance, we usually use the IN operator such as:

Field IN (value1, value2, value3), that is, Supplier IN ("FoodInc1", "FoodInc2", "FoodInc3")

To search an un-normalized database we do:

Value IN (field1, field2, field3), that is, "Food Inc" in (supplier1, supplier2, supplier3)

Note that we can extend the functionality of this code to search in multiple unrelated fields. For instance, we can search for the value "Mary" in the firstname, lastname, and address fields in the customer table to find a customer whose first name is Mary, or last name is Mary, or we have an address with the name Mary!

Code:
SELECT firstname, lastname, address
FROM customers
WHERE 'Mary' IN (firstname, lastname, address)

Result:

firstname	lastname	address
Mary	Demania	12 Madison Ave
Mary	Simmons	45 Burncliff Dr
Mary	Williams	7 Cherry Hill Road
Mary	Crawford	21 Aegean Dr

(5 row(s) returned)

112.   Create dynamic lists using the IN operator and subqueries
Generate a report of orders in which there is at least one non-discounted product
Discussion

The IN operator shows its real power when used with lists generated dynamically through SQL code. Instead of typing the values in the parenthesis, we can actually use SQL to create value lists automatically. This leads to the concept of subqueries, which we will discuss in detail in chapter 30, but we will go through a few examples here to understand the ultimate use of the IN operator.

In this specific example, management wants to have a report of orders in which no discount was extended for at least one of the products included in the order. Each order might contain multiple products, and for each product, we might or might not have extended a discount. In other words, the database is set up so that discounts are given per product in an order basis and not per order. This way, we have the flexibility to extend discounts on a product-by-product basis, which is a much more flexible way of doing business.

To answer this request, we need information from two different tables: the Orders table and the ProductsOrders table. The subquery in this case will generate a list of OrderIDs from the ProductsOrders table for which the discount = 0. Then, this list of OrderIDs will be used as filtering criteria by the IN operator in the Orders table. Therefore, we have dynamically created a list of values for the IN operator. There are 136 orders with at least one non-discounted product.

Code:
SELECT orderid, orderdate, shippeddate
FROM orders
WHERE orderid
IN (SELECT orderid FROM ProductsOrders WHERE (Discount) =0)

Result:

orderid	orderdate	shippeddate
2	2013-07-30	2013-08-04
5	2012-11-19	2012-11-24
7	2013-12-01	2013-12-06
24	2012-03-12	2012-03-17

(136 row(s) returned)

113. The IN operator with GROUP BY and HAVING in subqueries

Generate a report of orders for which the total extended discount was 0

Discussion

Continuing from the previous example, we now have a request to produce a report that will list orders in which all of the included products have a discount of zero. So, if four products are included in an order, the discount rate for all four of them should be zero. To reply to this request, we will again use the IN operator to look in the ProductsOrders table for OrderIDs of orders with zero total discounts. The problem here is that we cannot use the WHERE clause since it always runs first and excludes records before the SQL statement is executed. Our first goal is to sum up the discounts for each product in each order first. Our second concern is to somehow make calculations in the ProductsOrders table and find the sum of discount for every order. Third, we need to keep in the result set only orders with a total discount of zero, and filter out everything else. The final issue is that the filtering needs to happen after the results of the sum() function.

All of the above issues can be solved by using the IN operator, a subquery, the GROUP BY and HAVING clauses, and the sum() function as per the example below. In the example, the GROUP BY clause with the sum() function in the subquery will run first and produce a list of unique orders and their total discounts. From this list, the HAVING clause will keep only the ones with a zero total discount. Then, the SELECT statement in the subquery will generate a list of OrderIDs as filtered out by the HAVING clause. Finally, the WHERE clause from the main query will use the OrderIDs generated from the subquery to filter orders from the Orders table and produce a set of orders whose orderID matches the OrderID produced by the subquery.

At this point, we could easily answer the following question as well: Generate a report of orders for which the total extended discount was not 0. We can answer this in no time by replacing the IN operator with NOT IN!

Code:

```
SELECT orderid, orderdate, shippeddate
FROM orders
WHERE orderid
IN (SELECT orderid FROM ProductsOrders GROUP BY orderid HAVING sum(Discount) =0)
```

Result:

orderid	orderdate	shippeddate
836	2012-11-18	2012-11-23
390	2013-02-05	2013-02-10
273	2013-03-26	2013-03-31
356	2013-03-03	2013-03-08

```
(10 row(s) returned)
```

114. The IN operator with subqueries and dates

Find customers who have not placed any orders in the second half of 2013

Discussion

Our task in this scenario is to find customers who have not placed any orders in the second half of the year 2013. Management needs this information for initiating promotions to inactive customers. To achieve this task, we will use the NOT IN and BETWEEN operators and a subquery. Remember that the purpose of a subquery is always the same—to generate a list of values to be used by the IN operator. Here, the subquery will generate a list of CustomerIDs from the Orders table, which will be used by the main query to filter records from the Customers table. In total, 71 customers have not ordered anything during this six-month period.

Code:
SELECT *
FROM Customers
WHERE CustomerID NOT IN
(Select CustomerID FROM Orders WHERE
OrderDate BETWEEN '2013-6-1' AND '2013-12-1')

Result:

CustomerID	First Name	Last Name	Address	City
2	Mary	Demania	12 Madison Ave	New York
6	Michael	Demizio	23 Grove Rd	New York
7	Robert	Demaggio	34 Princeton Dr	New York
12	Jim	Devito	102 Lexington Ave	New York

(71 row(s) returned)

115. The IN operator with subqueries, dates, and date functions

Find customers who have not placed any orders in the year 2013

Discussion

Continuing from the previous example, the request now is to find customers who have not placed any orders in the year 2013. Of course, we do not track years separately in the orders table, but we can easily extract the year out of the OrderDate field using the year() function. Then, we can use it in the subquery as shown below. Only 36 customers have not placed any orders in the year 2013. This type of query is excellent to keep track of customer retention rates in a business.

Code:
SELECT *
FROM Customers
WHERE CustomerID NOT IN
(Select CustomerID FROM Orders WHERE
year(orderdate) = 2013)

Result:

CustomerID	First Name	Last Name	Address	City	State
2	Mary	Demania	12 Madison Ave	New York	NY
6	Michael	Demizio	23 Grove Rd	New York	NY
15	Pindar	Ames	23 Cornell Dr	New York	NY
19	Erin	Erin	28 Karrie Terrace	Los Angeles	CA

(36 row(s) returned)

CHAPTER 12 DISCUSSION QUESTIONS

1. What is the primary role of the IN operator?
2. What is the clause within which we must always use the IN operator?
3. Why is it a good idea to use IN instead of multiple OR operators?
4. What are the data types with which we can use the IN operator?
5. What is the purpose of the NOT IN operator?
6. Can we use the IN operator with dates?
7. Can we use date ranges with the IN operator?
8. How can we provide dynamic lists for the IN operator?
9. Can we use the IN operator to look for data in different tables?
10. Can we use the GROUP BY and HAVING clauses with the IN operator in a subquery?

CHAPTER 12 HANDS-ON EXERCISES

Chapter 12 Case 1:

Start SQL Server Management Studio. For each of the questions in this case you need to create a new query (Ctrl-N) and name it as per the instructions in each question. Submit your work to your instructor as one text file that contains all SQL statements or as per your instructor's directions.

1. The marketing department is asking for a report of all the customers in the States of New York, California, and Florida. Create a new query that includes all fields from the Customers table satisfying the marketing request. Order results by State ascending. Save the query as Chapter12_Case1_Q1.

Your result should look like:

CustomerID	First Name	Last Name	Address	City	State
16	Joseph	Anderson	34 Cortland Ave	Los Angeles	CA
17	Allen	Restad	72 Providence Dr	Los Angeles	CA
18	Charles	Zensons	23 Tampa Ave	Los Angeles	CA
19	Erin	Erin	28 Karrie Terrace	Los Angeles	CA
20	Lisa	Zartons	34 Home Ave	Los Angeles	CA

(100 row(s) returned)

2. Your supervisor needs a report of all the customers who do not reside in the States of Ohio and Texas. Create a new query that includes all fields from the Customers table satisfying your supervisor's request. Order results by state ascending. Save the query as Chapter12_Case1_Q2.

Your result should look like:

CustomerID	First Name	Last Name	Address	City	State
126	Christine	Lanci	28 Maplewood Ave	Phoenix	AZ
127	Lloyd	Latta	30 Miller Ave	Phoenix	AZ
128	Angelo	Lareous	11 Avon Ln	Phoenix	AZ
129	Cynthia	Papadopoulos	8 Upper Hillcrest Ave	Phoenix	AZ
130	Dolores	Mahoney	28 Parkwood Ave	Phoenix	AZ

(162 row(s) returned)

3. The shipping people called in and are asking for a report of all the orders processed by the SalesReps with IDs 2, 5, and 9. They want to check those orders again. Create a new query that includes all fields from the Orders table satisfying the request from shipping. Order results by SalesRepID ascending. Save the query as Chapter12_Case1_Q3.

Your result should look like:

OrderID	CustomerID	SalesRepID	ShipperID	OrderDate
151	110	2	2	2013-03-02
152	96	2	1	2014-08-31
153	177	2	2	2013-12-09
154	132	2	1	2012-01-27
155	56	2	2	2014-10-14

(317 row(s) returned)

4. The sales department is asking for a report of orders placed on the second, third and eleventh day of March 2014. Create a new query that includes all fields from the Orders table satisfying the request from sales. Order results by OrderDate ascending. Save the query as Chapter12_Case1_Q4.

Your result should look like:

OrderID	CustomerID	SalesRepID	ShipperID	OrderDate
98	105	1	2	2014-03-02
665	89	7	1	2014-03-02
835	17	8	3	2014-03-02
147	103	1	1	2014-03-03
542	124	6	2	2014-03-11

(6 row(s) returned)

5. The sales people need a list of customers who have not placed any orders so far so that they can market to them. Create a new query that includes the fields customerid, firstname and lastname from the Customers table and satisfies the sales people request. Save the query as Chapter12_Case1_Q5.

Your result should look like:

customerid	lastname	firstname
19	Erin	Erin
37	Cimo	Allan
40	Costa	Kelly
66	Webster	Arnold
69	Bigar	Cristopher

(11 row(s) returned)

Chapter 12 Case 2:

Start SQL Server Management Studio. For each of the questions in this case you need to create a new query (Ctrl-N) and name it as per the instructions in each question. Submit your work to your instructor as one text file that contains all SQL statements or as per your instructor's directions.

1. Your supervisor is asking for a list of sales representatives who reside in the zip codes 22459 and 12189. Create a new query that includes the FirstName, LastName, Address, City, State, and Zip fields from the SalesReps table and sort the results ascending by lastname. Save the query as Chapter12_Case2_Q1.

    Your result should look like:

FirstName	LastName	Address	City	State	Zip
John	Anderson	32 Colonial Street	Boston	MA	22459
Michael	Bernstein	21 Garden Ave	New York	NY	12189
Kenneth	Delaney	89 Edenburg Ave	New York	NY	12189
Andrew	Simmons	16 Greenway Street	New York	NY	12189
George	Spicer	90 Lenox Ave	Boston	MA	22459

    (8 row(s) returned)

2. The marketing department needs a list of orders for three particular customers: Andrew Demichele, Lisa Zartons, and William Teall. Create a new query that includes all fields from the Orders table satisfying the marketing request. Order results by customerID. Save the query as Chapter12_Case2_Q2.

    Your result should look like:

OrderID	CustomerID	SalesRepID	ShipperID	OrderDate	RequiredDate
43	5	1	1	2013-05-06	2013-05-16
115	5	1	3	2012-01-27	2012-02-06
264	5	3	2	2012-02-09	2012-02-19
756	5	8	2	2013-11-23	2013-12-03
963	20	10	1	2013-05-10	2013-05-20

    (20 row(s) returned)

3. The HR department is asking for a report of the sales representatives who do not have any orders in the last 15 days of December 2014, that is in the holiday period. HR feels these employees are not getting the help and training they need to be successful in their jobs. Create a new query that includes all fields from the SalesReps table satisfying the HR request. Order results by lastname ascending. Save the query as Chapter12_Case2_Q3.

    Your result should look like:

SalesRepID	FirstName	LastName	Title	Address	City
1	John	Anderson	Sales Reppresentative	32 Colonial Street	Boston
8	Michael	Bernstein	Sales Reppresentative	21 Garden Ave	New York
6	Kenneth	Delaney	Assistant Manager	89 Edenburg Ave	New York
5	Andrew	Simmons	Account Manager	16 Greenway Street	New York
3	George	Spicer	Assitant Director of Sales	90 Lenox Ave	Boston

    (8 row(s) returned)

4. Your supervisor is asking you to look for orphaned records in the orders table. That is, you need to check and see if there are any orders without associated customers. This would be very bad for the integrity of the database and if there are any they need to be deleted. Create a new query that includes all fields from the Orders table and save it as Chapter12_Case2_Q4.

Your result should look like:

```
(0 row(s) returned)
```

5. The marketing department is asking for a list of customers who placed orders after the holiday season and specifically in February and March 2014. They would like to know who these customers are so they can market to them and compensate for out of season sales drops. Create a new query that includes all fields from the Customers table and order the results by lastname asc. Save the query as Chapter12_Case2_Q5.

Your result should look like:

CustomerID	First Name	Last Name	Address	City	State
15	Pindar	Ames	23 Cornell Dr	New York	NY
50	Thomas	Andersen	52 Betwood Street	Orlando	FL
140	Peter	Anderson	22 Philip Street	New York	NY
147	Ricky	Anthopolis	45 Johnson Ave	New York	NY
68	Catherine	Bell	43 Alden Ave	Miami	FL

```
(54 row(s) returned)
```

CHAPTER 13
THE DISTINCT PREDICATE

The DISTINCT predicate is used to eliminate duplicate rows from the results of a SELECT statement. It belongs to a set of four predicates (ALL, TOP, DISTINCT, DISTINCTROW) which we use to manipulate the number of records returned from a SQL statement. All four of them are used right after the SELECT keyword, and all of them are optional. If we do not use a predicate with the SELECT statement, [ALL] is assumed by default.

SELECT [ALL] [TOP] [DISTINCT] [DISTINCTROW] field1, field2, … fieldn
FROM table

From the four predicates above, we will focus on DISTINCT in this chapter and TOP in the next one, since they are the two most useful ones. [ALL] is assumed as the default when no predicate is used and the DISTINCTROW has very specific applications. Specifically, the difference between DISTINCT and DISTINCTROW is that DISTINCT will look for unique values in the field or fields included in the SQL statement while DISTINCTROW will retrieve distinct records overall. We also need to know that the results of a query in which we use DISTINCT are not updatable while the results of a query in which we use DISTINCTROW are updatable. Also, keep in mind that DISTINCTROW might not be supported by other database engines like DB2, Oracle, or MySQL. To conclude, we should focus on understanding the DISTINCT and TOP predicates well because they are essential to retrieving the results we need in various scenarios.

The column on which we use the DISTINCT predicate will return only its unique values. When we apply the DISTINCT keyword on a combination of columns, lastname and firstname, for example—the database will return the unique combinations of their values. Let us see how this works through examples in our familiar customers and orders database.

116.   Run a SELECT statement without the DISTINCT predicate
Find cities in which we have customers
Discussion:
Using a classic SQL statement to retrieve the column "city" from the customers table will return multiple instances of the same city since it is logical to have multiple customers in the same city. For example, as we can see from the result set, New York appears as many times as the number of customers we have in this city. There are 201 records returned with multiple instances of various cities.

Code:
SELECT city
FROM customers

Result:

city
New York
New York
New York
New York

(201 row(s) returned)

117. Run a SELECT statement with the DISTINCT predicate on one column

Find unique cities in which we have customers

Discussion:

There are cases, however, in which we just want to obtain a report that shows only the unique or distinct names of the cities where we have customers. The business goal is to create a list of cities to know where we do business. Maybe we want to set up shipping centers in several regions. In this scenario, we would like New York to appear only once, Boston only once, and Los Angeles only once. This is a case where we use the DISTINCT predicate. This time, only 15 records returned, and the value for each city is unique. From this recordset, we know that the number of cities where we have customers is 15.

Code:

```
SELECT DISTINCT city
FROM customers
```

Result:

city
Albany
Boston
Chicago
Dallas
Denver

(15 row(s) returned)

118. Use DISTINCT on multiple columns

Finding unique customer names in various states

Discussion:

Experience indicates that DISTINCT works at its best when applied on a single column. However, if we want to apply DISTINCT on multiple columns, we need to know exactly what to expect. Let's work with our customers table and go through some examples to fully understand this concept.

Code Case 1:

If we run a simple SELECT statement such as:

```
SELECT firstname, state
FROM customers
WHERE firstname='John'
```

We will get four customers with a first name John. Actually, these are all the Johns we have in our customers table.

161

Result:

firstname	state
John	NY
John	TX
John	TX
John	CO

(4 row(s) returned)

Code Case 1:

If we include the DISTINCT clause such as:

SELECT DISTINCT firstname, state
FROM customers
WHERE firstname='John'

We will get only three customers with a first name John. This is because we told the database to return unique combinations of first names and states. In the previous result set, we have two Johns in Texas. When we use DISTINCT on both firstname and state, only one of the two will appear.

Result:

firstname	state
John	CO
John	NY
John	TX

(3 row(s) returned)

119. Getting more information beyond DISTINCT using GROUP BY
Find unique job titles and their corresponding numbers
Discussion:

Although it does not thematically belong here, your next logical thought is probably: Okay, I know how to retrieve unique values for names, states, job titles, and other fields. However, what is the total number I have from each? To answer this question, we need to use the GROUP BY clause, which we explore in detail in chapter 17. Here, we will use the job titles as an example to find the number of people holding each title.

As we can see from the result set, we have four sales managers and one of each of the other titles. We simply use one aggregate function count() and the GROUP BY clause to get the result we need. The "CountNumber" is the title we give ourselves to the counting column.

Code:
SELECT ContactTitle, Count(ContactTitle) AS CountNumber
FROM suppliers
GROUP BY ContactTitle

Result:

Contact Title	Count Number
Accounting Manager	1
Marketing Manager	1
Owner	1
Purchasing Director	1
Purchasing Manager	1
Sales Manager	4
Sales Representative	1

(7 row(s) returned)

CHAPTER 13 DISCUSSION QUESTIONS

1. What is the primary role of the DISTINCT predicate?
2. What other predicates similar to DISTINCT can be used to manipulate the number of rows retrieved?
3. Is DISTINCT a required predicate or an optional one?
4. Can we use the DISTINCT predicate on multiple columns?
5. What is the default predicate used if we do not use DISTINCT in the SQL statement?
6. If we use DISTINCT on one column what kind of values do we retrieve from that column?
7. If we use DISTINCT on multiple columns what kind of values do we retrieve from those columns?
8. Where in the SELECT statement do we place the DISTINCT predicate?
9. From the four possible predicates of the SELECT statement which two are the most useful?
10. What is the difference between DISTINCT and DISTINCTROW?

CHAPTER 13 HANDS-ON EXERCISES

Chapter 13 Case 1:

Start SQL Server Management Studio. For each of the questions in this case you need to create a new query (Ctrl-N) and name it as per the instructions in each question. Submit your work to your instructor as one text file that contains all SQL statements or as per your instructor's directions.

1. Your supervisor is asking for a list of unique states in which we have customers. Create a new query that satisfies your supervisor's request. Order results by State ascending. Save the query as Chapter13_Case1_Q1.

    Your result should look like:

state
AZ
CA
CO
DC
FL

    (10 row(s) returned)

2. The marketing department wants to prepare a nameday list so that they can send greeting cards to customers. They are asking you to give them a list of unique first names of customers. Create a new query that satisfies the marketing request. Order results by firstname ascending. Save the query as Chapter13_Case1_Q2.

    Your result should look like:

firstname
NULL
Alfred
Allan
Allen
Andrew

(71 row(s) returned)

3. The inventory people need a list of the different SKUs we have in the Products table. Create a new query that satisfies the inventory department request. Order results by SKU ascending. Save the query as Chapter13_Case1_Q3.

Your result should look like:

SKU
ADSE 2345
ADST 2345
ADSD 2345
ADSL 2345
ADST 2345

(17 row(s) returned)

4. The inventory people came back and they are now asking for a list that will display the unique SKUs as well as the number of products associated with each unique SKU. Create a query that satisfies this request and order results by SKU ascending. Save the query as Chapter13_Case1_Q4.

Your result should look like:

SKU	CountNumber
ADSE 2345	1
ADST 2345	1
ADSD 2345	1
ADSL 2345	1
ADST 2345	3

(17 row(s) returned)

5. The marketing people are back themselves asking for a list of unique first names of customers and their respective numbers so that they know how many customers they have for each nameday occasion. Create a query that satisfies this request and order results by firstname ascending. Save the query as Chapter13_Case1_Q5.

Your result should look like:

firstname	CountNumber
NULL	0
Alfred	3
Allan	2
Allen	3
Andrew	2

(71 row(s) returned)

Chapter 13 Case 2:

Start SQL Server Management Studio. For each of the questions in this case you need to create a new query (Ctrl-N) and name it as per the instructions in each question. Submit your work to your instructor as one text file that contains all SQL statements or as per your instructor's directions.

1. The inventory people need a list of unique states in which we have suppliers. Use the suppliers table and create a new query that satisfies the inventory department request. Order results by state ascending. Save the query as Chapter13_Case2_Q1.

   Your result should look like:

state
MA
NY
TX

   (3 row(s) returned)

2. The sales people are asking for a list of unique cities in which we have sales representatives. Use the SalesRep table to create a new query that satisfies the sales department request. Order results by city ascending. Save the query as Chapter13_Case2_Q2.

   Your result should look like:

city
Boston
Dallas
New York

   (3 row(s) returned)

3. The sales people are now asking for a list that will display the unique cities in which we have sales representatives as well as the number of sales reps in each city. Create a query that satisfies this request and order results by city ascending. Save the query as Chapter13_Case2_Q3.

   Your result should look like:

city	CountNumber
Boston	3
Dallas	2
New York	5

`(3 row(s) returned)`

4. The manager of sales people is asking for a list of unique discount levels from the productsorders table. He wants to have an idea of the various discounts the sales reps offer to the customers to close the sale. Create a new query that satisfies the inventory department request. Order results by discount level descending. Save the query as Chapter13_Case2_Q4.

Your result should look like:

Discount
0.20
0.15
0.00

`(3 row(s) returned)`

5. The sales manager is also asking for a report that will display the unique discount levels and the number of associated products for that unique discount. Create a query that satisfies this request and order results by discount level ascending. Save the query as Chapter13_Case2_Q5.

Your result should look like:

Discount	Product Number
0.00	140
0.15	1621
0.20	650

`(3 row(s) returned)`

CHAPTER 14
THE TOP PREDICATE

The TOP predicate is useful for selecting a specified number or a certain percentage of records from a data source like a table or query. It belongs to a set of four predicates (ALL, TOP, DISTINCT, DISTINCTROW) used to manipulate the number of records returned from a SQL statement. All four of them are used right after the SELECT keyword, and all of them are optional. If we do not use a predicate with the SELECT statement, [ALL] is assumed by default.

SELECT [ALL] [TOP] [DISTINCT] [DISTINCTROW] field1, field2, ... fieldn
FROM table

The TOP predicate used alone is not very useful since it does not return records in any special order; it simply returns the first n or n% of the records as they are stored in the table. However, when the TOP predicate is used with the ORDER BY, GROUP BY, and WHERE clauses, it shows its real potential and practicality.

120.   The TOP predicate alone with numbers
Retrieve 5 records from the products table
Discussion:
The TOP predicate in this example will return the first five records from the products table in the order these records are stored in the table. This process is practically useless for our business needs since it does not provide any special information at all. This example is given to demonstrate that TOP by itself will not produce any useful results.

Code:
SELECT TOP 5 productname, unitsinstock, unitsonorder
FROM Products

Result:

productname	unitsinstock	unitsonorder
Almonds, Hickory Smoked - 12 oz. Bag	40	5
Almonds, Roasted and Salted - 18 oz. Bag	32	0
Banana Chips - 20 oz. Bag	25	0
Berry Cherry in 8 oz. Bag	50	0
California Original Pistachios - 1 lb. Bag	35	0

(5 row(s) returned)

121.   The TOP predicate with ORDER BY and numbers
Find the five products with the most units in stock
Discussion:
In this example, the business goal is to find the five products with the highest levels of inventory. The use of the TOP predicate in combination with the ORDER BY clause can show its usefulness and practical application.
168

As you can see from the result set, the five products with the highest inventory levels appear first. We use the DESC keyword with the ORDER BY clause so that highest quantities appear first (see chapter 7 for the ORDER BY clause).

Code:
SELECT TOP 5 productname, unitsinstock, unitsonorder
FROM Products
ORDER BY unitsinstock DESC

Result:

productname	unitsinstock	unitsonorder
Berry Cherry in 8 oz. Bag	50	0
Artichokes in white sauce	50	0
Chocolate Chip Cookies	50	0
Biscuits with cream	49	0
Salsa Verde	49	0

(5 row(s) returned)

122.   The TOP predicate with ORDER BY and percentages

Retrieve 10% of the products with the highest prices

Discussion:

This time, management asked for the top 10% of the most expensive products in the inventory. We can easily reply to this request by using the TOP predicate with the ORDER BY clause as shown below. In SQL Server 2012, we use the word "10 PERCENT" and not "10%" with the TOP predicate.

Code:
SELECT TOP 10 PERCENT productname, productunitprice
FROM Products
ORDER BY productunitprice DESC

Result:

productname	productunitprice
Pepper Cheese Box 3.75 oz.	50.00
Coffee biscuits	50.00
Pizza croutons	49.00
Chocolate Chip Cookies	49.00
Fruit Dip	49.00
Mushroom Rolls	48.00
Lemon Biscuits	48.00

(7 row(s) returned)

In the products table we have 70 records and in the result set we have seven records. This is correct since we asked for 10% of the records.

123.   The TOP predicate with ORDER BY and dates

Find the 5 most recently hired employees

Discussion:

The TOP predicate is very useful when used with dates. In this example, we are looking for the five most recently hired employees in the corporation. We use the DESC keyword with ORDER BY to obtain this result. We could have used the ASC keyword to retrieve the 5 most senior employees of the corporation.

Code:

```
SELECT TOP 5 lastname, firstname, DateofHire
FROM SalesReps
ORDER BY DateofHire DESC
```

Result:

lastname	firstname	title
Anderson	John	Sales Reppresentative
Baker	Jim	Account Manager
Bernstein	Michael	Sales Reppresentative
Delaney	Kenneth	Assistant Manager
Simmons	Andrew	Account Manager

(5 row(s) returned)

124.   The TOP predicate with the GROUP BY clause

Find the 10 largest orders from customers

Discussion:

Let us assume that our manager wants to see the 10 largest orders received from our customers. The way to prepare this report would be to calculate order subtotals (multiply the quantity of each product with its price) for all of the products contained in one order and do a GROUP BY (see chapter 17) on the orderid, followed by a SORT DESC to get the largest orders. Then, we use the top predicate to retrieve only the ten largest orders.

Code:

```
SELECT TOP 10 orderid, Sum(([unitprice]*[quantity])) AS orderamount
FROM ProductsOrders
GROUP BY orderid
ORDER BY Sum(([unitprice]*[quantity])) DESC;
```

Result:

orderid	orderamount
354	576
944	574
609	530
308	512
404	510
353	490
169	477
547	462
932	455
433	441

```
(10 row(s) returned)
```

125. The TOP predicate with calculated fields and WHERE

Get the ten largest orders for a particular product
Discussion:

As in our previous discussion, we can, of course, use ORDER BY, DESC, TOP, and WHERE to create result sets that give us powerful information. In this scenario, we have been asked to prepare a report that contains the 15 largest orders for a particular product—for example "Almonds, Roasted and Salted - 18 oz. Bag" (the product with productid = 2).

Code:

```
SELECT TOP 10 orderid, productid, (unitprice*quantity) AS orderamount
FROM ProductsOrders
WHERE (productid=2)
ORDER BY (unitprice*quantity) DESC;
```

Result:

orderid	productid	orderamount
314	2	90
353	2	90
379	2	90
503	2	90
507	2	90
764	2	90
873	2	90
978	2	90
142	2	75
36	2	75

```
(10 row(s) returned)
```

CHAPTER 14 DISCUSSION QUESTIONS

1. What is the primary role of the TOP predicate?
2. What is the difference between TOP and TOP PERCENT?
3. What other predicates similar to TOP can be used to manipulate the number of rows retrieved?
4. Is TOP a required predicate or an optional one?
5. What is the default predicate if we do not specify one in the SQL statement?
6. Is TOP useful by itself?
7. What other SQL keywords can we use with TOP to retrieve useful results?
8. Where in the SELECT statement do we place the DISTINCT predicate?
9. What do we need to pay attention to when using TOP?
10. What are some data types with which we can use TOP?

CHAPTER 14 HANDS-ON EXERCISES

Chapter 14 Case 1:
Start SQL Server Management Studio. For each of the questions in this case you need to create a new query (Ctrl-N) and name it as per the instructions in each question. Submit your work to your instructor as one text file that contains all SQL statements or as per your instructor's directions.

1. The inventory people ask for a list of the five products with the highest quantities per unit. Create a new query that includes the ProductName, QuantityPerUnit, and ProductUnitPrice fields from the Products table and satisfies the inventory department request. Save the query as Chapter14_Case1_Q1.

Your result should look like:

productname	QuantityPerUnit	ProductUnitPrice
Chocolate Covered Cherries in 8 oz. Bag	35	37.00
Dark Chocolate Apricots in 20 oz. Bag	35	46.00
Roasted & Salted Almonds	35	19.00
Coconut Flavour Cream Wafers 10 oz.	35	38.00
Coconut Chocolate Chip Cookies	35	25.00

(5 row(s) returned)

2. The inventory people are back asking for a list that will display the top 15% of products with the highest product unit prices. Create a query that includes the ProductName, QuantityPerUnit, UnitsInStock, and ProductUnitPrice fields from the Products table and satisfies the inventory request. Save the query as Chapter14_Case1_Q2.

Your result should look like:

productname	QuantityPerUnit	UnitsInStock	ProductUnitPrice
Pepper Cheese Box 3.75 oz.	22	45	50.00
Coffee biscuits	30	24	50.00
Pizza croutons	20	44	49.00
Chocolate Chip Cookies	25	50	49.00
Fruit Dip	30	25	49.00

```
(11 row(s) returned)
```

3. The marketing department is asking for a list of the 10 most recent placed orders. Create a query that includes the OrderID, CustomerID, OrderDate, and ShippingCost from the Orders table that satisfies this request and save it as Chapter14_Case1_Q3.

Your result should look like:

OrderID	CustomerID	OrderDate	ShippingCost
4	165	2014-12-19	48
874	159	2014-12-16	39
165	120	2014-12-14	52
881	167	2014-12-12	44
628	157	2014-12-11	47

```
(10 row(s) returned)
```

4. The sales department is looking for a sample list that includes ten products from the Products table sorted by ProductName. They have many typos in the printed catalog and they want to check the entries in the database. Create a query that includes the ProductName, QuantityPerUnit, UnitsInStock, UnitsOnOrder, and ProductUnitPrice fields from the products table and satisfies this request. Save it as Chapter14_Case1_Q4.

Your result should look like:

ProductName	QuantityPerUnit	UnitsInStock	UnitsOnOrder	ProductUnitPrice
All-Purpose Marinade I	24	27	15	29.00
All-Purpose Marinade II	30	26	15	39.00
Almonds, Hickory Smoked - 12 oz. Bag	12	40	5	35.00
Almonds, Roasted and Salted - 18 oz. Bag	12	32	0	22.00
Apple Cinnamon Raisin Cookies	30	15	20	27.00

```
(10 row(s) returned)
```

5. The marketing department is asking for a list of the ten orders with the highest shipping cost. Customers have complained about shipping charges and there is an internal review in place now. Create a query that includes the OrderID, CustomerID, OrderDate, ShippedDate, and ShippingCost fields from the Orders table and satisfies this request. Save it as Chapter14_Case1_Q5.

Your result should look like:

OrderID	CustomerID	OrderDate	ShippedDate	ShippingCost
13	53	2012-02-10	2012-02-15	52
49	17	2013-07-07	2013-07-12	52
68	35	2012-09-03	2012-09-08	52
69	125	2012-02-24	2012-02-29	52
85	147	2012-04-30	2012-05-05	52

```
(10 row(s) returned)
```

Chapter 14 Case 2:

Start SQL Server Management Studio. For each of the questions in this case you need to create a new query (Ctrl-N) and name it as per the instructions in each question. Submit your work to your instructor as one text file that contains all SQL statements or as per your instructor's directions.

1. The HR department is looking for a list of the five most senior employees in the organization. Create a query that includes the FirstName, LastName, Title, and DateOfHire fields from the SalesReps table and satisfies this request. Save the query as Chapter14_Case2_Q1.

    Your result should look like:

FirstName	LastName	Title	DateOfHire
Michael	Bernstein	Sales Reppresentative	1991-05-25
Kenneth	Delaney	Assistant Manager	1995-05-10
John	Anderson	Sales Reppresentative	1999-01-01
Mary	Teall	Sales Director	2000-06-12
Jason	Vanderback	Sales manager	2001-05-12

```
(5 row(s) returned)
```

2. The sales department is looking for the ten most recently shipped orders. They had calls from customers that their orders have not arrived and they need to check what happened. Create a query that includes the OrderID, CustomerID, OrderDate, and ShippedDate fields from the Orders table and satisfies this request. Save it as Chapter14_Case2_Q2.

    Your result should look like:

OrderID	CustomerID	OrderDate	ShippedDate
4	165	2014-12-19	2014-12-24
874	159	2014-12-16	2014-12-21
165	120	2014-12-14	2014-12-19
881	167	2014-12-12	2014-12-17
628	157	2014-12-11	2014-12-16

```
(10 row(s) returned)
```

3. The marketing department has asked for a list of the 20 largest orders from our customers. Create a query that includes the OrderID, and a calculated field named OrderAmount from the ProductsOrders table and satisfies this request. Save the query as Chapter14_Case2_Q3.

Your result should look like:

OrderID	OrderAmount
354	576
944	574
609	530
308	512
404	510

(20 row(s) returned)

4. The marketing department is now asking for a report of the 20 largest orders for a particular product: California Original Pistachios - 1 lb. Bag. Create a query that includes the OrderID, and a calculated field named OrderAmount from the ProductsOrders table and satisfies this request. Save it as Chapter14_Case2_Q4.

Your result should look like:

OrderID	ProductID	OrderAmount
904	5	90
248	5	75
238	5	75
223	5	75
346	5	75

(20 row(s) returned)

5. The HR department is preparing for the employee of the year event and has asked for a list of the 3 sales representatives with the most orders. Create a query that includes the SalesRepID field, and a calculated field named CountOfOrders using the count() function from the Orders table that satisfies this request. Save the query as Chapter14_Case2_Q5.

Your result should look like:

SalesRepID	CountOfOrders
5	124
7	123
3	112

(3 row(s) returned)

CHAPTER 15
CALCULATED FIELDS

Calculated fields are temporary columns created using arithmetic operators such as (+, *, -, /, ^, Mod). You can create calculated fields in a variety of ways. For instance, you can multiply a numeric field by a certain number or a certain percentage, or you can multiply two numeric fields themselves. You can multiply two fields and divide the result by another field. You can also create calculated fields conditionally by using the iif() and case() functions. You can also generate powerful pieces of information by using calculated fields with aggregate functions. Of course, you can use calculated fields in a view with WHERE so that your calculations are applied only to a subset of records. You can also use calculated fields in the HAVING clause in a GROUP BY statement for filtering records after the aggregations from the GROUP BY clause are completed. Finally, you can use calculated fields with UPDATE statements to change hundreds or thousands of records instantly. The applications of calculated fields in databases are essential, and in this chapter, we will present you with multiple examples. However, we will deal with numeric calculations only. I have devoted two additional chapters on operations for dates and strings so that you can explore each in detail. The arithmetic operators available in SQL Server 2012 appear in the following table:

Operator	Meaning
+	Addition
*	Multiplication
-	Subtraction
/	Division
%	Remainder

When you use calculated fields remember that it is not a good practice to store calculated fields in tables. The third normal form rule of normalization says that all attributes should depend on the key. That is, all table fields need to be related to the entity they describe. That is, all customer fields need to be connected to the CustomerID PK field. A calculation used in a table is an ever changing attribute for the entity and this causes lot of trouble. The most appropriate place for a calculated field is within a view.

126.   Add a number to a numeric field
Create a product catalog with updated prices on the fly
Discussion:
The business goal here is to create a new product catalog that will appear on the corporate website for a promotional campaign. Management does not want the product prices in the underlying products table to change since this campaign will last only two weeks. We can easily create a query using the SQL code below and use it as the data source for our web catalog. Specifically, management asked to add $2 to the price of each product.

Code:

```
SELECT productname, productunitprice + 2 AS productprice
FROM Products
```

Result:

productname	productprice
Almonds, Hickory Smoked - 12 oz. Bag	37.00
Almonds, Roasted and Salted - 18 oz. Bag	24.00
Banana Chips - 20 oz. Bag	29.00
Berry Cherry in 8 oz. Bag	32.00

`(70 row(s) returned)`

127.   Add a percentage to a numeric field

Update product prices on the fly by a certain percentage

Discussion:

This time, due to increased replenishment costs (receiving goods from suppliers), our manager tells us to add a 2% markup for the product catalog we are sending out this month. We multiply by 1.02 and not by 0.02 since the latter will give us only the percentage increase and not the entire new price.

Code:

```
SELECT productname, productunitprice * (1.02) as productprice
FROM Products
```

Result:

productname	productprice
Almonds, Hickory Smoked - 12 oz. Bag	35.70
Almonds, Roasted and Salted - 18 oz. Bag	22.44
Banana Chips - 20 oz. Bag	27.54
Berry Cherry in 8 oz. Bag	30.60

`(70 row(s) returned)`

128.   Add two numeric columns

Calculate product inventory quantities

Discussion:

Management asks us for a report about product inventory quantities. Specifically, they want to know not only what units we have in the warehouse but how many are on order as well. To answer this request, we create a new column named TotalUnits, which is simply the sum of the units we have in stock plus the ones we have on order and have not arrived yet.

Code:

```
SELECT productname, unitsinstock, unitsonorder,
(unitsinstock + unitsonorder)
AS TotalUnits
FROM products
```

Result:

productname	unitsinstock	unitsonorder	TotalUnits
Almonds, Hickory Smoked - 12 oz. Bag	40	5	45
Almonds, Roasted and Salted - 18 oz. Bag	32	0	32
Banana Chips - 20 oz. Bag	25	0	25
Berry Cherry in 8 oz. Bag	50	0	50

(70 row(s) returned)

129. Multiply two columns and group their results

Find order totals by order

Discussion:

The request this time is to find order totals for all of the orders that we have had to date. Each order might contain multiple products with multiple quantities for each product. We first need to multiply product prices with quantities for every product in each order and sum the results. Then, we need to group by OrderID so that we can obtain the total for every order. A sample data set on which to make these calculations appears below. The order with OrderID = 1, contains three different products with prices of 15, 12, and 18 and quantities of 2, 3, and 5 respectively. We need to first multiply the product unit price times the quantity for each product, get the subtotals, and sum up the results for each order.

ProductsOrders			
OrderID	ProductID	UnitPrice	Quantity
1	1	15	2
1	2	12	3
1	3	18	5
2	1	15	2
2	3	18	8

Code:

```
SELECT OrderID, Sum([UnitPrice]*[quantity]) AS OrderSubtotal
FROM ProductsOrders
GROUP BY OrderID
```

Result:

OrderID	OrderSubtotal
593	69
925	8
23	38
238	175

(919 row(s) returned)

130. Subtract a percentage from a numeric column

Provide customers with a 20% discount on every product

Discussion:

Management decided to aggressively sell this month, and they have initiated a promotional campaign with a price discount of 20% for every product in the product catalog. We need to create a new product catalog, which the company wants to send out immediately. We can easily respond to this request using a calculated field as is shown in the code below:

Code:
SELECT ProductName, ProductUnitPrice * (1-0.2) as PromotionalPrice
FROM Products

Result:

Product Name	Promotional Price
Almonds, Hickory Smoked - 12 oz. Bag	28.0
Almonds, Roasted and Salted - 18 oz. Bag	17.6
Banana Chips - 20 oz. Bag	21.6
Berry Cherry in 8 oz. Bag	24.0

```
(70 row(s) returned)
```

131. How to display a currency symbol in calculated fields

Discussion:

SQL Server does not display the currency symbol in calculations even if the field on which calculations are made is of the money data type. In this example, we are creating a view in which we increase the value of the productunitprice field by 20%.

Code 1:
SELECT ProductUnitPrice* (1+0.2) AS ProductPrice
FROM products

Although the ProductUnitPrice field is of currency data type in the Products table, the resulting calculation is simply a number.

Result:

	Product Price
1	42.0
2	26.4
3	32.4
4	36.0
5	34.8

We can solve this problem by using the format function with the syntax

$$FORMAT(<value>, <format\_string>)$$

where value is the calculated field. For the format string we use the # character to designate any digit, and the 0 character to display a zero if a numeric value does not exist after the decimal placeholder.

Code2:
SELECT format((ProductUnitPrice * (1+0.2)),'$#,#.00') AS ProductPrice
FROM products

Result:

	ProductPrice
1	$42.00
2	$26.40
3	$32.40
4	$36.00
5	$34.80

(70 row(s) returned)

132.   Calculated fields with multiple conditions

Provide customers with different discounts based on the product supplier

Discussion:

A scenario of providing product discounts by filtering on supplier ids is fine for some cases, but it also has two major drawbacks. First, the same discount rate is applied to every supplier included in the WHERE clause. Second, discount rates can be applied only to suppliers included in the WHERE clause. In some cases, we might want to provide different discount rates for each supplier and include all products from all suppliers in the result set. Suppose we want to provide a 20% discount for products from SupplierID=1, 15% for those from SupplierID=2, 18% for those from SupplierID=3, and 25% for those from SupplierID=4. In addition, we might want to provide a 10% discount for all of the rest of the products regardless of supplier. The case() function comes to the rescue here, providing the flexibility to give us the results we need.

Code:

```
SELECT productname,
CASE
When SupplierID = 1 Then ProductUnitPrice*(1-0.2)
When SupplierID = 2 Then ProductUnitPrice*(1-0.15)
When SupplierID = 3 Then ProductUnitPrice*(1-0.18)
When SupplierID = 4 Then ProductUnitPrice*(1-0.25)
Else ProductUnitPrice*(1-0.1)
End
AS ProductPrice
FROM Products
```

Result:

productname	ProductPrice
Almonds, Hickory Smoked - 12 oz. Bag	28.00
Almonds, Roasted and Salted - 18 oz. Bag	17.60
Banana Chips - 20 oz. Bag	21.60
Berry Cherry in 8 oz. Bag	24.00
California Original Pistachios - 1 lb. Bag	23.20

(70 row(s) returned)

133.   How to use calculated fields with the iif() function

Determine employee bonus eligibility

Discussion:

In this example, we are looking for sales representatives who are eligible for a bonus. To be eligible for a bonus, a sales rep needs to have accumulated sales of $5,000 or more for the year. The SQL code in this example is long but easy. First, notice that we use three fields only: LastName, Bonus, and OrderDate. We use the OrderDate field to filter orders for 2014 only. Then, we use the lastname field with a GROUP BY clause to display results by employee name. The last field is that of the Bonus. Here, we use the iif() function with the syntax iif (expression, result if expression is true, result if expression is false) to actually make the calculations and determine bonus eligibility:

IIf(Sum([unitprice]*[quantity])>5000,'Bonus','No Bonus') AS Bonus

The iif() function above reads: If the total amount of orders serviced by the sales rep exceeds $5,000, give the sales rep a bonus. Otherwise, no bonus. The AS part means display this field name as "Bonus". Do not pay attention to the joins in this example since we only use them to get fields from three different tables. For a full overview of joins, see chapter 29.

Code:
```
SELECT SalesReps.LastName, IIf(Sum([unitprice]*[quantity])>5000,'Bonus','No Bonus') AS Bonus

FROM
(SalesReps INNER JOIN Orders ON SalesReps.SalesRepID = Orders.SalesRepID)

INNER JOIN ProductsOrders ON Orders.OrderID = ProductsOrders.OrderID

WHERE (((Orders.OrderDate) Between '2014/1/1' AND '2014/12/31'))

GROUP BY SalesReps.LastName
```

Result:

LastName	Bonus
Anderson	No Bonus
Baker	No Bonus
Bernstein	Bonus
Delaney	No Bonus

```
(10 row(s) returned)
```

134. Use calculated fields with GROUP BY and aggregate functions

Calculate total discount amounts by order

Discussion:

This time, we have a request to provide a report that will show the total discount amount for each order. Remember that each order might contain multiple products. In addition, for each product in the same order, we might have provided a different discount rate. Our goal is to calculate the discount amount for each product in each order and sum the results. To achieve this task, we will use the ProductsOrders table, which includes the unitprice (the one finally extended to the customer, not the one in the products table used for the product catalog), the quantity of each product, and the discount rate for each product. A sample from the table with two orders appears below:

ProductsOrders				
OrderID	ProductID	UnitPrice	Quantity	Discount
1	1	15	2	20%
1	2	12	3	0

1	3	18	5	15%
2	1	15	2	10%
2	3	18	8	15%

For each product in an order, we need to multiply the unit price by the quantity to get the amount invoiced for that product. Then, we multiply the result by the discount rate to get the total discount for each product in each order. Then, we sum all of the discount amounts in each order. Finally, we group on orderid so that we get the total discount amount by order.

Code:
```
SELECT OrderID, Sum((([UnitPrice]*[Quantity])*[Discount]) AS OrderDiscount
FROM ProductsOrders
GROUP BY OrderID
```

Result:

OrderID	OrderDiscount
593	10.35
925	1.2
23	6.1
238	27.75

(919 row(s) returned)

135.   Use a calculated field with an aggregate function

Calculate the average discount amount for all orders

Discussion:

Our business goal is to find the average discount amount we have given away for all of our orders. Discounts are excellent, but we need to keep track of them and evaluate them on a continuous basis. Fortunately, we can do this in no time by simply using the AVG (average) function to get the average amount from all the orders.

Code:
```
SELECT Avg([UnitPrice]*[Quantity]*[Discount]) AS AverageOrderDiscount
FROM ProductsOrders
```

Result:

AverageOrderDiscount
8.984508

Then, we can compare the above result with the actual average order amount using the code below. Now, we can make the conclusion that an average $9 discount for an average total order of $58 is an acceptable discount rate.

Code:
```
SELECT Avg([UnitPrice]*[Quantity]) AS AverageOrderAmount
FROM ProductsOrders
```

Result:

AverageOrderAmount
58

I know you noticed the number of decimals in the results above. We can decrease the number of decimals or eliminate them altogether by using the cast and convert functions. Actually, calculated fields are used extensively in combination with type conversion functions to format numbers in the most appropriate way. Here, we use the cast and convert functions to convert the decimal number to an integer. Both of them will produce the same result. For the full range of type conversion functions, read chapter 24, where they are explained in detail.

Code1 (using cast):
```
SELECT cast(avg([UnitPrice]*[Quantity]*[Discount]) AS int) AS AverageOrderDiscount
FROM ProductsOrders
```

Result:

AverageOrderDiscount
8

Code2 (using convert):
```
SELECT convert(int, avg([UnitPrice]*[Quantity]*[Discount])) AS AverageOrderDiscount
FROM ProductsOrders
```

Result:

AverageOrderDiscount
8

136. Storing the results of calculated fields with SELECT INTO

Storing total order amounts in a separate table

Discussion:

Sometimes, we need to store the results of our calculations in a backup, archive, or temporary table. This is very easy to achieve using SELECT INTO statements that were covered in the SELECT chapter. Storing results of calculated fields in production tables is not a good idea because these fields will interfere with normalization rules. However, for archiving purposes, we can go ahead.

In this example, we take the OrderID and OrderTotal fields from the ProductsOrders table and transfer their records in a new table named ArchivedOrders. Of course, the OrderTotal field is calculated from three different fields in the ProductsOrders table.

Code:
```
SELECT OrderID, SUM((unitprice*Quantity)*(1-Discount)) AS OrderTotal
INTO ArchivedOrders
FROM ProductsOrders
GROUP BY OrderID
```

Result:

The database will create a new table named ArchivedOrders. Go to the object explorer window, refresh your tables and you will be able to see your new table.

CHAPTER 15 DISCUSSION QUESTIONS

1. What are two goals of calculated fields?
2. Is it a good idea to store calculated fields in tables?
3. Why knowledge of the usage of calculated fields affects the design of the database?
4. What is the purpose of arithmetic operators?
5. How many arithmetic operators do we have in SQL Server 2012?
6. What is the best object (table, view) in which to use calculated fields?
7. How can we create calculated fields conditionally?
8. What is the difference between the iif() and case() functions?
9. Why does it make perfect sense to use calculated fields with UPDATE statements?
10. Can we use calculated fields with the WHERE and HAVING clauses? What is the difference?

CHAPTER 15 HANDS-ON EXERCISES

Chapter 15 Case 1:
Start SQL Server Management Studio. For each of the questions in this case you need to create a new query (Ctrl-N) and name it as per the instructions in each question. Submit your work to your instructor as one text file that contains all SQL statements or as per your instructor's directions.

1. The sales people embark on a sales effort for the next two days and they want all the product prices decreased by 20%. The new product catalog will be valid only for two days on the corporate web site. Then, the prices will go back to normal. Create a new query that includes the ProductName and the new price field from the Products table and satisfies the sales people request. Save the query as Chapter15_Case1_Q1.

   Your result should look like:

ProductName	NewPrice
Almonds, Hickory Smoked - 12 oz. Bag	28.00000
Almonds, Roasted and Salted - 18 oz. Bag	17.60000
Banana Chips - 20 oz. Bag	21.60000
Berry Cherry in 8 oz. Bag	24.00000
California Original Pistachios - 1 lb. Bag	23.20000

   (70 row(s) returned)

2. The accounts payable unit is conducting an internal audit and they are looking for product prices by quantity per unit. Divide the ProductUnitPrice by QuantityPerUnit to arrive at item prices so that accounts payable can better assess supplier prices. Create a new query that includes the ProductName, ProductUnitPrice, and QuantityPerUnit fields from the Products table and satisfies the accounts payable request. Save the query as Chapter15_Case1_Q2.

   Your result should look like:

Product Name	Product Unit Price	Quantity PerUnit	Price Per Unit
Almonds, Hickory Smoked - 12 oz. Bag	35.00	12	2.9166
Almonds, Roasted and Salted - 18 oz. Bag	22.00	12	1.8333
Banana Chips - 20 oz. Bag	27.00	12	2.25
Berry Cherry in 8 oz. Bag	30.00	15	2.00
California Original Pistachios - 1 lb. Bag	29.00	15	1.9333

`(70 row(s) returned)`

3. The marketing people need to print a new product catalog that contains updated prices, decreased by 15%, for the following suppliers: American Foods, LLC, Berkley Bakery Co., Nature's Food, Inc., and Old York Foods, Inc. Create a new query that includes the ProductName, ProductUnitPrice, and QuantityPerUnit fields from the Products table and satisfies the marketing request. Hint: First identify the SupplierID from the suppliers table and then use the case() function. The new report should contain the products from all suppliers. Save the query as Chapter15_Case1_Q3. Sort results by ProductName ascending.

Your result should look like:

productname	Product Unit Price	Quantity PerUnit	Product Price
All-Purpose Marinade I	29.00	24	24.650000
All-Purpose Marinade II	39.00	30	39.000000
Almonds, Hickory Smoked - 12 oz. Bag	35.00	12	35.000000
Almonds, Roasted and Salted - 18 oz. Bag	22.00	12	22.000000
Apple Cinnamon Raisin Cookies	27.00	30	27.000000

`(70 row(s) returned)`

4. Accounts payable is back and they need to verify what payments they are supposed to extend to suppliers. They are asking for a report that includes all open requisitions. To achieve this you need to multiply UnitsOnOrder by ProductUnitPrice to find out how much we have to pay. Create a new query that includes the ProductName, ProductUnitPrice, QuantityPerUnit, and UnitsOnOrder fields from the Products table and satisfies the accounts payable request. Save the query as Chapter15_Case1_Q4.

Your result should look like:

Product Name	Product Unit Price	Quantity PerUnit	UnitsOnOrder	Outstanding Payments
Almonds, Hickory Smoked - 12 oz. Bag	35.00	12	5	175.00
Almonds, Roasted and Salted - 18 oz. ...	22.00	12	0	0.00
Banana Chips - 20 oz. Bag	27.00	12	0	0.00
Berry Cherry in 8 oz. Bag	30.00	15	0	0.00
California Original Pistachios - 1 lb. Bag	29.00	15	0	0.00

`(70 row(s) returned)`

5. The order processing unit from the sales department is asking for a report that will list the total order amount by product. Select the ProductId field from the ProductsOrders table and create a calculated field named OrderTotal to satisfy the request. Save the new query as Chapter15_Case1_Q5.

Your result should look like:

ProductID	OrderTotal
23	1791.75
46	1651.50
69	1649.25
29	943.50
9	1389.00

(70 row(s) returned)

Chapter 15 Case 2:

Start SQL Server Management Studio. For each of the questions in this case you need to create a new query (Ctrl-N) and name it as per the instructions in each question. Submit your work to your instructor as one text file that contains all SQL statements or as per your instructor's directions.

1. The inventory people need a list of products that shows the difference between the quantities of units in stock minus the reorder levels. They need to see if we have any negative amounts which mean we need to order new products. Create a new query that includes the ProductName, ProductUnitPrice, UnitsInStock, and ReorderLevel fields from the Products table that satisfies the inventory people request. Sort results by ProductName ascending. Save the query as Chapter15_Case2_Q1.

    Your result should look like:

ProductName	ProductUnitPrice	UnitsInStock	ReorderLevel	UnitStatus
All-Purpose Marinade I	29.00	27	40	-13
All-Purpose Marinade II	39.00	26	35	-9
Almonds, Hickory Smoked - 12 oz. Bag	35.00	40	45	-5
Almonds, Roasted and Salted - 18 oz....	22.00	32	20	12
Apple Cinnamon Raisin Cookies	27.00	15	30	-15

    (70 row(s) returned)

2. The inventory people responsible for replenishing are asking for a report that will show how many units they need to order for each product. Create a new query that includes the ProductName, UnitsInStock, UnitsOnOrder, and ReorderLevel fields from the Products table that satisfies the inventory people request. Sort results by ProductName ascending. Save the query as Chapter15_Case2_Q2.

    Your result should look like:

ProductName	UnitsInStock	UnitsOnOrder	ReorderLevel	UnitsToOrder
All-Purpose Marinade I	27	15	40	2
All-Purpose Marinade II	26	15	35	6
Almonds, Hickory Smoked - 12 oz. Bag	40	5	45	0
Almonds, Roasted and Salted - 18 oz. Bag	32	0	20	12
Apple Cinnamon Raisin Cookies	15	20	30	5

    (70 row(s) returned)

3. The marketing department is asking for a report that will list the total amount of each order. They want the discount given for each product to be taken into consideration for the total. Select the OrderId field and

create a new calculated field named OrderTotal from the ProductsOrders table and group orders by OrderID. Save the query that satisfies the marketing department request as Chapter15_Case2_Q3.

Your result should look like:

OrderID	OrderTotal
1	24.00
2	184.50
3	190.05
4	38.25
5	214.00

(919 row(s) returned)

4. The sales director feels the sales reps went over the limit in providing discounts in order to get the sale. So he wants a report that will ignore the sales people discount if it is more than 15% and replace it with a discount of exactly 15%. Create a new query that includes the OrderID, ProductID, UnitPrice, and Discount from the ProductsOrders table and meets the sales director request. Name the new query as Chapter15_Case2_Q4. Hint: Use the iif() function.

Your result should look like:

OrderID	ProductID	Unit Price	Discount	Adjusted Discount
1	61	15	0.20	0.15
2	23	15	0.15	0.15
2	24	15	0.20	0.15
2	32	15	0.00	0.00
2	70	15	0.15	0.15

(2411 row(s) returned)

5. The marketing director wants to initiate a new campaign of generous discounts to customers. She just received a memo that the following suppliers have now discounted their products with the percentage shown: Home of Snacks, 25%, Mediterranean Foods, LLC, 20%, Nature's Food, Inc., 30%, and Old York Foods, Inc., 30%. The marketing manager wants to pass 80% of the wholesale discount received to her customers. For all other products, prices will remain the same. Create a new query that contains the productname field and a calculated field named ProductPrice from the Products table and satisfies the marketing director request. Name the query Chapter15_Case2_Q5. Hint: First identify the suppliers from the supplier table. Then calculate 80% of the supplier discount and finally use the case function.

Your result should look like:

productname	Product Price
Almonds, Hickory Smoked - 12 oz. Bag	28.000000
Almonds, Roasted and Salted - 18 oz. Bag	17.600000
Banana Chips - 20 oz. Bag	21.600000
Berry Cherry in 8 oz. Bag	24.000000
California Original Pistachios - 1 lb. Bag	23.200000

(70 row(s) returned)

CHAPTER 16
CONCATENATED FIELDS

Concatenating columns means nothing more than displaying the contents of two or more columns in one. The operation of concatenation happens through a view on the fly, and the resulting column and its contents are not saved in the underlying table. There are no special arithmetical or logical calculations involved. Simply put, if we want a view to display the contents of the first and last name fields as one, we just concatenate the two fields. Though the concept sounds simple, its applicability in every day work tasks is indispensable.

Concatenation in databases can achieve much more than simply displaying the contents of two or more columns together. We can create mailing labels, write letters with the correct punctuation, combine field data with plain text, perform conditional concatenation based on the values of any field, and use string and other functions for truly powerful results. To concatenate fields in SQL Server, we use the "+" character.

137.   Column concatenation without spaces
Put all customer address information in one field
Discussion:
We have a job to create mailing labels for letters to our suppliers. My experience indicates that most people will go to Word, connect to Excel or SQL Server, and go through multiple steps and a painful process to achieve this task. There is no need to go to this trouble since we can easily achieve this task using the database alone. Why do it in the database? In the future, we might need to create mailing labels only for a subset of our suppliers in the city of Boston or in the state of California. We can just modify our view_suppliers_labels, add the city field or the state field, and enter any criteria expressions we need.

I will show you how to use punctuation and spaces for formatting your concatenated columns so that you can do everything in SQL Server. In this example, we create a simple concatenation of four fields. Using this code, there will be no spaces between the field values in the result set.

Code:
```
SELECT  (address+city+state+zip) AS FullAddress
FROM Customers
```

Result:

FullAddress
11 Lark StreetNew YorkNY12189
12 Madison AveNew YorkNY12189
23 New Scotland AveNew YorkNY12189
22 Academy RoadNew YorkNY12189

```
(201 row(s) returned)
```

189

As you can see, the four fields are concatenated into one. However, the data is cramped in a continuous string of characters. We need to add spaces between the fields so that we can easily read them and print the results in a way that will make sense to USPS.

138.   Column concatenation with spaces

Put all customer address information in one field with spaces between values

Discussion:

In this example, we just add spaces between the concatenated columns. We use single quotes with a space between them to achieve this output. If we need to add two spaces between the fields, then we leave two spaces between the single quotes.

Code:
```
SELECT  (address +' '+ city +' '+ state +' '+ zip)  AS FullAddress
FROM Customers
```

Result:

FullAddress
11 Lark Street New York NY 12189
12 Madison Ave New York NY 12189
23 New Scotland Ave New York NY 12189
22 Academy Road New York NY 12189

```
(201 row(s) returned)
```

139.   Concatenation of columns and text

Writing custom letters in databases

Discussion:

What if we would like to write a letter using a database? We can combine plain text with field data with enough flexibility to write automatic letters! In the sample letter below notice how punctuation marks are enclosed in single quotes. Also, the SELECT statement is practically one field named "CustomerLetter".

Code:
```
SELECT 'Dear' + ' '+ (lastname +' ' + firstname) +'.' + ' '+ 'It is our pleasure to announce that we
reviewed your resume, and we have set up an interview time for you.  Can you please verify that
your address is' + ' ' + (address +' '+ City +' '+ State +' '+ Zip) + ' ' + 'to send you corporate policy
details and directions?'  AS CustomerLetter
FROM Customers
```

Result:

CustomerLetter
Dear Demarco John. It is our pleasure to announce that we reviewed your resume, and we have set up a...
Dear Demania Mary. It is our pleasure to announce that we reviewed your resume, and we have set up a...
Dear Demers George. It is our pleasure to announce that we reviewed your resume, and we have set up ...
Dear Demetriou Phillip. It is our pleasure to announce that we reviewed your resume, and we have set up...

```
(201 row(s) returned)
```

140.   Use the left() string function to concatenate a single character from a field

Displaying only the first letter from the customers' first names with the left() function.

Discussion:

Let's say we want to write a letter, but instead of using the complete first name of the customer, we only want the first letter to appear. We can achieve this result and more by using string (text) functions. In this example, we use the left() function, but we can use any function that suits our needs. Chapter 25 contains a plethora of examples on string manipulation. The left function in this example will extract the first character from the first name field.

Code:

```
SELECT 'Dear' + ' '+ (lastname + ' ' + left(firstname, 1)) +'.' + ' '+ 'Please complete the enclosed forms so
that we can ship your order to your country.' AS CustomerLetter
FROM Customers
```

Result:

CustomerLetter
Dear Demarco J. Please complete the enclosed forms so that we can ship your order to your country.
Dear Demania M. Please complete the enclosed forms so that we can ship your order to your country.
Dear Demers G. Please complete the enclosed forms so that we can ship your order to your country.
Dear Demetriou P. Please complete the enclosed forms so that we can ship your order to your country.

```
(201 row(s) returned)
```

141.   Use the upper(), left(), and substring() functions to uppercase the first character of a concatenated field

Uppercasing customer last names

Discussion:

The task of uppercasing the first character of a concatenated field might look very simple but it is not. We need to use three functions to achieve our goal as you can see in the code below. First, we use the left function to isolate the first character from the lastname field. Then we use the upper() function to capitalize this first character. Next, we use the substring() function to return all the characters in the lastname field starting with the second character. The number 50 which is the third argument of the substring() function indicates the limit of characters we will retrieve for the last name. That is, if the lastname field has fifteen characters, all fifteen will be returned. If the last name has sixty characters, then only the first fifty will be retrieved starting with the second character. Consult chapter 25 regarding string operations for a full understanding of the role of string functions.

Code:

```
SELECT 'Dear' + ' '+ upper(left(lastname,1))+ substring (lastname, 2, 50) + ' ' + firstname +'.' + ' ' +
'Please complete the enclosed forms so that we can ship your order to your country.' AS
CustomerLetter
FROM Customers
```

Result:

CustomerLetter
Dear Demarco John. Please complete the enclosed forms so that we can ship your order to your country.
Dear Demania Mary. Please complete the enclosed forms so that we can ship your order to your country.
Dear Demers George. Please complete the enclosed forms so that we can ship your order to your coun...
Dear Demetriou Phillip. Please complete the enclosed forms so that we can ship your order to your cou...
Dear Demichele Andrew. Please complete the enclosed forms so that we can ship your order to your c...

142. Concatenation with the concat() function

Concatenate customer order dates with shipping costs

Discussion:

Up until now we have concatenated text data with text data. What if we need to concatenate fields of different data types such as dates, numbers, and text? If we try to do that by using the + operator SQL Server will return an error as in the example below:

Code:

```
SELECT OrderDate + ' with ' +ShippingCost + ' shipping cost'
FROM Orders
```

Result:

```
Msg 402, Level 16, State 1, Line 1
The data types date and varchar are incompatible in the add operator.
```

However we can use the Concat() function with the syntax below to concatenate the various heterogeneous data types without any problems.

Concat(value1, value2, ..., valuen)

The cool thing about the concat() function is that it implicitly converts all the data types supplied to strings. Even null values are converted to empty strings so that they do not cause any errors in the concatenation. The concat() function needs at least two values to operate.

In the example below, we concatenate the OrderDate field with a date data type with the shipping cost with a numeric data type, with some text strings all at once!

Code:

```
SELECT concat(orderdate, ' with ', shippingcost, ' shipping cost') as LetterToTheCustomer
FROM Orders
```

Result:

LetterToTheCustomer
2013-11-11 with 36 shipping cost
2013-07-30 with 39 shipping cost
2013-07-04 with 34 shipping cost
2014-12-19 with 48 shipping cost

```
(1000 row(s) returned)
```

143. Conditional concatenation with the iif() function
Concatenating supplier fields using state as a condition
Discussion:
Sometimes, we might not want to apply the same concatenation rules for all of the records in the view. For example, we might want to create a certain letter for suppliers in NY and a somewhat different letter for everyone else, all in the same query. We can absolutely do this by using conditional statements and the iif() function in particular. However, someone might ask why we need to do this and not use simple criteria to do the same thing. First, in databases, we can achieve the same task in many different ways. There is always another less time-consuming and more effective way. Second, in this case, if we use a simple criterion such as (state = 'NY'), we only get the suppliers in NY. What we want is to send two different letters—one formatted for the state of NY and one for everyone else!

Using the iif(condition, true, false) function below, we tell the database to concatenate the companyname, contacttitle, and contactname fields if the state is NY. If it is not, we tell the database to concatenate only the contacttitle and contactname fields. This way, we can create two different sets of letters in the same view. Of course, we can use our imagination and modify the SQL statement below to use it for letters with plain text or any other concatenation task we need.

Code:
```
SELECT IIf((([State]='NY'),[Companyname]+' '+[ContactTitle]+' '+[Contactname], [ContactTitle]+' '+[Contactname]) AS MailTo
FROM Suppliers
```

Result:

MailTo
Sales Manager Pedro Adkins
Purchasing Manager John Marrey
Sales Manager Maria Hopkins
America's Greatest Snacks, Inc. Sales Manager Andrew Daves

```
(10 row(s) returned)
```

144. More powerful conditional concatenation with the case() function
Concatenating supplier columns different for each city
Discussion:
Now that we know conditional concatenation is possible, what if we want to create different letters for suppliers based on the city where they reside? Notice in the suppliers table that there are three cities: Boston, New York, and Dallas. Our task is to create a different letter for suppliers in each city using the same view. We can use the switch() function as shown below:

Code:

```
SELECT
CASE
When City = 'Boston'    Then 'Dear' +' '+ [contactname]+',' +' '+ 'for our current sale we offer a 10% discount in' +' '+ [city]
When City = 'Dallas'    Then 'Dear' +' '+ [contactname]+',' +' '+ 'for our current sale we offer a 25% discount in' +' '+ [city]
When City = 'New York'  Then 'Dear' +' '+ [contactname]+',' +' '+ 'for our current sale we offer a 30% discount in' +' '+ [city]
End
AS SupplierLetter
FROM Suppliers
```

Result:

SupplierLetter
Dear Pedro Adkins, for our current sale we offer a 10% discount in Boston
Dear John Marrey, for our current sale we offer a 10% discount in Boston
Dear Maria Hopkins, for our current sale we offer a 10% discount in Boston
Dear Andrew Daves, for our current sale we offer a 30% discount in New York
Dear Frank Baker, for our current sale we offer a 30% discount in New York

(10 row(s) returned)

CHAPTER 16 DISCUSSION QUESTIONS

1. What is the goal of field concatenation?
2. How many fields can we concatenate? Two, three, or more?
3. What is the most common character for field concatenation in databases?
4. Is there any arithmetic involved in field concatenation?
5. In what database object is it a good idea to use concatenated fields?
6. Can we concantenate plain text with field data?
7. Could you name a few practical examples of field concatenation?
8. Why is it useful to use string functions with concatenated fields?
9. What do we need to pay attention to when we use commas, periods, and other characters with concatenated fields?
10. How many functions are available for conditional concatenation and what is the difference between them?

CHAPTER 16 HANDS-ON EXERCISES

Chapter 16 Case 1:
Start SQL Server Management Studio. For each of the questions in this case you need to create a new query (Ctrl-N) and name it as per the instructions in each question. Submit your work to your instructor as one text file that contains all SQL statements or as per your instructor's directions.

1. The sales department is initiating a cross-selling campaign and is asking for mailing labels to send out to current customers. Create a new query that concatenates the FirstName, LastName, Address, City, State, and Zip fields from the customer table. Sort results by lastname ascending without including the lastname in the result set. Save the query as Chapter16_Case1_Q1.

   Your result should look like:

MailingLabel
Nicholas Ackerman 5 Buckingham Dr Dallas TX 52347
Alfred Allen 29 Water Street New York NY 12189
Pindar Ames 23 Cornell Dr New York NY 45357
Thomas Andersen 52 Betwood Street Orlando FL 89754
Joseph Anderson 34 Cortland Ave Los Angeles CA 94...

   (201 row(s) returned)

2. The sales department is asking again for mailing labels. This time they want only the first letter of the customer FirstName to appear in the label followed by a period. Create a new query that concatenates the FirstName, LastName, Address, City, State, and Zip fields from the customer table. Sort results by lastname ascending without including the lastname in the result set. Save the query as Chapter16_Case1_Q2.

   Your result should look like:

MailingLabel
N. Ackerman 5 Buckingham Dr Dallas TX 52347
A. Allen 29 Water Street New York NY 12189
P. Ames 23 Cornell Dr New York NY 45357
T. Andersen 52 Betwood Street Orlando FL 89754
J. Anderson 34 Cortland Ave Los Angeles CA 94851

(201 row(s) returned)

3. The HR department needs mailing labels to send out letters containing employee W-2s. Create a new query that concatenates the FirstName, LastName, Title, Address, City, State, and Zip fields from the SalesRep table. The LastName field needs to be capitalized. Sort results by lastname ascending without including the lastname in the result set. Save the query as Chapter16_Case1_Q3.

Your result should look like:

MailingLabel
Anderson John Sales Reppresentative 32 Colonial Street Boston MA 22459
Baker Jim Account Manager 5 Ormond Street Dallas TX 52347
Bernstein Michael Sales Reppresentative 21 Garden Ave New York NY 12189
Delaney Kenneth Assistant Manager 89 Edenburg Ave New York NY 12189
Simmons Andrew Account Manager 16 Greenway Street New York NY 12189

(10 row(s) returned)

4. The marketing people want to send a mail card to customers announcing the availability of a new product line. The letter should be worded: Dear firstname, space lastname. Our company has just received a new line of products. If interested, please return this card and we will send you our new catalog at the following address (address space City space State space Zip). Create a new query that satisfies the request of the marketing people and sort results by lastname ascending without including lastname in the result set. Save the query as Chapter16_Case1_Q4.

Your result should look like:

Letter
Dear Nicholas, Ackerman. Our company has just received a new line of products. If interested, please retu...
Dear Alfred, Allen. Our company has just received a new line of products. If interested, please return this c...
Dear Pindar, Ames. Our company has just received a new line of products. If interested, please return this ...
Dear Thomas, Andersen. Our company has just received a new line of products. If interested, please retur...
Dear Joseph, Anderson. Our company has just received a new line of products. If interested, please return...

(201 row(s) returned)

5. The sales people from the Boston office want to send a thank you letter to customers. For the customers in the city of Boston they want the mailing label to include the FirstName, Address, City, State, and Zip fields. For everyone else they want the label to include the FirstName, LastName, Address, City, State, and Zip fields. Create a new query that satisfies the marketing request. Sort results by lastname ascending without including the lastname in the result set. Save the query as Chapter16_Case1_Q5.

Your result should look like:

MailingLabel
Nicholas Ackerman 5 Buckingham Dr Dallas TX 52347
Alfred Allen 29 Water Street New York NY 12189
Pindar Ames 23 Cornell Dr New York NY 45357
Thomas Andersen 52 Betwood Street Orlando FL 89754
Joseph Anderson 34 Cortland Ave Los Angeles CA 94...

```
(201 row(s) returned)
```

Chapter 16 Case 2:

Start SQL Server Management Studio. For each of the questions in this case you need to create a new query (Ctrl-N) and name it as per the instructions in each question. Submit your work to your instructor as one text file that contains all SQL statements or as per your instructor's directions.

1. The HR department needs mailing labels for a letter to all employees in the organization. Create a new query that concatenates the Title, FirstName, LastName, Address, City, State, and Zip fields from the SalesReps table. Sort results by lastname ascending. Save the query as Chapter16_Case2_Q1.

   Your result should look like:

MailingLabel
Sales Reppresentative John Anderson 32 Colonial Street Boston MA 22459
Account Manager Jim Baker 5 Ormond Street Dallas TX 52347
Sales Reppresentative Michael Bernstein 21 Garden Ave New York NY 12189
Assistant Manager Kenneth Delaney 89 Edenburg Ave New York NY 12189
Account Manager Andrew Simmons 16 Greenway Street New York NY 12189

```
(10 row(s) returned)
```

2. The director of inventory wants to send out a letter to suppliers asking for a reduction in their prices by 5%. The letter should be worded: "Dear [contactname], due to the recent downturn in the market we would like to ask for a 5% discount for the products we buy from you. Please let us know within the week if this is a possibility." Create a new query that satisfies the request of the inventory director, sort results by contactname ascending without including contactname in the result set. Save the query as Chapter16_Case2_Q2.

   Your result should look like:

SupplierLetter
Dear Andrew Daves, due to the recent downturn in the market we would like to ask for a 5% discount for the...
Dear Frank Baker, due to the recent downturn in the market we would like to ask for a 5% discount for the pr...
Dear George Casey, due to the recent downturn in the market we would like to ask for a 5% discount for the ...
Dear John Marrey, due to the recent downturn in the market we would like to ask for a 5% discount for the pr...
Dear Julia Ford, due to the recent downturn in the market we would like to ask for a 5% discount for the prod...

```
(10 row(s) returned)
```

3. The president of the company wants to send out a letter of appreciation to employees hired before 12/31/2000 to invite them to a special evening dinner. The letter should be worded: "Dear [firstname], you

are now working with us for more than ten years and the company highly appreciates your work and loyalty. You are invited to our family dinner this Friday night at 6:30 PM. Create a new query that satisfies the request of the president, sort results by lastname ascending without including lastname in the result set. Save the query as Chapter16_Case2_Q3.

Your result should look like:

EmployeeLetter
Dear John, you are now working with us for more than ten years and the company highly appreciates your work...
Dear Michael, you are now working with us for more than ten years and the company highly appreciates your w...
Dear Kenneth, you are now working with us for more than ten years and the company highly appreciates your ...
Dear Mary, you are now working with us for more than ten years and the company highly appreciates your work...

```
(4 row(s) returned)
```

4. The sales director needs to send a letter to sales reps with information about upcoming events so that they can perform better in their sales quests. For each state the instructions are different but you need to create one SQL statement that contains all three letters. Specifically:

    a. For NY: Dear [firstname], Our major competitor cut prices by 15%. Cut our own prices by up to 20% but not more.

    b. For MA: Dear [firstname], Start introducing our new product immediately before any of our competitors enters the market with their own updated products.

    c. For TX: Dear [firstname], We were able to get significant discounts from our suppliers and as such try to increase market share by reducing our current prices by 20% for the next two months.

    Create a new query that satisfies the request of the sales director, sort results by lastname ascending without including lastname in the result set. Save the query as Chapter16_Case2_Q4.

    Your result should look like:

SalesRepLetter
Dear John, Start introducing our new product immediately before any of our competitors enters the market wi...
Dear Jim, We were able to get significant discounts from our suppliers and as such try to increase market sh...
Dear Michael, Our major competitor cut prices by 15%. Cut our own prices by up to 20% but not more.
Dear Kenneth, Our major competitor cut prices by 15%. Cut our own prices by up to 20% but not more.
Dear Andrew, Our major competitor cut prices by 15%. Cut our own prices by up to 20% but not more.

```
(10 row(s) returned)
```

5. The marketing director wants to send a letter to customers announcing new discounts for next month. The letter should be worded: Dear [firstname], space [lastname]. For the next 30 days only, take the opportunity to obtain our product at the generous discount rate of [

    a. 15% for the customers in NY state

    b. 20% for the customer in Texas,

    c. 25% for customers in Florida

    d. 20% for California

    Create a new query that satisfies the request of the marketing director and sort results by lastname ascending without including lastname in the result set. Limit the results of the query to contain only customers from the states of NY, TX, FL, and CA. Save the query as Chapter16_Case2_Q5.

Your result should look like:

CustomerDiscountLetter
Dear Nicholas Ackerman. For the next 30 days only, take the opportunity to obtain our product at the genero...
Dear Alfred Allen. For the next 30 days only, take the opportunity to obtain our product at the generous discou...
Dear Pindar Ames. For the next 30 days only, take the opportunity to obtain our product at the generous disco...
Dear Thomas Andersen. For the next 30 days only, take the opportunity to obtain our product at the generous...
Dear Paul Anderson. For the next 30 days only, take the opportunity to obtain our product at the generous di...

(125 row(s) returned)

CHAPTER 17
THE GROUP BY CLAUSE

The GROUP BY clause is one of the foggiest keywords for both beginners and intermediate database professionals and users. Because of its intricacies, users and developers do not have a clear understanding of the circumstances when the GROUP BY clause is used. In this chapter, we have two goals: First, to understand in detail how and when the GROUP BY clause should be used, and second, to understand exactly what results to expect from it. The fundamental goal of the GROUP BY clause is to summarize data. The general syntax of the GROUP BY clause appears below but you do not need to memorize it since we will explore the role of each option in detail in the subsequent examples. Notice that in the statement below the WHERE, HAVING, and ORDER BY clauses are optional. However, we always need to use an aggregate function (sum, avg, min, max, etc.) in conjunction with the GROUP BY clause.

SELECT fields, aggregate function (field or calculated field)
FROM table
WHERE criteria (optional)
GROUP BY field(s)
HAVING criteria (optional)
ORDER BY field – (optional)

Before we do anything else, let's have a look at the table below which I prepared especially for this chapter. It is a simple table with only twelve records about customers and their orders. The goal is to run the GROUP BY examples on this table and give you the ability to do the calculations manually so that you know exactly how every result is obtained. The name of the table is tbls_customersgr.

First, notice that there are four customers in total. Second, the customer, Mr. Mahoney, ordered twice: orders 57 and 502. Third, the rest of the three customers have one order only. Fourth, Mr. Riegert has one order with one product only, but he ordered two units of it. Fifth, orders 57, 494, 502, and 509 contain multiple products. Sixth, dark chocolate is a product included in two orders (in 57 and 509). At this point, we are ready to go through our first example.

PK	Last Name	OrderID	OrderDate	Product Name	Unit Price	Quantity
1	Riegert	1	2013-11-06	Dried Red Tart Cherries Gift Box - 6 oz	15	2
2	Mahoney	57	2012-05-29	Dark Chocolate Apricots in 20 oz. Bag	28	5
3	Mahoney	57	2012-05-29	Mushrooms Sauce	5	2
4	Mahoney	57	2012-05-29	Chocolate Chip Brownie	15	1
5	Martin	494	2013-09-30	Traditional Swedish Cookies, 5.25 oz	5	5
6	Martin	494	2013-09-30	Cream and honey biscuits	32	3
7	Mahoney	502	2014-08-03	Sesame Crackers in 20 oz. Pack	15	3
8	Mahoney	502	2014-08-03	Roasted No-Salt Almonds	15	1
9	Spicer	509	2013-09-17	Dark Chocolate Apricots in 20 oz. Bag	28	3
10	Spicer	509	2013-09-17	Corn Chips Bag	15	2
11	Spicer	509	2013-09-17	Oatmeal Raisin Walnut Cookies	8	3
12	Spicer	509	2013-09-17	All-Purpose Marinade II	15	2

tbls_customersgr

145. The GROUP BY clause on one column and one aggregated field

Retrieve the total product units ordered by customer

Discussion:

In this scenario, the objective is to calculate the total units of products ordered by each customer. There are only two fields used in the SQL code below. LastName is the field on which we apply the GROUP BY clause, and TotalUnits is the aggregated field that results from applying the sum() function on the Quantity column.

Code:

```
SELECT LastName, SUM(quantity) AS TotalUnits
FROM tbls_customersgr
GROUP BY LastName
```

Result:

Last Name	Total Units
Mahoney	12
Martin	8
Riegert	2
Spicer	10

(4 row(s) returned)

146. The GROUP BY clause on one column and one aggregated-calculated field

Retrieve the total order amount by customer

Discussion:

In this scenario, we have a request from management to calculate the total order amounts by customer to create a list with our best customers. There are two fields used in the SQL code. LastName is the field on which we apply the GROUP BY clause. TotalUnits is the aggregated field. However, this time, the aggregation occurs on the result of the multiplication of two columns. It is necessary to multiply the unitprice with the quantity columns to retrieve the total for each product in each order and then, sum the results by customer lastname.

Code:
```
SELECT LastName, SUM(unitprice*quantity) AS OrderTotal
FROM tbls_customersgr
GROUP BY LastName
```

Result:

LastName	OrderTotal
Mahoney	225
Martin	121
Riegert	30
Spicer	168

(4 row(s) returned)

We see some interesting results here. First, since we grouped by customer last name, the result set produced four records, which is the exact number of unique customers we have in the tbls_customersgr table. We need to check the results to verify the database made the calculations correctly. We use Mahoney as an example.

LastName	Unit Price	Quantity	UnitPrice* Quantity
Mahoney	15	1	15
Mahoney	15	3	45
Mahoney	15	1	15
Mahoney	5	2	10
Mahoney	28	5	140
		SUM()	225

First, the database will do the multiplication of (unitprice * quantity) as we defined it in the calculated field named OrderTotal. This means that the database will multiply the price of each product ordered * its quantity ordered for all products in all orders for the particular customer. Then, it will simply SUM()results since we used the sum() function. Doing the calculations manually, we arrived at 225 for Mr. Mahoney, which is the same number the database produced for this customer.

147.   The GROUP BY clause on one column and two aggregated fields

Find total and average order amounts by customer

Discussion:

In this scenario, the goal is to produce a report that will show the total and average order amounts grouped by customer. There are three fields used in the SQL code: LastName, OrderTotal, and AvgOrder. The lastname is the field used with the GROUP BY clause. The fields OrderTotal and AvgOrder are the two aggregated fields.

Code:
```
SELECT lastname, SUM(unitprice*quantity) AS OrderTotal, AVG(unitprice*quantity) AS AvgOrder
FROM tbls_customersgr
GROUP BY lastname
```

Result:

lastname	OrderTotal	AvgOrder
Mahoney	225	45
Martin	121	60.5
Riegert	30	30
Spicer	168	42

(4 row(s) returned)

148.   The GROUP BY clause on one column, one aggregated field, and WHERE

Find total order amounts for a subset of customers

Discussion:

Sometimes, we want to exclude certain records from our aggregate calculations. In these cases, we can use the WHERE clause to exclude records we are not interested in working with. Using WHERE, we exclude records before the GROUP BY clause takes effect. Therefore, if we have a source dataset and use WHERE, the GROUP BY clause takes effect on the remaining records only. Later, you will learn the use of HAVING, which is a filtering statement like WHERE that takes effect after the GROUP BY calculates the summarized field values.

In this example, we look for order totals by customer, but we want to exclude the orders from our customer Spicer. Mr. Spicer has only one order with orderid = 509. We use three fields in this SQL statement: Lastname, OrderTotal, and OrderID. LastName is the GROUP BY field, OrderTotal the aggregated field, and OrderID the filtering field. The order from Mr. Spicer will be filtered before the GROUP BY clause takes effect.

Code:

```
SELECT LastName, SUM(unitprice*quantity) AS OrderTotal
FROM tbls_customersgr
WHERE orderid <> 509
GROUP BY LastName
```

Result:

LastName	OrderTotal
Mahoney	225
Martin	121
Riegert	30

(3 row(s) returned)

149.   The GROUP BY clause on one column, one aggregated field, and HAVING

Find customer orders with total order amount exceeding $100

Discussion:

In this example, we want to exclude from the result set all customers whose order totals are less than $100. However, we do not know beforehand who these customers are. We need to run the GROUP BY clause, find the totals, and exclude those below $100. This is exactly the case in which HAVING is used. Using HAVING with GROUP BY is a powerful and flexible way to filter records. By the way, we use the HAVING clause only in conjunction with the GROUP BY clause. Looking at the result set, we can see that only three customers appear. The customer named Riegert does not appear because his order total is only 30.

Code:

SELECT LastName, SUM(unitprice*quantity) AS OrderTotal
FROM tbls_customersgr
GROUP BY LastName
HAVING SUM(unitprice*quantity)>100

Result:

LastName	OrderTotal
Mahoney	225
Martin	121
Spicer	168

(3 row(s) returned)

150.   The GROUP BY clause on one column, one aggregated field, WHERE and HAVING

Calculate order totals above $100 excluding a subset of products

Discussion:

In this example, pay attention to the combined use of WHERE and HAVING. We want to calculate customer order totals, but we want to exclude from the result set customers whose order totals are less than $100. In addition, we want to exclude the calculation amounts related to the product "Chocolate Chip Brownie". Perhaps management wants to see how customer order amounts differ if this product is excluded from their orders. Maybe they are thinking of discontinuing this particular product.

In general, when it comes to filtering records in GROUP BY statements, we need to make some quick decisions: Do we need to use WHERE, HAVING, or a combination of the two? Your way of thinking should always be the same: Use the WHERE clause to exclude records that you do not want to be included in the aggregate calculations, and use HAVING to exclude values after the aggregations by GROUP BY are made. In this case, we use WHERE to exclude the product "Chocolate Chip Brownie" from the recordset, and we use GROUP BY to create the aggregations on whatever records remain. After the aggregations are made, the HAVING clause takes effect to exclude order totals less than $100. The bottom line is that in the SQL statement below, the WHERE clause will run first, then the GROUP BY, and finally the HAVING clause.

Code:

SELECT LastName, SUM(unitprice*quantity) AS OrderTotal
FROM tbls_customersgr
WHERE productname <> 'Chocolate Chip Brownie'
GROUP BY LastName
HAVING SUM(unitprice*quantity)>100

Result:

LastName	OrderTotal
Mahoney	210
Martin	121
Spicer	168

(3 row(s) returned)

151.   The GROUP BY clause with WHERE, HAVING, and ORDER BY

Sorting customer order totals

Discussion:

In this example, we put together all of the statements we learned about GROUP BY up to this point and introduce the ORDER BY clause. When the ORDER BY clause is used with GROUP BY, it takes effect after the database makes the calculations resulting from the GROUP BY clause. Furthermore, in this example, we exclude from the calculations a particular order with orderid=509.

Code:

```
SELECT LastName, SUM(unitprice*quantity) AS OrderTotal
FROM tbls_customersgr
WHERE orderid <> 509
GROUP BY LastName
HAVING SUM(unitprice*quantity)>100
ORDER BY Lastname DESC
```

Result:

LastName	OrderTotal
Martin	121
Mahoney	225

(2 row(s) returned)

152.   The GROUP BY clause with NULLS

Calculate average customer order amounts with and without nulls

Discussion:

For the purposes of this example, open the table tbls_customersgr for editing and enter the value "NULL" for the unitprice for Dark Chocolate Appricots for OrderID=57. The idea is to demonstrate exactly what happens when nulls exist in data needed for calculations in GROUP BY clauses. Using 3 records in this table, you can check the results manually and learn so that when you deal with 5,000 records, you know exactly what to do.

tbls_customersgr					
LastName	OrderID	OrderDate	ProductName	UnitPrice	Quantity
Mahoney	57	2012/5/29	Dark Chocolate Apricots in 20 oz. Bag	NULL	5
Mahoney	57	2012/5/29	Mushrooms Sauce	5	2
Mahoney	57	2012/5/29	Chocolate Chip Brownie	15	1

Let us run two pieces of code:

Code:
SELECT OrderID, Avg((([unitprice]*[quantity])) AS AverageOrderAmount
FROM tbls_customersgr
GROUP BY OrderID

Result with null values:

OrderID	AverageOrderAmount
1	30
57	12.5
494	60.5
502	30
509	42

(5 row(s) returned)

Now replace the deleted unit price for Dark Chocolate Appricots at $28 and run the SQL statement again:

Code:
SELECT OrderID, Avg((([unitprice]*[quantity])) AS AverageOrderAmount
FROM tbls_customersgr
GROUP BY OrderID

Result without null values:

OrderID	AverageOrderAmount
1	30
57	55
494	60.5
502	30
509	42

(5 row(s) returned)

As you can see from the first result set, all of the calculations look right except for orderid = 57. In this case, the database gave us an average of 12.5 with null values and an average of 55 without null values. In other words, it takes into consideration only the two products in that order and leaves out the third—the one with the missing quantity. I will not express an opinion whether this is correct or not. I simply want you to know that when missing data exists, aggregate functions will ignore the missing values. Some people might argue that this is correct because if we do not have data for an item, it should not be included in the calculations. Others might say that when missing data exists, aggregate functions should take this into consideration.

We will not miss the forest for the trees in this case. Instead of becoming bogged down by database peculiarities and arguing indefinitely, the most effective action when you make calculations like multiplications or when you use the GROUP BY clause is to first check your fields for missing data. It takes a few seconds to check for nulls (chapter 23), and you will not have to worry how aggregate functions will handle your data.

153. The GROUP BY clause on multiple columns

Find order totals grouped by customer and order number at the same time

Discussion:

Sometimes, you want to have a more detailed view of your data. For example, you might want to find order totals by customer and OrderID at the same time. You can easily achieve this with GROUP BY. Since you grouped first by last name and then by OrderID, orders will be totaled by lastname first, followed by OrderID. You can reverse the order of grouping or add more grouping fields according to the level of the detail you would like to see.

Code:

```
SELECT lastname, OrderID, SUM([unitprice]*[quantity]) AS OrderTotal
FROM tbls_customersgr
GROUP BY lastname, OrderID
```

Result:

lastname	OrderID	OrderTotal
Riegert	1	30
Mahoney	57	165
Martin	494	121
Mahoney	502	60
Spicer	509	168

(5 row(s) returned)

CHAPTER 17 DISCUSSION QUESTIONS

1. What is the basic goal of the GROUP BY clause in relational databases?
2. Are aggregate functions optional or required with the GROUP BY clause?
3. Can we use multiple aggregate fields with the GROUP BY clause?
4. Can we summarize values in multiple fields with the GROUP BY clause?
5. What do we need to pay attention to when we have null values in the fields we use aggregate functions?
6. How exactly the WHERE clause works with GROUP BY sql statements?
7. What is the purpose of the HAVING clause in GROUP BY statements?
8. Are the HAVING and WHERE clauses mandatory or optional with GROUP BY?
9. On the other hand, can we use the HAVING clause without the GROUP BY clause?
10. Which one takes precedence? The WHERE clause or the HAVING clause?

CHAPTER 17 HANDS-ON EXERCISES

Chapter 17 Case 1:
Start SQL Server Management Studio. For each of the questions in this case you need to create a new query (Ctrl-N) and name it as per the instructions in each question. Submit your work to your instructor as one text file that contains all SQL statements or as per your instructor's directions.

1. The inventory people are asking for a report that will display the total shipping cost by shipping company (hint: group by ShipperID) for all orders in the Orders table. Create a new query that satisfies the inventory people request. Save the query as Chapter17_Case1_Q1.

   Your result should look like:

ShipperID	TotalShipping
3	8274
1	18331
2	14969

   (3 row(s) returned)

2. The marketing people are asking for a report that will provide the number of orders placed by each customer (hint: group by CustomerID) in the Orders table. Create a new query that satisfies the marketing people request. Save the query as Chapter17_Case1_Q2.

   Your result should look like:

CustomerID	NumberOfOrders
1	7
2	4
3	6
4	9
5	4

   (190 row(s) returned)

3. The marketing people are now asking for a report that will provide the number of customers by zip code in the Customers table. Create a new query that satisfies the marketing people request. Save the query as Chapter17_Case1_Q3.

Your result should look like:

Zip	NumberOfCustomers
11882	12
12110	4
12189	19
21214	13
22459	14

(17 row(s) returned)

4. The marketing people became a pain in the neck and they are now asking for a report that will provide the average, minimum, and maximum shipping cost of orders by customer from the Orders table (Hint: group by CustomerID). Create a new query that satisfies the marketing people request. Save the query as Chapter17_Case1_Q4.

Your result should look like:

CustomerID	MinShippingCost	AvgShippingCost	MaxShippingCost
23	38	43.6666666666667	52
46	39	44.8333333333333	52
192	46	46	46
92	36	43.1666666666667	52
115	37	39	42

(190 row(s) returned)

5. The marketing people are back and they now want the same report as in question four excluding however any customers with an average shipping cost of more than 40. Create a new query that satisfies the marketing people request. Save the query as Chapter17_Case1_Q5.

Your result should look like:

CustomerID	MinShippingCost	AvgShippingCost	MaxShippingCost
115	37	39	42
29	32	39.8571428571429	50
169	31	39.3333333333333	49
75	31	39.125	51
109	31	38.75	49

(190 row(s) returned)

CHAPTER 17

Chapter 17 Case 2:
Start SQL Server Management Studio. For each of the questions in this case you need to create a new query (Ctrl-N) and name it as per the instructions in each question. Submit your work to your instructor as one text file that contains all SQL statements or as per your instructor's directions.

1. The sales department is asking for a report that will provide the total product quantity by productID for all order items in the table ProductsOrders. Create a new query that satisfies the sales people request. Sort results by TotalProductUnitsSold descending. Save the query as Chapter17_Case2_Q1.

   Your result should look like:

ProductID	TotalProductUnitsSold
38	164
33	159
35	150
55	149
53	149

   (70 row(s) returned)

2. The marketing people are asking for a report listing the most successful products in terms of overall sales. Specifically, they are asking for a report that will provide the total order amount by productID for all order items in the table ProductsOrders. Do not take into consideration any product discounts given to customers. Sort results by TotalOrderAmount DESC. Create a new query that satisfies the marketing people request. Save the query as Chapter17_Case2_Q2.

   Your result should look like:

ProductID	TotalOrderAmount
31	4640
39	4448
17	4088
37	3744
50	3696

   (70 row(s) returned)

3. Accounts payable is asking for a report that will provide the min, average, and max shipping cost by shipper id for all orders in the Orders table. Create a new query that satisfies the accounts payable request. Save the query as Chapter17_Case2_Q3.

   Your result should look like:

ShipperID	MinShippingCost	AvgShippingCost	MaxShippingCost
3	31	42.2142857142857	52
1	31	42.1402298850575	52
2	31	40.6766304347826	52

   (3 row(s) returned)

210

4. The marketing people are again asking for a report that will provide the total order amount by productID for all order items in the table ProductsOrders. However, this time they want the products with productIDs 1,14,15, and 28 to be excluded from the results. They also want to see order totals by product above $2000. Do not take into consideration any product discounts given to customers. Create a new query that satisfies the marketing people request. Save the query as Chapter17_Case2_Q4.

Your result should look like:

ProductID	TotalOrderAmount
23	2100
52	2268
26	2310
12	3668
35	2250

(23 row(s) returned)

5. The marketing people need one additional report that will provide the total order amount for each product within each order in the ProductsOrders table. This time you need the results aggregated by OrderId first and then by ProductID within each order. Do not include any sorting in your query and do not take into consederation any discounts extended to customers. Save the query as Chapter17_Case2_Q5.

Your result should look like:

OrderID	ProductID	TotalOrderAmount
1	61	30
2	23	60
2	24	15
2	32	45
2	70	90

(2411 row(s) returned)

CHAPTER 18
AGGREGATE FUNCTIONS

Aggregate functions like sum(), avg(), count(), count(*), max(), and min() have the main goal of summarizing data and converting this data into useful pieces of information. Aggregate functions process values from a table column to produce a summary value, whether a summation, an average, or a maximum value.

Aggregate functions are often used on calculated fields (chapter 15) which fields are themselves the result of the multiplication, summation, or division of two or more fields.

With aggregate functions, you need to pay attention to any null values in your data. In this chapter, you will understand well the effect of null values on aggregate calculations. However, no matter how much knowledge you have regarding the behavior of aggregate functions with null values, you should have one goal in mind: To eliminate null values from the columns on which you conduct aggregations. In other words, you need to develop a habit to examine your data for nulls before you even use aggregate functions. Of course, advanced developers by design do not allow null values in their tables. They use default values and constraints to avoid nulls altogether.

Finally, aggregate functions are extremely useful when combined with the GROUP BY clause. We examined GROUP BY in the previous chapter and are now ready to go a step further, using it with aggregate functions to observe the power of the results obtained.

In this chapter, we will use aggregate functions with calculated fields, the GROUP BY clause, the WHERE clause, the HAVING clause, and a few operators so that you learn the combined use of aggregate functions. For the purposes of this chapter, we have created a special table called tbls_customersag with only 20 records so that you can check the results against the dataset, make calculations manually, and fully understand the effects of aggregate functions. Before you start the examples in this chapter, open this table to understand its structure and have a look at its 20 records.

154.   The count() function
Count the number of orders
Discussion:
The count() function, will calculate the number of records in a dataset as soon as it is used on a field that contains no null values. In practice, the count() function is usually applied on the primary key of the table since it is the one field that is certain not to contain nulls. In this example, we use it on the OrderID field, which is not the primary key, but I use it to show you the different results produced by count() in the subsequent examples. The count() function returned the number of records in the table, i.e. 20. We can be certain of one thing from this result: The OrderID field does not contain any null values since the number returned from the count() function is equal to the number of records in the table.

Code:
```
SELECT count(orderid) as NumberofOrders
FROM tbls_customersag
```

Result:

NumberofOrders
20

`(1 row(s) returned)`

155. The count() and count(*) functions in comparison
Count the number of records in a table using count(*)
Discussion:

In this scenario, the objective is to understand the differences between Count(), Count(*), and count() DISTINCT so that you can take full advantage of them in your data tasks. For this purpose, I have temporarily deleted the name of customer Davis from the table tbls_customersag. Now, we have 20 records in the table with the last name of a customer missing.

tbls_customersag					
CustID	LastName	OrderID	ProductID	UnitPrice	Quantity
1	*	4	55	15	3
2	Sterling	60	56	12	5
3	Sterling	60	21	15	4

* Deleted the lastname "Davis" from the table.

Let's use the count() function first. As you can see from the result set, the number returned is 19. This is because we used count() on the lastname field in which a value is missing. Consequently, while the table contains 20 records, we received only 19. You do not need to worry about these intricacies if you follow a simple piece of advice: Any time you work with aggregate functions, calculated fields, or GROUP BY, check your records for null values, and make the necessary edits and replacements (see chapter 23 for details on null values). Then, you do not need to worry about the intricacies of how aggregate functions or calculated fields behave with missing data.

Code:
SELECT count(lastname) as NumberofCustomers
FROM tbls_customersag

Result:

NumberofCustomers
19

`(1 row(s) returned)`

Now, let's use the count(*) function. As you can see from the result set, the count(*) function returned the correct result of 20 records in the table.

Code:
SELECT count(*) as NumberofCustomers
FROM tbls_customersag

Result:

NumberofOrders
20

(1 row(s) returned)

Now, let's use count() with DISTINCT. As you can see from the result set, the number of unique customers returned is 9. We know already however, that we have 9 unique customers in the table. This time, the count() function returned 9 because it ignored the "NULL" customer from the count.

Code:

SELECT count(distinct lastname) As CountUniqueCustomers
FROM tbls_customersag

Result:

CountUniqueCustomers
9

(1 row(s) returned)

Open the tbls_Customersag table and reinsert the value "Davis" for CustID = 1.

tbls_customersag*					
CustID	LastName	OrderID	ProductID	UnitPrice	Quantity
1	Davis	4	55	15	3
2	Sterling	60	56	12	5
3	Sterling	60	21	15	4

* Reinserted the lastname "Davis" in the table.

156.   The count() function with DISTINCT

Count the number of unique orders from customers

Discussion:

In this example, we want to calculate the number of unique orders in this table. We have many customers and some of them have multiple orders. The proper way to accomplish this is to use COUNT and DISTINCT together on the OrderID field. From the result set below, notice that the number of unique orders produced is 15, which is exactly what we need.

Code:

SELECT Count (Distinct OrderID) as NumberofOrders FROM tbls_customersag

Result:

NumberofOrders
15

(1 row(s) returned)

157. The count() function with the GROUP BY clause

Count the number of orders by customer

Discussion:

The business goal is to calculate the number of orders by customer. We can answer this quickly by using the count() function with the GROUP BY clause. From the result set, you obtain two pieces of information. First, you know that you have 9 unique customers in the dataset of 20 records. Second, you have a count of the number of orders by each customer.

Code:

```
SELECT lastname, count(orderid) as NumberofOrders
FROM tbls_customersag
GROUP BY lastname
```

Result:

lastname	NumberofOrders
Currier	1
Davis	2
Johnson	4
Madsen	1
McGrath	1
Miller	2
Ming	2
Powers	4
Sterling	3

(9 row(s) returned)

158. The AVG() function

Calculate the average order amount by customer

In this example we calculate the number of orders and the average order amount by customer. Some customers might have many orders but with minimal order amounts. If we depend on the number of orders only, we might miss some good customers with big orders, and our marketing promotions might be off target. Calculating the average order amount solves this problem.

Code:

```
SELECT lastname, count(orderid) as NumberofOrders, AVG(unitprice*quantity)
AS AvgOrderAmount
FROM tbls_customersag
GROUP BY lastname
```

Result:

lastname	NumberofOrders	AvgOrderAmount
Currier	1	30
Davis	2	60
Johnson	4	18.75
Madsen	1	30

(9 row(s) returned)

159. The avg() function with the WHERE clause

Calculate the number of orders and average order amounts for specific customers

Discussion:

We have the flexibility to use the WHERE clause with aggregate functions to manipulate the result set and retrieve the exact pieces of information we need. Using WHERE will cause the database engine to first eliminate records per the WHERE clause and perform any calculations on the remaining ones. In this particular example, we exclude two customers using the NOT IN operator.

Code:

```
SELECT lastname, count(orderid) as NumberofOrders, AVG(unitprice*quantity)
AS AvgOrderAmount
FROM tbls_customersag
WHERE lastname NOT IN ('Johnson', 'Madsen')
GROUP BY lastname
```

Result:

lastname	NumberofOrders	AvgOrderAmount
Currier	1	30
Davis	2	60
McGrath	1	10
Miller	2	25

(7 row(s) returned)

160. The sum() function

Calculate the number of orders, average, and total order amounts by customer

Discussion:

Here, we use everything we have written in the previous example and add the sum() function to calculate the total order amount by customer. We are still excluding two customers from the calculations using the NOT IN operator in the WHERE clause.

Code:

```
SELECT lastname, count(orderid) as Num, avg(unitprice*quantity)
AS Avg, sum(unitprice*quantity) AS Total
FROM tbls_customersag
WHERE lastname NOT IN ('Johnson', 'Madsen')
GROUP BY lastname
```

Result:

lastname	Num	Avg	Total
Currier	1	30	30
Davis	2	60	120
McGrath	1	10	10
Miller	2	25	50

(7 row(s) returned)

161.   The min() function
Calculate the minimum order amount by customer
Discussion:
Let's assume we now have to compute the minimum order amount for each customer. We can achieve this using the code below:

Code:
SELECT lastname, count(orderid) as Num, min(unitprice*quantity) AS Min, avg(unitprice*quantity)
AS Avg, sum(unitprice*quantity) AS Total
FROM tbls_customersag
WHERE lastname NOT IN ('Johnson', 'Madsen')
GROUP BY lastname

Result:

lastname	Num	Min	Avg	Total
Currier	1	30	30	30
Davis	2	45	60	120
McGrath	1	10	10	10
Miller	2	20	25	50

(7 row(s) returned)

162.   The max() function
Calculate the maximum value of customer orders
Discussion:
The max() function will calculate the value of the biggest order for each customer, and it will report just that in the result set.

Code:
SELECT lastname, count(orderid) as Num, min(unitprice*quantity) AS Min, avg(unitprice*quantity)
AS Avg, max(unitprice*quantity) AS Max, sum(unitprice*quantity) AS Total
FROM tbls_customersag
WHERE lastname NOT IN ('Johnson', 'Madsen')
GROUP BY lastname

Result:

lastname	Num	Min	Avg	Max	Total
Currier	1	30	30	30	30
Davis	2	45	60	75	120
McGrath	1	10	10	10	10
Miller	2	20	25	30	50

(7 row(s) returned)

163.   The Standard Deviation and Variance functions

Calculate the standard deviation and variance of customer order amounts

Discussion:

Using SQL, we can do much more than the usual arithmetic calculations. Actually, we can even perform some statistical analysis. In this example, we are looking for the standard deviation and variance of order amounts from each customer. In the SQL code, we used the convert() function (see chapter 24 for more details) to avoid multiple decimals for the standard deviation column. In the result set, Currier and McGrath have only one order and, as it is logical, no variance and standard deviation can be calculated. From a business point of view, customers Davis, Sterling, and Powers are prone to making orders that vary a lot in size.

Code:

```
SELECT lastname, count(orderid) as Num, min(unitprice*quantity) AS Min, avg(unitprice*quantity)
AS Avg, max(unitprice*quantity) AS Max, sum(unitprice*quantity) AS Total, convert(SmallInt,
var(unitprice*quantity)) As stdev, var(unitprice*quantity) as var
 FROM tbls_customersag
WHERE lastname NOT IN ('Johnson', 'Madsen')
GROUP BY lastname
```

Result:

lastname	Num	Min	Avg	Max	Total	stdev	var
Currier	1	30	30	30	30	NULL	NULL
Davis	2	45	60	75	120	450	450
McGrath	1	10	10	10	10	NULL	NULL
Miller	2	20	25	30	50	50	50
Ming	2	60	60	60	120	0	0
Powers	4	15	31	45	124	218	218
Sterling	3	30	50	60	150	300	300

```
(7 row(s) returned)
```

164.   Aggregate functions with GROUP BY and HAVING

Calculate order amounts and filter records based on results of aggregate functions

Discussion:

This time, our manager wants a report that shows the number of orders, minimum, average, maximum, and total order amounts calculated by customer. In addition, he wants products with productID 13, 56, and 30 to not participate in the calculations. He wants us to exclude from the result set any customers with total order amounts of less than $100. He also wants us to exclude from the calculations any customers with average order amounts of less than $40. Finally, he wants us to exclude from the calculations any customers with a standard deviation in their order amounts of 20 and above, but the standard deviation calculation should not appear in the result set.

The above sounds complicated, and it is complicated to a degree. Still, it is not difficult to achieve. I would like you to learn to follow a process when it comes to complicated SQL statements. This process involves the incremental building of the SQL statement instead of trying to think about everything at once. Essentially, we will build the solution one step at a time.

Our first step in any complicated problem involving SQL is to try to identify the fields. In this example, we need seven fields to do our job, and this step is straightforward. The SELECT statement with the seven fields appears below. We include the type conversion function convert() so that we restrict the number of decimals for the standard deviation field.

SELECT lastname, count(orderid) as Num, min(unitprice*quantity) AS Min, avg(unitprice*quantity) AS Avg, max(unitprice*quantity) AS Max, sum(unitprice*quantity) AS Total, convert(smallint, stdev(unitprice*quantity)) As stdev
FROM tbls_customersag

Since our manager wants results produced by customer, we add the GROUP BY clause on lastname.

SELECT lastname, count(orderid) as Num, min(unitprice*quantity) AS Min, avg(unitprice*quantity) AS Avg, max(unitprice*quantity) AS Max, sum(unitprice*quantity) AS Total, convert(smallint, stdev(unitprice*quantity)) As stdev
FROM tbls_customersag
GROUP BY lastname

Our next step is to exclude products with productID 13, 56, and 30. For this task, we make use of the WHERE clause with the NOT IN operator (chapter 12) as it appears below:

SELECT lastname, count(orderid) as Num, min(unitprice*quantity) AS Min, avg(unitprice*quantity) AS Avg, max(unitprice*quantity) AS Max, sum(unitprice*quantity) AS Total, convert(smallint, stdev(unitprice*quantity)) As stdev
FROM tbls_customersag
WHERE productID NOT IN (13,56,30)
GROUP BY lastname

The next step is to exclude from the result set any customers with total order amounts of less than $100 or any customers with average order amounts of less than $40. Here, we make use of the HAVING clause, which is the filtering clause you can use to filter records after aggregate calculations have been performed. The code will now look like this:

SELECT lastname, count(orderid) as Num, min(unitprice*quantity) AS Min, avg(unitprice*quantity) AS Avg, max(unitprice*quantity) AS Max, sum(unitprice*quantity) AS Total, convert(smallint, stdev(unitprice*quantity)) As stdev
FROM tbls_customersag
WHERE productID NOT IN (13,56,30)
GROUP BY lastname
HAVING sum(unitprice*quantity) > 100 AND avg(unitprice*quantity) > 40

The final step in building the SQL statement is to exclude from the calculations any customers with a standard deviation in their order amounts of 20 and above but without including the standard deviation calculation in the result set. In the SQL code below, we took out the expression convert(smallint, stdev(unitprice*quantity)) from the SELECT statement and put it in the HAVING clause. This way, the filtering happens, but the standard deviation calculations do not appear in the result set.

Code:

```
SELECT lastname, count(orderid) as Num, min(unitprice*quantity) AS Min, avg(unitprice*quantity)
AS Avg, max(unitprice*quantity) AS Max, sum(unitprice*quantity) AS Total FROM tbls_customersag
WHERE productID NOT IN (13,56,30)
GROUP BY lastname
HAVING sum(unitprice*quantity) > 100 AND avg(unitprice*quantity) > 40 AND convert(smallint,
stdev(unitprice*quantity)) < 20
```

After all of the filtering, only one customer out of nine satisfied all of the criteria.

Result:

lastname	Num	Min	Avg	Max	Total
Ming	2	60	60	60	120

(1 row(s) returned)

CHAPTER 18 DISCUSSION QUESTIONS

1. What is the main goal of aggregate functions?
2. Name four aggregate functions and their corresponding roles.
3. Can we use aggregate functions with calculated fields?
4. What is the clause that greatly enhances the usefulness of aggregate functions?
5. Why do we need to pay attention to null values when using aggregate functions?
6. How can we avoid null values by design?
7. What is the difference between the Count() and Count(*) aggregate functions?
8. What solution do we need to employee to count distinct records in a table?
9. What other clauses can we use with aggregate functions to greatly improve their usefulness?
10. What statistical functions can we use in SQL Server 2012?

CHAPTER 18 HANDS-ON EXERCISES

Chapter 18 Case 1:
Start SQL Server Management Studio. For each of the questions in this case you need to create a new query (Ctrl-N) and name it as per the instructions in each question. Submit your work to your instructor as one text file that contains all SQL statements or as per your instructor's directions.

1. The sales people are asking for the total number of customers in the customer table. Create a new query that satisfies the sales people request. Save the query as Chapter18_Case1_Q1.

   Your result should look like:

NumberofCustomers
201

   (1 row(s) returned)

2. The sales people are back asking for a report that will display the number of customers by city. Create a new query that satisfies the sales people request and sort results by number of customers descending. Save the query as Chapter18_Case1_Q2.

   Your result should look like:

city	NumberofCustomers
Los Angeles	31
New York	27
Boston	14
Chicago	14
Dallas	13

   (15 row(s) returned)

3. The sales people are now asking for a report that will display the number of customers by city excluding customers from NY State. Create a new query that satisfies the sales people request and sort results by number of customers descending. Save the query as Chapter18_Case1_Q3.

Your result should look like:

city	NumberofCustomers
Los Angeles	31
Boston	14
Chicago	14
Dallas	13
Denver	13

(13 row(s) returned)

4. The sales people are now asking for a report that will display the number of customers by city excluding customers from NY State. In addition, the report should exclude any cities with less than 10 customers. Create a new query that satisfies the sales people request and sort results by number of customers descending. Save the query as Chapter18_Case1_Q4.

Your result should look like:

city	NumberofCustomers
Los Angeles	31
Boston	14
Chicago	14
Dallas	13
Denver	13

(10 row(s) returned)

5. The sales people are now asking for a report that will display the number of customers by zip code excluding customers from NY State. In addition, the report should exclude any zip codes with less than 10 customers. Create a new query that satisfies the sales people request and sort results by number of customers descending. Save the query as Chapter18_Case1_Q5.

Your result should look like:

zip	NumberofCustomers
56789	10
88987	12
11882	12
53289	12
21214	13

(10 row(s) returned)

Chapter 18 Case 2:

Start SQL Server Management Studio. For each of the questions in this case you need to create a new query (Ctrl-N) and name it as per the instructions in each question. Submit your work to your instructor as one text file that contains all SQL statements or as per your instructor's directions.

1. The sales department is asking for a report that will display the total number of products by supplier in the Products table. Group on the SupplierID. Create a new query that satisfies the sales people request. Save the query as Chapter18_Case2_Q1.

    Your result should look like:

SupplierId	NumberofProducts
1	10
2	9
3	7
4	6
5	8

    (10 row(s) returned)

2. The marketing department is asking for a report that will provide the minimum, average, maximum, and total product units sold. Create a new query that satisfies the marketing people request. Save the query as Chapter18_Case2_Q2. Hint: Use the ProductsOrders table.

    Your result should look like:

MinSold	AverageSold	MaxSold	TotalUnitsSold
1	3	6	8429

    (1 row(s) returned)

3. The marketing department is again asking for a report that will provide the minimum, average, maximum, and total product units sold but grouped by ProductID this time. Sort results by ProductID ascending. Create a new query that satisfies the marketing people request and save it as Chapter18_Case2_Q3.

    Your result should look like:

ProductID	MinSold	AverageSold	MaxSold	TotalUnitsSold
1	1	3	6	97
2	1	3	6	145
3	1	3	6	132
4	1	3	6	117
5	1	2	6	88

    (70 row(s) returned)

4. The marketing department is now asking for a report that will provide the minimum, average, maximum, and total product units sold grouped by ProductID. In addition, results should exclude products with product IDs in the range 35 to 70. The boundaries of 35 and 70 should be excluded as well Sort results by ProductID ascending. Create a new query that satisfies the marketing people request and save it as Chapter18_Case2_Q4.

    Your result should look like:

ProductID	MinSold	AverageSold	MaxSold	TotalUnitsSold
1	1	3	6	97
2	1	3	6	145
3	1	3	6	132
4	1	3	6	117
5	1	2	6	88

(34 row(s) returned)

5. The marketing department is finally asking for a report that will provide the minimum, average, maximum, and total product units sold grouped by ProductID. In addition, results should exclude products with product IDs in the range 35 to 70. Moreover, the query should exclude Products with total units sold less than 100. Sort results by ProductID ascending. Create a new query that satisfies the marketing people request and save it as Chapter18_Case2_Q5.

Your result should look like:

ProductID	MinSold	AverageSold	MaxSold	TotalUnitsSold
2	1	3	6	145
3	1	3	6	132
4	1	3	6	117
6	1	3	6	121
8	1	3	6	114

(29 row(s) returned)

CHAPTER 19
CROSSTABING IN SQL SERVER 2012

Crosstab views have a reputation of being complicated and intricate objects. This should not be the case. You can really work efficiently with crosstab views once you recognize their basic structure. In essence, to create a crosstab view, you use three basic fields. One field will function as the column heading, the second as the row heading, and the third as the value field. The value field is the actual field on which calculations occur using aggregate functions like sum(), avg(), count(), count(*), max(), and min(). From the previous chapter, you know very well how to work with aggregate functions. Let us apply this knowledge in crosstab views.

Suppose you want to calculate order totals by state and year. In other words, you would like to know how much you sold in every state in every year. Since you know already that to create a crosstab view, you need to have a field as a column heading, a field as a row heading, and a value field, your view will look like this in its most basic design:

	Year
State	Value

When you run the view, since you have multiple states and years in your data, your result set will look like this:

	Year1	Year2	Year3
State1	Value	Value	Value
State2	Value	Value	Value
State3	Value	Value	Value

The state row field will expand automatically to include data for as many states as you have in your database. Unfortunately, in SQL Server 2012, the year field will not expand automatically to include as many columns as the number of years you have in your data. We need to define manually the number of years that we would like to see in the result set. The value field will present the sum of order amounts for all of the combinations of years and states.

The above diagram represents the basic structure of a crosstab view in SQL Server 2012. However, you have a couple of bonuses at this point. Once you understand how crosstab views work in SQL Server 2012, you also understand how pivot tables work in Excel, how pivot charts summarize data, and even how OLAP cubes work in a data warehouse environment. You definitely have an advantage over someone who creates pivot tables and charts without full knowledge of data summaries under the hood. In the following examples, we start with basic crosstabbing techniques and incrementally add functionality that will make your crosstab views powerful tools for your work.

Working with crosstab views usually involves the joining of multiple tables. We might need a field from the customers table, a field from the orders table, and a field from the products table. Since joins are not the focus of this chapter, I would like to spare you the intricacies of joining tables and focus on the actual crosstab views themselves. That is why the examples in this chapter are based on a view purposely made for this chapter. Its name is "View_CrosstabBase" from which we will take all the fields we need to work with. Of course, I also provide chapter 29 toward the end of the book to explain joins so that you can professionally work with joined tables.

165.   A crosstab view with three fields - example 1

Find total sales by state and year

Discussion:

As you can see from the SQL code, we use three fields (CustomerState, OrderYear, OrderTotal) to create this very informative crosstab view. The first is the CustomerState field, which we use for the row headings. The second is the OrderYear field, which we use for the column headings. The third field is the value field, which we call OrderTotal. This is a calculated field in the View_CrosstabBase that sums the unitprice * the quantity of each product for each of our customer orders.

Code:
```
SELECT *
FROM
(SELECT CustomerState, OrderYear, OrderTotal FROM View_CrosstabBase)
AS Crosstab
PIVOT (sum(OrderTotal)
FOR OrderYear IN ([2012], [2013], [2014]))
AS CrossTabTable
```

Looking at the results below, we can quickly understand and compare sales volumes by each state and each year. For example, the biggest sales revenues come from California, and they grow year by year. In Florida, we need to have a look at our business since sales dropped a lot for 2014. This is the power of crosstab views. We get summarized results in seconds.

Result:

CustomerState	2012	2013	2014
AZ	2849	2386	3460
CA	12216	13364	14919
CO	1961	3326	1937
DC	3020	3351	3102
FL	4439	4736	3413
MA	1999	2020	859
NY	8584	6089	7188
OH	2353	4924	3076
PA	1525	1781	1738
TX	5284	9187	5310

```
(10 row(s) returned)
```

166. A crosstab view with three fields—example 2

Find total sales by city and year

Discussion:

Our business manager is very happy with the comprehensive sales report we provided by state and year. Now that she knows what our database can do, she asks for an additional report that will show sales by city and year. To achieve this, it will take us about three seconds to replace the state field with the city field in our view, and our new crosstab view is ready!

Code:

```
SELECT *
FROM
(SELECT CustomerCity, OrderYear, OrderTotal FROM View_CrosstabBase)
AS Crosstab
PIVOT (sum(OrderTotal)
FOR OrderYear IN ([2012], [2013], [2014]) )
AS CrossTabTable
```

Result:

CustomerCity	2012	2013	2014
Albany	1199	1214	1356
Boston	1999	2020	859
Chicago	2353	4924	3076
Dallas	2691	4174	3292
Denver	1961	3326	1937
Houston	2593	5013	2018
Los Angeles	5725	8570	10118
Miami	1965	2775	1380
New York	7385	4875	5832
Orlando	2474	1961	2033

(15 row(s) returned)

167. The issue of uniqueness of values in crosstab views

Find total sales by customer and year

Discussion:

Now, our supervisor asks for additional detail. Specifically, he wants a sales report by customer and year. Again, in a few seconds, we replace the city field from the previous example with lastname and presumably, we are done!

Unfortunately, that isn't the case this time! Our problem is that multiple customers might have the same last names. Since we are grouping on the last name field, all of the customers with the same lastname will be grouped together! This is a very common problem in crosstab views when using the GROUP BY clause. Consequently, I would like you to develop a process to think thoroughly about the uniqueness of values when using the GROUP BY clause. For instance, you should think about the possibility of having the same last name in your data for multiple customers. The same is true for city fields since the same city name might refer to multiple distinct cities, as is the case with Portland, Oregon and Portland, Maine. We will see how we can solve this problem in the next example with concatenated fields.

In addition, notice from the result set that there are some blank values. For example, there are blank values for Ames in 2012 and 2013. These blanks mean that Ames has not placed any orders in 2012 and 2013 respectively.

Code:
```
SELECT *
FROM
(SELECT CustomerLastName, OrderYear, OrderTotal FROM View_CrosstabBase)
AS Crosstab
PIVOT (sum(OrderTotal)
FOR OrderYear IN ([2012], [2013], [2014]))
AS CrossTabTable
```

Result:

CustomerLastName	2012	2013	2014
Ackerman	120	32	207
Ames	NULL	NULL	871
Andersen	350	NULL	393
Anderson	965	924	1434
Anthopolis	220	240	48
Aversa	469	NULL	NULL
Baker	255	482	617
Balfur	100	313	75

```
(171 row(s) returned)
```

168.   Looking for uniqueness: crosstab views with concatenated fields

Find total sales by customer and year displaying full customer names

Discussion:

In the previous example, we discussed that the results of the crosstab view might have been incorrect because multiple distinct customers might have the same last name. In this example, we need to make sure that we summarize sales volumes by unique customers. The knowledge acquired from the concatenated fields chapter (chapter 16) comes in handy here. In this example, we will GROUP BY the field resulting from the concatenation of the last and first name fields of the customers to obtain accurate results.

I know what you are thinking: What if there are customers with the same last and first names? This is a real possibility and we have three ways to solve this problem depending on its nature. First, if two customer entries pertain to the same customer, (there are duplicated records in the data set), read chapter 22 on duplicate and orphaned records to explore a range of solutions.

Second, if the two customer entries pertain to two different customers, we can add middle names, zip codes, and even part of the address information to the concatenated expression to obtain unique results.

Third, to avoid this problem in its conception, we can add to the customer table a unique multiple-field index on the last and first name fields so that values of customers with the same last and first names are not accepted at all in the table. See chapter 3 for the exact syntax of multiple-field indexes.

I have created an additional problem on purpose: When you look at the result set in this example, you will notice that the first record is blank! If this is the case, go immediately to your record set, and check the values of the fields you use in the concatenated expression for blanks. You will notice that customer "Corelli" does not have a first name entry! Add a first name for this customer, and your blank record will disappear when you run your crosstab again.

Code:

```
SELECT *
FROM
(SELECT CustomerLastName + ' ' + CustomerFirstName AS CustomerName, OrderYear, OrderTotal
FROM View_CrosstabBase)
AS Crosstab PIVOT (sum(OrderTotal)
FOR OrderYear IN ([2012], [2013], [2014]))
AS CrossTabTable
```

Result:

CustomerName	2012	2013	2014
NULL	90	1131	240
Ackerman Nicholas	120	32	207
Ames Pindar	NULL	NULL	871
Andersen Thomas	350	NULL	393
Anderson Joseph	110	575	477
Anderson Paul	371	72	513
Anderson Peter	484	277	444
Anthopolis Ricky	220	240	48

(190 row(s) returned)

169. Limit the number of rows in crosstab views using WHERE

Find total sales by state and year for certain states only

Discussion:

All of the crosstab views we have examined to this point produce summaries counting every record in the underlying database table or view. Experience shows, however, that in the vast majority of cases, we will make calculations on a subset of data. We can use the WHERE clause to filter the data we want to cross tabulate. The WHERE clause always affects the number of records returned from a view whether this view is a simple SELECT or a crosstab one. In this specific example, the goal is to provide sales volumes by state and year, including only the states CA, FL, and NY in the calculations. We can use the WHERE clause in conjunction with the IN operator to get exactly the results we need.

Code:
```
SELECT *
FROM
(SELECT CustomerState, OrderYear, OrderTotal FROM View_CrosstabBase
WHERE CustomerState IN ('CA', 'NY', 'FL'))
AS Crosstab
PIVOT(sum(OrderTotal)
FOR OrderYear IN ([2012], [2013], [2014]))
AS CrossTabTable
```

Result:

CustomerState	2012	2013	2014
CA	12216	13364	14919
FL	4439	4736	3413
NY	8584	6089	7188

(3 row(s) returned)

170.   Limit the number of columns in crosstab views using PIVOT IN

Find total sales by state and year for specific years

Discussion:

In the previous example, we discussed how we can use the WHERE clause to define the states included in the crosstab results. We learned how to limit the number of rows in a crosstab view, but there is a way to limit the number of columns as well.

For instance, what if our dataset contains sales data for the last ten years, and we do not want to include all of them in our crosstab results? We might want to see only the last two years. In this scenario, we are looking to control the number of columns appearing in the crosstab results. To achieve this task, we can use the PIVOT IN statement. In this particular example, we only want to see sales volumes for the years 2013 and 2014.

Code:
```
SELECT *
FROM
(SELECT CustomerState, OrderYear, OrderTotal FROM View_CrosstabBase)
AS Crosstab
PIVOT (sum(OrderTotal)
FOR OrderYear IN ([2013], [2014]))
AS CrossTabTable
```

Result:

CustomerState	2013	2014
AZ	2386	3460
CA	13364	14919
CO	3326	1937
DC	3351	3102
FL	4736	3413
MA	2020	859

(10 row(s) returned)

230

171.   Filter crosstab views using any field for criteria

Find total sales by state and year excluding the cities of Albany

Discussion:

In the previous two examples of filtering crosstab views, we used the WHERE clause on the state field and the PIVOT IN on the year field. Both of these fields are part of the crosstab view. The state field is used for rows, and the year field for columns. I would like you to know, however, that you can use any field in your dataset to filter records in a crosstab view without this field being an integral part of the crosstab view. You simply designate it as a "WHERE" field in a WHERE clause as it appears in the SQL code below. In this particular example, the business goal is to obtain sales volumes by year and state excluding from the results those sales that happened in the cities of Albany. We know in the United States we have 28 cities named Albany and we want to exclude sales volumes from those cities in particular. Compare the sales figures for NY State now that we excluded Albany with those in example 165 where the sales from the city of Albany where included. The sales volume in this example is lower as it has been expected.

Code:
```
SELECT *
FROM
(SELECT CustomerState, OrderYear, OrderTotal FROM View_CrosstabBase
WHERE CustomerCity NOT IN ('Albany'))
AS Crosstab
PIVOT (sum(OrderTotal)
FOR OrderYear IN ([2012], [2013], [2014]))
AS CrossTabTable
```

Result:

CustomerState	2012	2013	2014
AZ	2849	2386	3460
CA	12216	13364	14919
CO	1961	3326	1937
DC	3020	3351	3102
FL	4439	4736	3413
MA	1999	2020	859
NY	7385	4875	5832
OH	2353	4924	3076
PA	1525	1781	1738
TX	5284	9187	5310

(10 row(s) returned)

172.   Conditional processing of crosstab views using the iif() function

Calculate discounted sales volumes depending on revenue volumes

Discussion:

Our business assignment in the first example of this chapter was to give our manager a print out of total of sales by state and year. Now, our task is a little bit more complicated. Management wants to know what the sales volumes would have been if they gave a 10% discount to customers in states with total sales of more than $10,000. In addition, they want to know the sales volumes if they gave a discount of 5% to customers in states with total sales of less than $10,000. And they want to see all results in one report. This is not a problem at all. The key here is to use the iif() function with the crosstab view. Using the code below, we ask the database to apply a 10% discount if total sales are more than $10,000 or to apply a 5% discount if total sales are less than $10,000.

Code:
```
SELECT *
FROM
(SELECT CustomerState, OrderYear,
iif(ordertotal>10000, ordertotal*0.9, OrderTotal*0.95)
AS Ordertotal
FROM View_CrosstabBase)
AS Crosstab
PIVOT (Sum(Ordertotal)
FOR OrderYear IN ([2012], [2013], [2014]))
AS CrossTabTable
```

Result:

CustomerState	2012	2013	2014
AZ	2706.55	2266.70	3287.00
CA	11605.20	12695.80	14173.05
CO	1862.95	3159.70	1840.15
DC	2869.00	3183.45	2946.90
FL	4217.05	4499.20	3242.35
MA	1899.05	1919.00	816.05
NY	8154.80	5784.55	6828.60
OH	2235.35	4677.80	2922.20
PA	1448.75	1691.95	1651.10
TX	5019.80	8727.65	5044.50

(10 row(s) returned)

173. Conditional crosstab views using the CASE function

Calculate order totals for "expensive" and "inexpensive" products

Discussion:

This time, management wants to know the contribution to the total sales volume of products selling above $25 per unit and the contribution of products selling below $25 per unit. Depending on the results we give them, they will change their sales priorities to focus more on products that will generate the most sales for the company. In addition, they would like to have the results by year so that they can also distinguish any trends in sales volumes. We can use the CASE function to provide the custom categories exactly the way management has asked. We can clearly see from the result set that inexpensive products produce the highest sales volumes.

Code:
```
SELECT *
FROM
(SELECT
CASE
WHEN unitprice >= 25 THEN 'Expensive Products Total Sales'
WHEN unitprice < 25 THEN  'Inexpensive Product Total Sales'
END
AS UnitPrice,
OrderYear, OrderTotal FROM View_CrosstabBase)
AS Crosstab
PIVOT (sum(OrderTotal)
FOR OrderYear IN ([2012], [2013], [2014]))
AS CrossTabTable
```

Result:

UnitPrice	2012	2013	2014
Inexpensive Product Total Sales	31886	35908	33158
Expensive Products Total Sales	12344	15256	11844

```
(10 row(s) returned)
```

CHAPTER 19 DISCUSSION QUESTIONS

1. What is the purpose of crosstab queries in SQL Server?
2. How many fields do we need for a basic crosstab query?
3. What is the purpose of the PIVOT statement in crosstab queries?
4. What keyword do we use to create the columns in crosstab queries in SQL Server?
5. What is the purpose of the GROUP BY clause in cross tab queries?
6. Why do we need to pay attention to the uniqueness of values in the GROUP BY field?
7. What is the meaning of blank values in the results of crosstab queries? Is this a database issue or a business fact?
8. What clause do we use to limit the number of rows in crosstab queries?
9. How do we limit the number of columns in crosstab queries?
10. What conditional functions can we use with crosstab queries? What results can we achieve with these conditional functions that are not possible otherwise?

CHAPTER 19 HANDS-ON EXERCISES

Chapter 19 Case 1:

Start SQL Server Management Studio. For each of the questions in this case you need to create a new query (Ctrl-N) and name it as per the instructions in each question. Submit your work to your instructor as one text file that contains all SQL statements or as per your instructor's directions.

1. The management of the company needs a report that will provide the total order amount by city and year. The three years to be included in the crosstab query will be 2012, 2013, and 2014. Use the view "View_CrosstabBase" for your crosstabbing calculations. Create a new query that satisfies the managerial request and name it Chapter19_Case1_Q1.

   Your result should look like:

CustomerCity	2012	2013	2014
Albany	1199	1214	1356
Boston	1999	2020	859
Chicago	2353	4924	3076
Dallas	2691	4174	3292
Denver	1961	3326	1937

   (15 row(s) returned)

2. The management of the company is now asking for the same report as in question 1 but they want to see results that exclude the cities of Albany, Boston, and Dallas. Create a new query that satisfies the managerial request and name it Chapter19_Case1_Q2.

   Your result should look like:

CustomerCity	2012	2013	2014
Chicago	2353	4924	3076
Denver	1961	3326	1937
Houston	2593	5013	2018
Los Angeles	5725	8570	10118
Miami	1965	2775	1380

(12 row(s) returned)

3. The management now wants a report like the one you created in question 2 that will show what the sales volumes would have been if they gave a 10% discount to customers in cities with total sales of more than $5,000 and 5% to customers in cities with total sales of less than $5,000. Create a new query that satisfies the managerial request and name it Chapter19_Case1_Q3.

Your result should look like:

CustomerCity	2012	2013	2014
Chicago	2235.35	4677.80	2922.20
Denver	1862.95	3159.70	1840.15
Houston	2463.35	4762.35	1917.10
Los Angeles	5438.75	8141.50	9612.10
Miami	1866.75	2636.25	1311.00

(12 row(s) returned)

4. The management is really very happy with all this useful information. They now need the same report you created in question 3 but to exclude the year 2012. Create a new query that satisfies the managerial request and name it Chapter19_Case1_Q4.

Your result should look like:

CustomerCity	2013	2014
Chicago	4677.80	2922.20
Denver	3159.70	1840.15
Houston	4762.35	1917.10
Los Angeles	8141.50	9612.10
Miami	2636.25	1311.00

(12 row(s) returned)

5. Finally, the management requests a report that will provide the total sales amounts by employee seniority and year. Specifically, they want you to provide sales volumes for sales reps hired between 1995 and 2000 and those hired after 2001. The three years to be included in the crosstab query will be 2012, 2013, and 2014. Use the view "View_CrosstabBase" for your crosstabbing calculations. HINT: Use the CASE function. Create a new query that satisfies the managerial request and name it Chapter19_Case1_Q5.

Your result should look like:

SalesRepExperience	2012	2013	2014
NULL	4122	5589	5683
Experienced Sales Reps Total Sales	26461	31526	26227
Senior Sales Reps Total Sales	13647	14049	13092

```
(3 row(s) returned)
```

Chapter 19 Case 2:

Start SQL Server Management Studio. For each of the questions in this case you need to create a new query (Ctrl-N) and name it as per the instructions in each question. Submit your work to your instructor as one text file that contains all SQL statements or as per your instructor's directions.

1. The marketing department is asking for a report that will provide the total order amount by ProductName and year. The three years to be included in the crosstab query will be 2012, 2013, and 2014. Use the view "View_CrosstabBase" for your crosstabbing calculations. Save the query as Chapter19_Case2_Q1.

    Your result should look like:

ProductName	2012	2013	2014
All-Purpose Marinade I	392	560	560
All-Purpose Marinade II	915	750	255
Almonds, Hickory Smoked - 12 oz. Bag	600	180	675
Almonds, Roasted and Salted - 18 oz. Bag	660	975	540
Apple Cinnamon Raisin Cookies	552	540	696

    ```
    (67 row(s) returned)
    ```

2. The marketing department is now asking for the same report as in question 1 but they want to see results that exclude the products "Chili salsa", "Coffee biscuits", and "Crispy Pears". Create a new query that satisfies this request. Save the query as Chapter19_Case2_Q2.

    Your result should look like:

ProductName	2012	2013	2014
All-Purpose Marinade I	392	560	560
All-Purpose Marinade II	915	750	255
Almonds, Hickory Smoked - 12 oz. Bag	600	180	675
Almonds, Roasted and Salted - 18 oz. Bag	660	975	540
Apple Cinnamon Raisin Cookies	552	540	696

    ```
    (64 row(s) returned)
    ```

3. The marketing department now wants a report like the one you created in step 2 that will also show what the sales volumes would have been if they gave a 10% discount for products with a product price above $30 and a 5% discount for products costing less than $ 30. This way marketing can do some scenario analysis. Create a new query that satisfies the managerial request and name it Chapter19_Case1_Q3. Create a new query that satisfies the sales people request. Save the query as Chapter19_Case2_Q3.

    Your result should look like:

ProductName	2012	2013	2014
All-Purpose Marinade I	372.40	532.00	532.00
All-Purpose Marinade II	869.25	712.50	242.25
Almonds, Hickory Smoked - 12 oz. Bag	570.00	171.00	641.25
Almonds, Roasted and Salted - 18 oz. Bag	627.00	926.25	513.00
Apple Cinnamon Raisin Cookies	524.40	513.00	661.20

(64 row(s) returned)

4. The marketing people are now asking for the same report you created in question 3 but to exclude the year 2012. Create a new query that satisfies the latest marketing people request. Save the query as Chapter19_Case2_Q4.

Your result should look like:

ProductName	2013	2014
All-Purpose Marinade I	532.00	532.00
All-Purpose Marinade II	712.50	242.25
Almonds, Hickory Smoked - 12 oz. Bag	171.00	641.25
Almonds, Roasted and Salted - 18 oz. Bag	926.25	513.00
Apple Cinnamon Raisin Cookies	513.00	661.20

(64 row(s) returned)

5. The marketing people are asking for a report that will provide the total sales amounts by product price range and year. Specifically, they want you to provide sales volumes for products priced between $1 and $10, $11-$20, $21-$30 and more than $31. The three years to be included in the crosstab query will be 2012, 2013, and 2014. Use the view "View_CrosstabBase" for your crosstabbing calculations. HINT: Use the CASE function. Create a new query that satisfies this request and save it as Chapter19_Case2_Q5.

Your result should look like:

Price 11-20	26894	31702	28786
Price > 31	6016	6016	4256
Price 1-10	2022	1852	2128
Price 21-30	9298	11594	9832

(4 row(s) returned)

CHAPTER 20
CONDITIONAL DATA MANIPULATION

The iif(), and case() functions are the most useful and practical functions for conditional data manipulation in SQL Server 2012.

What exactly do we mean by conditional data processing? Let's assume we have a customer database we use for promotional campaigns. We might decide we want to provide different discount levels for customers in the Northeast, Midwest, West, Southeast, and Southwest states. Since we do not have region information in our database, we need to create multiple SELECT views for these categories and apply the appropriate discount for each region. Using conditional data processing, on the other hand, will enable us to do our job in just one view.

You might be thinking at this point that it does not bother you to create four views to do your job. What matters in the end is getting the job done. I totally agree. However, what will happen after a couple of years at work is that you will end up with several hundred views. In the end, you will not remember what was what, and you will be afraid to delete even one of them since you no longer know what it was used for. During the last almost twenty years, I have seen this happen countless times with departmental databases.

To encourage you to use conditional processing, let me give you another example. Let's say we have a database in which we store our products, along with the corresponding suppliers. Every now and then, our suppliers send us updated prices, and we need to update our own product catalog as well. We have only 20 suppliers and 200 products in our database, and we need to update our prices every few weeks.

Of course, thinking logically, suppliers will provide us with different price updates. Some of them will increase their prices by 3%, some by 5%, some by 3.5%, some by 4%, ending up with four clusters in this example. Still, we will have to create four update queries and include the specific calculated fields for the updates and specific criteria so that the appropriate supplier products are updated and with the correct percentages.

Furthermore, every time we have price updates, we will need to modify our current update queries, modify their criteria, and calculate new prices for the updates. We will end up with an unmanageable number of views even for this simple scenario. Using conditions, on the other hand, we can do the job very effectively using just a single view!

A final point on conditional statements: Those who understand conditional statements will produce much better database designs and entity relationship diagrams since they know in advance what needs to be stored and what can be produced automatically by the database.

174.   Using the iif() and case() functions with two simple conditions
Produce a product catalog with special discounts for one product only
Discussion:
We received an urgent message from the inventory department saying we have a large quantity of Chocolate Fudge which needs to go out into the market fast. We only have a few hours to produce a new product catalog for this week and send it to our customers. All of the product prices in the catalog should remain the same

except for Chocolate Fudge, which will be reduced by 50%. We must not make this percentage change right in the table because this price will be valid only for a week.

Solution 1: using the iif() function

We can solve this problem using an iif() function as in the code below. The translation of the iif() function in this example says: For the product with productid = 14, change the value of the field ProductUnitPrice by 50%, and for the rest of the products in the catalog, leave the price as is in the table. Notice that we have changed the title of the ProductUnitPrice field to appear as "ProductPrice" in this week's catalog. Finally, notice in the result set that the price of Chocolate Fudge is now $20.50 in the view, while it remains $41 in the products table.

Code:

```
SELECT ProductID, ProductName, QuantityPerUnit,
iif([productid]=14,[productunitprice]*0.5,[productunitprice]) AS ProductPrice
FROM Products
```

Result:

ProductID	ProductName	QuantityPerUnit	ProductPrice
12	Chocolate Covered Cherries in 8 oz. Bag	35	37.0
13	Chocolate Blueberries in 10 oz. Bag	25	29.0
14	Chocolate Fudge	28	20.5
15	Chocolate Blueberries in 10 oz. Bag	28	24.0

(70 row(s) returned)

Solution 2: using the case() function

There is no need to use the case function in this case since there is only one very simple condition. However, I would like to show you its syntax and how it works with respect to an iif() function. There is no doubt that the case() function is much cleaner and comprehensible than the iif() function. This becomes more evident as the number of conditions goes up.

Code:

```
SELECT ProductID, ProductName, QuantityPerUnit,
case
WHEN productid = 14 THEN   productunitprice*0.5
WHEN productid <>14 THEN   productunitprice
END
AS ProductPrice
FROM Products
```

Result:

ProductID	ProductName	QuantityPerUnit	ProductPrice
12	Chocolate Covered Cherries in 8 oz. Bag	35	37.0
13	Chocolate Blueberries in 10 oz. Bag	25	29.0
14	Chocolate Fudge	28	20.5
15	Chocolate Blueberries in 10 oz. Bag	28	24.0

(70 row(s) returned)

175.   Using the iif() and case() functions with two conditions but multiple criteria

Provide discounts for customers in NY, TX, and CA only

Discussion:

This time, management initiates a new promotional campaign. They want to offer a 20% discount to customers in large states such as NY, TX, and CA and 10% to everyone else around the country. They want a list of customers and their corresponding discount rates for review.

Solution 1: using the iif() function

Using the iif() function becomes a bit more complicated this time and requires two OR operators. The iif() function translates to: If the customer is in NY, CA, or TX, provide him or her with a discount of 20%. Otherwise, provide the customer with a discount of 10%.

Code:

```
SELECT State, lastname, firstname,  OrderTotal,
IIf([state]= 'NY' Or [state]= 'CA' Or [state]= 'TX',0.20,0.10)
AS Discount
FROM View_Conditions
```

Result:

State	lastname	firstname	OrderTotal	Discount
NY	Riegert	Joanne	30	0.20
DC	Read	Lisa	210	0.10
AZ	Moore	Gerald	231	0.10
MA	Davis	Catherine	45	0.10
CA	Irving	Barbara	253	0.20

```
(919 row(s) returned)
```

Solution 2: using the case() function

The use of the case function with two conditions and multiple criteria is again more legible than using the iif() function and, therefore, easily editable if we need to update our criteria later on. Notice in this piece of code how we use the "ELSE" keyword to designate a discount of .10 to all other states except NY, CA, and TX.

Code:

```
SELECT State, lastname, firstname,  OrderTotal,
CASE
WHEN state= 'NY' Or state= 'CA' Or state = 'TX' THEN  0.20
ELSE  0.10
END
AS Discount
FROM View_Conditions
```

Result:

State	lastname	firstname	OrderTotal	Discount
NY	Riegert	Joanne	30	0.20
DC	Read	Lisa	210	0.10
AZ	Moore	Gerald	231	0.10
MA	Davis	Catherine	45	0.10
CA	Irving	Barbara	253	0.20

(919 row(s) returned)

176. Working with multiple conditions using nested iif() functions and the case() function

Determine discount amounts based on customer past sales volumes

Discussion:

Our sales manager wants to provide order discounts to customers based on their historical total sales volume with the company. Thus, if a customer has a certain recorded sales volume, the next time she orders, she will get a predetermined discount rate regardless of her new order amount.

If the historical total order amount for a customer is less than $200, that customer will receive no discounts. If it is between $200 and $300, the customer will get a 5% discount. If it is between $300 and $500, the customer will get a 10% discount. For anything above that, our manager will offer a generous 25% discount to the customer. Our job is to create a datasheet that will list customers and show the corresponding discount rate for each customer.

Solution 1: using nested iif() functions

Our first option, and not the one recommended, is to use a series of nested iif() functions as shown below — four iif() functions, one inside the other to accomplish our goal. However, the use of nested iif() functions is a convoluted process. Moreover, if we need to change the business logic in our statement by adding additional categories, the task is not a clear and clean preposition. The problem originates from the fact that the iif() function takes only two arguments. For more outcomes or categories, we need to nest, which, in turn, results in complicated statements. You can go down to ten nested iif functions in SQL Server 2012.

Code:
```
SELECT lastname, firstname, OrderTotal,
iif(ordertotal<200,0,
iif(ordertotal>=200 And ordertotal<300, 0.05,
iif(ordertotal>=300 And ordertotal<500, 0.10, 0.25)))
AS Discount
FROM View_Conditions
```

241

Result:

lastname	firstname	OrderTotal	Discount
Riegert	Joanne	30	0.00
Read	Lisa	210	0.05
Moore	Gerald	231	0.05
Davis	Catherine	45	0.00
Irving	Barbara	253	0.05
Lanci	Christine	378	0.10

(919 row(s) returned)

Solution 2: using the case() function

In this example, the immediate observation is that with the case() function our logic becomes instantly apparent to us and anyone else who will need to edit the SQL statement later on. The cleanliness of the SQL statement is obvious:

Code:
```
SELECT lastname, firstname, ordertotal,
CASE
WHEN ordertotal < 200                        THEN      0
WHEN ordertotal >= 200 and ordertotal < 300  THEN      0.05
WHEN ordertotal > 300 and ordertotal <= 500  THEN      0.10
WHEN ordertotal > 500                        THEN      0.25
END
AS Discount
FROM View_Conditions
```

Result:

lastname	firstname	OrderTotal	Discount
Riegert	Joanne	30	0.00
Read	Lisa	210	0.05
Moore	Gerald	231	0.05
Davis	Catherine	45	0.00
Irving	Barbara	253	0.05
Lanci	Christine	378	0.10

(919 row(s) returned)

177.   Using the ELSE keyword with the case() function

Calculate customer discounts based on location

Discussion:

This time, the task is to provide specific customer discounts in specific states. At the same time a general discount percentage should be extended to all customers in states not included in the discounted state list. We can achieve this task by using the ELSE keyword as part of the last expression in a case() function. This last expression will evaluate true for every state not included in NY, AZ, CO, FL, and MA, and we will extend a 10% discount to customers in all other states.

Code:
```
SELECT state, lastname, firstname, ordertotal,
CASE
WHEN state = 'NY'    THEN        0.20
WHEN state = 'AZ'    THEN        0.15
WHEN state = 'CO'    THEN        0.12
WHEN state = 'FL'    THEN        0.18
WHEN state = 'MA'    THEN        0.18
ELSE 0.10
END
AS Discount
FROM View_Conditions
```

Result:

state	lastname	firstname	ordertotal	Discount
NY	Riegert	Joanne	30	0.20
DC	Read	Lisa	210	0.10
AZ	Moore	Gerald	231	0.15
MA	Davis	Catherine	45	0.18
CA	Irving	Barbara	253	0.10
AZ	Lanci	Christine	378	0.15

```
(919 row(s) returned)
```

178. Using case() function with WHERE, IN, and ORDER BY
Calculate discounted order totals based on customer sales volume
Discussion:

Our goal now is to calculate sales totals for specific customer categories. The cool thing is that these categories do not yet exist but we will obtain them by calculating customer order amounts. The policy is to offer discounts only to customers with order totals between $200 and $500. In addition, we want to extend these discounts only to customers in AZ, CO, TX, and FL. To achieve this goal we use the WHERE clause with the IN operator to exclude customers from all other states.

Code:
```
SELECT OrderID, lastname, firstname, State,
CASE
WHEN ordertotal>= 200 and ordertotal < 300  THEN        ordertotal*(1-0.1)
WHEN ordertotal> 300 and ordertotal <= 500  THEN        ordertotal*(1-0.15)
WHEN ordertotal> 500                        THEN        ordertotal*(1-0.2)
ELSE   ordertotal
END
AS DiscountedOrders
FROM View_conditions
WHERE state in ('AZ', 'CO', 'TX', 'FL')
ORDER BY ordertotal DESC
```

243

Result:

OrderID	lastname	firstname	State	DiscountedOrders
944	Corelli	NULL	TX	459.20
308	Darek	Matthew	CO	409.60
404	Crandil	Joseph	TX	408.00
932	Weinberger	Fred	FL	386.75
457	Williams	Mary	TX	369.75
747	Crondos	Kenneth	TX	368.05

```
(301 row(s) returned)
```

179.   Using case() with calculated fields

Produce product categories based on product prices

Discussion:

Now, the request we have from management is to provide a product list categorized arbitrarily by price. That is, they want to see a product list that specifies each product as "economical", "moderate", and "expensive" based on its price. Although we carry no such field in the database, we can absolutely create the list in seconds by using a case() function combined with calculated fields. In essence, we calculate the unit price times its quantity per unit to get the total price we pay, and then we assign categories based on price. For instance, if the price falls between $500 and $1000, we designate these products as "moderately" priced. We can save this view and update it at will if management wants more, less, or otherwise defined categories.

Code:

```
SELECT ProductName, UnitsInStock, UnitsOnOrder,
CASE
WHEN ProductUnitPrice*QuantityPerUnit < 500  THEN  'Economical'
WHEN ProductUnitPrice*QuantityPerUnit >= 500 AND  ProductUnitPrice*QuantityPerUnit<1000
THEN  'Moderate'
WHEN ProductUnitPrice*QuantityPerUnit >= 1000 THEN  'Expensive'
END
as PricingCategory
FROM Products
ORDER BY  ProductUnitPrice*QuantityPerUnit DESC
```

Result:

ProductName	UnitsInStock	UnitsOnOrder	PricingCategory
Chocolate Chunk Cookies, 9....	15	20	Expensive
Dark Chocolate Apricots in 2...	38	0	Expensive
Buttermilk Muffins	31	0	Expensive
Coffee biscuits	24	0	Expensive

```
(70 row(s) returned)
```

180.   Using case() with aggregate functions

Calculate employee commissions and bonuses based on their sales volume

Discussion:

There are multiple tasks in this example. First, we need to calculate employee commissions as a percentage of their sales. Second, we need to calculate employee bonuses based again on sales volumes. Third, we need to add commission and bonus amounts. Fourth, we need to make these calculations only for 2014.

Do not be intimidated by the long SQL statement. It is long but not as tough as it looks. In two minutes, you will have a total grasp of it. First, notice we use only three fields in this SQL statement: lastname, orderdate, and CommissionAndBonus. We use the lastname field as is. For the orderdate field, we use the function year() to extract the year part of the date. The CommissionAndBonus field will be the result of the case() function calculations.

Next, notice that we use sum() and case(), one after the other. We use the sum() function to obtain the total order amounts sold by our salesperson. Since we do not have a field for order totals in the database (correctly, since we can calculate them), we need to multiply the quantity of each product sold by its price in every order and sum() the results. Then, we use the case() function to assign commissions and bonuses according to sales volumes.

Next, we have a FROM statement but do not pay attention to the joins since SQL Server will create the joins automatically when we paste this code in a view and look at its design. We devote a whole chapter on joins (chapter 29).

In the final part of the SQL statement, we group by employee and year since we need to have commissions and bonuses shown by employee and year. We filter the year by using the HAVING clause as we examined in our "GROUP BY" chapter.

In the end, the whole view is reduced to three fields: lastname and year by which we group by and the commissionandbonus field on which we apply the sum() aggregate function.

Code:
```
SELECT LastName, Year(OrderDate) AS OrderYear,
SUM
(
CASE
WHEN (UnitPrice*quantity) < 5000  THEN  (UnitPrice*quantity)*(0.1) + 500
WHEN (UnitPrice*quantity) >= 5000 AND  (UnitPrice*quantity) <10000   THEN
(UnitPrice*quantity)*(0.15) + 1000
WHEN (UnitPrice*quantity) >= 10000 AND  (UnitPrice*quantity) <15000  THEN
(UnitPrice*quantity)*(0.2) + 3000
WHEN (UnitPrice*quantity) >= 15000  THEN    (UnitPrice*quantity)*(0.25) + 5000
END
)
AS CommissionAndBonus

FROM SalesReps INNER JOIN (Orders INNER JOIN ProductsOrders ON Orders.OrderID =
ProductsOrders.OrderID) ON SalesReps.SalesRepID = Orders.SalesRepID

GROUP BY LastName, Year(OrderDate)
HAVING (((Year(OrderDate))=2014))
ORDER BY Sum(UnitPrice*quantity) DESC
```

Result:

LastName	OrderYear	CommissionAndBonus
Bernstein	2014	50068.30
Simmons	2014	51064.20
Vanderback	2014	43506.50
Anderson	2014	41464.10
Baker	2014	39452.00
Spicer	2014	38934.40
Teall	2014	35924.40
Delaney	2014	40420.70
Zensons	2014	34410.50
Williams	2014	23755.10

```
(10 row(s) returned)
```

181.   Using case() with update views

Update multiple product prices from multiple suppliers conditionally

Discussion:

Now, this is an occasion where a case() function will show its true and unique power. When we combine it with update statements, we can produce highly effective updates that otherwise would have required multiple update views to obtain.

In this example, we want to update 70 products from ten suppliers, and for each supplier, we apply a different update percentage. Those percentages start from 2% all the way up to 11%, as you can see from the SQL code below. By combining the case() function with the UPDATE statement, we can do everything in one single view. We can save this view and use it every time we need to update our prices. Even if we do not receive price updates for one or some of the suppliers, we can leave the code as is and simply do not use any percentage updates for that supplier. We can just write: ProductUnitPrice = ProductUnitPrice.

Code:

```
UPDATE tbls_Products_Upd
SET ProductUnitPrice =
CASE
WHEN supplierid=1     THEN ProductUnitPrice*(1.1)
WHEN supplierid=2     THEN ProductUnitPrice*(1.08)
WHEN supplierid=3     THEN ProductUnitPrice*(1.07)
WHEN supplierid=4     THEN ProductUnitPrice*(1.05)
WHEN supplierid=5     THEN ProductUnitPrice*(1.03)
WHEN supplierid=6     THEN ProductUnitPrice*(1.02)
WHEN supplierid=7     THEN ProductUnitPrice*(1.03)
WHEN supplierid=8     THEN ProductUnitPrice*(1.07)
WHEN supplierid=9     THEN ProductUnitPrice*(1.11)
WHEN supplierid=10    THEN ProductUnitPrice*(1.08)
END
```

Result:

```
(70 row(s) affected)
```

182.   Using case() with crosstab views

Create a crosstab view that calculates order totals for "big" and "small" cities

Discussion:

This time, we have a request from management to calculate sales volumes by year and, at the same time, categorize results by small and big cities in the country. They told us specifically that they want to see combined sales volumes for big cities like New York and Los Angeles and combined sales volumes for every other city in which we do business. This is an excellent occasion to combine the power of the case() function with the flexibility of crosstab views. Instead of pivoting by the city field as we did in the crosstab views chapter, we use the case() function right in the PIVOT statement to create city categories of our own imagination and creativity.

Code:
```
SELECT *
FROM
(SELECT
CASE
WHEN CustomerCity IN ('New York', 'Los Angeles')  THEN    'BigCities'
WHEN CustomerCity NOT IN ('New York', 'Los Angeles')  THEN    'SmallCities'
END
AS UnitPrice,
OrderYear, OrderTotal FROM View_CrosstabBase)
AS Crosstab
PIVOT
(
sum(OrderTotal)
FOR OrderYear IN ([2012], [2013], [2014])
)
AS CrossTabTable
```

Result:

UnitPrice	2012	2013	2014
BigCities	13110	13445	15950
SmallCities	31120	37719	29052

(2 row(s) returned)

CHAPTER 20 DISCUSSION QUESTIONS

1. What are the business goals of conditional data manipulation?
2. Which are the basic two functions for conditional data manipulation?
3. Why the undersdanding of conditional statements leads to better entity relationship diagrams?
4. How many conditions can we process with an iif() function?
5. How many conditions can we process with the case() function?
6. Can we process multiple conditions with iif() functions?
7. When we have multiple conditions is it better to use the case() or the iif() function?
8. What is the meaning of the ELSE keyword in the case() function?
9. Can we use calculated fields within the case() function?
10. What is the benefit of using case() with crosstab queries?

CHAPTER 20 HANDS-ON EXERCISES

Chapter 20 Case 1:
Start SQL Server Management Studio. For each of the questions in this case you need to create a new query (Ctrl-N) and name it as per the instructions in each question. Submit your work to your instructor as one text file that contains all SQL statements or as per your instructor's directions.

1. The marketing department initiates a new campaign to provide customers with discount coupons. The customers in NY and CA will receive 20% discounts while the customers in the rest of the country 25%. Create a query that will contain the firstname, lastname, address, city, and zip fields from the customer table and include a field that will show the actual discount the customer will get. You must use the iif() function to get your result. Save the query as Chapter20_Case1_Q1.

Your result should look like:

firstname	lastname	address	city	state	zip	CouponDiscount
John	Demarco	11 Lark Street	New York	NY	12189	20%
Mary	Demania	12 Madison Ave	New York	NY	12189	20%
George	Demers	23 New Scotland Ave	New York	NY	12189	20%
Phillip	Demetriou	22 Academy Road	New York	NY	12189	20%
Andrew	Demichele	14 Glandel Ave	New York	NY	12189	20%

(201 row(s) returned)

2. Create the same outcome as in question 1 but using the case() function this time. Save the query as Chapter20_Case1_Q2.

Your result should look like:

firstname	lastname	address	city	state	zip	CouponDiscount
John	Demarco	11 Lark Street	New York	NY	12189	20%
Mary	Demania	12 Madison Ave	New York	NY	12189	20%
George	Demers	23 New Scotland Ave	New York	NY	12189	20%
Phillip	Demetriou	22 Academy Road	New York	NY	12189	20%
Andrew	Demichele	14 Glandel Ave	New York	NY	12189	20%

(201 row(s) returned)

3. The management wants to extend a special bonus to employees based on seniority. Employees with 5 years or less in the company will receive $2500, between five and ten years $5,000, and beyond 10 years $7500. Create a new query that includes the firstname, lastname, title, dateofhire fields as well as one additional field to show the associated bonus. Save the query as Chapter20_Case1_Q3. HINT: use the datediff() function in the following way datediff(yyyy, dateofhire, GetDate()) to find the difference in years between today's date and the date the employee was hired. See chapter 26 for more information on date functions.

Your result should look like:

firstname	lastname	title	dateofhire	Bonus
John	Anderson	Sales Reppresentative	1999-01-01	$7,500
Mary	Teall	Sales Director	2000-06-12	$7,500
George	Spicer	Assitant Director of Sales	2004-05-15	$5,000
Phillip	Zensons	Sales Reppresentative	2001-06-10	$7,500
Andrew	Simmons	Account Manager	2006-05-11	$5,000

(10 row(s) returned)

4. For the next two days a new pricing promotion will be extended to customers. Specifically, for the products with ProductID = 2, 15, 17, and 19 a 20% discount will be extended. For all the other products a standard 10% discount will be given. Create a new query that will include the ProductName and updated ProductUnitPrice from the products table. Save the query as Chapter20_Case1_Q4.

Your result should look like:

ProductName	ProductUnitPrice
Almonds, Hickory Smoked - 12 oz. Bag	31.50000
Almonds, Roasted and Salted - 18 oz. Bag	17.60000
Banana Chips - 20 oz. Bag	24.30000
Berry Cherry in 8 oz. Bag	27.00000
California Original Pistachios - 1 lb. Bag	26.10000

(70 row(s) returned)

5. At the marketing department they need a report that will list the number of customers in "big" and "small" cities in the states of NY, CA, and TX. "Big" cities are considered to be the cities of New York, Los Angeles, and Houston. Every other city in those states is considered to be a "small" city. The results need to be crosstabbed by state. Create a new query on the customers table that satisfies the marketing people request and save it as Chapter20_Case1_Q5. Hint: Enclose the field state in brackets such as [state] so that the SQL engine does not confuse it for a system keyword.

Your result should look like:

NumberOfCustomers	NY	CA	TX
Big cities	27	31	12
Small Cities	4	17	13

(2 row(s) returned)

Chapter 20 Case 2:

Start SQL Server Management Studio. For each of the questions in this case you need to create a new query (Ctrl-N) and name it as per the instructions in each question. Submit your work to your instructor as one text file that contains all SQL statements or as per your instructor's directions.

1. For the next couple of days the products California Original Pistachios - 1 lb. Bag, Choice Apricots - 16 oz. Bag, and Cran Raisin Mix in 17 oz. are on sale with a generous discount of 20%. The sales people are asking for a new product catalog to reflect these discounts which will be valid for only two days. Create a new query that includes the fields ProductID, ProductName, QuantityPerUnit, and the calculated field you need from the products table and satisfies the sales people request. Order the results by ProductID ascending. Save the query as Chapter20_Case2_Q1. You must use the logical iif() function. Hint: use the IN operator within the iif() function.

    Your result should look like:

ProductID	ProductName	QuantityPerUnit	NewProductPrice
1	Almonds, Hickory Smoked - 12 oz. Bag	12	35.00000
2	Almonds, Roasted and Salted - 18 oz. ...	12	22.00000
3	Banana Chips - 20 oz. Bag	12	27.00000
4	Berry Cherry in 8 oz. Bag	15	30.00000
5	California Original Pistachios - 1 lb. Bag	15	23.20000

    (70 row(s) returned)

2. Achieve the exact same results as in question 1 by using the case() function this time. Save the query as Chapter20_Case2_Q2.

    Your result should look like:

ProductID	ProductName	QuantityPerUnit	NewProductPrice
1	Almonds, Hickory Smoked - 12 oz. Bag	12	35.00000
2	Almonds, Roasted and Salted - 18 oz. ...	12	22.00000
3	Banana Chips - 20 oz. Bag	12	27.00000
4	Berry Cherry in 8 oz. Bag	15	30.00000
5	California Original Pistachios - 1 lb. Bag	15	23.20000

    (70 row(s) returned)

3. The marketing people are initiating a new campaign so that the company can get rid of high inventory items. In this respect, create a new product catalog with the following discounts: 20% discount for products with units in stock below 20, 25% discount for products with units in stock greater than 20 and

less than 30, 30% discount for products with units in stock greater than 30 and less than 40, and 35% discount for products with units in stock greater than 40. Create a new query that includes the fields ProductName, UnitsInStock, and the calculated field you need from the products table and satisfies the marketing people request. Order the results by ProductID ascending. Save the query as Chapter20_Case2_Q3.

Your result should look like:

ProductName	UnitsInStock	NewProductPrice
Almonds, Hickory Smoked - 12 oz. Bag	40	22.750000
Almonds, Roasted and Salted - 18 oz. Bag	32	15.400000
Banana Chips - 20 oz. Bag	25	20.250000
Berry Cherry in 8 oz. Bag	50	19.500000
California Original Pistachios - 1 lb. Bag	35	20.300000

(70 row(s) returned)

4. The marketing people are amazingly happy from your report in question 3. However, someone from replenishment pointed out that the report though amazing does not make perfect business sense. They propose we need to add to the units in stock the units we have on order to arrive at what we actually have in inventory even though the units on order are not physically in yet. Consequently, recreate the query in question 3 summing the units in stock and the units on order to provide the corresponding discounts. The new query should include the fields ProductName, QuantityPerUnit, UnitsInStock, UnitsOnOrder, and the the calculated field you need from the products table and satisfies the replenishing people request. Save the query as Chapter20_Case2_Q4.

Your result should look like:

ProductName	QuantityPerUnit	UnitsInStock	UnitsOnOrder	NewProductPrice
Almonds, Hickory Smoked - 12 oz. Bag	12	40	5	22.750000
Almonds, Roasted and Salted - 18 oz....	12	32	0	15.400000
Banana Chips - 20 oz. Bag	12	25	0	20.250000
Berry Cherry in 8 oz. Bag	15	50	0	19.500000
California Original Pistachios - 1 lb. Bag	15	35	0	20.300000

(70 row(s) returned)

5. The management of the company is asking for a report identical to that in question 4. However, this time they want to see the actual discount extended (for example 20%, 25%, 30%) for each product instead of the new price of the product. Create a new query that satisfies the management's request and save it as Chapter20_Case2_Q5.

Your result should look like:

Product Name	Quantity Per Unit	Units In Stock	Units On Order	Discount Extended
Almonds, Hickory Smoked - 12 oz. Bag	12	40	5	35%
Almonds, Roasted and Salted - 18 oz...	12	32	0	30%
Banana Chips - 20 oz. Bag	12	25	0	25%
Berry Cherry in 8 oz. Bag	15	50	0	35%
California Original Pistachios - 1 lb. Bag	15	35	0	30%

(70 row(s) returned)

CHAPTER 21
UNION OPERATIONS

The primary goal of the UNION statement is to combine records from multiple data sets. In this respect, you can merge records from two or more SQL statements, from a SQL statement and a table, or from two or more tables. In contrast to popular belief, you can combine records with fields of different data types and sizes in SQL Server. In addition, the fields do not have to be similar in content or name! The number of fields, however, does need to be the same. The UNION operator will return no duplicate records, while the UNION ALL operator will return all records from the combined data sets.

The UNION operator is not just a dull SQL statement that we use to combine records from multiple tables. You will see throughout this chapter that you can combine it with clauses like WHERE, ORDER BY, and GROUP BY, operators like IN, NOT IN, and BETWEEN, and even subqueries for powerful results. Understanding the UNION operator will enable you to perform operations and achieve results that other database users could not even imagine possible.

In this chapter, we will work with two customer tables under the assumption that we have two distribution centers with one as our main center and the other as a regional center. For the most part, customers order from one of the two distribution centers. However, just to complicate our scenario a bit, we do have customers who will order from both. Consequently, we need to pay attention to how customer records are merged in order to exclude duplicate ones.

We will use two tables: The tbls_customers_un1 table with 201 records and the tbls_customers_un2 table with 20 records. Fifteen of the customers in the tbls_customers_un2 table are included in the tbls_customers_un1 table as well, while five are unique customers. The similarities or dissimilarities of data among tables are important for UNION statements, as we shall see in a second.

183.   The UNION operator with similar fields
Combine unique customer records from two datasets
Discussion:
In this example, we use a simple UNION statement to combine customer records from the two distribution centers. Notice that the number of customers returned is 206. This is because we combined 201 customers from the first table and 20 from the second. Since 15 customers are identical in both tables, and we use the UNION operator, we will only get 206 unique customers. If we used the UNION ALL operator, we would get 221 records.

Code:

```
SELECT lastname, firstname, city, state, zip
FROM tbls_customers_un1
UNION
SELECT lastname, firstname, city, state, zip
FROM tbls_customers_un2
```

Result:

lastname	firstname	city	state	zip
Ackerman	Nicholas	Dallas	TX	52347
Allen	Alfred	New York	NY	12189
Ames	Pindar	New York	NY	45357
Andersen	Thomas	Orlando	FL	89754

```
(206 row(s) returned)
```

184.   The UNION operator with dissimilar fields

Combine customer and supplier records from two different tables

Discussion:

Here, we demonstrate the ability of the UNION statement to combine data from two dissimilar tables. Notice the different field names from the customer and supplier tables. In addition, check the numbers. We get all of the customers from the customers table (201) and all of the suppliers (10) from the suppliers table.

Code:

```
SELECT lastname, firstname, city, state, zip
FROM customers
UNION
SELECT companyname, contactname, city, state, zip
FROM suppliers
```

Result:

lastname	firstname	city	state	zip
Ackerman	Nicholas	Dallas	TX	52347
Allen	Alfred	New York	NY	12189
American ...	John Marrey	Boston	MA	22459
American I...	Maria Hopkins	Boston	MA	22459

```
(211 row(s) returned)
```

185.   Using multiple UNION operators

Combine records from two customer tables and a supplier table

Discussion:

We can use UNION to merge records from multiple data sources. In this example, we employ two UNION statements to merge data from three data sources. Notice that while the first two SELECT statements contain identical fields, the third one uses different ones. Also, we must pay attention to our numbers. The first table (tbls_customers_un1) contains 201 records, the second (tbls_customers_un2) 20, and the third (suppliers) 10. We have a total of 231 records, but our result set contains only 216. This is correct since we have 15 identical customers. Consequently, the final result is 231-15 = 216 records.

Code:

```
SELECT lastname, firstname, city, state, zip
FROM tbls_customers_un1
UNION
SELECT lastname, firstname, city, state, zip
FROM tbls_customers_un2
UNION
SELECT companyname, contactname, city, state, zip
FROM suppliers
```

Result:

lastname	firstname	city	state	zip
Ackerman	Nicholas	Dallas	TX	52347
Allen	Alfred	New York	NY	12189
American ...	John Marrey	Boston	MA	22459
American ...	Maria Hopkins	Boston	MA	22459

(216 row(s) returned)

186. The UNION ALL operator

Combine customer records from two data sources and allow duplicates to appear

Discussion:

The UNION operator will exclude duplicate records. The UNION ALL operator will include duplicate records. Have a look at the number of records returned. In this case, it should be 201 + 20 for a total of 221, and this is exactly what we get. (Remember we have 201 records in the tbls_customer_un1 table and 20 in the tbls_customers_un2 table).

Code:

```
SELECT lastname, firstname, city, state, zip
FROM tbls_customers_un1
UNION ALL
SELECT lastname, firstname, city, state, zip
FROM tbls_customers_un2
```

Result:

lastname	firstname	city	state	zip
Demarco	John	New York	NY	12189
Demania	Mary	New York	NY	12189
Demers	George	New York	NY	12189
Demetriou	Phillip	New York	NY	12189

(221 row(s) returned)

187. Using UNION with ORDER BY

Sort customer records correctly when using UNION

Discussion:

The ORDER BY clause should be used at the end of the whole SQL statement when using UNION operators, not after the individual SQL statements.

255

Code:

```
SELECT lastname, firstname, city, state, zip
FROM tbls_customers_un1
UNION
SELECT lastname, firstname, city, state, zip
FROM tbls_customers_un2
ORDER BY lastname
```

Result:

lastname	firstname	city	state	zip
Ackerman	Nicholas	Dallas	TX	52347
Allen	Alfred	New York	NY	12189
Ames	Pindar	New York	NY	45357
Andersen	Thomas	Orlando	FL	89754

```
(206 row(s) returned)
```

188.   Using UNION with WHERE

Create customer lists with filtering criteria using WHERE

Discussion:

In this example, notice we use the WHERE clause in each individual SELECT statement. We can absolutely use multiple WHERE clauses to get exactly what we need from the individual data sets. In this example, we wanted to get only customers from New York from the first table and customers from Texas from the second.

Code:

```
SELECT lastname, firstname, city, state, zip
FROM tbls_customers_un1
WHERE state = 'NY'
UNION
SELECT lastname, firstname, city, state, zip
FROM tbls_customers_un2
WHERE state ='TX'
ORDER BY state
```

Result:

lastname	firstname	city	state	zip
Allen	Alfred	New York	NY	12189
Ames	Pindar	New York	NY	45357
Anderson	Peter	New York	NY	12189
Anthopolis	Ricky	New York	NY	12189

```
(31 row(s) returned)
```

189. A trick with UNION and the aggregate function count()

Display total customer numbers dynamically

Discussion:

Here, we use a trick to display all of the customer records from the tbls_customers_un1 table and a total row at the end of the recordset. We can do this by using a single SQL statement and UNION. Notice in the second SQL statement we use quotes instead of fields to satisfy the UNION requirement of having the same number of fields in both statements. In addition, notice that we start the name of the first field of the second SQL statement with a "z", which has no other meaning but to force the total row to appear last in the recordset since z is the last letter in the alphabet. Finally, for our trick to succeed, we need to use the ORDER BY clause on the first field of the first SQL statement.

Code:

```
SELECT lastname, firstname, city, state, zip, CustomerID
FROM tbls_customers_un1
UNION
SELECT
'zTotal customer count', '', '', '', '', Count(CustomerID)
FROM tbls_customers_un1
ORDER BY lastname ASC
```

Result:

lastname	firstname	city	state	zip	CustomerID
Zensons	Charles	Los Angeles	CA	94851	18
Zentons	Lauren	Los Angeles	CA	94851	21
Zinter	Stephen	Philadelphia	PA	56789	48
zTotal customer count					201

```
(202 row(s) returned)
```

190. Using UNION with SELECT INTO

Combine customer data from multiple tables and save the combined dataset dynamically in a different table

Discussion:

This is a very useful way to get data from multiple data sources and save it in one different table. We can use SELECT INTO to pull this off. Pay attention to the number of records. It has to be 206 (201 from the first table and 5 from the second) since we are asking for unique records to be moved. If we want to move everything, we can use UNION ALL and duplicate records will be included.

Code:

```
SELECT lastname, firstname, city, state, zip INTO Temp_UnionTable1
FROM tbls_customers_un1
UNION
SELECT lastname, firstname, city, state, zip
FROM tbls_customers_un2
```

Result:

```
(206 row(s) affected)
```

191.   Using UNION with INSERT INTO

Combine records from multiple data sources, filter them, and append them into an existing table

Discussion:

There are occasions in which we need to combine data from multiple sources (tables or queries) and append it in an existing table. We can use INSERT INTO and UNION to accomplish these tasks. The table "TempTable_Union_InsertInto" used in this example needs to exist before we run the SQL statement. Notice in the CREATE TABLE statement below the usage of the identity specification so that the values of the primary key start at 1 and go up automatically by 1.

Code1:

```
CREATE TABLE TempTable_Union_InsertInto
(
CustomerID int PRIMARY KEY identity (1,1),
lastname varchar (50),
firstname varchar (50),
city varchar (50),
state varchar (50),
zip varchar (10)
);
```

Notice in the code below how we use the WHERE clause to filter the records we want to transfer.

Code2:

```
INSERT INTO TempTable_Union_InsertInto (lastname, firstname, city, state, zip)
SELECT lastname, firstname, city, state, zip
FROM tbls_customers_un1
WHERE state = 'NY'
UNION
SELECT lastname, firstname, city, state, zip
FROM tbls_customers_un2
WHERE state = 'NY'
```

Result:

(36 row(s) affected)

192.   Using UNION with GROUP BY within each SELECT statement

Combine customer data from all distribution centers, count the totals, and show in the view the center they came from

Discussion:

Here, we use a number of tricks and functions to arrive at the result we need. First, notice we use a GROUP BY clause in both SQL statements to group our customers by state. Second, we use the count() function to calculate the number of customers by state. Third, we create a field of our own ("Main" and "Regional") in the beginning of each of the two SQL statements to display customer numbers according to the distribution center they belong. Finally, we use the ORDER BY clause to sort results by state for easy comparison of numbers.

Code:

```
SELECT 'Main' As DisCenter, state, count(CustomerID) AS Customers
FROM customers
GROUP BY state
UNION
SELECT 'Regional' As Center, state, Count(CustomerID) AS Customers
FROM tbls_customers_un2
GROUP BY state
ORDER BY STATE
```

Result:

DisCenter	state	Customers
Main	AZ	13
Main	CA	48
Main	CO	13
Main	DC	12
Main	FL	21
Main	MA	14
Main	NY	31
Regional	NY	20

```
(11 row(s) returned)
```

193. Using UNION with two subqueries to filter records for aggregations

Compare customer numbers from two distribution centers

Discussion:

Our goal this time is to compare customer numbers from the two distribution centers, but we only want to see states from the "Main" center for which corresponding states exist in the "regional" center. As "main" center we consider customers from the table "tbls_customers_un1" and as a regional center we consider customers from the table "tbls_customers_un2"

To achieve the desired comparison, we need a subquery in the first SELECT statement. The subquery in the first SELECT statement will search for matching states in the table in the second SELECT statement.

Code:

```
SELECT 'Main' As DisCenter, state, count(CustomerID) AS Customers
FROM tbls_customers_un1
WHERE State in (SELECT state from tbls_customers_un2)
GROUP BY state
UNION
SELECT 'Regional' As Center, state, Count(CustomerID) AS Customers
FROM tbls_customers_un2
GROUP BY state
ORDER BY STATE
```

Result:

DisCenter	state	Customers
Main	NY	31
Regional	NY	20

`(2 row(s) returned)`

194.   Trick for knowing which table the row came from when using UNION

Discussion:

In certain occasions with UNION operators it is useful to know the source table for each record in the result set. In this example, we combine data from the suppliers and customers table but we want to know who is a customer and who is a supplier. To achieve this we simply add a text entry in each of the SQL statements used with the UNION operator.

Code:

```
SELECT lastname, firstname, city, state, zip, 'customer' AS TypeOfContact
FROM customers
UNION
SELECT companyname, contactname, city, state, zip, 'supplier'
FROM suppliers
```

Result:

lastname	firstname	city	state	zip	TypeOfContact
Ackerman	Nicholas	Dallas	TX	52347	customer
Allen	Alfred	New York	NY	12189	customer
American Foods,....	John Marrey	Boston	MA	22459	supplier
American Imports...	Maria Hopkins	Boston	MA	22459	supplier
America's Greate...	Andrew Daves	New York	NY	12189	supplier

`(211 row(s) returned)`

CHAPTER 21 DISCUSSION QUESTIONS

1. What is the basic goal of the UNION operator?
2. Can we combine the results of a table and a query using the UNION operator?
3. When using the UNION operator to combine two or more tables, do we need to have the same number of fields?
4. When using the UNION operator to combine two or more tables, do we need to have the same data types and sizes of fields in both tables?
5. Which operator returns duplicate values? UNION or UNION ALL?
6. Can we use the ORDER BY clause with UNION and multiple SQL statements? Where should we place it in the SQL statement?
7. Can we use the WHERE clause with UNION and multiple SQL statements? Where should we place it in the SQL statement? How many WHERE clauses can we use within a UNION statement?
8. Can we use different criteria for each of the WHERE clauses used in the SQL statements combined with the UNION operator?
9. What trick can we use to indicate the source table of each record in the result of the UNION statement?
10. What difference it will make if we use the GROUP BY clause within each SQL statement with the UNION operator or if we use the GROUP BY clause outside all SQL statements with a UNION operator?

CHAPTER 21 HANDS-ON EXERCISES

Chapter 21 Case 1:
Start SQL Server Management Studio. For each of the questions in this case you need to create a new query (Ctrl-N) and name it as per the instructions in each question. Submit your work to your instructor as one text file that contains all SQL statements or as per your instructor's directions.

1. The sales people are asking for a new product catalog that will combine records from the Products and tbls_ProductsUnion tables. They also want the new catalog to contain only the ProductName field. Create a new query that satisfies the sales people request and save it as Chapter21_Case1_Q1. Why do you think the resulting recordset contains 76 records?

    Your result should look like:

productname
All-Purpose Marinade I
All-Purpose Marinade II
Almonds, Hickory Smoked - 12 oz. Bag
Almonds, Roasted and Salted - 18 oz. Bag
Apple Cinnamon Raisin Cookies

    (76 row(s) returned)

2. The sales people are back asking for a new report that will again combine the Products and tbls_ProductsUnion tables. They want the new report to contain the ProductName, SupplierID, and ProductUnitPrice fields. Create a new query that satisfies the sales people request and save it as

Chapter21_Case1_Q2. Why do you think the resulting recordset contains 80 records?

Your result should look like:

productname	SupplierID	Product Unit Price
All-Purpose Marinade I	9	29
All-Purpose Marinade II	10	39
Almonds, Hickory Smoked - 12 oz. Bag	1	35
Almonds, Roasted and Salted - 18 oz. Bag	1	22
Apple Cinnamon Raisin Cookies	7	27

(80 row(s) returned)

3. After your explanation from question 2, the sales people are explicitly asking for a new report that will combine ALL the products in the Products table with ALL the products in the tbls_ProductsUnion table. They want the new report to contain the ProductName, SupplierID, and ProductUnitPrice fields. Create a new query that satisfies the sales people request and save it as Chapter21_Case1_Q3. Why do you think the resulting recordset contains again 80 records? What is the explanation here?

Your result should look like:

productname	SupplierID	Product Unit Price
Almonds, Hickory Smoked - 12 oz. Bag	1	35
Almonds, Roasted and Salted - 18 oz. Bag	1	22
Banana Chips - 20 oz. Bag	1	27
Berry Cherry in 8 oz. Bag	1	30
California Original Pistachios - 1 lb. Bag	1	29

(80 row(s) returned)

4. The sales people are really happy with your ability to provide them with combined information. Now, they are asking for a report that will combine the products from suppliers 1, 2, and 3 from the Products table and suppliers 2, 5, and 10 from the tbls_ProductsUnion table. They want the new report to contain the ProductName, SupplierID, and ProductUnitPrice fields. They also need the report to be sorted by ProductName ascending. Create a new query that satisfies the sales people request and save it as Chapter21_Case1_Q4.

Your result should look like:

productname	SupplierID	Product Unit Price
Almonds, Hickory Smoked - 12 oz. Bag	1	35
Almonds, Roasted and Salted - 18 oz. Bag	1	22
Banana Chips - 20 oz. Bag	1	27
Berry Cherry in 8 oz. Bag	1	30
California Original Pistachios - 1 lb. Bag	1	29

(27 row(s) returned)

5. The sales people now need a report that will combine the products from suppliers 1 through 5 from the Products table and suppliers 1 through 5 from the tbls_ProductsUnion table. They want the new report to contain the ProductName, SupplierID, and ProductUnitPrice fields. They also need the report to be sorted

by ProductName ascending. Create a new query that satisfies the sales people request and save it as Chapter21_Case1_Q5.

Your result should look like:

productname	SupplierID	ProductUnitPrice
Almonds, Hickory Smoked - 12 oz. Bag	1	35
Almonds, Roasted and Salted - 18 oz. Bag	1	22
Banana Chips - 20 oz. Bag	1	27
Banana Glazed Chips 35 lb. bag	1	30
Berry Cherry in 8 oz. Bag	1	30

(44 row(s) returned)

Chapter 21 Case 2:
Start SQL Server Management Studio. For each of the questions in this case you need to create a new query (Ctrl-N) and name it as per the instructions in each question. Submit your work to your instructor as one text file that contains all SQL statements or as per your instructor's directions.

1. The marketing people are asking for a list of contact information from Customers, Suppliers, and SalesReps so they can send out an end of the year thank you note. Create a new query that includes the fields lastname, firstname, city, state, zip from the Customers and SalesReps tables and the fields companyname, contactname, city, state, zip from the Suppliers table. Save the query as Chapter21_Case2_Q1.

Your result should look like:

lastname	firstname	city	state	zip
Ackerman	Nicholas	Dallas	TX	52347
Allen	Alfred	New York	NY	12189
American Foods, LLC.	John Marrey	Boston	MA	22459
American Imports Inc.	Maria Hopkins	Boston	MA	22459
America's Greatest Snacks, Inc.	Andrew Daves	New York	NY	12189

(221 row(s) returned)

2. The marketing people are back asking you to create a new table that contains all the records from question 1. Desing a new query which creates a new table with all the records from the Customers, Suppliers, and SalesReps tables and the fields specified in question 1. Save the query as Chapter21_Case2_Q2.

Your result should look like:
(221 row(s) affected)

3. The inventory department asks for a report that will list the number of products by stock keeping unit (sku) in the Products_Local and Products_regional tables. They want the report to differentiate between product units in the local warehouse and the regional warehouse. Create a new query that satisfies the inventory people request and save it as Chapter21_Case2_Q3.

Your result should look like:

Location	sku	NumberOfProducts
Local	ADSE 2345	1
Local	ADST 2345	1
Local	ASDT-3456	1
Local	ADSD 2345	1
Local	ADSL 2345	1

(20 row(s) returned)

4. The inventory people liked the report you created for them in question 3. Now, they want the same report of product units by sku without however differentiating between local and regional warehouses. Create a new query that satisfies the inventory people request and save it as Chapter21_Case2_Q4.

Your result should look like:

sku	NumberOfProducts
ADSE 2345	1
ADST 2345	1
ASDT-3456	1
ADSD 2345	1
ADSL 2345	1

(20 row(s) returned)

5. The director of inventory is super happy with the reports you provided. They have a final request. They need a report identical to the one in question 4 with the following additions: First, they need to include only products with ProductUnitPrices between $20 and $35. Second, they want to include products with a total count by sku of more than 1. Create a new query that satisfies the inventory people request and save it as Chapter21_Case2_Q5.

Your result should look like:

sku	NumberOfProducts
ADST 2345	2
ASDT-3456	3
DKLS-4732	4
EPDA-2345	4
KTRT-4589	6

(9 row(s) returned)

CHAPTER 22
DUPLICATE, ORPHANED, and UNRELATED RECORDS

This chapter focuses on four specific learning goals: The identification of duplicate, orphaned, related, and unrelated records. Orphaned and duplicate records will affect your database integrity, while related and unrelated records will affect your business decisions.

Orphaned records occur when there are no primary key values for corresponding foreign key values in a one-to-many relationship. For example, in a relationship between customers and orders, you might have orders without corresponding customers. This scenario can occur if referential integrity for this relationship is not set (see chapter 4). This will allow a user to delete a customer without any warning that there are existing orders for this customer. Alternatively, it might allow a user to enter an order without first entering a customer.

We need to have referential integrity on in order to avoid the occurrence of orphaned records. Yet, what happens when we already have orphaned records in the database? There are two solutions with orphaned records. The first is to delete orphaned records from the database which means we first have to find them. In this chapter, there will be plenty of examples to locate orphaned records. The second scenario might occur if we need to keep orphaned records such as past orders in the database. In this case, we have to enter their corresponding customer information. In any case, we must be able to retrieve orphaned records.

A second common occurrence in business databases is duplicate records. In this chapter, you will learn several techniques to isolate and deal with duplicate records, which are not, by the way, synonymous with identical records. Two customer records might be duplicates even if they have the same name but different address information. So, you will learn how to find duplicate records based on the values of one, two, or multiple fields.

A third case involves unrelated records. For example, we might have customers in the database who have not placed an order for quite some time. These customers have no related orders in the orders table. This is a business and not a database problem. However, we need to act, and we have two choices for inactive customers. The first is to use a marketing campaign to entice them to start buying again. If this is not feasible, we might want to delete them from the database or move them to a historical customer table. To delete or move these records, we need to be able to find them first.

The fourth scenario is that of related records. We might want to know how many customers placed orders over a period of a year, month, or quarter. In other words, we want to know how many customers have related order entries in the orders table. In this chapter, you will learn how to quickly identify these customers to increase the effectiveness of your business operations.

Finally, so that you can check your numbers, you will use the table named tbls_orders, which contains a number of orphaned and duplicate records. Specifically, the records with OrderID = 8, 45, 254, 820, 993 are duplicate records. In addition, there are two records with null OrderIDs, which I put in to make our work a bit more complicated.

SECTION 1 – DUPLICATE RECORDS

195. Find duplicate records in a table based on the values of one field

Find duplicate customer orders based on the value of the orderID

Discussion:

In this example, we are looking for records in the tbls_Orders table that have the same value for the OrderID field. We also use the count(*) function to calculate the number of duplicate records for each OrderID value. Remember that this example will give us duplicate field values and not necessarily duplicate records. Though the OrderID values are the same, the rest of the fields in the returned records might have different values. Still, it is very useful to know how to search for duplicate values on one field. As you can see from the result set, two records have null values for the OrderID. In addition, there are two instances of duplicate records for OrderIDs with values 8, 45, 254, and 820. Finally, the OrderId with value 993 appears in three records in the table.

Code:

```
SELECT OrderID, Count(*) AS NumberofDuplicates
FROM tbls_Orders
GROUP BY OrderID
HAVING count(*)>1
```

Result:

OrderID	NumberofDuplicates
NULL	2
8	2
45	2
254	2
820	2
993	3

(6 row(s) returned)

196. Find duplicate records in a table based on the values of two fields

Find duplicate customer orders based on the values of OrderID and CustomerID

Discussion:

In this example, we are looking for duplicate records based on the values of OrderID and CustomerID. If the values of the OrderID and CustomerID are the same for at least two records, they will appear in the result set as duplicates. In addition, the count(*) function is used to calculate the number of records with identical OrderID and CustomerID values. We can replace the two fields used in this example with any fields on which we would like to look for duplicate values. Keep in mind that while two records might have matching values for two fields, this does not necessarily mean that they have identical values for the rest of their fields. This code will allow us to locate potential duplicate records based on the values of two fields. We need to examine the individual records to verify that they are indeed duplicates.

Code:

```
SELECT OrderID, CustomerID, Count(*) AS NumberofDuplicates
FROM tbls_Orders
GROUP BY OrderID, CustomerID
HAVING count(*)>1
```

Result:

OrderID	CustomerID	NumberofDuplicates
820	46	2
8	71	2
45	93	2
993	99	3
254	198	2

(5 row(s) returned)

197. Find duplicate records in a table based on the values of multiple fields

Find duplicate customer orders based on the values of multiple fields

Discussion:

In this example, we are looking for duplicate records based on the values of eight fields. In other words, if the values of eight fields of at least two records are identical, those records will appear as duplicates. Of course, with eight identical values, two records will most probably be duplicate entries. Notice that there are two identical records for OrderIDs with values 8, 45, 254, and 820, while there are three identical records for OrderID = 993.

Code:

```
SELECT Count(*) AS NumberofDuplicates, OrderID, CustomerID, SalesRepID, ShipperID,
OrderDate, RequiredDate, ShippedDate, ShippingCost
FROM tbls_Orders
GROUP BY OrderID, CustomerID, SalesRepID, ShipperID, OrderDate, RequiredDate, ShippedDate,
ShippingCost
HAVING count(*)>1
```

Result:

NumberofDuplicates	OrderID	CustomerID	SalesRepID	ShipperID	OrderDate
2	8	71	3	1	2014-04-01
2	45	93	1	3	2012-10-23
2	254	198	3	2	2012-07-15
2	820	46	8	1	2014-09-04
3	993	99	10	2	2012-10-14

(5 row(s) returned)

198. Find and display all duplicate records in a table

Find and display all duplicate records in the Orders table

Discussion:

In the previous examples, we were able to find duplicate records in the table but display only one instance from each in the result set. There are cases, however, in which we will want to display all instances from all duplicate records. We can achieve this goal by using a subquery. In this example, we will display all instances of all duplicate records based on the values of the OrderID field, or put it another way, based on the values of one field.

Code:
SELECT *
FROM tbls_Orders WHERE OrderID IN(
SELECT OrderID
FROM tbls_Orders
GROUP BY OrderID
HAVING count(*)>1)
ORDER BY OrderID

Result:

OrderID	CustomerID	SalesRepID	ShipperID	OrderDate
8	71	3	1	2014-04-01
8	71	3	1	2014-04-01
45	93	1	3	2012-10-23
45	93	1	3	2012-10-23
254	198	3	2	2012-07-15
254	198	3	2	2012-07-15
820	46	8	1	2014-09-04
820	46	8	1	2014-09-04
993	99	10	2	2012-10-14
993	99	10	2	2012-10-14
993	99	10	2	2012-10-14

(11 row(s) returned)

SECTION 2 – ORPHANED RECORDS

199. What are orphaned records and how to deal with them

In the figure below, there are five orders in the Orders table with OrderIDs from 1 to 5. For the first four orders, there are corresponding customers in the Customers table. For orders with OrderID=5, there does not exist a corresponding customer in the database. This is an order that belongs to no one. The record in the Orders table with OrderID=5 is called an orphaned record.

CUSTOMERS		ORDERS		
CustID	**Name**	**OrderID**	**CustID**	**OrderDate**
1	John	1	2	9/10/2009
2	Mary	2	2	10/10/2010
3	George	3	1	11/10/2010
4	Stacy	4	3	11/11/2010
		5	7	11/15/2010

A reason for this might be that when the database was created and relationships established, referential integrity was not set. The immediate consequence is that a user of the database deleted the customer with CustomerID=7 either by mistake or on purpose. Although the customer record is gone, his or her orders are still in the database, useless and compromising data integrity. Another reason might be that a user received an order from a new customer. The correct process would have been to check if the customer existed and then enter the order. If referential integrity is off a representative can enter an order without an existing customer. To avoid orphaned records, referential integrity should be set for a relationship between two tables.

200. Find orphaned records using a subquery

Find orders for which there are no customers using a subquery
Discussion:
Let us assume that we want to set on referential integrity for the relationship between the Customers and Orders tables (chapter 4). If SQL Server does not allow us to do this, our first action should be to look for orphaned records in the Orders table or in the table in the many side of the relationship. We can use the code below to do just that. As you can see in the result set, there are three orders (OrderID= 1500, 1501, and 1502) that came up as orphaned records. This in turn means that the customers with CustomerID values of 250, 251, and 252 do not exist in the Customers table. If we open the customers table, we will not find any customers with these CustomerID values.

Code:
```
SELECT *
FROM tbls_Orders
WHERE CustomerID
NOT IN (SELECT CustomerID from Customers)
```

Result:

OrderID	CustomerID	SalesRepID	ShipperID	OrderDate
1500	250	11	2	2012-01-20
1501	251	12	2	2012-11-18
1502	252	14	3	2013-02-05

(3 row(s) returned)

201. Find orphaned records using a join

Find orders for which there are no customers using a join

Discussion:

There is a second and faster way to locate orphaned records in a table. Specifically, we can use a LEFT join (chapter 29) between Customers and tbls_Orders to locate any orphaned records in the tbls_Orders table. As you can see, the result set is identical to the one using a subquery in the previous example.

Code:
SELECT *
FROM tbls_Orders
LEFT JOIN Customers ON tbls_Orders.CustomerID = Customers.CustomerID
WHERE Customers.CustomerID Is Null

Result:

OrderID	CustomerID	SalesRepID	ShipperID	OrderDate
1500	250	11	2	2012-01-20
1501	251	12	2	2012-11-18
1502	252	14	3	2013-02-05

(3 row(s) returned)

202. Delete orphaned records using a subquery

Delete orders for which there are no customers using a subquery

Discussion:

We can use a subquery to find and delete orphaned records in one step. In the code below, we use the DELETE statement to delete orders in the tbls_Orders1 table for which there are no customers in the customers table. The subquery will isolate CustomerID values in the tbls_Orders1 table for which there are no corresponding CustomerID values in the Customers table. Notice that the CustomerID is the primary key in the Customers table and the foreign key in the tbls_Orders1 table. In this example we will first create the tbls_Orders1 table which is an exact copy of the tbls_Orders table.

Code1:
SELECT *
INTO tbls_Orders1
FROM tbls_Orders

Result:
(1008 row(s) affected)

Code2:
DELETE
FROM tbls_Orders1
WHERE CustomerID
NOT IN (SELECT CustomerID FROM Customers)

Result:
```
(3 row(s) affected)
```

203.   Delete orphaned records using a join

Delete orders for which there are no customers using a join

Discussion:

We can also use a LEFT join to isolate and delete orphaned records in a table. Notice the WHERE clause in the code below which looks for CustomerID values in the LEFT JOIN with a null value, i.e. CustomerID or foreign key values in the tbls_Orders2 table for which no primary key values exist in the customers table. Joins work faster than subqueries especially on indexed fields, and while they are more complicated, their use might well be justified in cases with many records. However, this does not mean that a join will always be faster than a subquery. The bottom line is that we have the option to isolate and delete orphaned records using joins. In this example we first create the tbls_Orders2 table, an exact copy of the tbls_Orders table.

Code1:
```
SELECT *
INTO tbls_Orders2
FROM tbls_Orders
```

Result:
```
(1008 row(s) affected)
```

Code2:
```
DELETE tbls_Orders2
FROM tbls_Orders2
LEFT JOIN Customers ON tbls_Orders2.CustomerID = Customers.CustomerID
WHERE (Customers.CustomerID Is Null)
```

Result:
```
(3 row(s) affected)
```

SECTION 3 – UNRELATED RECORDS

The knowledge to locate unrelated records is fundamental in database applications. It allows us to reply to questions such as: How many customers have not placed any orders? How many students have not taken classes this semester? What sales reps did not have sales last week? So, we are looking for customers who have no orders (maybe over a period of time) knowing that there is a one-to-many relationship between customers and orders. Keep in mind that finding customers without orders is not a problematic situation when it comes to database integrity; it is simply a business fact. However, finding orders without customers represents a database integrity problem, and we call these orphaned records.

204.   Find unrelated records using a subquery

Find customers for whom there are no orders using a subquery

Discussion:

In this example, we use a subquery with the NOT IN operator to find customers who have not placed any orders. Technically, we are looking for records in the customers table that have no related records in the Orders table. In other words, we are looking for CustomerID values (1, 2, 3 etc.) in the Customers table, which do not

271

exist in the Orders table. Put it yet in another way, we are looking for primary key values (CustomerID) in the customers table with no corresponding foreign key values (CustomerIDs) in the Orders table.   The code appears below:

Code:
SELECT *
FROM Customers
WHERE CustomerID
NOT IN (SELECT CustomerID from tbls_Orders)

Result:

CustomerID	First Name	Last Name	Address	City	State	Zip	Country
19	Erin	Erin	28 Karrie Terrace	Los Angeles	CA	94851	USA
37	Allan	Cimo	24 Crestwood CT	New York	NY	45357	USA
40	Kelly	Costa	45 Sixth Ave	Philadelphia	PA	56789	USA
66	Arnold	Webster	53 Southern Blvd	Miami	FL	88987	USA

```
(11 row(s) returned)
```

205.   Find unrelated records using a subquery and criteria

Find customers for whom there are no orders using date criteria

Discussion:

In the previous example, you learned how to identify customers without orders for all sales years in the database. This is excellent knowledge, but in actual business practice, you will need some additional criteria to derive insightful pieces of information. For example, we might want to know what customers have not placed any orders in the last year, quarter, month, or even week. Alternatively, we might want to know what customers from NY have not placed any orders in the last two months. It is possible to use criteria to extract these amazing pieces of information fast and efficiently. In this example, we are looking for customers who have not placed any orders in 2013. As you can see from the result set, we have 36 such customers. Of course, we can use the vast arsenal of date functions in the upcoming chapter 26 to extract any time period we feel we need to look into.

Code:
SELECT *
FROM Customers
WHERE CustomerID NOT IN
(SELECT CustomerID
FROM tbls_Orders
WHERE OrderDate BETWEEN '2013/1/1' AND '2013/12/31')

Result:

CustomerID	First Name	Last Name	Address	City
2	Mary	Demania	12 Madison Ave	New York
6	Michael	Demizio	23 Grove Rd	New York
19	Erin	Erin	28 Karrie Terrace	Los Angeles
28	Colin	Bousher	14 Hurst Ave	Los Angeles

```
(36 row(s) returned)
```

SECTION 4 – RELATED RECORDS

206.   Find related records using a subquery

Find customers who placed orders

Discussion:

There will be occasions in your work in which you will need to find related records. In other words, you might want to find customers who placed orders, suppliers who sent raw materials, or products that sold some units. In this example, we are looking for customers who placed at least one order. Since we know from previous examples that out of the 201 customers, 11 never placed any orders, we would expect to retrieve 190 records. This is exactly the result from the following code. Remember that we can add additional criteria to identify customers who placed orders in certain periods such as years, quarters, or months, as we will see in the next example.

Code:

```
SELECT *
FROM Customers
WHERE CustomerID
IN (SELECT CustomerID from tbls_Orders)
```

Result:

CustomerID	FirstName	LastName	Address	City
1	John	Demarco	11 Lark Street	New York
2	Mary	Demania	12 Madison Ave	New York
3	George	Demers	23 New Scotlan...	New York
4	Phillip	Demetriou	22 Academy Ro...	New York
5	Andrew	Demichele	14 Glandel Ave	New York

(190 row(s) returned)

207.   Find related records using a subquery and criteria

Find customers who placed orders during the 4th quarter of 2013

Discussion:

In this scenario, we are looking for customers who placed orders in the 4th quarter of 2013. Notice that we use two date functions, datepart() and year(), to extract the quarter and year out of the OrderDate field respectively. Using the subquery and the two date functions, we are able to extract exactly the information we need about our customers. As we can see from the result set there are 82 customers who have not placed any orders in the fourth quarter of 2013. This list of customers can definitely help in our marketing and promotional campaigns, and we can retrieve it in seconds.

Code:

```
SELECT *
FROM Customers
WHERE CustomerID
IN (SELECT CustomerID from tbls_Orders WHERE
DatePart(q , OrderDate) = 4 AND  year(OrderDate) = 2013)
```

Result:

CustomerID	FirstName	LastName	Address	City	State
1	John	Demarco	11 Lark Street	New York	NY
4	Phillip	Demetriou	22 Academy Road	New York	NY
5	Andrew	Demichele	14 Glandel Ave	New York	NY
7	Robert	Demaggio	34 Princeton Dr	New York	NY

(82 row(s) returned)

CHAPTER 22 DISCUSSION QUESTIONS

1. How do we call the records for which there are no primary key values for corresponding foreign key values?
2. How do we call the records for which there are no foreign key values for corresponding primary key values?
3. When referential integrity is off what kind of risk do we incur? End up with orphaned, duplicate, related or unrelated records?
4. If referential integrity is on can we still end up with duplicate records in the database? Why yes or why not?
5. What techniques can we use to identify orphaned records in the database?
6. What do we mean by duplicate records? For two records to be duplicates do they need to have identical data?
7. If we have customers without orders is this a database integrity problem or a business problem?
8. If we have orders without customers is this a database integrity problem or a business problem?
9. What kind of action do we need to take when we find orphaned records in the database?
10. What kind of action do we need to take when we find unrelated records in the database?

CHAPTER 22 HANDS-ON EXERCISES

Chapter 22 Case 1:
Start SQL Server Management Studio. For each of the questions in this case you need to create a new query (Ctrl-N) and name it as per the instructions in each question. Submit your work to your instructor as one text file that contains all SQL statements or as per your instructor's directions.

1. The department of accounts receivable has notified IT that something is not right with the orders presented for payment. It looks like some of them are repeated entries and we risk paying them twice. They are asking you to find duplicate records in the table tble_Orders based on the values of the fields CustomerID, SalesRepID, and ShipperID. Your report should also include the number of instances of repeated records. Create a new query that satisfies the accounts receivable request and save it as Chapter22_Case1_Q1.

Your result should look like:

CustomerID	Sales RepID	ShipperID	Numberof Duplicates
1	4	1	2
3	4	1	2
8	5	2	2
9	7	2	2
11	3	1	2

(94 row(s) returned)

2. The accounts receivable people are happy with your report but they want to make sure that what they do makes business sense. In this respect, it might be natural for the same customer to have ordered through the same sales person, and used the same shipping company multiple times. To account for this fact and make sure they identify only duplicate records they are asking you to find duplicate records in the table

tble_orders based on the values of all fields. Your report should also include the number of instances of duplicate records. Create a new query that includes all fields from the tble_Orders table and satisfies the accounts receivable request. Save the query as Chapter22_Case1_Q2. (Hint: Do not include the OrderID in the list of fields in your code since it is the primary key and it will always have a unique value.)

Your result should look like:

CustomerID	SalesRepID	ShipperID	OrderDate	RequiredDate	ShippedDate	ShippingCost	NumberofDuplicates
126	2	2	2012-06-15	2012-06-25	2012-06-15	35	2
139	2	2	2013-11-11	2013-11-21	2013-11-11	36	2
177	10	1	2014-08-12	2014-08-22	2014-08-12	35	2
194	3	1	2014-04-19	2014-04-29	2014-04-19	46	2

(4 row(s) returned)

3. Human Resources called in and they say they are trying to calculate commissions for sales people but some orders refer to sales reps they cannot find in the database. Check to see why the HR people cannot find the sales representatives in the SalesReps table and why they appear as processing orders in the tble_Orders table. Make a list of all orders for which no sales reps exist in the SalesReps table. Create a new query that includes all fields from the tble_Orders table and satisfies the HR people request. Save it as Chapter22_Case1_Q3.

Your result should look like:

OrderID	CustomerID	SalesRepID	ShipperID	OrderDate	RequiredDate
256	129	11	1	2012-09-16	2012-09-26
257	27	12	2	2012-03-20	2012-03-30
258	124	15	2	2012-03-12	2012-03-22
259	8	12	1	2014-07-27	2014-08-06
260	38	11	1	2012-12-27	2013-01-06

(18 row(s) returned)

4. The sales director thinks that some of the sales people are not very aggressive in the market with the result of them missing commissions and the company sales. He asks for a report that lists the sales people without sales for the month of December 2014 using order records from the tble_Orders table. Create a new query that includes all fields from the SalesReps table and satisfies the sales director request. Save it as Chapter22_Case1_Q4.

Your result should look like:

SalesRepID	FirstName	LastName	Title	Address	City	State
4	Phillip	Zensons	Sales Reppresentative	32 Camberland Street	New York	NY

(1 row(s) returned)

5. The sales director is now asking for a report of sales people who actually had sales in the month of December 2014. Create a new query that includes all fields from the SalesReps table and satisfies the sales director request. Save it as Chapter22_Case1_Q5. Use the tble_Orders table to check for placed orders.

Your result should look like:

SalesRepID	FirstName	LastName	Title	Address	City	State
1	John	Anderson	Sales Reppresentative	32 Colonial Street	Boston	MA
2	Mary	Teall	Sales Director	14 Highland Ave	Boston	MA
3	George	Spicer	Assitant Director of Sales	90 Lenox Ave	Boston	MA
5	Andrew	Simmons	Account Manager	16 Greenway Street	New York	NY

(9 row(s) returned)

Chapter 22 Case 2:

Start SQL Server Management Studio. For each of the questions in this case you need to create a new query (Ctrl-N) and name it as per the instructions in each question. Submit your work to your instructor as one text file that contains all SQL statements or as per your instructor's directions.

1. The sales people are asking for a report of any shipping companies which have not shipped any orders for us for the records we have in the tble_Orders table. Create a query that includes all fields from the ShippingCompanies table and satisfies the sales people request. Name the query as Chapter22_Case2_Q1.

   Your result should look like:

ShipperID	CompanyName	City	State	Phone
4	US Postal Service	Philadelphia	PA	438-433-8998

   (1 row(s) returned)

2. The sales people are back asking for a report that will list any shipping companies that have not been used in the shipping of our orders for the records we have in the tble_Orders table and for the last six months of 2014. Create a query that includes all fields from the ShippingCompanies table and satisfies the sales people request. Name the query as Chapter22_Case2_Q2. Why is the result the same as in question 1?

   Your result should look like:

ShipperID	CompanyName	City	State	Phone
4	US Postal Service	Philadelphia	PA	438-433-8998

   (1 row(s) returned)

3. The sales people are now asking for a report that will list any orders in the tble_Orders table without any associated shipping companies. Create a query that includes all fields from the tble_Orders table and satisfies the sales people request. Name the query as Chapter22_Case2_Q3. What is the meaning of 0 rows returned?

   Your result should look like:
   (0 row(s) returned)

4. The sales people need a report that will list all the shipping companies that participated in the shipping of at least one order from the records we have in the tble_Orders table. Create a query that includes all fields from the ShippingCompanies table and satisfies the sales people request. Name the query as

Chapter22_Case2_Q4.

Your result should look like:

ShipperID	CompanyName	City	State	Phone
1	Federal Unites	Los Angeles	CA	451-237-4387
2	CHL	New York	NY	518-589-4990
3	United Postal	Boston	MA	546-437-3989

(3 row(s) returned)

5. Finally, the sales people want a report that will list all the shipping companies that shipped our orders in the last fifteen days of December 2014. Use historical order data from the tble_Orders table. Create a query that includes all fields from the ShippingCompanies table and satisfies the sales people request. Name the query as Chapter22_Case2_Q5.

Your result should look like:

ShipperID	CompanyName	City	State	Phone
1	Federal Unites	Los Angeles	CA	451-237-4387

(1 row(s) returned

CHAPTER 23
WORKING WITH NULLS

There are three concepts you need to understand null values in full: First, a zero (0) value is not a null value. It means that there is a value, and it is zero. Second, a zero-length string, also called an empty string, is not a null value. It means that there should be a value, but there is none. Third, a null value means that we do not know whether there should be a value or not.

Zero-length strings are designated by typing two single quotation marks with no space between them (''). Null values contain the entry *NULL*. The best way to avoid tricky and problematical situations with nulls and zero-length values is to avoid them altogether. When designing a new database, we can assign default values to fields that users might leave blank. For example, for a customer middle name, we can set a default value of 'NA' when none is entered. For existing databases, we can run effective update statements (chapter 27 in this book) to replace null and empty string values with default values.

Null values will affect your calculations in aggregate functions, searching expressions, union operations, and will leave doubts about the validity of your results. Let us explore in detail all of the scenarios around nulls and the ways to eliminate them. For this chapter, so that you can verify the effects of null values and zero-length strings, I have created a table called "ProductsN" which contains only ten records. Using these ten records, you will be able to verify your calculations and learn to work with nulls effectively. Then, you will be able to apply the same techniques to thousands of records.

208.   Looking for nulls using the IS NULL expression
Find products whose stock keeping unit codes (SKUs) are null
Discussion:
Our task is to find all products for which the SKU code is missing. Of course, with only ten products, we can just eye the table and tell right away that there are four SKU codes missing. Let us try to write the code to retrieve them and see if the database agrees. In this example, we are looking for null values using the criterion "IS NULL" in the WHERE clause, and as you can see, the SQL statement returned four records.

Code:
SELECT productID, productname, productunitprice, SKU
FROM tbls_ProductsN
WHERE SKU IS NULL

Result:

productID	productname	productunitprice	SKU
3	Banana Chips (Zero-Length)	30	NULL
4	Berry Cherry (Zero-Length)	30	NULL
71	Almonds (Null)	NULL	NULL
72	Almonds Roasted (Null)	NULL	NULL

(4 row(s) returned)

209. Looking for nulls using the ISNULL() function

Display the word "nothing" for products with null SKUs

Discussion:

We can use the ISNULL() function to find nulls in a field and replace them with any character string or expression we like. In the code below, we are looking for NULL values in the SKU field and we replace them on the fly with the 'Nothing' string. We have a total of four replacements. We can use the ISNULL() function with number fields as well to assign a value of our liking where a null value might exist. The general syntax of the ISNULL() function is

$$ISNULL \text{ (field, replacement value)}$$

Code:

```
SELECT ProductID, productname, productunitprice, ISNULL(SKU,'Nothing') AS SKUCheck
FROM tbls_ProductsN
ORDER BY SKU
```

Result:

ProductID	productname	productunitprice	SKUCheck
3	Banana Chips (Zero-Length)	30	Nothing
4	Berry Cherry (Zero-Length)	30	Nothing
71	Almonds (Null)	NULL	Nothing
72	Almonds Roasted (Null)	NULL	Nothing
5	California Original Pistachios - 1 lb. Bag	29	PDK-2347

```
(10 row(s) returned)
```

210. Calculations with nulls

Calculate product inventory subtotals where some values are nulls

Discussion:

In this example, we want to multiply the field ProductUnitPrice with the QuantityPerUnit to calculate the value of our inventory by product. In the ProductsN table, there are blank values for both the ProductUnitPrice and the QuantityPerUnit fields. Let's see how our result set will come up.

Code:

```
SELECT productID, productname, (productunitprice*quantityperunit) As Subtotal
FROM tbls_ProductsN
ORDER BY (productunitprice*quantityperunit) DESC
```

Result:

As you can see, for the records with null values for either one of the two multiplied fields, there will be no result. This will have consequences in our inventory results since at least for productid=72, we know that we do have 25 units on hand. Since their price is missing, the inventory report will be erroneous. To avoid this situation, we need to make it a habit to look for nulls before we do any calculations.

productID	productname	Subtotal
6	Choice Apricots - 16 oz. Bag	800
10	Raw Sunflower Seeds in 19 oz. Bag	625
9	Dried Cranberries - 34 oz.	525
4	Berry Cherry (Zero-Length)	450
5	California Original Pistachios - 1 lb. Bag	435
7	Cran Raisin Mix in 17 oz. Bag	372
3	Banana Chips (Zero-Length)	360
8	Dried Blueberries - 1 lb. Bag	280
71	Almonds (Null)	NULL
72	Almonds Roasted (Null)	NULL

(10 row(s) returned)

211. Using sum() with null values

Calculate the total inventory value

Discussion:

The situation becomes even worse when we use aggregate functions since we cannot see the empty field values to realize we have missing data. When aggregate functions encounter null values, they will leave them out of the calculations altogether and report only on known values.

In this case, products with productID 71 and 72 will be missing from the calculations. For productid=72, we have no quantity or price data, and we do not know if this is correct or not. For productid=71, we know that we have a quantity on hand = 25 but no price, and our results are definitely wrong. The best way to avoid the above situations is to check the data for nulls and make every effort to fill in the missing values.

Code:

```
SELECT SUM(productunitprice*quantityperunit) As Total
FROM tbls_ProductsN
```

Result:

	Total
1	3847

(1 row(s) returned)

212. Using count() with nulls

Count the number of products in the inventory correctly

Discussion:

As I have mentioned countless times in this book, our primary goal is to rid the database of nulls by replacing them with concrete values in our tables such as 'NA' for text fields or zeros for numeric ones. Now, our goal is to calculate the number of products in our inventory table. If we apply the count() function on the SKU field, we will get six records. This is because the four null values in the SKU field have not been counted!

Code:

```
SELECT Count(SKU) As CountSKUs
FROM tbls_ProductsN
```

Result:

	CountSKUs
1	6

(1 row(s) returned)

Discussion:

My recommendation to this problem is to use count() or other arithmetic functions on fields that, by default, do not allow nulls in their values. For example, we could use count() on the ProductID field which is the primary key of the table.

Code:

```
SELECT Count(ProductID) As CountSKUs
FROM tbls_ProductsN
```

Result:

	CountSKUs
1	10

(1 row(s) returned)

Discussion:

Another solution for correct counts is to use the count(*) function, which will return the actual number of records in the table independently of any null values in any field.

Code:

```
SELECT Count(*) As CountRecords
FROM tbls_ProductsN
```

Result:

	CountRecords
1	10

(1 row(s) returned)

213.   Leaving nulls out of the result set

Find products for which the SKU code is not null

Discussion:

We can obtain a list of products that do not contain null values in the SKU field by using the IS NOT NULL expression. The IS NOT NULL expression is not a panacea to null values problems. The real solution would be to use UPDATE statements to replace null values with concrete values such as 'NA' for text or zeros for numeric fields. As we have expected, the SQL statement returned six records with non-null values for the SKU field.

Code:

```
SELECT productID, productname, productunitprice, SKU
FROM tbls_ProductsN
WHERE SKU IS NOT NULL
```

Result:

productID	productname	productunitprice	SKU
5	California Original Pistachios - 1 lb. Bag	29	PDK-2347
6	Choice Apricots - 16 oz. Bag	32	PDK-2347
7	Cran Raisin Mix in 17 oz. Bag	31	PDKLS-1889
8	Dried Blueberries - 1 lb. Bag	28	PDKLS-1889
9	Dried Cranberries - 34 oz.	35	PDK-2347
10	Raw Sunflower Seeds in 19 oz. Bag	25	PDKLS-1889

```
(6 row(s) returned)
```

214. Permanently replace nulls using an update statement
Use UPDATE to replace null values in the SKU field
Discussion:
We can replace the null values in the SKU field by using the UPDATE statement with the WHERE clause and the IS NULL expression. As you can see from the result set, the database will replace the four existing null values in the SKU field. (check chapter 27 for an in depth look at the update statement).

We will create a copy of the tbls_ProductsN table before we apply the UPDATE statement.

Code:
```
SELECT *
INTO temp_tbls_ProductsN
FROM tbls_ProductsN
```

Result:
```
(10 row(s) affected)
```

Code:
```
UPDATE temp_tbls_ProductsN
SET SKU = 'NA'
WHERE SKU IS NULL
```

Result:
```
(4 row(s) affected)
```

CHAPTER 23 DISCUSSION QUESTIONS

1. What do we mean by a null value in a table cell?
2. Is a null value the same as a zero (0) value?
3. Is a null value the same as a zero length string? What is the difference?
4. How can we designate a zero length string?
5. If we look at data in a table can we distinguish which cells contain null values?
6. What is the best strategy to avoid problematic situations with null values?
7. How can we avoid the presence of null values when we design a new database?
8. How can we eliminate null values from an existing database?
9. How do null values affect calculations with aggregate functions?
10. Why is it a good idea to use the IsNull() function? What kind of results does it produce?

CHAPTER 23 HANDS-ON EXERCISES

Chapter 23 Case 1:
Start SQL Server Management Studio. For each of the questions in this case create a new query (Ctrl-N) and name it as per the instructions in each question. Submit your work to your instructor as one text file that contains all SQL statements or as per your instructor's directions.

1. The marketing people have initiated a marketing campaign which includes repeated written letters to customers. They have many of those letters coming back with an "undeliverable" notice. It looks like the state is missing from many of the addresses they have in their database. They are asking you to help them identify who are the customers with missing states in the database. Create a new query that includes all the fields from the tble_CustomersN table and satisfies the marketing people request. Save the query as Chapter23_Case1_Q1.

   Your result should look like:

CustomerID	First Name	Last Name	Address	City	State
7	Robert	Demaggio	34 Princeton Dr	New York	NULL
13	David	Vanderback	91 Fifth Ave	New York	NULL
20	Lisa	Zartons	34 Home Ave	Los Angeles	NULL
47	Patricia	Woods	18 Turner DR	Philadelphia	NULL
58	Veronica	Martin	22 Stanwick Street	Miami	NULL

   (11 row(s) returned)

2. The marketing people are now asking for a list of customers with the following fields from the tble_CustomersN table: CustomerID, lastname, firstname, city, State, and zip. For the state field they want the value to appear as "State does not exist" whenever there is no state value. Create a new query that satisfies the marketing people request and name it Chapter23_Case1_Q2.

   Your result should look like:

284

CustomerID	lastname	firstname	city	StateCheck	zip
1	Demarco	John	New York	NY	12189
2	Demania	Mary	New York	NY	12189
3	Demers	George	New York	NY	12189
4	Demetriou	Phillip	New York	NY	12189
5	Demichele	Andrew	New York	NY	12189
6	Demizio	Michael	New York	NY	12189
7	Demaggio	Robert	New York	State does not exist	12110

(201 row(s) returned)

3. The marketing people need some statistics on the number of bad records they have. Specifically they need to know how many states actually have values in the table. Use the count() function on the state field of the tble_CustomersN table to provide them with an answer. Create a new query that satisfies this request and save it as Chapter23_Case1_Q3.

Your result should look like:

CountState
190

(1 row(s) returned)

4. The marketing people need the number of the total records they have in the table tble_CustomersN. Create a new query that satisfies this request and save it as Chapter23_Case1_Q4.

Your result should look like:

CountState
201

(1 row(s) returned)

5. The marketing people finally need a list of customers for which the state field is not null. Create a new query that includes all the fields from the tble_CustomersN table and satisfies the marketing people request. Save it as Chapter23_Case1_Q5.

Your result should look like:

CustomerID	FirstName	LastName	Address	City	State	Zip	Country
1	John	Demarco	11 Lark Street	New York	NY	12189	USA
2	Mary	Demania	12 Madison Ave	New York	NY	12189	USA
3	George	Demers	23 New Scotlan Ave	New York	NY	12189	USA
4	Phillip	Demetriou	22 Academy Road	New York	NY	12189	USA
5	Andrew	Demichele	14 Glandel Ave	New York	NY	12189	USA

(190 row(s) returned)

Chapter 23 Case 2:

Start SQL Server Management Studio. For each of the questions in this case create a new query (Ctrl-N) and name it as per the instructions in each question. Submit your work to your instructor as one text file that contains all SQL statements or as per your instructor's directions.

1. The inventory people think there are missing values for the quantity field in the table tble_ProductsOrdersN. They would like to know which are the records with no quantity entries. Create a new query that will include the fields ProductID, OrderID, UnitPrice, and Quantity from this table and satisfies the request. Save the query as Chapter23_Case2_Q1.

    Your result should look like:

ProductID	OrderID	UnitPrice	Quantity
23	5	NULL	NULL
26	5	NULL	NULL
3	6	NULL	NULL
23	25	NULL	NULL
2	36	15	NULL

    (117 row(s) returned)

2. Seeing the report from question 1 the inventory people notice right away that there are null values in the UnitPrice field as well. They need a new report that will count the null values in the UnitPrice field in the table tble_ProductsOrdersN. Save the query as Chapter23_Case2_Q2.

    Your result should look like:

NumberOfNulls
150

    (1 row(s) returned)

3. The inventory people are asking for some aggregate calculations to better plan for inventory replenishment. Specifically, they need your help for a report that will provide the total number of orders, the total order amount, and the average order amount by product. Create a new query on the table tble_ProductsOrdersN that satisfies the inventory people request and sort results by Product ID ascending. Save the query as Chapter23_Case2_Q3.

    Your result should look like:

ProductID	NumberOfOrders	AvgOrder	TotaAmount
23	39	49.6875	795
46	40	49.125	1965
69	36	54	1890
29	20	57.6315789473684	1095
9	34	46.8181818181818	1545

    (70 row(s) returned)

4. The inventory people are back and are very politely indicating to you that the numbers you provided appear to be off according to some written records they have. Your mind immediately goes to null values.

Check to see if there are any null values for the fields UnitPrice or Quantity. Create a new query that includes all the fields from the tble_ProductsOrdersN table and shows the records with null values for the UnitPrice and Quantity fields. Save the query as Chapter23_Case2_Q4.

Your result should look like:

OrderID	ProductID	UnitPrice	Quantity	Discoun
2	23	NULL	4	0.15
5	23	NULL	NULL	0.15
5	26	NULL	NULL	0.15
5	69	NULL	3	0.2
6	3	NULL	NULL	0.15

`(204 row(s) returned)`

5. Now that you know you have 204 records with null values for the UnitPrice or Quantity fields or both you need to recreate the report requested by the inventory people in question 1. However, this time you need to make sure you leave out any null values from your calculations. Create a new query that satisfies the inventory people request and save it as Chapter23_Case2_Q5. What conclusion do you make when you compare the numbers from questions 3 and 1?

Your result should look like:

ProductID	NumberOfOrders	AvgOrder	TotaAmount
23	37	49.6875	795
46	40	49.125	1965
69	36	54	1890
29	20	57.6315789473684	1095
9	34	46.8181818181818	1545

`(70 row(s) returned)`

CHAPTER 24
TYPE CONVERSION FUNCTIONS

Type conversion functions are an excellent tool in the arsenal of the database power user and developer. Unfortunately, they usually go underneath the radar screen of even advanced users because their functionality is not apparent or because they use other methods to accomplish the same result. For instance, to convert a column from a text data type to number data type, some users go to the table design and force a change there.

There are three problems with this approach: First, by changing the field data type forcefully, data might be lost. Second, if something goes wrong, there is no turning back to the original data. Third, database administrators might not allow a change to the design of the back-end database. The solution is to use type conversion functions to change data types on the fly without affecting the table design. In SQL Server 2012, we have two type conversion functions at our disposal: cast() and convert().

The generic syntax for the cast() function is :

CAST (expression AS data_type [(length)])

The generic syntax for the convert() function is:

CONVERT (data_type [(length)] , expression [, style])

215.   Convert numbers to Tinyint size using cast() and convert()
Convert numbers to Tinyint size
Discussion:
In this example, we will use the cast() function to convert numbers with decimals to a number between 0 and 255.

Code1:
SELECT cast(245.234 AS TinyInt) AS ConvertedNumber

We can achieve the same result using the convert() function:
Code2:
SELECT convert(TinyInt, 245.234) AS ConvertedNumber

Result:

ConvertedNumber
245

(1 row(s) returned)

216.   Convert numbers to SmallInt size using cast() and convert()

Convert numbers to SmallInt

Discussion:

A SmallInt data type will hold numbers between -32,768 to 32,767 with no decimals. Consequently, if we want to convert the number 10234.2345 to a SmallInt data type, we can write:

Code:

SELECT cast(10234.234 AS SmallInt) AS ConvertedNumber

We can achieve the same result using the convert() function:

Code2:

SELECT convert(SmallInt,10234.234) AS ConvertedNumber

Result:

ConvertedNumber
10234

(1 row(s) returned)

217.   Convert text to date data types using cast() and convert()

Convert text to a date data type

Discussion:

We might have inherited or imported date data in text format like "November 21 2014" or even "21 November 2014". We want to store this text data in a date field so that we can take full advantage of the range of date functions in our disposal to manipulate date data (chapter 26). This is very important since we can summarize information by any time interval we would like such as by year, semester, month, week etc. We can conveniently use the cast() and convert() functions to achieve our goal. Keep in mind that SQL server future end year is 2049. This means that if you write 39 it means 2039 but if you write 59 it means 1959. Consequently, it is always a good idea to use four digit years.

Code 1 using cast():

SELECT cast('November 21 2014' AS date) AS ConvertedDate

Code 2 using convert():

SELECT convert(date, 'November 21 2014') AS ConvertedDate

Result:

ConvertedDate
2014-11-21

(1 row(s) returned)

We continue this example using the year() function to extract the year out of the converted date field. We can now use the year value to aggregate data by year such as retrieve order totals by year. Refer to chapter 26 for a full list of date functions. The bottom line is we have managed to extract very specific information out of plain text data.

Code:

SELECT year(cast('November 21 2014' AS date)) AS ConvertedDate

Result:

ConvertedDate
2014

(1 row(s) returned)

218. Convert numeric data to text using cast() and convert()

Convert numeric data to text

Discussion:

Let us assume that the previous DBA used the smallint data type to store zip codes. Zip codes as numbers might behave oddly in situations where we need to concatenate them for example with address names and numbers. The safest way is to convert them to text before any concatenations as we can see below.

Code 1 using cast():

SELECT cast(12456 AS char(5)) AS ConvertedText

Code 2 using convert():

SELECT convert(char(5), 12456) AS ConvertedText

Result:

ConvertedText
12456

(1 row(s) returned)

CHAPTER 24 DISCUSSION QUESTIONS

1. What is the purpose of type conversion functions?
2. Why is it better to change the data type of a field on the fly rather than forcing a change in the design of the table?
3. Can we use type conversion functions to change text data to numeric data and vice versa?
4. What are the two main type conversion functions in SQL Server?
5. What is the range of numbers an integer data type can hold?
6. What is the syntax of the convert() function?
7. What is the syntax of the cast() function?
8. What is the future end year for SQL Server 2012? Why is this important?
9. Why is it a good idea to convert zip codes to a text data type?
10. What is a reason to convert text such as "November 12, 2014" to a date data type such as "2014-11-12"?

CHAPTER 24 HANDS-ON EXERCISES

Chapter 24 Case 1:

Start SQL Server Management Studio. For each of the questions in this case create a new query (Ctrl-N) and name it as per the instructions in each question. Submit your work to your instructor as one text file that contains all SQL statements or as per your instructor's directions.

1. The inventory people want to make calculations and they need the UnitPrice field values to appear without decimals. They do not want any changes in the original data in the tble_Orders_Conversion table. Create a new query that contains the fields OrderID, city, state, zip, orderdate, shippingcost, and unitprice from the tble_Orders_Conversion table. The unit price field in this query should not have any decimal values. Use the cast() function to achieve your result. Save the query as Chapter24_Case1_Q1.

   Your result should look like:

OrderID	city	state	zip	orderdate	shippingcost	unitprice
1	San Diego	CA	33521	May 21 2011	40	15
2	Orlando	FL	89754	May 21 2011	47	15
3	Albany	NY	45357	May 21 2011	52	8
4	Albany	NY	45357	May 21 2011	52	15
5	Albany	NY	45357	June 15 2012	52	15

   (20 row(s) returned)

2. Achieve the same result as in question 1 using the convert() function. Save the query as Chapter24_Case1_Q2.

   Your result should look like:

3. The marketing people need to send out letters to customers and they need to time those letters based on the values in the order date field. However, when they try to use the dates in the order date field they have trouble because the values are in text format. Create a new query that contains the fields OrderID, city, state, zip, orderdate, shippingcost, and unitprice from the tble_Orders_Conversion table. The order date field in this query should be a date value in the format yyyy-mm-dd. Use the convert() function to achieve your result. Save the query as Chapter24_Case1_Q3.

Your result should look like:

OrderID	city	state	zip	NewOrderDate	shippingcost	unitprice
1	San Diego	CA	33521	2011-05-21	40	15.015
2	Orlando	FL	89754	2011-05-21	47	15.09
3	Albany	NY	45357	2011-05-21	52	8.02
4	Albany	NY	45357	2011-05-21	52	15.02
5	Albany	NY	45357	2012-06-15	52	15.01

(20 row(s) returned)

4. The marketing people need to retrieve the year value out of the order date field because they want to perform calculations based on year totals. Create a new query that contains the fields OrderID, city, state, zip, orderdate, shippingcost, and unitprice from the tble_Orders_Conversion table. Convert the order date field to a date value as you did in question 3 and then extract the year out of this field. Save the query as Chapter24_Case1_Q4.

Your result should look like:

OrderID	city	state	zip	OrderYear	shippingcost	unitprice
1	San Diego	CA	33521	2011	40	15.015
2	Orlando	FL	89754	2011	47	15.09
3	Albany	NY	45357	2011	52	8.02
4	Albany	NY	45357	2011	52	15.02
5	Albany	NY	45357	2012	52	15.01

(20 row(s) returned)

5. The sales people need a report that calculates order totals for customer. However, when they try to multiply the unitprice field with the quantity field they get errors. Convert the quantity field in the appropriate format so that the sales people can perform their calculations. Create a new query that contains the last name and first name fields from the tble_Orders_Conversion table as well as the calculated field that you need. Name the query Chapter24_Case1_Q5.

Your result should look like:

lastname	firstname	OrderTotal
Wagner	Anthony	90.03
Bittel	David	251.0293
Grady	July	218.118
Knortz	Kelly	30.024
Trindan	Luis	138.19

(8 row(s) returned)

Chapter 24 Case 2:

Start SQL Server Management Studio. For each of the questions in this case create a new query (Ctrl-N) and name it as per the instructions in each question. Submit your work to your instructor as one text file that contains all SQL statements or as per your instructor's directions.

1. The sales people need to change the ProductUnitPrice field to extend new prices to customers but they have trouble implementing these changes because the ProductUnitPrice field is of the text data type. Create a new query that contains the ProductName, QuantityPerUnit, ProductUnitPrice, UnitsInStock, UnitsOnOrder fields from the tble_Products_Conversion table. The ProductUnitPrice field should not have any decimal values. Use the cast() function to achieve your result. Save the query as Chapter24_Case2_Q1.

Your result should look like:

ProductName	QuantityPerUnit	ProductUnitPrice	UnitsInStock	UnitsOnOrder
Almonds, Hickory Smoked - 12 oz. Bag	12	35	30	5
Almonds, Roasted and Salted - 18 oz. Bag	12	22	15	0
Banana Chips - 20 oz. Bag	12	23	25	0
Berry Cherry in 8 oz. Bag	15	30	35	0
California Original Pistachios - 1 lb. Bag	15	29	35	10

(15 row(s) returned)

2. Achieve the same result as in question 1 using the convert() function. Save the query as Chapter24_Case2_Q2.

Your result should look like

ProductName	QuantityPerUnit	ProductUnitPrice	UnitsInStock	UnitsOnOrder
Almonds, Hickory Smoked - 12 oz. Bag	12	35	30	5
Almonds, Roasted and Salted - 18 oz. Bag	12	22	15	0
Banana Chips - 20 oz. Bag	12	23	25	0
Berry Cherry in 8 oz. Bag	15	30	35	0
California Original Pistachios - 1 lb. Bag	15	29	35	10

(15 row(s) returned)

3. The sales people need to create some reports using the CatalogLastUpdated date field but they have difficulty since the field data is of the text data type. Create a new query that contains the ProductName, ProductUnitPrice, UnitsInStock, UnitsOnOrder, and CatalogLastUpdated fields from the

tble_Products_Conversion table. The CatalogLastUpdated field should have the format "yyyy-mm-dd". Save the query as Chapter24_Case2_Q3.

Your result should look like:

Product Name	Product Unit Price	Units In Stock	Units On Order	Catalog Last Updated
Almonds, Hickory Smoked - 12 oz. Bag	35.01	30	5	2012-11-13
Almonds, Roasted and Salted - 18 oz. Bag	22.02	15	0	2012-12-10
Banana Chips - 20 oz. Bag	23.02	25	0	2012-01-14
Berry Cherry in 8 oz. Bag	30.12	35	0	2012-01-18
California Original Pistachios - 1 lb. Bag	29.01	35	10	2012-03-20

(15 row(s) returned)

4. Continuing with the request in question 3 the sales people need to extract the year out of the CatalogLastUpdated field. Create a new query that contains all the fields from question 3 and satisfies the sales people request. Convert the CatalogLastUpdated field to a date field as you did in step 2 and then extract the year out of this field. Save the query as Chapter24_Case2_Q4.

Your result should look like:

Product Name	Product Unit Price	Units In Stock	Units On Order	Catalog Last Updated
Almonds, Hickory Smoked - 12 oz. Bag	35.01	30	5	2012
Almonds, Roasted and Salted - 18 oz. Bag	22.02	15	0	2012
Banana Chips - 20 oz. Bag	23.02	25	0	2012
Berry Cherry in 8 oz. Bag	30.12	35	0	2012
California Original Pistachios - 1 lb. Bag	29.01	35	10	2012

(15 row(s) returned)

5. The inventory people need a report that will show the product name and its corresponding total units in inventory. To achieve this they try to add the fields UnitsInStock and UnitsOnOrder but they receive an error. Create a new query on the tble_Products_Conversion table that will help the inventory people achieve the result they need. Save the query as Chapter24_Case2_Q5.

Your result should look like:

Product Name	Total Inventory Units
Almonds, Hickory Smoked - 12 oz. Bag	35
Almonds, Roasted and Salted - 18 oz. Bag	15
Banana Chips - 20 oz. Bag	25
Berry Cherry in 8 oz. Bag	35
California Original Pistachios - 1 lb. Bag	45

(15 row(s) returned)

CHAPTER 25
WORKING WITH STRINGS

It is now time to enter the amazing world of string functions and text manipulation. Text functions produce output that is impossible to generate without them. They should be in the toolbox of every database user since lack of such knowledge has direct effects on database and table design. In other words, extra fields might be inserted in tables when not needed. In this chapter, we will explore a multitude of practical examples of how to use such functions. For a list of all the string functions available in SQL Server 2012, please see the table at the end of this chapter. For a full reference of string functions please go to http://technet.microsoft.com/en-us/library/ms181984.aspx.

219. Capitalize field values using the upper() function
Capitalize the first and last names of customers using upper()

Discussion:

The general syntax of the upper() function is shown below. It takes just one argument, and it will capitalize the contents of the field on which it is applied. Upper() will capitalize all of the characters in the field, leaving any existing capital characters unchanged.

upper(field name)

Code:

SELECT Upper(lastname) AS LastName, Upper(firstname) AS FirstName, city, state, zip
FROM customers

Result:

LastName	FirstName	city	state	zip
DEMARCO	JOHN	New York	NY	12189
DEMANIA	MARY	New York	NY	12189
DEMERS	GEORGE	New York	NY	12189
DEMETRIOU	PHILLIP	New York	NY	12189

(201 row(s) returned)

220. Capitalize only the first character in a field using the upper(), left(), and substring() functions
Capitalize the first character in the lastname field

Discussion:

In this example we first use the left function to isolate the first character from the lastname field. Then we use the upper() function to capitalize this first character. Next, we use the substring() function to return all the characters in the lastname field starting with the second character. The number 50 which is the third argument of the substring() function indicates the limit of characters we will retrieve. That is, if the lastname field has fifteen characters, all fifteen will be returned. If however, it has sixty, then only the first fifty will be retrieved starting with the second character. In this example, we assume last names are up to 50 characters long.

Code:

```
SELECT upper(left(lastname,1))+ substring (lastname, 2, 50) AS LastName, city, state, zip
FROM customers
```

Result:

LastName	city	state	zip
Demarco	New York	NY	12189
Demania	New York	NY	12189
Demers	New York	NY	12189
Demetriou	New York	NY	12189

(201 row(s) returned)

Another way to achieve this task would be to replace its third argument with the function len(lastname) in which case the len() function will count the number of characters and provide the substring() function their actual number. It will produce the same result with the above.

Code:

```
SELECT upper(left(lastname,1))+ substring (lastname, 2, len(lastname)) AS LastName, city, state, zip
FROM customers
```

221. Convert field values to lowercase using the lower() function

Convert the first and last names of our customers to lowercase

Discussion:

The lower() function takes only one argument—the field name—and results in converting all characters of a field to lowercase. Its general syntax is:

$$lower(field\ name)$$

In this particular example, we use it to convert both the first and last names of our customers to lowercase as you can see in the example below:

Code:

```
SELECT lower(lastname) AS LastName, lower(firstname) AS FirstName, city, state, zip
FROM customers
```

Result:

LastName	FirstName	city	state	zip
demarco	john	New York	NY	12189
demania	mary	New York	NY	12189
demers	george	New York	NY	12189
demetriou	phillip	New York	NY	12189

(201 row(s) returned)

222.   Retrieve any number of characters from the beginning of a field using the left() function

Retrieve the first four characters of the SKU code

Discussion:

In some situations, the data in our database is well formatted, and we do not have to resort to combinations of functions such as left() and charindex(), as we shall see later on, to retrieve a substring from a string in a field. For example, if the letter part of the SKU code in our products table is always of length 4 (PDKS-2345), we simply use the left function to retrieve the first four characters in this field. The left() function takes two arguments—the field name and the number of characters we would like to retrieve.

left(fieldname, number of characters to retrieve)

Code:

SELECT productid, productname, left(sku,4) AS SKU4
FROM Products

Result:

productid	productname	SKU4
1	Almonds, Hickory Smoked - 12 oz. Bag	PDKL
2	Almonds, Roasted and Salted - 18 oz. Bag	PDKL
3	Banana Chips - 20 oz. Bag	PDKL
4	Berry Cherry in 8 oz. Bag	PDK-

(70 row(s) returned)

223.   Retrieve any number of characters starting from the end of a field using the right() function

Retrieve the last four characters of the SKU code

Discussion:

In this example, instead of retrieving the first four characters of the SKU code, we would like to get the last four, which, by the way, represent the number part of our SKUs (PDKS-2345). If the SKU field is well formatted, we can use the right() function to achieve this task very easily. By well formatted, we mean the number part of the SKU will always have four digits. Otherwise, we will run into trouble with the right() function. The right() function takes two arguments—the field name and the number of characters we would like to retrieve.

right(fieldname, number of characters to retrieve)

Code:

SELECT productid, productname, right(sku,4) AS SKU4
FROM Products

Result:

productid	productname	SKU4
1	Almonds, Hickory Smoked - 12 oz. Bag	2332
2	Almonds, Roasted and Salted - 18 oz. Bag	2344
3	Banana Chips - 20 oz. Bag	2347
4	Berry Cherry in 8 oz. Bag	2589

(70 row(s) returned)

224.   Count the number of characters in a field using the len() function

Count the number of characters in the sku field

Discussion:

There are occasions in which we like to count the number of characters for a field in every record in the database. This is especially useful when we want to change the data type of a field or when we want to decrease its length. If we work with extraction, transformation, and loading (ETL) tools, this function is particularly useful to know exactly what is happening instead of making guesses and ending up with truncated values. The len() function is especially easy to use, it takes just one argument, and its general syntax appears below. Notice that the len() function will not count any trailing blank values in the field.

len(field name)

In this particular example, we count the number of characters in the sku field of the products table. Notice from the output that the result of the function for each record is different. We can then sort ascending or descending to display the shortest or lengthiest entries first in the output.

Code:

```
SELECT productid, productname, len(sku) AS CountSKUChars
FROM Products
```

Result:

productid	productname	CountSKUChars
1	Almonds, Hickory Smoked - 12 oz. Bag	10
2	Almonds, Roasted and Salted - 18 oz. Bag	11
3	Banana Chips - 20 oz. Bag	11
4	Berry Cherry in 8 oz. Bag	8

```
(70 row(s) returned)
```

225.   Find the position of a character in a string evaluating from the beginning of a string using the charindex() function

Find the number of characters occurring before the "-" character in the SKUs field

Discussion:

In business, we use stock keeping unit codes (SKU) to assign a unique code to products. In our products table, we do have an SKU field. This code consists of some letters and a hyphen followed by some numbers like PDKLS-3483. The letter part of the code before the hyphen signifies some larger category, and we might be required to create a report listing only the letter part of the SKU codes. Our problem is that the number of letters in the SKU is not always the same. At least this is what happened in my own experience. So, how can we get the string part of the SKU independent of the number of characters it consists of? To complete this task effectively, we first use the charindex() function to determine the position of the hyphen in the string (PDKLS-3483). Its general syntax appears below:

charindex(character to find ,field to search [, starting character])

In this example, we use charindex('-',sku,1) to look for the "-" character in the SKU field starting from the first character. Notice that we cannot use the charindex() function on text, ntext, and image fields.

Code:

SELECT productid, productname, sku, charindex('-',sku,1) AS PartSKU
FROM Products

Result:

productid	productname	sku	PartSKU
1	Almonds, Hickory Smoked - 12 oz. Bag	PDKLS-2332	6
2	Almonds, Roasted and Salted - 18 oz. Bag	PDKLSD-2344	7
3	Banana Chips - 20 oz. Bag	PDKLSD-2347	7
4	Berry Cherry in 8 oz. Bag	PDK-2589	4
5	California Original Pistachios - 1 lb. Bag	PDK-2347	4

(70 row(s) returned)

226. Find the position of a blank space evaluating from the beginning of a string using the charindex() function

Find the number of characters occurring before a blank space in the SKU field

Discussion:

For this example, I have purposely created an additional problem for us: Some of the hyphens separating the letter code of the SKU from the number code are missing because they were not typed correctly during data entry. We can still use the charindex() function to find the position of those blanks. Notice the WHERE clause, which is there so that the result set includes only SKU codes with spaces between letter and number codes and not those with hyphens. Pay attention also to the fact that for productids 41, and 42 the charindex() function found the first blank space in the beginning of the field, at position 1, and that is why these records have been returned. They would have been returned anyway since they do have a blank space later on as well.

Code:

SELECT productid, productname, sku, charindex(' ', sku, 1) AS PartSKU
FROM Products
WHERE charindex (' ', sku, 1) <> 0

Results:

productid	productname	sku	PartSKU
41	Banana Bisquits	ADSE 2345	1
42	Chocolate Bisquits	ADST 2345	1
43	Cocoa and Hazelnut Biscuits	ADSD 2345	5
44	Cream and honey biscuits	ADSL 2345	5

(7 row(s) returned)

227. Extract a substring from any part of a field

Extract part of the product name

Discussion:

In this example we want to extract five characters from the ProductName field starting at the fifth character. We can achieve this using the substring() function which takes three arguments. The first is the actual field name from which we will extract the substring, the second the starting character, and the third how many characters to extract.

substring (field name, where to start, how many characters to retrieve)

The code below will extract five characters from the productname field starting from the fifth one. The fifth character will be included in the retrieved expression as they will any spaces, periods, or other characters after that.

Code:

SELECT substring (productname, 5, 5)
FROM Products

Result:

ProductName
nds,
nds,
na Ch
y Che
fomi

(70 row(s) returned)

228.   Extract a substring ending in a special character like a hyphen from within a string

Extract the letter part of the SKU field

Discussion:

We can dynamically extract a substring ending in a special character from within a string. To do this, we use the left() and charindex() functions together. First, we use the charindex() function on the SKU field to obtain the numeric value of the exact position of the "hyphen" in the SKU field.

Code:

SELECT productid, productname, sku, charindex('-', sku) AS PartSKU
FROM Products

Result:

productid	productname	sku	PartSKU
1	Almonds, Hickory Smoked - 12 oz. Bag	PDKLS-2332	6
2	Almonds, Roasted and Salted - 18 oz....	PDKLSD-2344	7
3	Banana Chips - 20 oz. Bag	PDKLSD-2347	7
4	Berry Cherry in 8 oz. Bag	PDK-2589	4

(70 row(s) returned)

Then, we use the left() function, which takes two arguments. The first is the field, and the second is the number of characters to be returned. For the second argument we insert the expression charindex('-',sku). The whole expression below will retrieve the text part of the SKU including the hyphen independently of the number of characters it contains.

left(sku, charindex('-', sku))

Code:

SELECT productid, productname, sku, left(sku, charindex('-', sku)) AS PartSKU
FROM Products

Result:

productid	productname	sku	PartSKU
1	Almonds, Hickory Smoked - 12 oz. Bag	PDKLS-2332	PDKLS-
2	Almonds, Roasted and Salted - 18 oz. Bag	PDKLSD-2344	PDKLSD-
3	Banana Chips - 20 oz. Bag	PDKLSD-2347	PDKLSD-
4	Berry Cherry in 8 oz. Bag	PDK-2589	PDK-

(70 row(s) returned)

What if we want to exclude the hyphen? It is possible but we need a trick. The problem is that I messed up the data really well on purpose to simulate all possible problematic situations. That is, the sku code might have a blank in front of it, at the end, between the letters and numbers, a hyphen might exist or not, and letters and numbers do not have the same length. This is the rationale:

If we run the charindex() by itself, it will produce the following results. As you can see we have multiple 0s for some skus instead of the number that indicates the position of the hyphen. Why? Because some skus have no hyphens! Let us see what happens next.

Code:
```
SELECT charindex('-', sku) AS PartSKU
FROM Products
```

Result:

PartSKU
0
0
0
0
0
0
0
5
5
5

(70 row(s) returned)

To exclude the hyphen from the result set we need to add -1 at the end of the charindex() function. As you can see from the result set below, the -1 in the charindex() function creates negative numbers. This is a problem because the left function will not work with negative numbers. The cause of the negative numbers is the absence of hyphens in some SKU codes.

Code:
```
select charindex('-', sku)-1 AS PartSKU
FROM Products
```

Result:

PartSKU
-1
-1
-1
-1
-1
-1
-1
4
4
4

(70 row(s) returned)

Consequently, before we apply the left() function we need to exclude the sku codes without a hyphen. To do that, we use the code below which is actually the solution to the problem. It is but we still have a problem. As you can see in the result set the sku codes without a hyphen where excluded since now we have only 63 records. How can we retrieve the rest of them? This is the topic of the next example.

Code:
```
SELECT productid, productname, sku, left(sku,charindex('-', sku)-1) AS PartSKU
FROM Products
WHERE charindex('-', sku) > 0
```

Result:

productid	productname	sku	PartSKU
1	Almonds, Hickory Smoked - 12 oz. Bag	PDKLS-2332	PDKLS
2	Almonds, Roasted and Salted - 18 oz. Bag	PDKLSD-2344	PDKLSD
3	Banana Chips - 20 oz. Bag	PDKLSD-2347	PDKLSD
4	Berry Cherry in 8 oz. Bag	PDK-2589	PDK

(63 row(s) returned)

229. Extract a substring ending in a blank space
Extract the letter part of the SKU field just before a blank space
Discussion:
In this example, we extract the letter code of the SKU before a space. That is, we extract a substring that ends in a space from a string.

Code:
```
SELECT productid, productname, sku, left(sku, charindex(' ', sku)) AS PartSKU
FROM Products
WHERE charindex(' ', sku) <> 0
```

Result:

productid	productname	sku	PartSKU
41	Banana Bisquits	ADSE 2345	
42	Chocolate Bisquits	ADST 2345	
43	Cocoa and Hazelnut Biscuits	ADSD 2345	ADSD
44	Cream and honey biscuits	ADSL 2345	ADSL
45	Mushrooms Sauce	ADST 2345	ADST
46	Artichokes in white sauce	ADST 2345	ADST
47	Chocolate Chip Cookies	ADST 2345	ADST

```
(7 row(s) returned)
```

230. Remove blank spaces from the beginning of a field using the Ltrim() function

Remove blank spaces from the beginning of the product name field

Discussion:

The ltrim() function takes only one argument and is extremely easy and useful. It will simply eliminate any blank spaces from the beginning of the values of a field. For instance, in this example, we are not certain if there are blank spaces at the start of the field for some product names. We can simply use the ltrim() function to make certain there are not. The ltrim() function will eliminate any blank spaces if they exist. If there are no blank spaces for this field in some records, it will leave those values unchanged. Besides, blank spaces affect how other functions such as charindex() work. We can use the ltrim() function to make sure we count correctly from the beginning of the field.

Code:

```
SELECT productid, ltrim(productname) AS LeftTrimmedName, sku
FROM Products
```

Result:

productid	LeftTrimmedName	sku
1	Almonds, Hickory Smoked - 12 oz. Bag	PDKLS-2332
2	Almonds, Roasted and Salted - 18 oz. Bag	PDKLSD-2344
3	Banana Chips - 20 oz. Bag	PDKLSD-2347
4	Berry Cherry in 8 oz. Bag	PDK-2589

```
(70 row(s) returned)
```

231. Remove spaces from the end of a field using the Rtrim() function

Remove blank spaces from the end of the product name field

Discussion:

The Rtrim() function takes one argument, and its main job is to eliminate blank spaces from the end of a field. If there are no blank spaces, it will leave the field values unchanged. In addition, blank spaces affect how other functions work, for example the Right() function. Using the Rtrim() function, we make sure we count correctly from the end of the field.

Code:

```
SELECT productid, Rtrim(productname) AS RightTrimmedName, sku
FROM Products
```

Result:

productid	Right Trimmed Name	sku
1	Almonds, Hickory Smoked - 12 oz. Bag	PDKLS-2332
2	Almonds, Roasted and Salted - 18 oz. Bag	PDKLSD-2344
3	Banana Chips - 20 oz. Bag	PDKLSD-2347
4	Berry Cherry in 8 oz. Bag	PDK-2589

```
(70 row(s) returned)
```

232. Insert a space before or after a field

Insert a blank space in the beginning and end of the product name field

Discussion:

This time, we have the opposite task. Instead of using the Ltrim(), and Rtrim() functions to remove blank spaces from the beginning or end of a field, we want to add a blank space. To achieve this task, we use concatenation characters like '+' to add a space in the beginning and end of the productname field. You can read a whole chapter in this book on concatenation, which you can consult for multiple concatenation techniques (chapter 16).

Code:

```
SELECT productid, (' ' +productname + ' ')  AS SpacedName, sku
FROM Products
```

Result:

productid	SpacedName	sku
1	Almonds, Hickory Smoked - 12 oz. Bag	PDKLS-2332
2	Almonds, Roasted and Salted - 18 oz. Bag	PDKLSD-2344
3	Banana Chips - 20 oz. Bag	PDKLSD-2347
4	Berry Cherry in 8 oz. Bag	PDK-2589

```
(70 row(s) returned)
```

233. Use the space() function to insert any number of spaces dynamically before or after a field

Insert ten blank spaces in the beginning and end of the product name field

Discussion:

In some cases, we might want to add multiple blank spaces in the beginning or at the end of the same field. Using concatenation characters to achieve this task will be a very messy affair. Instead, we can use the space() function to achieve the same outcome as we do in the example below:

Code:

```
SELECT productid, (space(10)+ productname + space(10))  AS SpacedName, sku
FROM Products
```

Result:

productid	SpacedName	sku
1	Almonds, Hickory Smoked - 12 oz. Bag	PDKLS-2332
2	Almonds, Roasted and Salted - 18 oz. Bag	PDKLSD-2344
3	Banana Chips - 20 oz. Bag	PDKLSD-2347
4	Berry Cherry in 8 oz. Bag	PDK-2589

```
(70 row(s) returned)
```

234. Change field values using the Replace() function
Replace part of supplier's SKU codes dynamically
Discussion:
The replace() function provides us with great flexibility for our work. Let us suppose that one of our suppliers has recently updated the SKU coding they use, and we need to do the same for their products in our own database. From now on, products with the SKU letter codes "PDK" need to be updated to "PDS". Keep in mind that PDKSs and PDKRs need to remain as they are untouched. In addition, the number part of the SKU code needs to remain untouched. So, "PDK-2389" needs to become "PDS-2389". Consequently, we need to isolate the exact letter code "PDK", replace it with PDS, and leave the trailing numbers untouched. This is a job for the replace function. Its basic syntax appears below:

replace(field name, string to search for, string to replace with)

For example the expression
replace(sku, 'pdk-', 'pds-')

will replace "pdk-" with "pds-". The way we work when it comes to updates is to isolate the records to be updated first. We write a SELECT statement to isolate the records to be updated. Then, we write the update statement against those records only. This way, just in case something goes sideways, we know which records are affected. This logic is demonstrated below with two consecutive SQL statements:

Code:
SELECT productid, productname, sku
FROM Products
WHERE left(sku, 4) = 'PDK-'

Result:

productid	productname	sku
4	Berry Cherry in 8 oz. Bag	PDK-2589
5	California Original Pistachios - 1 lb. Bag	PDK-2347

(2 row(s) returned)

Here we actually replace on the fly: Notice that no records will be updated in the back end table. If we need to update the actual records in the table we will use an UPDATE statement instead of the SELECT below.

Code:
SELECT productid, productname, replace(sku, 'pdk-', 'pds-') As skuUpdated
FROM Products
WHERE left(sku, 4) = 'PDK-'

Result:

productid	productname	skuUpdated
4	Berry Cherry in 8 oz. Bag	pds-2589
5	California Original Pistachios - 1 lb. Bag	pds-2347

(2 row(s) returned)

235.   Reverse the order of characters in a field using the Reverse() function

Reverse the order of characters in the SKU field in the products table

Discussion:

The Reverse() function is easy to use, and it takes only one argument as its syntax shows below. It will return a string in which the character order is reversed.

$$Reverse(field)$$

In this example, we apply it on the SKU field in the products table, and we see from the output that the number part of the SKU now appears first. Of course, this happens dynamically, and the actual data in the table will not be affected.

Code:

SELECT productid, Reverse(sku) As ReverseSKU
FROM Products

Result:

productid	ReverseSKU
1	2332-SLKDP
2	4432-DSLKDP
3	7432-DSLKDP
4	9852-KDP

(70 row(s) returned)

	Function Name	Syntax/Explanation
1.	ASCII	ASCII(Character string)
2.	CHAR	CHAR (Integer number)
3.	CHARINDEX	CHARINDEX (expressionToFind ,expressionToSearch [,
4.	CONCAT	CONCAT (string_value1, string_value2 [, string_valueN])
5.	DIFFERENCE	DIFFERENCE (character_expression , character_expression)
6.	FORMAT	FORMAT (value, format [, culture])
7.	LEFT	LEFT (character_expression, NumberOfCharacterstoReturn)
8.	LEN	LEN (character_expression)
9.	LOWER	LOWER (character_expression)
10.	LTRIM	LTRIM (character_expression)
11.	NCHAR	NCHAR (integer_expression)
12.	PATINDEX	PATINDEX ('%pattern%' , expression)
13.	QUOTENAME	QUOTENAME ('character_string' [, 'quote_character'])
14.	REPLACE	REPLACE (character_expression , character_pattern , character_replacement)
15.	REPLICATE	REPLICATE (character_expression ,integer_expression)
16.	REVERSE	REVERSE (character_expression)
17.	RIGHT	RIGHT (character_expression , integer_expression)
18.	RTRIM	RTRIM (character_expression)
19.	SOUNDEX	SOUNDEX (character_expression)
20.	SPACE	SPACE (integer_expression)
21.	STR	STR (float_expression [, length [, decimal]])
22.	STUFF	STUFF (character_expression , start , length , replaceWith_expression)
23.	SUBSTRING	SUBSTRING (expression ,start , length)
24.	UNICODE	UNICODE ('ncharacter_expression')
25.	UPPER	UPPER (character_expression)

Source: http://technet.microsoft.com/en-us/library/ms181984.aspx

CHAPTER 25 DISCUSSION QUESTIONS

1. What function can we use to capitalize field values?
2. What do we need to do to capitalize only the first character in a field value?
3. What is the purpose of the lower() function?
4. What is the purpose of the left() function?
5. What function do we use if we need to retrieve only the last four characters from a field?
6. What function can we use to count the number of characters in a field?
7. What function can we use to find the position of a character or a blank space in a string?
8. What functions do we use to remove spaces from the beginning or the end of strings?
9. What function can we use to enter any number of spaces before or after a field value?
10. When we update field values using the replace() function are those updates permanent in the back-end table?

CHAPTER 25 HANDS-ON EXERCISES

Chapter 25 Case 1:
Start SQL Server Management Studio. For each of the questions in this case create a new query (Ctrl-N) and name it as per the instructions in each question. Submit your work to your instructor as one text file that contains all SQL statements or as per your instructor's directions.

1. The sales people need to create mailing labels to send out letters to customers. They want the first name of the customer capitalized for emphasis. Create a new query that contains the FirstName, LastName, City, State, and Zip fields from the customer table that satisfies the sales people request. Save the query as Chapter25_Case1_Q1.

   Your result should look like:

Firstname	LastName	City	State	Zip
JOHN	Demarco	New York	NY	12189
MARY	Demania	New York	NY	12189
GEORGE	Demers	New York	NY	12189
PHILLIP	Demetriou	New York	NY	12189
ANDREW	Demichele	New York	NY	12189

   (201 row(s) returned)

2. The marketing people need to send out letters to customers but they fear that some of the addresses are too long and they might exceed the space limit they have on a special pamphlet they are preparing. They are asking you to provide a report which shows the customers whose address exceeds twenty (20) characters. Create a new query that contains the FirstName, LastName, city, state, and zip fields from the customers table and satisfies the sales people request. Save the query as Chapter25_Case1_Q2.

   Your result should look like:

FirstName	LastName	city	state	zip
Kenneth	Crondos	Houston	TX	53289
Stephanie	Elser	San Jose	CA	36945
Cynthia	Papadopoulos	Phoenix	AZ	44895

(3 row(s) returned)

3. The marketing people are back asking for a list of customers for whom it is certain there are no blank spaces in front of the FirstName or the LastName fields because any blank spaces interfere with the alignment of the various paragraphs in the personalized brochures they are preparing. Create a new query that contains the FirstName, LastName, City, State, and Zip fields from the customers table and satisfies the marketing people request. Save the query as Chapter25_Case1_Q3.

Your result should look like:

FirstName	LastName	City	State	Zip
John	Demarco	New York	NY	12189
Mary	Demania	New York	NY	12189
George	Demers	New York	NY	12189
Phillip	Demetriou	New York	NY	12189
Andrew	Demichele	New York	NY	12189

(201 row(s) returned)

4. The marketing people are very happy with the list you provided them in question 3. They have a final request that will help the graphic designers who are working on the pamphlet. Specifically they need five blank spaces for all customers at the end of the Zip field. Create a new query that contains the FirstName, LastName, City, State, and Zip fields from the customers table and satisfies the marketing people request. Save the query as Chapter25_Case1_Q4.

Your result should look like:

FirstName	LastName	City	State	Zip
John	Demarco	New York	NY	12189
Mary	Demania	New York	NY	12189
George	Demers	New York	NY	12189
Phillip	Demetriou	New York	NY	12189
Andrew	Demichele	New York	NY	12189

(201 row(s) returned)

5. The marketing people need a report that contains the FirstName, LastName, City, State, and Zip fields from the customers table. However, for the customers in the state of NY they want the whole name of the state to appear such as "New York" instead of the abbreviation "NY". Create a new query that satisfies the marketing people request without changing the state values in the back-end customers table. Save the query as Chapter25_Case1_Q5.

Your result should look like:

FirstName	LastName	City	State	Zip
John	Demarco	New York	New York	12189
Mary	Demania	New York	New York	12189
George	Demers	New York	New York	12189
Phillip	Demetriou	New York	New York	12189
Andrew	Demichele	New York	New York	12189

(201 row(s) returned)

Chapter 25 Case 2:

Start SQL Server Management Studio. For each of the questions in this case create a new query (Ctrl-N) and name it as per the instructions in each question. Submit your work to your instructor as one text file that contains all SQL statements or as per your instructor's directions.

1. The sales people need to create a new product catalog. Specifically, they need a catalog that contains the ProductName and ProductUnitPrice fields from the table tble_Products_Strings. For the Product name field they need only the portion of the name up until the dash to appear and not any weight information about the product. Create a new query that satisfies the sales people request and save it as Chapter25_Case2_Q1.

    Your result should look like:

NewProductName	ProductUnitPrice
Almonds, Hickory Smoked -	35.00
Almonds, Roasted and Salted -	22.00
Banana Chips -	27.00
Berry Cherry -	30.00
California Original Pistachios -	29.00

    (13 row(s) returned)

2. The sales people are back asking for another product catalog. They again need the product catalog to contain the ProductName and ProductUnitPrice fields from the tble_Products_Strings table but this time they want the "oz." notation to be replaced by "grams." Create a new query that satisfies the sales people request and save it as Chapter25_Case2_Q2.

    Your result should look like:

NewProductName	ProductUnitPrice
Almonds, Hickory Smoked - 12 grams. Bag	35.00
Almonds, Roasted and Salted - 18 grams. Bag	22.00
Banana Chips - 20 grams. Bag	27.00
Berry Cherry - in 8 grams. Bag	30.00
California Original Pistachios - 1 lb. Bag	29.00

    (13 row(s) returned)

3. The supplierID field has the format XXX-XXX or XXXX-XXX with the first three or four numbers indicating the region of the supplier while the last three digits representing the product family the supplier is

manufacturing for us. The production people need a list that includes the ProductName and SupplierID fields fields from the tble_Products_Strings table. For the supplierID field they only need the region indicator to appear. They do not want any dashes to appear at the end of the SupplierID field. Create a new query that satisfies the production people request and save it as Chapter25_Case2_Q3.

Your result should look like:

SupplierID	ProductName
1111	Almonds, Hickory Smoked - 12 oz. Bag
1111	Almonds, Roasted and Salted - 18 oz. Bag
1111	Banana Chips - 20 oz. Bag
112	Berry Cherry - in 8 oz. Bag
112	California Original Pistachios - 1 lb. Bag

(13 row(s) returned)

4. The inventory people liked very much the report you created for the production people in question 3 and they want a similar report which will include the total the value of inventory on hand by supplier region. Create a new query that satisfies the inventory people request and save it as Chapter25_Case2_Q4.

Your result should look like:

SupplierRegion	TotalValueInStock
1111	2779
1119	3805
112	3963
115	1609

(4 row(s) returned)

5. The inventory people are really amazed by the information you were able to give them. They now have one additional request. They need a report that will total the value of inventory on hand by product family. Create a new query with the fields ProductFamily and TotalValueInStock from the tble_Products_Strings table that satisfies the inventory people request and save it as Chapter25_Case2_Q5.

Your result should look like:

ProductFamily	TotalValueInStock
121	3404
122	2671
123	1554
141	1419
143	3108

(5 row(s) returned)

CHAPTER 26
WORKING WITH DATES

Date functions enable us to perform a superior level of work in multiple database tasks. For instance, we can create advanced reports by extracting the year or month out of a date field, and then, we can summarize data based on those years or months. Second, we can extract the quarters out of a date range and create a crosstab query showing our data by quarter. Third, we can create projected order fulfillment cycle times by adding, say, two business days to the order date field and comparing our projections with the actual shipped dates for quality control. Fourth, we can use date functions as default field values to a table field to record the exact date and time a record was inserted. Fifth, with date functions, we can convert numerical date values such as 9/20/2014 to actual named values such as September 20, 2014. Sixth, we can combine date functions with aggregate functions for exceptional data calculations and summaries. Seventh, our level of knowledge on date functions will have a direct effect on the quality of our database design since we can avoid date fields that we can create automatically from other date fields. These examples are just a small part of what we can do with date functions. The main point is that date functions do not just represent additional knowledge; they are required for truly exceptional work.

236.   Find orders within two dates
Discussion:

In this example we want to produce a list of orders between the dates of 1/1/2014 and 6/30/2014. There are two ways to achieve this task. We can use the inequality and equality predicates or the BETWEEN AND operator. Of course you remember that the BETWEEEN AND operator is inclusive which means the boundary dates will be included in the result set.

Code (using BETWEEN AND):
```
SELECT *
FROM Orders
WHERE OrderDate BETWEEN '2014/1/1' AND '2014/6/30'
ORDER BY OrderDate ASC
```

Code (using inequality and equality predicates):
```
SELECT *
FROM Orders
WHERE OrderDate>= '2014/1/1' AND OrderDate<= '2014/6/30'
ORDER BY OrderDate
```

Result:

OrderID	CustomerID	SalesRepID	ShipperID	OrderDate	RequiredDate	ShippedDate
581	143	6	2	2014-01-02	2014-01-12	2014-01-07
431	29	5	1	2014-01-03	2014-01-13	2014-01-08
146	144	1	3	2014-01-04	2014-01-14	2014-01-09
473	160	5	2	2014-01-04	2014-01-14	2014-01-09

```
(165 row(s) returned)
```

237.   Find orders outside two dates

Discussion:
To find orders outside two dates we need to use equality and inequality predicates as in the code below. Notice how we use the OR operator when we want to find outside date ranges.

Code:
```
SELECT *
FROM Orders
WHERE OrderDate<= '2014/1/1' OR OrderDate >= '2014/6/30'
ORDER BY OrderDate
```

Result:

OrderID	CustomerID	SalesRepID	ShipperID	OrderDate	RequiredDate	ShippedDate
351	56	4	1	2012-01-14	2012-01-24	2012-01-19
380	193	4	3	2012-01-15	2012-01-25	2012-01-20
76	113	1	2	2012-01-15	2012-01-25	2012-01-20
854	80	9	2	2012-01-15	2012-01-25	2012-01-20

```
(835 row(s) returned)
```

238.   Set default field values using the GetDate() function

Discussion:
The GetDate() function will output the system date and time, and it is frequently used as the default value for a date field. For example, if we open the SalesReps table, we will notice that there is a field called DateInserted with a default value of GetDate(). This means that every time a record is inserted in this table, the system date and time will be recorded in this field. We can also use GetDate() to capture the date and time as in the statement below:

Code:
```
SELECT GetDate() as CurrentTimeAndDate
```

Result:

CurrentTimeAndDate
2013-08-29 14:19:03.323

```
(1 row(s) returned)
```

239.   Find the latest order by customer using the max() function

Discussion:
The sales people are asking for a report that shows the latest order for each customer. Specifically, they want to see a list that contains the last name, first name, and latest order date for each customer. There is a plethora of solutions here but we will go for the simplest one.

Solution 1:
We can quickly identify the latest order by using the max() function and the group by clause but the problem is we will not see the customer first and last names:

313

Code 1:
```
SELECT customerID, max(OrderDate) As LatestOrder
FROM Orders
GROUP BY customerID
```

Result 1:

customerID	LatestOrder
23	2014-09-29
46	2014-09-09
192	2014-08-12
92	2014-03-27
115	2014-10-16

```
(190 row(s) returned)
```

Solution 2 (practically wrong in most cases):
If we need the name of the customer to show we can go with a solution like the one below with the max() function, an INNER JOIN (chapter 29), and the GROUP BY clause. This solution is conceptually correct but practically wrong because in most cases we have multiple customers with the same last name. Even if you concatenate the customers' first and last names and use the group by clause on the concatenated name, you might still get wrong results because some customers will have the same first and last names. Notice that we already have 171 records returned from the 190 in the previous example.

Code 2 (wrong in most cases):
```
SELECT lastname, Max(Orders.OrderDate) AS MaxOfOrderDate
FROM Customers INNER JOIN Orders ON Customers.CustomerID = Orders.CustomerID
GROUP BY lastname
```

Result 2:

lastname	MaxOfOrderDate
Ackerman	2014-07-29
Ames	2014-10-30
Andersen	2014-04-18
Anderson	2014-12-10

```
(171 row(s) returned)
```

Solution 3 (Simple and correct solution)
In this example we use the group by clause on the first name, last name, and customerid fields combined. There is no way to mess up results since the CustomerID field is the primary key (PK) in the customer table and thus unique for each customer.

Code 3
```
SELECT Customers.CustomerID, Customers.LastName, Customers.FirstName,
Max(Orders.OrderDate) AS LatestOrderDate
FROM Customers INNER JOIN Orders ON Customers.CustomerID = Orders.CustomerID
GROUP BY Customers.CustomerID, Customers.LastName, Customers.FirstName
```

Result 3

CustomerID	LastName	FirstName	LatestOrderDate
1	Demarco	John	2014-01-09
2	Demania	Mary	2014-06-07
3	Demers	George	2013-06-07
4	Demetriou	Phillip	2014-09-28
5	Demichele	Andrew	2013-11-23

(190 row(s) returned)

240. Calculate the difference between two dates using the datediff() function.

Discussion:

We can calculate the number of days between two dates using the datediff(DatePart, StartDate, EndDate) function. Notice from the table below the rich array of options we have for the Datediff() function. Check the table at the end of this chapter for a list of all possible values for the datepart argument of the datediff() function.

Code:

```
SELECT DateDiff(d, '2014/5/15', '2014/6/30')  As NumberOfDays
```

Result:

NumberOfDays
46

(1 row(s) returned)

241. Count the number of orders by business day of the week and within a specific quarter.

Discussion:

In this example, we calculate the number of orders by business day of the week within a specific quarter. Check how we use the datepart(DatePart, Date) function in conjunction with the IN operator in the WHERE clause to isolate the business days only. By default the week in SQL Server starts on Sunday and consequently Monday will be the second (2) day, Tuesday the third (3), and Friday the sixth (6). Also, check how we use the weekday 'dw' datepart argument in the datepart() function in the SELECT statement. Check the table at the end of this chapter for a list of all possible values for the datepart argument of the datepart() function.

Code:

```
SELECT datepart(dw, orderdate) As BusinessDay, Count(OrderID) AS NumberOfOrders
FROM Orders
WHERE year(orderdate) = 2014 AND datepart(q, orderdate) = 2 AND datepart(dw, orderdate) IN
(2,3,4,5,6)
GROUP BY datepart(dw, orderdate)
```

Result:

BusinessDay	NumberOfOrders
2	12
3	9
4	13
5	8
6	12

(5 row(s) returned)

242.   Count the number of orders by non-business days of the week and by quarter within a specific year

Discussion:

In this example, we are looking for the number of orders in non-business days of the week, that is, Saturdays and Sundays. We also want to present results grouped by quarter within a specific year. Notice in the code below how we use the datepart(datepart, datefield) function in the WHERE clause to isolate the non-business days of the week (Saturday and Sunday). Sunday in SQL Server is the first (1) day of the week and thus Saturday is the seventh (7). Notice how we use the datepart() function to group twice by quarter "q" and by weekday "dw". Check the table at the end of this chapter for a list of all possible values for the datepart argument of the datepart() function.

Code:

```
SELECT datepart(q, orderdate) As Quarter, datepart(dw, orderdate) As NonBusinessDay,
Count(OrderID) AS NumberOfOrders
FROM Orders
WHERE year(orderdate) = 2014 AND datepart(dw, orderdate) IN (1,7)
GROUP BY datepart(q, orderdate), datepart(dw, orderdate)
```

Result:

Quarter	NonBusinessDay	NumberOfOrders
1	1	12
2	1	11
3	1	13
4	1	16
1	7	13
2	7	12
3	7	16
4	7	3

(8 row(s) returned)

243.   List orders within a month using the datepart() function

Discussion (month):

This time the request is to create a simple list of all orders in June 2014. We can respond to this request by using the datepart(datepart, datefield) function to extract the month from the OrderDate field and the year(datefield) function to extract the year. Notice the usage of "m" for the interval argument in the datepart() function. Check the table at the end of this chapter for a list of all possible values for the datepart argument of the datepart() function.

Code:
```
SELECT *
FROM Orders
WHERE DatePart(m, [OrderDate]) =6 AND year(Orderdate) = 2014
ORDER BY OrderDate
```

Result:

OrderID	CustomerID	SalesRepID	ShipperID	OrderDate
40	109	5	1	2014-06-01
178	95	2	2	2014-06-01
319	11	3	1	2014-06-02
60	175	1	2	2014-06-03
856	17	9	2	2014-06-04

```
(22 row(s) returned)
```

Of course we could obtain the same result by leaving out the functions and just use absolute date intervals which are fine since what matters is to get the job done.

Code:
```
SELECT *
FROM Orders
WHERE OrderDate BETWEEN '2014/6/1' AND '2014/6/30'
ORDER BY OrderDate
```

244. Count the number of orders by each day of the month using the datepart() function

Discussion:

But then, why do we need to learn about functions? Because if our manager asks to count the number of orders by day within June 2014 we will need to use the DatePart(datepart, datefield) function to respond as in the example below. Check the table at the end of this chapter for a list of all possible values for the datepart argument of the datepart() function.

Code:
```
SELECT DatePart(d,OrderDate) AS Day, Count(OrderID) AS NumberOfOrders
FROM Orders
WHERE Year([OrderDate])=2014 AND DatePart(m,[OrderDate]) = 6
GROUP BY DatePart(d,[OrderDate])
ORDER BY DatePart(d,[OrderDate])
```

Result:

As you can see from the result set, we obtain the total number of orders for each of the 31 days in June 2014 where we had any orders. We have fifteen records below because we did not have orders every single day of the month.

Day	NumberOfOrders
1	2
2	1
3	1
4	1
6	2
7	2

(15 row(s) returned)

245.   Count the number of orders by week using the datepart() function

Discussion:

In this example we calculate the number of orders within each one of the 52 weeks of the calendar year 2014. Notice from the SQL code that we only have two output fields (Week and NumberofOrders) while we use the year([OrderDate]) field in the WHERE clause to limit the results within the year 2014. This is a quick way to identify order numbers and look for seasonality effects in our sales patterns. Check the table at the end of this chapter for a list of all possible values for the datepart argument of the datepart() function.

Code:

```
SELECT DatePart(ww,[OrderDate]) AS Week, Count(OrderID) AS NumberOfOrders
FROM Orders
WHERE (((Year([OrderDate]))=2014))
GROUP BY DatePart(ww,[OrderDate])
```

Result:

Week	NumberOfOrders
1	4
2	8
3	3
4	6
5	7

(21 row(s) returned)

246.   Count the number of orders every Monday for the last three months using the datepart() function

Discussion:

What if we have a request from marketing to count the number of orders for a specific day of the week and for a period of three months? It can be absolutely done and it is much less complicated than it sounds. First we use the DatePart(datepart, datefield) function twice to extract the month and the week day from the Orderdate field. Then we use the Year() and Datepart() functions in the WHERE clause to isolate the year to 2014, the quarter to the first quarter of the year, and the weekday to Monday since by default in SQL Server the week starts on Sunday which is day 1. Then, we group the results by month and day to arrive at the desired outcome.   This way we can calculate all the orders for any specific day of the week and any period we would like. Check the table at the end of this chapter for a list of all possible values for the datepart argument of the datepart() function.

Code:

```
SELECT DatePart(m,[OrderDate]) As month, DatePart(dw,[OrderDate]) AS Day,  Count(OrderID)
AS NumberOfOrders
FROM Orders
WHERE year(OrderDate) = 2014  AND  datepart(q, ([OrderDate])) = 1  AND datepart(w,
([OrderDate])) = 2
GROUP BY DatePart(m,[OrderDate]), DatePart(w,[OrderDate])
ORDER BY DatePart(m,[OrderDate])
```

Result:

month	Day	NumberOfOrders
1	2	2
2	2	3
3	2	7

(3 row(s) returned)

247. Calculate order totals for the same week in different years using the year() and datepart() functions

Discussion:

Management is asking for a report of order totals for the week before Christmas for all the years for which we have data in the database. Practically, we are talking about week 50 out of the 52 weeks for the whole year. For this request we need to group order totals first by year and secondly by week since we also need to show the difference of sales among the weeks 50 in each year. We use the Year(datefield) function to extract the year out of the OrderDate field. Notice that we use the Datepart(datepart, datefield) function to extract the week since there is no week() function in SQL Server. Finally, notice how we use the DatePart() function in the WHERE clause to make sure we have results only for weeks that equal 50. This results in some very interesting time series analysis. Check the table at the end of this chapter for a list of all possible values for the datepart argument of the datepart() function.

Code:

```
SELECT Year([orderdate]) AS [Year], DatePart(ww,[OrderDate]) AS Week, Sum(unitprice*quantity)
AS OrderTotal
FROM View_Invoices
WHERE (((DatePart(ww,[OrderDate]))=50))
GROUP BY Year([orderdate]), DatePart(ww,[OrderDate])
```

Result:

Year	Week	OrderTotal
2012	50	1158
2013	50	1074
2014	50	990

(3 row(s) returned)

248. Calculate order totals by year using the year(), and datepart() functions

Discussion (year function):

On many occasions, we want to extract the year out of a date field to create aggregate summaries of our data. One way to achieve this task is to use the year() function, which takes only one argument. Its general syntax is:

Year(date)

In this example, we want to calculate order totals by year. We use the year() function to extract the year out of the OrderDate field in combination with the sum() aggregate function to calculate order totals.

Code:

```
SELECT year(OrderDate) AS Year, sum(unitprice*quantity) AS OrderTotal
FROM View_Invoices
GROUP BY Year(OrderDate)
```

Result:

Year	OrderTotal
2013	51164
2014	45002
2012	44230

(3 row(s) returned)

Discussion (datepart function):

We could also extract the year from a date field using the datepart() function. The datepart() function has two arguments. Its syntax appears below:

datepart(datepart, datefield)

The datepart argument indicates the date part we want to extract from the date field. For example, we would use "yyyy" to extract the year or "q" to extract the quarter. Check the table at the end of this chapter for a list of all possible values for the datepart argument of the datepart() function.

Code:

```
SELECT datepart(yyyy, OrderDate) AS Year, SUM(unitprice*quantity) AS OrderTotal
FROM View_Invoices
GROUP BY datepart(yyyy, OrderDate)
```

Result:

Year	OrderTotal
2013	51164
2014	45002
2012	44230

(3 row(s) returned)

249. Calculate order totals by quarter for a specific year using the datepart() function

Discussion:

The business goal in this example is to create a quarterly sales report for the year 2014. To achieve this task, we need to use two date functions. First, we will use the year() function to extract the year from the orderdate field and use this expression in the WHERE clause with an equality predicate "=". This way, we make certain that our resulting recordset contains orders only for the year 2014. Then, we can use the datepart(datepart, datefield) function to group by our order totals by quarter.

Code:

```
SELECT datePart(q,[OrderDate])  AS Quarter, sum(unitprice*quantity) AS OrderTotal
FROM View_Invoices
WHERE Year(orderdate) = 2014
GROUP BY DatePart(q , [OrderDate])
```

Result:

Quarter	OrderTotal
3	11856
1	12709
4	9555
2	10882

(4 row(s) returned)

250.   Calculate monthly order and discount totals for a specific year using the month(), datename() and datepart() functions

Discussion (with month):

The business goal in this example is to calculate order and associated discount totals by month for the year 2014. Management wants to have a look at the numbers to check the discount percentages forwarded by the sales reps. There are three different ways to achieve this result depending on the date function we use. Notice that in all three examples, the rationale is the same: We will use the year() function to isolate the year from the orderdate field and use this expression in the WHERE clause. Then, we need to use a function to isolate the month from the orderdate field so that we can group by month within the year 2014. Finally, we will use two calculated fields (OrderTotal and TotalDiscount) to calculate the order and discount totals for each month.

Discussion with the month() function:

In this first alternative, we will use the month function to extract the month from the orderdate field. The month() function has only one argument, and its syntax appears below:

month(datefield)

Code:

```
SELECT month(OrderDate) AS [Month], Sum(unitprice*quantity) AS OrderTotal,
Sum((([unitprice]*[quantity])*[Discount]) AS TotalDiscount
FROM View_Invoices
WHERE year(orderdate) = 2014
GROUP BY month(OrderDate)
```

Result:

Month	OrderTotal	TotalDiscount
1	4012	669.70
2	3607	554.15
3	5090	805.55
4	5376	780.75

(12 row(s) returned)

Discussion (with monthname):

The management is not very happy with our first report because the month numbers confused them, and they could not quickly discern the corresponding month name. They now ask us to provide them with another report showing actual month names. We can do this immediately using the datename() function. Notice how we use the month(orderdate) function in the ORDER BY clause to have the months appear in the correct order. For a full list of all the arguments for the datename function please refer to the end of this chapter.

Code:

```
SELECT datename(m,OrderDate) AS [Month], sum(unitprice*quantity) AS OrderTotal,
sum(([unitprice]*[quantity])*[Discount]) AS TotalDiscount
FROM View_Invoices
WHERE year(orderdate) = 2014
GROUP BY datename(m,OrderDate), month([OrderDate])
ORDER BY month([OrderDate])
```

Result:

Month	OrderTotal	TotalDiscount
January	4012	669.70
February	3607	554.15
March	5090	805.55
April	5376	780.75
May	2280	364.90

(12 row(s) returned)

Discussion (with datepart):

We can also use the datepart() function to achieve the same result except that we will get numerals instead of month names. In other words, the result will be identical with that of the month() function. The only real difference is that the month function is much simpler, and we do not need to remember the "m" argument of the datepart() function.

Code:

```
SELECT datepart(m, OrderDate) AS [Month], sum(unitprice*quantity) AS OrderTotal,
Sum(([unitprice]*[quantity])*[Discount]) AS TotalDiscount
FROM View_Invoices
WHERE year(orderdate) = 2014
GROUP BY datepart(m, OrderDate), month([OrderDate])
ORDER BY datepart(m, OrderDate)
```

Result:

Month	OrderTotal	TotalDiscount
1	4012	669.70
2	3607	554.15
3	5090	805.55
4	5376	780.75

(12 row(s) returned)

251.   Count the number of orders by day of the week for the whole year using the datepart() function

Discussion:

The goal here is to count the number of orders by day of the week for the whole year. That is, how many orders we had in total on Mondays, how many on Tuesdays, how many on Wednesdays etc. Notice how we use the day of the week argument ("dw") in the DatePart(datepart, dategield) function to isolate the days of the week and then group by them. Remember that by default in SQL Server the week starts on Sunday = 1.   As you can see from the result set, we obtain some very useful information indeed. For example, that we have the most orders on Wednesday (day 4), followed by Sunday (day 1).

Code:

SELECT DatePart(dw,[OrderDate]) AS Day, Count(OrderID) AS NumberOfOrders
FROM Orders
WHERE (((Year([OrderDate]))=2014))
GROUP BY DatePart(dw,[OrderDate])

Result:

Day	NumberOfOrders
1	52
2	44
3	45
4	62
5	47
6	46
7	44

(7 row(s) returned)

Of course we could obtain the names of the days using the datename(datepart, date field) function as in the code below. Please see the table at the end of the chapter for all possible arguments of the datename() function.

Code:

SELECT DateName(dw,[OrderDate]) AS Day, Count(OrderID) AS NumberOfOrders
FROM Orders
WHERE (((Year([OrderDate]))=2014))
GROUP BY DateName(dw,[OrderDate])

Result:

Day	NumberOfOrders
Friday	46
Monday	44
Saturday	44
Sunday	52
Thursday	47
Tuesday	45
Wednesday	62

(7 row(s) returned)

CHAPTER 26

252.   Count the number of orders by day of the year using the datepart() function

Discussion:

In this example, we calculate the number of orders by day of the year. We have 365 days per year and by using the "y" datepart argument we can isolate the number of orders by the day of the year. Very useful data for some time series analysis throughout the year. Notice from the result set, we see that from the 365 days of the year we had orders only on 222 days.

Code:

```
SELECT DatePart(y,OrderDate) AS Day, Count(OrderID) AS NumberOfOrders
FROM Orders
WHERE Year([OrderDate])=2014
GROUP BY DatePart(y,[OrderDate])
ORDER BY DatePart(y,[OrderDate])
```

Result:

Day	NumberOfOrders
2	1
3	1
4	2
5	2
7	2

(222 row(s) returned)

253.   Anniversaries: Find past anniversaries using the LIKE operator.

Discussion:

Let us assume we need a list of orders for today's date which is 10/22/2014. Practically, we need to find all orders which occurred on 10/22 of each year in our order history. A very easy and flexible way to achieve this is by using the LIKE operator as in the code below. As you can see from the result set, we had four past orders the 22nd of October. Notice that we put the percent character in the year part of the date. Moving the percent to the month or day part of the date we can achieve some additional interesting results.

Code:

```
SELECT OrderID, CustomerID, OrderDate
FROM Orders
WHERE OrderDate Like '%-10-22'
```

Result:

OrderID	CustomerID	OrderDate
16	20	2013-10-22
579	20	2013-10-22
658	139	2013-10-22
904	11	2013-10-22

(4 row(s) returned)

254.   Anniversaries: Find future anniversaries using the DateAdd() function.

Discussion:

In this case we need to find the future date at which our sales representatives complete 20 years of service. We can do this by using the DateAdd(datepart, number, date field) function which takes three arguments. In this case we use the "yyyy" datepart argument and we add 20 years to the DateOfHire field. For a full list of the options for the datepart argument please see the DateAdd() table at the end of this chapter.

Code:

```
SELECT firstname, lastname, DateAdd(yyyy, 20 , DateOfHire) AS Anniversary20yr
FROM SalesReps
```

Result:

firstname	lastname	Anniversary20yr
John	Anderson	2019-01-01
Mary	Teall	2020-06-12
George	Spicer	2024-05-15
Phillip	Zensons	2021-06-10

(10 row(s) returned)

255.   Anniversaries: Finding upcoming anniversaries within a specific period.

Discussion:

We would like to create a list of employees with a birthday within a specific month of the year. We can do this by using the datepart (datepart, datefield) function twice; first to show the day of the employee's birthday as you can see in the SELECT statement and second to isolate the month of the year as you can see in the WHERE clause. In this specific example, we are looking for employee birthdays in the month of April. As you can see from the result set, we have four employees with birthdays in the month of April. We also get to know the exact day of their birthday within the month.

Code:

```
SELECT firstname, lastname, title, datepart(d, dateofbirth) As DayOfBirth
FROM SalesReps
WHERE datepart(m, dateofbirth) = 4
```

Result:

firstname	lastname	title	DayOfBirth
John	Anderson	Sales Reppresentative	15
George	Spicer	Assitant Director of Sales	4
Phillip	Zensons	Sales Reppresentative	3
Gerald	Williams	Sales Reppresentative	1

(10 row(s) returned)

256.   Anniversaries: Calculate time elapsed such as employment length using the DateDiff() function

Discussion:

We have a request from management to calculate the number of employment years for each of our employees. We can use the DateDiff(datepart, start date, end date) function to calculate the elapsed time between the employee's date of hire and today's date. We use the "yyyy" option to display the interval in years and the GetDate() function to obtain today's date from which we will subtract the date of hire.

Code:

```
SELECT firstname, lastname, DateDiff(yyyy, DateOfHire, GetDate()) AS YearsEmployed
FROM SalesReps
```

Result:

firstname	lastname	YearsEmployed
John	Anderson	14
Mary	Teall	13
George	Spicer	9
Phillip	Zensons	12

```
(10 row(s) returned)
```

257.   Anniversaries: Calculating Employee Age

Discussion:

This time we would like to calculate the ages of our employees. We can do this using the DateDiff(datepart, start date, end date) function which subtracts the start date from the end date and provides the difference in years, months, quarters or in any other period we need. Refer to the end of this chapter for all possible interval settings for the DateDiff() function. In this particular example, we see the age in years and that is why we use the "yyyy" setting.

Code:

```
SELECT firstname, lastname, title, DateDiff(yyyy, DateOfBirth, GetDate())  As Age
FROM SalesReps
```

Result:

firstname	lastname	title	Age
John	Anderson	Sales Reppresentative	53
Mary	Teall	Sales Director	23
George	Spicer	Assitant Director of Sales	30
Phillip	Zensons	Sales Reppresentative	35

```
(10 row(s) returned)
```

258.   Calculate order processing cycle times using the DateDiff() function

Discussion:

Customer service has reported to management that customers are complaining about shipping. Specifically, they complain that it takes a lot of time to receive their orders after they complete the ordering process. Management is trying to determine the cause, and they need our help. They want to know if the problem is internal as a result of packaging and payment processing or if the problem is external as a result of the shipping company. They suspect the problem is internal, and they tell us to produce a report that lists how many days it takes for an order to ship from the time it has been received.

We can do this by using the datediff() function. The datediff() function takes three arguments and the general syntax of the function appears below. The datepart argument is a string that will determine in what interval we want to find the difference between start date and end date. For instance, we might want to calculate the difference in days, weeks, months, or years. Please refer to the end of this chapter for a full list of values for the datepart argument. As you can see from the code below, we calculate the difference between orderdate and shippeddate in days. In other words, how many days elapsed between receiving and shipping an order? The results are not good at all. It takes a full five days to get the orders out from our factory for the month of September 2014.

DateDiff(datepart, start date, end date)

Code:
SELECT OrderID, datediff(d, orderdate, shippeddate) AS CycleTime
FROM Orders
WHERE year(orderdate) = 2014 AND month(orderdate) = 9

Result:

OrderID	CycleTime
14	5
65	5
77	5
109	5
116	5

(39 row(s) returned)

259. Establish policies on expected shipping dates using the DateAdd() function

Discussion:
Management is not very happy to see that it takes five days to ship an order. This means that customers will receive their orders in about ten to fifteen days total. This is unacceptable because we are in the food industry, and our products need to arrive fresh. So, management asks for our help again to produce a timetable that will list the expected shipping dates for orders. Management has determined that it should take two days at most for any order to ship, and they have established a corporate policy to be strictly enforced. We can produce target shipping dates using the dateadd() function. It takes three arguments, and its general syntax appears below:

dateadd(datepart, number, date field)

The datepart argument is a string like "d", "m", or "yyyy" determining the time interval we want to add. For instance, if we want to add days to a date, we use the "d" value. If we want to add years, we use the "yyyy" value for the datepart argument. (For a full list of the values for the datepart argument, please refer to the table at the end of this chapter). The number argument is the actual number of time intervals we want to add. If we want to add 15 days, for example, we use the number 15. Finally, the date field argument is the date field to which we want to add a number of days, months, or years. In the code below, we add 2 days to the orderdate field:

Code:
SELECT OrderID, dateadd(d, 2, orderdate) AS PolicyShipmentDate
FROM Orders
WHERE year(orderdate) = 2014 AND month(orderdate) = 9

Result:

OrderID	PolicyShipmentDate
14	2014-09-12
65	2014-09-12
77	2014-09-24
109	2014-09-14
116	2014-09-30

(39 row(s) returned)

Datediff() function argument settings	
datepart	Abbreviations
year	yy, yyyy
quarter	qq, q
month	mm, m
dayofyear	dy, y
day	dd, d
week	wk, ww
hour	hh
minute	mi, n
second	ss, s
millisecond	ms
microsecond	mcs
nanosecond	ns

Table 1: Arguments for the DateDiff() function

Source: http://technet.microsoft.com/en-us/library/ms189794.aspx

DatePart(), DateName(), and DateAdd() argument settings	
datepart	Abbreviations
year	yy, yyyy
quarter	qq, q
month	mm, m
dayofyear	dy, y
day	dd, d
week	wk, ww
weekday	dw, w
hour	hh
minute	mi, n
second	ss, s
millisecond	ms
microsecond	mcs
nanosecond	ns

Table 2: DatePart arguments

Source: http://technet.microsoft.com/en-us/library/ms174420.aspx
Source: http://technet.microsoft.com/en-us/library/ms174395.aspx

CHAPTER 26 DISCUSSION QUESTIONS

1. What is the usefulness of date functions in database tasks? Can you give a couple of examples?
2. Can we extract the month out of a date field? How many date functions can we use to achieve this result?
3. What function can we use to retrieve the name of the month (such as January) instead of its number (that is, 1)?
4. Why deep knowledge of date functions leads to better table design?
5. Why do we want to use date functions as default values in table fields?
6. What are the two functions we can use to extract quarters out of date fields?
7. How many functions can we use to extract the day out of a date field?
8. What is the purpose of the DateDiff() function? How many arguments does it take? Which ones are the most useful in practice?
9. What function can we use to add date intervals to a date field? Why is a function like this one useful?
10. What is the difference between "mmm" and "mmmm"? Hint: Refer to the appendix at the end of the chapter.

CHAPTER 26 HANDS-ON EXERCISES

Chapter 26 Case 1:

Start SQL Server Management Studio. For each of the questions in this case create a new query (Ctrl-N) and name it as per the instructions in each question. Submit your work to your instructor as one text file that contains all SQL statements or as per your instructor's directions.

1. The accounts receivable director is asking for report that will list the Order totals for all the years for which we have data in the database. Create a new query on the tble_Dates table with the fields "Year" and "OrderTotal" that satisfies the director's request and save it as Chapter26_Case1_Q1. Do not take into consideration any given discounts.

    Your result should look like:

Year	OrderTotal
2013	51164
2014	45002
2012	44230

    (3 row(s) returned)

2. The accounts receivable director wants to concentrate on the year 2014. He wants a report that lists the total value of orders by month for the year 2014. Create a new query on the tble_Dates table with the fields "Month" and "OrderTotal" that satisfies the director's request and save it as Chapter26_Case1_Q2. Do not take into consideration any given discounts and make sure the director sees month names and not month numbers. In addition month names should be in the correct order starting in January and ending in December.

    Your result should look like:

Month	OrderTotal
January	4012
February	3607
March	5090
April	5376
May	2280

(12 row(s) returned)

3. The director is very happy with the reports you have provided him. Now he needs a report that will list the total shipping cost by CustomerCity and month in the year 2014. He needs the results pivoted so that he obtains a much better value from the data. Create a new query on the tble_Dates table that satisfies the director's request and save it as Chapter26_Case1_Q3.

Your result should look like:

CustomerCity	January	February	March	April	May	June	July	August	Septemb
Phoenix	429	534	563	181	741	861	316	432	801
Miami	549	229	213	276	34	96	307	488	523
Los Angeles	839	1001	2201	999	792	1897	1631	882	1657
San Jose	600	189	257	131	404	207	138	333	405
Albany	309	298	314	358	NULL	NULL	168	188	361

(15 row(s) returned)

4. The accounts receivable director is back asking for a report that will list the total order amount by quarter in the year 2014. Create a new query on the tble_Dates table that satisfies the director's request and save it as Chapter26_Case1_Q4. Do not take into consideration any given discounts. Quarters should be displayed in the correct order, that is, 1,2,3, and 4.

Your result should look like:

Quarter	OrderTotal
1	12709
2	10882
3	11856
4	9555

(4 row(s) returned)

5. The accounts receivable director is really amazed by the pieces of information you are able to provide him. He now needs a report that will list the quantity of products sold by sales representative and quarter in the year 2014. Create a new query on the tble_Dates table that satisfies the director's request and save it as Chapter26_Case1_Q5.

Your result should look like:

SalesRepLastName	1	2	3	4
Vanderback	191	279	267	234
Zensons	280	264	209	133
Spicer	266	218	138	319
Anderson	165	211	268	239
Simmons	221	235	284	274

```
(10 row(s) returned)
```

Chapter 26 Case 2:
Start SQL Server Management Studio. For each of the questions in this case create a new query (Ctrl-N) and name it as per the instructions in each question. Submit your work to your instructor as one text file that contains all SQL statements or as per your instructor's directions.

1. The sales department is asking for a report that will list the Total Order Amount by customer state and by week for the month of April 2014. Create a new query on the tble_Dates table that satisfies the sales people request and save it as Chapter26_Case2_Q1. HINT: April 2014 had five weeks. Do not take into consideration any given discounts.

   Your result should look like:

CustomerState	14	15	16	17	18
AZ	NULL	NULL	NULL	243	NULL
CA	477	237	48	NULL	465
CO	300	NULL	333	257	NULL
DC	248	148	NULL	105	NULL
FL	NULL	NULL	393	337	NULL
MA	NULL	NULL	NULL	NULL	20
NY	NULL	253	168	184	NULL
OH	NULL	105	NULL	474	NULL
TX	188	393	NULL	NULL	NULL

```
(9 row(s) returned)
```

2. The sales department is impressed with your data and they are now asking for the Total Order Amount by the same week in the years 2012, 2013, and 2014. Specifically, they need the report for the week just before Christmas taking into consideration that a year has 52 weeks. Create a new query on the tble_Dates table that satisfies the sales people request and save it as Chapter26_Case2_Q2. Do not take into consideration any given discounts for your calculations.

   Your result should look like:

Year	Week	TotalOrderAmount
2012	50	1158
2013	50	1074
2014	50	990

```
(3 row(s) returned)
```

3. The sales people are asking for a report that will list the total order amount by city for the months of January, May, and September in the year 2014. Create a new query on the tble_Dates table that satisfies the

sales people request and save it as Chapter26_Case2_Q3. Order results by total order amount so that bigger amounts show first. HINT: we are looking for totals by city for the three months together and not for totals by city and by month. Do not take into consideration any given discounts for your calculations.

Your result should look like:

customercity	TotalOrderAmount
New York	2476
Los Angeles	2149
Phoenix	1281
Philadelphia	758
Washington	669

(14 row(s) returned)

4. The shipping director set a new rule that all orders should arrive to the customer within ten days of the order date. She needs a report that includes the OrderID, customerlastname, orderdate, and the RequiredArrivalDate fields from the tble_Dates table where the Required ArrivalDate field is ten days after the order field. She will compare these results with what actually happened. Create a new query that satisfies the director's request and save it as Chapter26_Case2_Q4.

Your result should look like:

OrderID	customerlastname	orderdate	RequiredArrivalDate
42	Stoll	2014-04-19	2014-04-29
43	Demichele	2013-05-06	2013-05-16
43	Demichele	2013-05-06	2013-05-16
43	Demichele	2013-05-06	2013-05-16
44	Ford	2014-10-16	2014-10-26

(2411 row(s) returned)

5. The HR director is asking for a report that will list the name of the sales representative and the number of years he or she is with the company. Create a new query on the tble_Dates table that satisfies the director's request and save it as Chapter26_Case2_Q5.

Your result should look like:

Salesreplastname	NumberOfYears
Anderson	15
Baker	8
Bernstein	23
Delaney	19
Simmons	8

(10 row(s) returned)

CHAPTER 27
UPDATE SQL STATEMENTS

Update statements are powerful tools for the advanced user, administrator, and developer. They provide astonishing flexibility and control to complete a task in minutes for which we would otherwise need hours. For example, suppose we have a database of 100 suppliers and a few thousand products associated with each supplier. Every week, due to promotional campaigns, pricing strategies, and replenishment costs, our suppliers might change their prices and since their products constitute our own raw materials we need to update our own prices. After all, the only constant in business is change. Change will affect your operations, and, in the end, your data. Since this is true, you must be ready for lightning speed changes to your operational data.

Your suppliers will never update their product prices at the same time and at the same percentage rates. This scenario is valid only for theoretical books. What actually happens is that suppliers will send you a price update when their business operations dictate, and this update will most probably be different from everyone else's. So, how do you account for situations like this? You can use flexible update statements that you can reuse effectively. This chapter starts with simple examples and ends up with powerful conditional updates for manipulating your data.

Keep in mind that you cannot undo the results of update statements. Consequently, my advice and my own policy are to first use a SELECT statement to check the records to be updated and then, run the update itself. This is actually common industry practice. We never run an update statement in the blind. The general syntax of an update statement is shown below:

UPDATE table
SET fieldvalue1 = value1, fieldvalue2 = value2, fieldvalue3 = value3…
[WHERE condition]

We can also run updates on views (updateable ones). We might construct a dataset having data from multiple tables and run the update against the view. In addition, we can update a table based on the values of another table or view. We can easily achieve this by using subqueries. Update statements are highly efficient for operations. Before we delve into examples, let's make sure we understand what cascade updates are and how they work in SQL Server 2012.

260. What are cascade updates, how to use them, and what they mean

There are cases in which we have to update the values of primary keys in your tables. Usually, these changes are mandated by entities external to the organization, such as the government. For example, up until now, we might have used the social security number of an employee as the primary key for the employees table. As a result, SSN functioned as the foreign key for all related tables for that employee (sales, HR records etc.) Now, the government steps in and says that we cannot do that anymore. This means that we have to change the SSN value for the employee in the employees table, and, most importantly, we need to change all of its occurrences in related tables. So, if this employee worked for us for 10 years, he might have 260 paystub records in the HR table. We might actually have thousands of references that we need to update for this employee.

Doing so manually is an impossible task, especially if we have several thousand employees. This is where cascade updates come in. Cascade updates will allow us to change the value of the primary key in the primary table, and the database will change all of its occurrences automatically, as a foreign key, in related tables. Let's go through a simple graphical example using a customer database to see how cascade updates work.

Customers			Orders		
CustID	Name		OrderID	CustID	OrderDate
1	John		1	2	9/10/2012
2	Mary		2	2	10/10/2012
3	George		3	1	11/10/2012
4	Stacy		4	3	11/11/2012

Products_Orders			Products		
OrderID	ProductID	Quantity	ProductID	ProductName	
1	2	2	1	A	
2	2	5	2	B	
3	1	3	3	C	
4	2	4	4	D	

In the figure above, let's assume that we need to change Mary's primary key value from 2 to 222. First, we need to turn cascade updates on for the relationship between customers and orders (technical explanation follows shortly). Then, we can simply change the primary key value 2 to the value 222. The database will ask us to confirm the action, and once the updates are completed, this is how the same tables will look:

Customers			Orders		
CustomerID	Name		OrderID	CustomerID	OrderDate
1	John		1	222	9/10/2012
222	Mary		2	222	10/10/2012
3	George		3	1	11/10/2012
4	Stacy		4	3	11/11/2012

Products_Orders			Products		
OrderID	ProductID	Quantity	ProductID	ProductName	
1	2	2	1	A	
2	2	5	2	B	
3	1	3	3	C	
4	2	4	4	D	

Notice how the database automatically changed all of the references of CustomerID=2 to 222 in the Orders table. I strongly recommend having cascade updates turned off except when you actually want to make changes to primary key values. This is a precaution in case an end user changes the value of a primary key by accident. To set cascade updates on for a relationship is pretty straightforward and easy in SQL Server 2012. Just follow the steps below:

1. Expand the node of the database with which you are working. In the node "Database Diagrams" double click the database diagram. For our sample database the diagram is called "ERD_Diagram".

2. This will open up the relationships window as shown below:

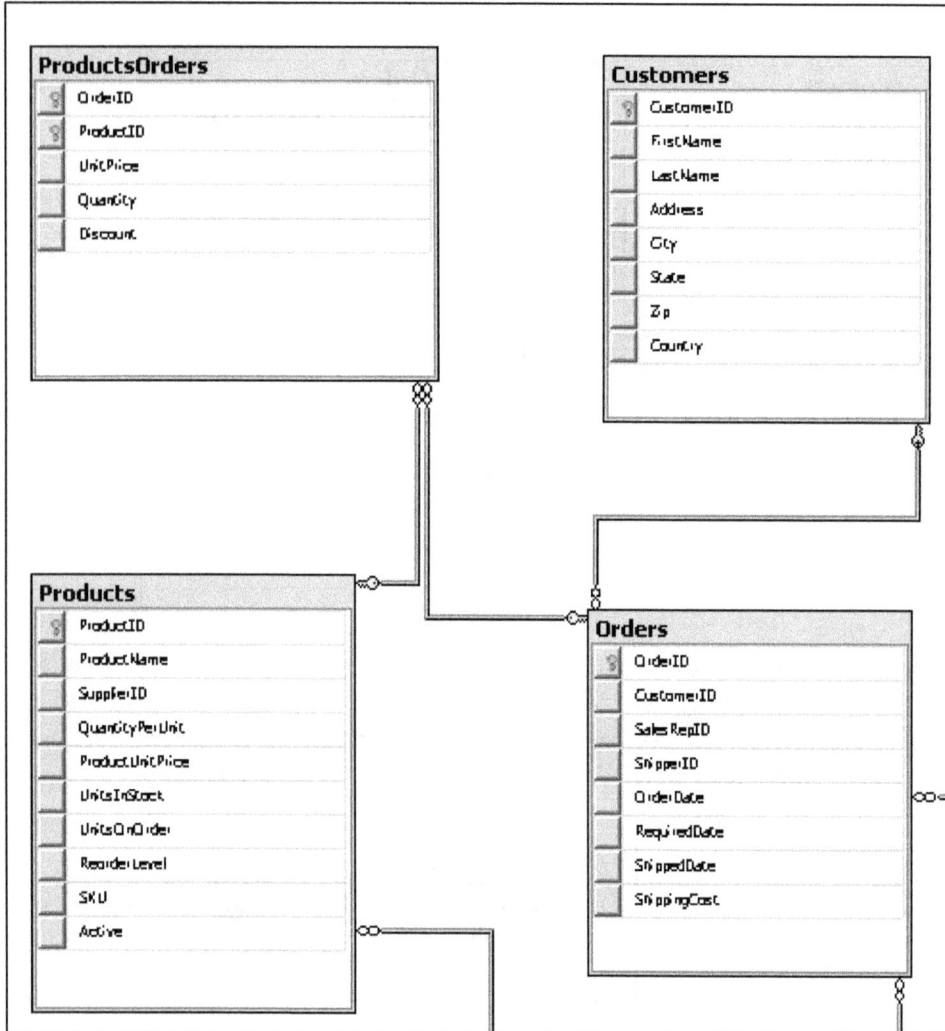

3. Right click on the relationship line between customers and orders. The following relationships window will appear:

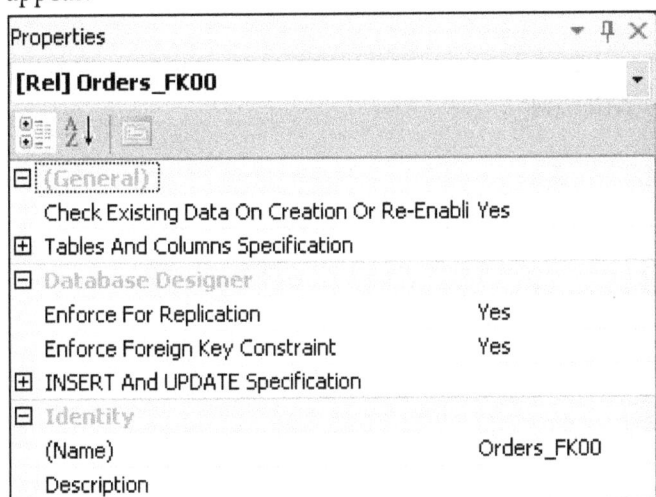

```
Properties                          ▼ ⁴ ✕

[Rel] Orders_FK00                              ▼

⊟ (General)
    Check Existing Data On Creation Or Re-Enabli  Yes
⊞ Tables And Columns Specification
⊟ Database Designer
    Enforce For Replication              Yes
    Enforce Foreign Key Constraint       Yes
⊞ INSERT And UPDATE Specification
⊟ Identity
    (Name)                               Orders_FK00
    Description
```

4. Expand the node "INSERT And UPDATE Specification". For the "Update Rule" select the "Cascade" option and you are all set. The relationship between Customers and Orders is ready for Cascade Updates. This implies that if you change the CustomerID primary key value for any of the customers in the customer's table, the corresponding CustomerID foreign key values will change in the Orders table.

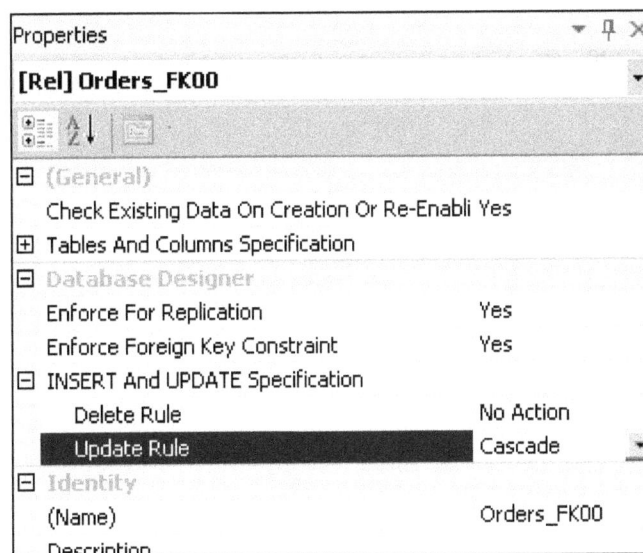

```
Properties                          ▼ ⁴ ✕

[Rel] Orders_FK00                              ▼

⊟ (General)
    Check Existing Data On Creation Or Re-Enabli  Yes
⊞ Tables And Columns Specification
⊟ Database Designer
    Enforce For Replication              Yes
    Enforce Foreign Key Constraint       Yes
⊟ INSERT And UPDATE Specification
    Delete Rule                          No Action
    Update Rule                          Cascade    ▼
⊟ Identity
    (Name)                               Orders_FK00
    Description
```

Remember to edit the relationship again and turn off "Cascade Updates" once the records are updated.

261.   Update a single field value in a single record
Update address information for a single customer
Discussion:
In this example, our goal is to update the address information for one of our customers. Notice the criteria in the view. They need to uniquely identify the customer we want to update. We use a SELECT statement to

make absolutely certain that we do not have another customer with the same first and last names and then we will apply the update statement.

```
SELECT *
FROM tbls_customers_Upd
WHERE lastname = 'Demizio' AND firstname = 'Michael'
```

Code:
```
UPDATE tbls_Customers_Upd
SET Address = '12 Lark Street'
WHERE lastname = 'Demizio' AND firstname = 'Michael'
```

Result:
```
(1 row(s) affected
```

262.   Update multiple field values in a single record
Update address and city information for a single customer
Discussion:
Our job now is to update both the address and city information for a customer. In other words, we will update two fields of the same record. The criteria remain the same, but notice how the two fields that we are updating are separated by a comma in the SET part of the code.

```
SELECT *
FROM customers
WHERE lastname = 'Demizio' AND firstname = 'Michael'
```

Code:
```
UPDATE tbls_Customers_Upd
SET Address = '12 Lark Street', city = 'Albany'
WHERE lastname = 'Demizio' AND firstname = 'Michael'
```

Result:
```
(1 row(s) affected
```

263.   Update a field value in multiple records
Update zip codes for all customers in a certain city
Discussion:
This time we want to update the zip code values for all of our customers in Denver, Colorado. It might look simple, but we need to pay attention and make sure the city of Denver does not exist in any other States. If it does, we need to add one more criterion in the WHERE clause to identify the state as well. Always run a SQL statement in advance to make sure your operation will affect the records you intend it to affect.

```
SELECT *
FROM tbls_Customers_Upd
WHERE city = 'Denver'
```

Code:
```
UPDATE tbls_Customers_Upd
SET zip = '22215'
WHERE city = 'Denver'
```

Result:
```
(13 row(s) affected
```

264. Update multiple field values in multiple records

Update city, zip, and address information for all customers in Dallas, Texas

Discussion:

Because of erroneous data entry, customers that show up from Denver, Colorado are actually from Tucson, Arizona. Consequently, we have to update their zip, city, and state information. Consequently, we need to update multiple field values in multiple records in the database. This is possible by using multiple update values in the SET clause of the update statement. We must always check our criteria in the WHERE clause to make sure they identify the records we want to update.

```
SELECT *
FROM tbls_Customers_Upd
WHERE city = 'Denver'
```

Code:
```
UPDATE tbls_Customers_Upd
SET zip = '22730', city = 'Tucson', state = 'AZ'
WHERE city = 'Denver'
```

Result:
```
(13 row(s) affected
```

265. Update using calculated values

Update product prices increasing them by a certain percentage

Discussion:

One of our suppliers has sent us updated prices, and we need to increase our own product prices by 5% for the products from this supplier. Notice the calculated field in the SET clause and in the WHERE clause. Notice that instead of the supplier name, we will use the supplier ID to make sure we identify the correct product records for this supplier. This is common practice in databases for criteria in the WHERE clause because primary key values are unique. Therefore, we do not need to worry if we have two suppliers with the same name in the database. Finally, notice in this example that we work with the view "View_SupplierPrices" which combines the information of suppliers and their products. Running update statements against views is fine and sometimes desirable because they provide us with just the information we need rather than looking at huge tables. In this particular example, our supplier, "Home of Snacks", has increased prices by 5%, and we will increase our own prices by the same amount.

```
SELECT *
FROM View_SupplierPrices
WHERE supplierID = 1
```

Code:

UPDATE View_SupplierPrices

SET ProductUnitPrice = ProductUnitPrice * (1+0.05)

WHERE supplierID = 1

Result:

(10 row(s) affected)

266. Update conditionally using the case() function

Update product prices using different update conditions for every supplier

Discussion:

As you might expect, in everyday work scenarios, our suppliers, customers, and partners do not set up meetings to send us uniform and standardized information just so that we can have a nice time with our operations. Instead, they send us their own percentage increases and not at the same time. So, what can we do to take care of this business fact in minutes instead of making it an operational and administrative nightmare? The solution is to combine the powers of the update statement and the case() function. As you can see below, our suppliers sent us percentage updates ranging from 2% all the way up to 15%. Using the update statement with the case() function, we obtain the following: First, using just one statement, we can take care of all of the particular updates in seconds. Second, the statement is so clean that it is reusable the next time we need to do the same job. Third, suppose that some of our suppliers have not sent us any updates. We can leave the statement below as is and update the ProductUnitPrice with itself as is the case with supplierID=5 where nothing is updated.

Code:

UPDATE tbls_Products_Upd

SET ProductUnitPrice =

CASE

WHEN supplierid=1   THEN ProductUnitPrice*(1.1)

WHEN supplierid=2   THEN ProductUnitPrice*(1.05)

WHEN supplierid=3   THEN ProductUnitPrice*(1.1)

WHEN supplierid=4   THEN ProductUnitPrice*(1.05)

WHEN supplierid=5   THEN ProductUnitPrice

WHEN supplierid=6   THEN ProductUnitPrice*(1.02)

WHEN supplierid=7   THEN ProductUnitPrice*(1.03)

WHEN supplierid=8   THEN ProductUnitPrice*(1.05)

WHEN supplierid=9   THEN ProductUnitPrice*(1.15)

WHEN supplierid=10   THEN ProductUnitPrice*(1.1)

END

Result:

(70 row(s) affected)

267. Update records in a table using criteria from another table or view

Update the products table using criteria from the suppliers table

Discussion:

In this example, our goal is to update prices in the tbls_products_Upd table using criteria from the suppliers table. We can achieve this using a subquery. The subquery will retrieve supplier ids from the suppliers table and will update the corresponding product prices in the tbls_products_Upd table. Specifically, the subquery will retrieve supplier ids for suppliers in Boston or Dallas and feed those ids in the WHERE clause of the main update statement.

Let me explain this point a bit more. The business request is to update product prices from suppliers in Boston and Dallas by 20% for everything coming from that direction. Our problem is that the tbls_products_Upd table does not contain any city information. Even so, we can satisfy management by using the subquery below:

Code:
```
UPDATE tbls_Products_Upd
SET ProductUnitPrice = ProductUnitPrice * (1+0.20)
WHERE SupplierID IN
(SELECT SupplierID FROM Suppliers
WHERE city= 'Boston' or city = 'Denver')
```

Result:
```
(26 row(s) affected
```

CHAPTER 27 DISCUSSION QUESTIONS

1. What is the basic goal of update statements?
2. Can we undo the result of an update statement if we change our mind?
3. What is a good safety strategy to follow before we use an update statement?
4. What is the role of cascade updates in relational databases?
5. Why it is a good idea to keep cascade updates off and use them only when needed?
6. Can you provide an example situation in which it makes sense to use cascade updates?
7. Can we update multiple values in a single record with a single SQL statement?
8. Can we update multiple values in multiple records by using a single SQL statement?
9. What function can we use to update records based on multiple conditions?
10. What technique can we use to update records in one table using criteria from another table?

CHAPTER 27 HANDS-ON EXERCISES

Chapter 27 Case 1:
Start SQL Server Management Studio. For each of the questions in this case create a new query (Ctrl-N) and name it as per the instructions in each question. Submit your work to your instructor as one text file that contains all SQL statements or as per your instructor's directions.

1. The inventory people want to change the UnitsOnOrder quantity from 0 to 5 for the Almonds, Roasted and Salted - 18 oz. Bag product with productid=2. Create a new query on the table tble_Products_UPD that satisfies the inventory people request and save it as Chapter27_Case1_Q1.

   Your result should look like:
   (1 row(s) affected)

2. The inventory people now want to change the ProductUnitPrice and UnitsInStock to 32 and 30 respectively for the product Banana Chips - 20 oz. Bag with ProductID = 3. Create a new query on the table tble_Products_UPD that satisfies the inventory people request and save it as Chapter27_Case1_Q2.

   Your result should look like:
   (1 row(s) affected)

3. The replenishing department just called in and notified us that we need to add five dollars to the price of all products from the supplier with SupplierID = 5. Create a new query on the table tble_Products_UPD that satisfies this request and save it as Chapter27_Case1_Q3.

   Your result should look like:
   (8 row(s) affected)

4. The purchasing department just called and informed us that we need to make the following changes for the supplier with SupplierID = 3. Create a new query on the table tble_Products_UPD that satisfies this request

and save it as Chapter27_Case1_Q4.

    a.   Change the QuantityPerUnit to 35.
    b.   Add 12 dollars to the price of each of the products.
    c.   Change the ReorderLevel to 15.

       Your result should look like:
       (7 row(s) affected)

5.   The purchasing department called in again and informed us that the supplier with SupplierID = 5 increased their prices by 7.5%. Now we need to increase our own prices by the same amount. Create a new query on the table tble_Products_UPD that satisfies this request and save it as Chapter27_Case1_Q5.

   Your result should look like:
   (8 row(s) affected)

Chapter 27 Case 2:

Start SQL Server Management Studio. For each of the questions in this case create a new query (Ctrl-N) and name it as per the instructions in each question. Submit your work to your instructor as one text file that contains all SQL statements or as per your instructor's directions.

1.   HR called in and said that the city for employee Anderson John is wrong and it needs to be changed to "Los Angeles". Create a new query on the tble_SalesReps_UPD table that satisfies the HR request and save it as Chapter27_Case2_Q1.

   Your result should look like:
   (1 row(s) affected)

2.   HR called in again and said that for the employee John Thomas the zip code needs to be updated to 83044 and the date of hire to 5/10/2008. Create a new query on the tble_SalesReps_UPD table that satisfies the HR request and save it as Chapter27_Case2_Q2.

   Your result should look like:
   (1 row(s) affected)

3.   The sales people are asking for a ten dollar increase to the price of all products with a ProductUnitPrice lower than $30. Create a new query on the table tble_Products_UPD that satisfies this request and save it as Chapter27_Case2_Q3.

   Your result should look like:
   (28 row(s) affected)

4.   The purchasing people called in and reported that some of our suppliers changed their prices. Now we need to change our own prices as follows:

For supplierid=1 the price should go up by 20%

For supplierid=3 the price should go up by 10%

For supplierid=7 the price should go up by 4%

For supplierid=9 the price should go up by 8%

Create a new query on the tble_ Products _UPD table that satisfies the purchasing people request and save it as Chapter27_Case2_Q4. You need to be able to do all the updates using a single query.

Your result should look like:

```
(70 row(s) affected)
```

5. The sales people are asking us to decrease by $4 the prices of the products in the tble_ Products _UPD table for which the extended price to the customer in the ProductsOrders table equals or exceeds $32. Create a new query that satisfies the sales people request and save it as Chapter27_Case2_Q5.

    Your result should look like:

    ```
    (4 row(s) affected)
    ```

CHAPTER 28
DELETE STATEMENTS

The principal role of delete statements is to remove multiple records in one operation. Instead of deleting table rows manually, we use delete statements to delete many of them with one SQL statement. The general syntax of a delete statement appears below, and while it looks simple, it can become an amazing tool when coupled with criteria and subqueries.

> DELETE
> FROM table
> WHERE criteria

As with update statements, we cannot undo the results of delete statements. Thus, once we delete a set of records, there is no way to get them back. Consequently, we should have a solid backup strategy just in case we made a mistake. In this chapter, we will see how to easily move records to other tables before deleting them. Furthermore, it is professional practice to run a SELECT statement first to determine if its result set contains the records we want to delete and then, run the delete statement. Before we run any code in this chapter, we should learn about the role of cascade deletes. For all of the examples in this chapter, cascade deletes are off, and we should keep them off in our databases as well unless we specifically want to take advantage of their functionality in specific situations. We want cascade deletes off so that we do not accidentally delete a record in a table and then the database deletes all related records in related tables.

268.   What are cascade deletes, how to use them, and what they mean

In order to understand cascade deletes in full, let's work with the record of a customer from five years ago who is no longer in business. We want to delete this customer from the database so that it does not come up in our query results.

We could simply go to the customers table and try to delete this record. However, if there are associated orders with this customer, the database will not allow us to delete it since we would end up with orphaned records in the orders table. Referential integrity rules do not allow this to happen, and we would not be able to delete the customer. For a full explanation of referential integrity, check chapter 4. Understanding referential integrity is a must for all database professionals and users. To delete this customer manually, we should first go to the orders table and delete all of the orders associated with this customer. However, since we also have a many-to-many relationship between Orders and Products, we first need to go to the Products_Orders table and delete the respective records of Orders and Products for that customer. If we need to delete the customer Mary from the database, we need to do the following in the order provided:

Customers table

CustomerID	First Name	Last Name
1	John	Demarco
2	Mary	Demania
3	George	Demers
4	Phillip	Demetriou

Orders table

OrderID	CustomerID	Sales RepID	ShipperID	OrderDate	RequiredDate
982	2	10	1	2014-06-07	2014-06-17
609	2	6	2	2014-05-09	2014-05-19
538	2	6	3	2012-06-21	2012-07-01
353	2	4	1	2012-05-11	2012-05-21

ProductsOrders table

OrderID	ProductID	Unit Price	Quantity	Discount
353	1	15	4	0.20
353	2	15	6	0.20
353	11	15	1	0.20
353	20	15	3	0.15
353	27	15	5	0.20
353	31	32	5	0.15
353	51	15	3	0.15

1. Delete from the Products_Orders table all of the records with orderid 353, 538, 609, and 982. For example, order 353 contains products 1, 2, 11, 20, 27, 31, and 51.
2. Delete from the Orders table the orders with orderid = 353, 538, 609, and 982 since they all belong to Mary.
3. Finally, delete Mary's record with CustomerID = 2 from the Customer table.

Even in this simple scenario, deleting a customer is an involved process. Imagine the scenario where you have hundreds of customers with thousands of associated orders. It would be humanly impossible to remove customers manually.

This is where cascade deletes come in. By using cascade deletes, we can delete a customer in the primary table, and the database itself will delete all references to that customer in all related tables. In this example, if cascade deletes are on, when we delete Mary from the customers table, the database will automatically delete all of Mary's references in the Orders and Product_Orders tables reliably and at once. To turn cascade deletes on, follow these steps:

1. Expand the node of the database with which you are working. In the node "Database Diagrams" double click the database diagram. For our sample database the diagram is called "ERD_Diagram".

2. This will open up the relationships window as shown below:

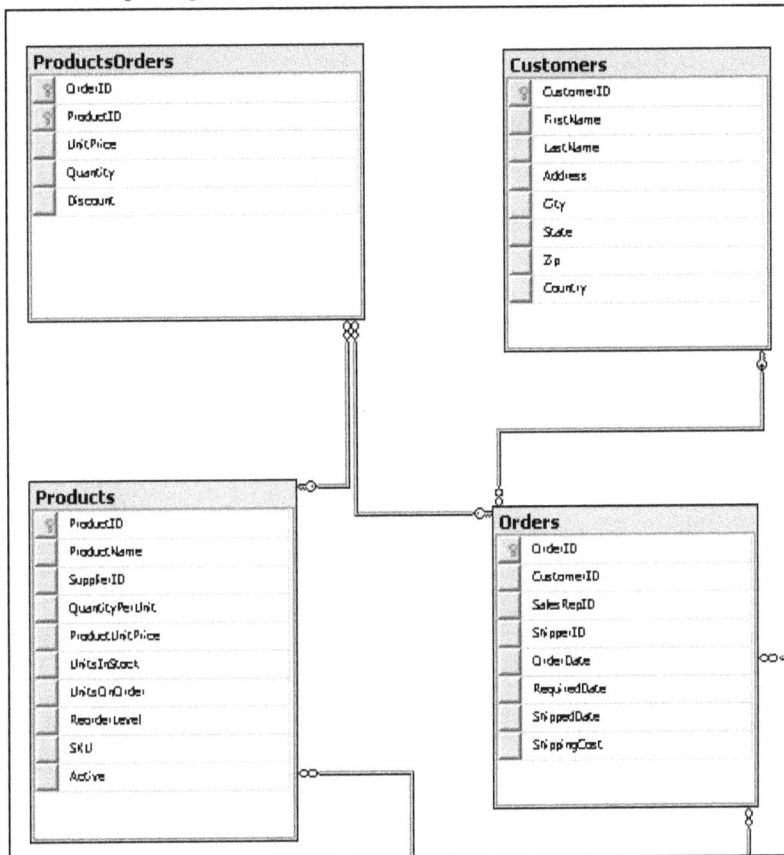

3. Right click on the relationship line between customers and orders. The following relationships window will appear:

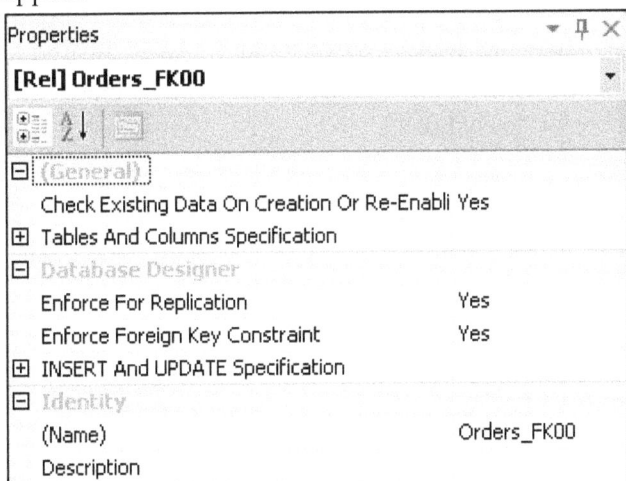

4. Expand the node "INSERT And UPDATE Specification". For the "Delete Rule" select the "Delete" option and you are all set. The relationship between Customers and Orders is ready for Cascade Deletes. You need to set cascade deletes for the relationship between the tables Orders and ProductsOrders. Once the setting has been completed for both relationships, if you delete Mary from the customers table, all its

related orders will be deleted from the customers table and all related records in the ProductsOrders tables will be deleted as well.

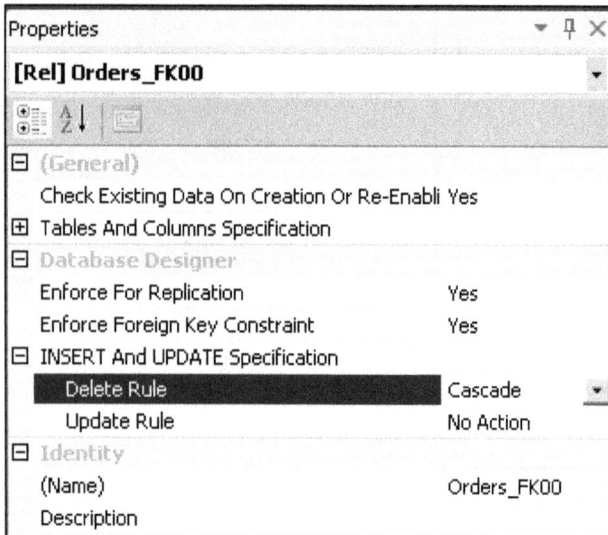

Remember to edit the relationship again and turn off "Cascade Deletes" once the records are updated. For the purposes of this chapter, cascade deletes are off. In addition, we will be working on the tbls_Orders_DEL table, which is just a copy of the Orders table in which we can delete records at will.

269. Delete a single record in a table

Delete a specific customer's order

Discussion:

The goal in this example is to delete a single order from a single customer. That is, we need to delete a single record from the Orders table. Notice how we use the OrderID as the criterion in the WHERE clause. The OrderID is the primary key of the Orders table, and it will uniquely identify the record for deletion. Try to use primary key values for criteria instead of fields such as customer names, which might have duplicates in the table with the result of deleting records you do not intend to delete. In addition, always run a SELECT beforehand or a SELECT INTO so that you can identify or backup your data respectively. I will show you how you can use the SELECT INTO to make a temporary table for deleted data.

Step 1: Run a SELECT statement
Code:
```
SELECT *
FROM tbls_Orders_Del
WHERE orderid = 20
```

Step 2: Run the DELETE statement
Code:
```
DELETE
FROM tbls_Orders_Del
WHERE orderid = 20
```

Result:
```
(1 row(s) affected
```

270. Delete multiple records in a table

Delete all orders for a specific customer

Discussion:

In this example, we want to delete all orders for customerid= 2, i.e. Mary. To achieve this task, we will use the CustomerID field in the WHERE clause, which is the primary key for the customers table and the foreign key in the orders table.

Step 1: Run a SELECT statement to uniquely identify and verify records for deletion.
Code:

```
SELECT *
FROM tbls_Orders_Del
WHERE customerid = 2
```

Step 2: Run the DELETE statement
Code:

```
DELETE
FROM tbls_Orders_Del
WHERE customerid = 2
```

Result:
```
(1 row(s) affected
```

271. Delete records in a certain date range

Delete multiple orders from multiple customers within a date range

Discussion:

This is an example of how we can use date criteria to delete orders within a specified date range.

Step 1: Run a SELECT statement
Code:

```
SELECT *
FROM tbls_Orders_Del
WHERE orderdate BETWEEN '2012/10/15' AND '2012/10/17'
```

Step 2: Run the DELETE statement
Code:

```
DELETE
FROM tbls_Orders_Del
WHERE orderdate BETWEEN '2012/10/15' AND '2012/10/17'
```

Result:
```
(2 row(s) affected
```

272. Delete duplicate records while controlling if you want to delete the earliest or the latest ones

Delete earliest or latest duplicate customer orders

Discussion:

Let's discuss the setup of this example so that you can understand it in detail. First, in the table tbls_Orders_DEL, records with orderid 1001, 1002, and 1003 are duplicates. Specifically, the record with orderid

349

= 1 is identical to 1001, the record with orderid = 988 is identical to 1002, and the record with orderid = 990 is identical to 1003. Keep in mind that these records have identical field values but different primary keys values.

The burning question is which records we should delete; the earliest ones or the latest ones? We know that a record with a lesser orderid value was entered before a record with a higher orderid value since the primary key is an auto increment. In the following example, we discuss both alternatives in detail. In any case, the four steps to follow appear below:

Step 1: Run a SELECT statement to uniquely identify and verify records for deletion.
The SQL statement below will SELECT the records with smaller orderid values. Notice we use a subquery to obtain what we need. In the main SELECT statement, we select all orders from the tbls_Orders_Del table that do not belong in the subquery. The subquery itself will fetch the duplicate records with the maximum orderid values (1001, 1002, and 1003). The main SELECT statement will fetch what is left from the six duplicated records, i.e. 1, 988, and 990. We can also use the NOT IN operator instead of the "<>" inequality predicate to obtain the same results. I know it is counter intuitive to use max() to get the earliest records, but max() is used in the subquery to identify duplicates with maximum primary key values. Then, the main SELECT statement will fetch all duplicates not in the subquery.
Code:

```
SELECT *
FROM tbls_Orders_Del AS T2
WHERE OrderID <>
(SELECT Max(OrderID)
FROM tbls_Orders_Del AS T1
WHERE T2.CustomerID = T1.CustomerID AND T2.SalesRepID = T1.SalesRepID AND T2.ShipperID
= T1.ShipperID AND T2.OrderDate = T1.OrderDate)
```

Result:

OrderID	CustomerID	SalesRepID	ShipperID	OrderDate	RequiredDate	ShippedDate	ShippingCost
1	139	2	2	2013-11-06	2013-11-21	2013-11-11	36
988	145	10	1	2014-03-21	2014-04-05	2014-03-26	39
990	160	10	1	2012-05-17	2012-06-01	2012-05-22	48

```
(3 row(s) returned)
```

This SQL statement will select the latest duplicate records:
Code:

```
SELECT *
FROM tbls_Orders_Del AS T2
WHERE OrderID <>
(SELECT Min(OrderID)
FROM tbls_Orders_Del AS T1
WHERE T2.CustomerID = T1.CustomerID AND T2.SalesRepID = T1.SalesRepID AND T2.ShipperID
= T1.ShipperID AND T2.OrderDate = T1.OrderDate)
```

Result:

OrderID	CustomerID	SalesRepID	ShipperID	OrderDate	RequiredDate	ShippedDate	ShippingCost
1001	139	2	2	2013-11-06	2013-11-21	2013-11-11	36
1002	145	10	1	2014-03-21	2014-04-05	2014-03-26	39
1003	160	10	1	2012-05-17	2012-06-01	2012-05-22	48

```
(3 row(s) returned)
```

Step 2: Run the DELETE statement
Code:
DELETE tbls_Orders_Del
FROM tbls_Orders_Del AS T2
WHERE OrderID <>
(SELECT Min(OrderID)
FROM tbls_Orders_Del AS T1
WHERE T2.CustomerID = T1.CustomerID AND T2.SalesRepID = T1.SalesRepID AND T2.ShipperID = T1.ShipperID AND T2.OrderDate = T1.OrderDate)

Result:
```
(3 row(s) affected
```

273.   Delete ALL duplicate records (originals plus duplicates) that have the same field values and same primary key values
Delete all duplicate customer orders including original and duplicate orders
Discussion:
In this example, our goal is to delete all duplicate orders, including the original orders. We are working on the table below (tbls_Orders_Del2) where six records are identical such as records with orderids 1, 3, and 5. The records with orderid = 2 and 4 are unique and should not be touched.

OrderID	CustomerID	SalesRepID	ShipperID	OrderDate	RequiredDate	ShippedDate	ShippingCost
1	139	2	2	2013-11-06	2013-11-21	2013-11-11	36
2	184	2	1	2013-07-25	2013-08-09	2013-07-30	39
3	137	2	2	2013-06-29	2013-07-14	2013-07-04	34
4	165	2	1	2014-12-14	2014-12-29	2014-12-19	48
5	123	2	2	2012-11-14	2012-11-29	2012-11-19	40
5	123	2	2	2012-11-14	2012-11-29	2012-11-19	40
3	137	2	2	2013-06-29	2013-07-14	2013-07-04	34
1	139	2	2	2013-11-06	2013-11-21	2013-11-11	36

Step 1: Run a SELECT statement to uniquely identify and verify records for deletion.
Code:
SELECT *
FROM tbls_Orders_DEL2
WHERE orderid IN(
SELECT OrderID
FROM tbls_Orders_DEL2
GROUP BY OrderID, CustomerID, ShipperID, OrderDate
HAVING count(*)>1)

Result:

OrderID	CustomerID	SalesRepID	ShipperID	OrderDate	RequiredDate	ShippedDate	ShippingCost
1	139	2	2	2013-11-06	2013-11-21	2013-11-11	36
3	137	2	2	2013-06-29	2013-07-14	2013-07-04	34
5	123	2	2	2012-11-14	2012-11-29	2012-11-19	40
5	123	2	2	2012-11-14	2012-11-29	2012-11-19	40
3	137	2	2	2013-06-29	2013-07-14	2013-07-04	34
1	139	2	2	2013-11-06	2013-11-21	2013-11-11	36

(6 row(s) returned)

Step 2: Run the DELETE statement
Code:
```
DELETE
FROM tbls_Orders_DEL2
WHERE OrderID IN(
SELECT OrderID
FROM tbls_Orders_DEL2
GROUP BY OrderID, CustomerID, ShipperID, OrderDate
HAVING count(*)>1)
```

Result:
(6 row(s) affected)

274.   Use SELECT INTO to back up records before deleting them
Create a temp table to back up customers' orders before deleting them
Discussion:
In this example, we delete records from the tbls_Orders_DEL table but just in case we need these records later on, we back them up on the fly in a new table using the SELECT INTO statement. Alternatively, If we want to append the deleted records in a historical table, we can easily do so by using the INSERT INTO statement.

Code:
```
SELECT * INTO TempTable1
FROM tbls_Orders_Del
WHERE orderdate
BETWEEN '2012/8/15' AND '2012/9/15'
```

Result:
(17 row(s) affected)

Code:
```
DELETE
FROM tbls_Orders_Del
WHERE orderdate
BETWEEN '2012/8/15' AND '2012/9/15'
```

Result:
(17 row(s) affected)

275. Delete records in a table based on values in a different table using a subquery

Delete records from the orders table using criteria from the customers table

Discussion:

This time, we have a request from management to delete all orders in the city of Los Angeles for a customer whose last name is "Orlando". The problem is we do not have a city field or a last name field in the tbls_orders_del table. To achieve this task we use a subquery to delete records in the tbls_orders_Del table using criteria from the Customers table!

Step 1: Run a SELECT statement to uniquely identify and verify records for deletion.
Code:

```
SELECT *
FROM tbls_Orders_DEL
WHERE CustomerID IN
(SELECT CustomerID FROM Customers
WHERE city= 'Los Angeles' AND lastname = 'Orlando')
```

Result:

OrderID	CustomerID	SalesRepID	ShipperID	OrderDate	RequiredDate	ShippedDate	ShippingCost
414	153	4	2	2013-03-15	2013-03-30	2013-03-20	32
493	153	5	1	2014-10-31	2014-11-15	2014-11-05	51
749	153	8	2	2014-03-21	2014-04-05	2014-03-26	39
202	153	2	2	2014-04-03	2014-04-18	2014-04-08	38
215	153	2	1	2013-07-29	2013-08-13	2013-08-03	51
237	153	3	2	2012-05-10	2012-05-25	2012-05-15	42

```
(6 row(s) returned)
```

Step 2: Run the DELETE statement
Code:

```
DELETE
FROM tbls_Orders_DEL
WHERE CustomerID IN
(SELECT CustomerID FROM Customers
WHERE city= 'Los Angeles' AND lastname = 'Orlando')
```

Result:
```
(6 row(s) affected)
```

276. Delete records in a table based on calculations in a different table

Delete Orders with total sales above $500

Discussion:

This time, the request from management is to delete all orders with a grand total of more than $500. We will resort to the Products_Orders table to make calculations and use the calculated fields as criteria to delete orders in the tbls_Orders_Del table. It sounds like a big deal, but it is not.

A sample dataset from the ProductsOrders table appears below. Notice the pairs of OrderIDs and ProductIDs so that you know what product is included in what order. For example, order 2 contains products 32 and 70. Order 3 contains products 26, 27, 43, and 51.

To be able to comply with the request of management, we first need to calculate order subtotals by multiplying unitprice*quantity. Once we have the order subtotals, we need to calculate order totals. To do this, we use the SUM() function and the GROUP BY clause. Finally, since we only want order totals which exceed $500, we use the HAVING clause with ">500" as the criterion. Please note that we use HAVING instead of WHERE since HAVING is applied after the records are grouped while WHERE is applied before they are grouped and so it is useless in this case.

Table ProductsOrders

orderid	productid	unitprice	quantity	discount
2	23	15	4	0.15
2	24	15	1	0.20
2	32	15	3	0.00
2	70	15	6	0.15
3	26	22	3	0.20
3	27	15	2	0.15
3	43	15	5	0.15
3	51	15	4	0.20

Step 1: Run a SELECT statement to uniquely identify and verify records for deletion.
Code:

```
SELECT
FROM tbls_Orders_DEL
WHERE OrderID IN(
SELECT Sum([unitprice]*[quantity]) AS totalOrder
FROM ProductsOrders
GROUP BY OrderID
HAVING Sum([unitprice]*[quantity])>500)
```

Result:

OrderID	CustomerID	SalesRepID	ShipperID	OrderDate	RequiredDate	ShippedDate	ShippingCost
510	186	5	3	2013-12-21	2014-01-05	2013-12-26	32
512	79	5	2	2013-10-10	2013-10-25	2013-10-15	48
530	117	5	1	2014-03-02	2014-03-17	2014-03-07	42
574	128	6	1	2014-06-19	2014-07-04	2014-06-24	47
576	191	6	2	2012-09-18	2012-10-03	2012-09-23	33

(5 row(s) returned)

Step 2: Run the DELETE statement
Code:

```
DELETE
FROM tbls_Orders_DEL
WHERE OrderID IN(
SELECT Sum([unitprice]*[quantity]) AS totalOrder
FROM ProductsOrders
GROUP BY OrderID
HAVING Sum([unitprice]*[quantity])>500)
```

Result:
(5 row(s) affected)

CHAPTER 28 DISCUSSION QUESTIONS

1. What is the basic goal of delete statements in relational databases?
2. Can we undo the results of delete statements just in case we deleted records by mistake?
3. What is a good strategy to follow before we use a delete statement?
4. What is the role of cascade deletes in relational databases?
5. Why it is a good idea to keep cascade deletes off and use them only when needed?
6. Can you provide an example of a business occasion in which it makes sense to use cascade deletes?
7. If we have duplicate records in a table how can we choose to delete the earliest or latest ones?
8. How can we delete all duplicate records in a table using a single SQL statement?
9. What SQL command can we use to backup records in a different table before we delete them from the current one?
10. What technique can we use to delete records in one table while using criteria from a different table?

CHAPTER 28 HANDS-ON EXERCISES

Chapter 28 Case 1:
Start SQL Server Management Studio. For each of the questions in this case create a new query (Ctrl-N) and name it as per the instructions in each question. Submit your work to your instructor as one text file that contains all SQL statements or as per your instructor's directions.

1. The inventory people want you to delete from the table **tble_Products_DEL** the product "Dried Blueberries - 1 lb. Bag". Create a new query that satisfies the department's request and save it as Chapter28_Case1_Q1.

   Your result should look like:
   (1 row(s) affected)

2. The inventory people are back and they want you to delete from the **tble_Products_DEL table** all the products with prices between $15 and $19. Create a new query that satisfies the department's request and save it as Chapter28_Case1_Q2.

   Your result should look like:
   (8 row(s) affected)

3. The inventory people are very happy with your work because you saved them a lot of time. Now, they want to delete additional records from the **tble_Products_DEL** table but they need a backup copy of it before they proceed. Create a new query that creates a backup copy of the products table and save it as Chapter28_Case1_Q3. Save the backup table as TempProductsDEL.

   Your result should look like:
   (61 row(s) affected)

4. The management of the company decided to suspend operations with the suppliers from Dallas after a government directive for potential pollutants in their products. They want you to delete all the products in

the tble_Products_DEL table from suppliers in the city of Texas. Create a new query that satisfies the management's request and save it as Chapter28_Case1_Q4.

Your result should look like:
```
(7 row(s) affected)
```

5. Prices in the Northeast went way out of control and the management decided to replace the suppliers there with others from the Southeast of the country. Create a new query that deletes all products in the tble_Products_DEL table from suppliers in the states of NY and MA and save it as Chapter28_Case1_Q5.

Your result should look like:
```
(54 row(s) affected)
```

Chapter 28 Case 2:
Start SQL Server Management Studio. For each of the questions in this case create a new query (Ctrl-N) and name it as per the instructions in each question. Submit your work to your instructor as one text file that contains all SQL statements or as per your instructor's directions.

1. The sales department called in and said that the customer Zartons Lisa from Los Angeles does not exist and they ask you to remove her related orders from the tble_Orders_DEL table. Create a new query that satisfies this request and save it as Chapter28_Case2_Q1.

Your result should look like:
```
(9 row(s) affected)
```

2. The sales department sent us a message that the processed orders from the sales rep with ID=2 and shipping cost = 36 were a mistake and we need to delete them from the tble_Orders_DEL table. Create a new query that satisfies the sales people request and save it as Chapter28_Case2_Q2.

Your result should look like:
```
(4 row(s) affected)
```

3. The sales people want us to delete the orders with an order date before 12/31/2012 from the table tble_Orders_DEL since they only clutter the database. Create a new query that satisfies the HR request and save it as Chapter28_Case2_Q3.

Your result should look like:
```
(311 row(s) affected)
```

4. The sales manager called in and is asking us to delete all orders from the table tble_Orders_DEL put in by any sales rep from the city of Dallas. Create a new query that satisfies the request of the manager and save it as Chapter28_Case2_Q4. HINT: You need to use a subquery to achieve this result.

Your result should look like:

(105 row(s) affected)

5. The shipping people are asking us to delete all orders from the table tble_Orders_DEL placed between 1/1/2014 and 1/31/2014 through any shipping company in the city of Boston. Create a new query that satisfies this request and save it as Chapter28_Case2_Q5.

    Your result should look like:

    (5 row(s) affected)

CHAPTER 29
WORKING WITH JOINS

The power of joins is a bit of a hidden jewel in the world of databases and data analysis. Developers and power users alike stay away from a good understanding of joins, mostly because they perceive them as complicated and impractical concepts. Both beliefs are false. You must understand joins to understand databases, and they are actually easy to use. They just look complicated. Devoting some time to understanding the remarkable muscle of joins will transform the way you work and give you amazing flexibility in your everyday work tasks. In this chapter, we will look at practical applications of joins through realistic scenarios. In fact, this is the only way someone could convince me to use joins: Show me what they can actually do in practice.

In relational databases, we keep data in separate tables. We keep supplier information in the suppliers table, customers in the customer table, and orders in an orders table. This is what we call the physical structure or design of the database. This is done so that normalization rules apply in the database where we keep our business transactions (orders, quotations, invoices). What we are interested in, however, are the conceptual invocations from a relational database. We would like to generate and send out information, such as invoices, in a way that makes sense for our customers and for us. In this respect, joins are links that we establish between or among tables with the goal of retrieving related information.

In this chapter, we will explore the use of inner, left, and right joins. Among these three, inner joins are the most commonly used in practice. Left joins are useful in certain business scenarios, while right joins can be used to check the integrity of the database and identify any orphaned records.

277.   Inner Joins
Find customers who have orders in the orders table
Discussion:
Let us assume our supervisor has a very simple request: She wants a report of customers who actually ordered something from us. The customers table might include people who asked for quotations, leads, or it might include customers who have not ordered anything for some time. How can we answer this request? We can go back to the chapter about duplicate, orphaned, and related records and use a subquery such as:

Code:
```
SELECT *
FROM Customers
WHERE CustomerID
IN (SELECT CustomerID from tbls_Orders)
```

Result:
Notice the number of customers returned is only 190. However, in the customers table, there are 201 customers. So, 11 customers have not had any orders at all for the historical data we have.

CustomerID	First Name	Last Name	Address	City
1	John	Demarco	11 Lark Street	New York
2	Mary	Demania	12 Madison Ave	New York
3	George	Demers	23 New Scotland Ave	New York
4	Phillip	Demetriou	22 Academy Road	New York
5	Andrew	Demichele	14 Glandel Ave	New York

```
(190 row(s) returned)
```

We can achieve the same result using a join. Let's create a new query in design view and add the customers and orders tables. There is a one-to-many relationship between customers and orders. For one customer, there might be multiple orders, but each order definitely belongs to one customer.

Right-click on the relationship line between customers and orders. The following dialog box will appear. By default, SQL Server 2012 will join two tables through an inner join or, in other words, include records from each table where there is a common CustomerID value. By the way, CustomerID is the primary key (PK) in the customers table and the foreign key (FK) in the orders table.

This is the case of an inner join. Notice that an inner join will give us the customers who have orders. If there are any customers without orders, they will not appear in the result set. In addition, if there are any orders without associated customers, they will not appear either. Only where the two tables match on the CustomerID records will be returned. The SQL code for the inner join appears below. Notice that the database returned 1000 records. This is because there are 1000 cases in which the CustomerID in the customers table has an associated CustomerID in the orders table. The eleven customers without a CustomerID in the orders table will not appear in the result set of this inner join.

Code:

SELECT FirstName, LastName, Address, OrderDate, ShippingCost

FROM Customers

INNER JOIN Orders ON Customers.CustomerID = Orders.CustomerID

Result:

FirstName	LastName	Address	OrderDate	ShippingCost
John	Demarco	11 Lark Street	2012-06-10	34
John	Demarco	11 Lark Street	2013-06-09	40
John	Demarco	11 Lark Street	2012-11-07	34
John	Demarco	11 Lark Street	2012-03-23	49

```
(1000 row(s) returned)
```

Discussion:

The initial request, however, was to present a list of unique customers who have orders. We do not need any repeated customer names in the result set. To achieve this, we need an inner join and a GROUP BY clause by last name, first name, and address fields. We choose to GROUP BY the last name, first name, and address fields under the assumption that there are no two different customers with the same last name, same first name, and same address information. Notice how the number of customers returned is the same as that returned by the subquery we used in the beginning of this example.

Code:

SELECT FirstName, LastName, Address

FROM Customers

INNER JOIN Orders ON Customers.CustomerID = Orders.CustomerID

GROUP BY FirstName, LastName, Address

ORDER BY LastName

Result:

FirstName	LastName	Address
Nicholas	Ackerman	5 Buckingham Dr
Pindar	Ames	23 Comell Dr
Thomas	Andersen	52 Betwood Street
Joseph	Anderson	34 Cortland Ave
Paul	Anderson	90 Lenox Ave

```
(190 row(s) returned)
```

278.   Left Joins

List all customers whether they have orders or not

Discussion:

There are cases in which we do not want to retrieve only the matching records from two related tables. For instance, we might want to list all customers from the customers table and their associated orders where they exist. In this case, the output of our query will list all records from the customers table and their associated orders in the orders table. For customers without orders, it will return blank values for fields from the orders table such as the OrderDate and ShippingCost fields.

The figure below shows the design for an inner join, which is the default join type when we create a view in SQL Server 2012.

Right-click on the relationship line between customers and orders. The Joins dialog box comes up. Change the join type to "Select All Rows from Customers"

The query design now changes to:

A left join will output all customers from the customers table and any related orders from the orders table based on matches on the CustomerID field. If there are any customers without orders, they will still appear in the result set. If there are any orders without associated customers, they will not appear in the result set. Notice the relationship arrow that now has a point toward the Orders table. This is the visual sign that there is a left join relationship between these two tables.

Code:
SELECT lastname, firstname, Address, OrderDate, ShippingCost
FROM Customers LEFT JOIN Orders ON Customers.CustomerID = Orders.CustomerID

Result:
Note that the database returned 1011 records. This is because there are 1000 records in which the CustomerID in the customers table has an associated CustomerID in the orders table. In addition, we have 11 customers without a CustomerID in the orders table, but they will appear in the result set because this is a left join. Notice the blank values for the OrderDate and ShippingCost for some of the customers without any orders.

lastname	firstname	Address	OrderDate	ShippingCost
Demarco	John	11 Lark Street	2012-06-10	34
Demarco	John	11 Lark Street	2013-06-09	40
Demarco	John	11 Lark Street	2012-11-07	34
Demarco	John	11 Lark Street	2012-03-23	49

```
(1011 row(s) returned)
```

279. Right Joins

List all orders including those without customers

Discussion:

In this scenario, we want to produce a list of all orders from the orders table with any matching customer information if they exist. If a record from the orders table has a matching record in the customers table, this is fine and should actually be the case for all orders. If our query returns any records in which the fields from the customers table are blank, these are orphaned records. This means that we have orders without customers, and the integrity of our database is compromised. Let's start with an inner join view and see how we can change it to a right join one.

Right-click the relationship line between customers and orders. The Joins dialog box comes up. Change the join type to "Select All Rows from Orders".

▫ᴢ	Remo<u>v</u>e	
▷ᴢ	<u>S</u>elect All Rows from Customers	
◻◈	Se<u>l</u>ect All Rows from Orders	
🖺	P<u>r</u>operties	Alt+Enter

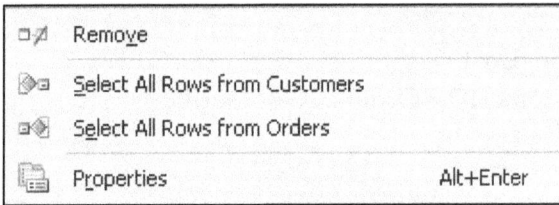

This is how the right join will look like:

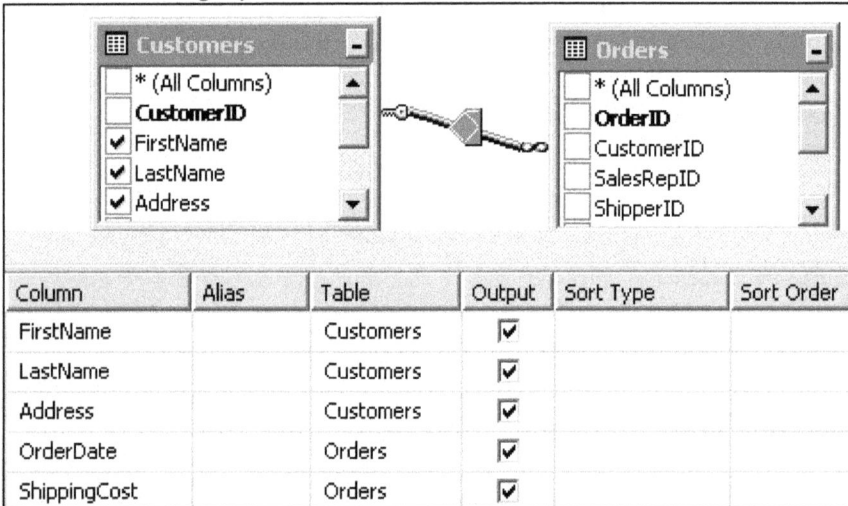

A right join will output all of the orders from the orders table and any related customers from the customers table based on matches on the CustomerID field. If there are any orders without customers, they will still appear in the result set. These orders are considered orphaned records, and they need to be investigated very closely and eliminated from the database. We cannot have orders without customers because first, it does not make sense and second, because our database integrity is compromised. Maybe these were orders belonging to existing customers and entered with the wrong CustomerID as the foreign key while referential integrity was not on. If this is the case, change the value of the CustomerID field in the orders table to associate them with existing customers in the customers table. If we cannot find any customers to associate the orphaned orders, we must delete them from the database.

Notice the relationship arrow that now has a point toward the customers table. This is the visual sign that there is a relationship with a right join between these two tables.

Code:
SELECT lastname, firstname, Address, OrderDate, ShippingCost
FROM Customers
RIGHT JOIN Orders ON Customers.CustomerID = Orders.CustomerID;

Result:
Notice that the database returned 1000 records. This is because there are 1000 records in which the CustomerID in the orders table has an associated CustomerID in the customers table. As you know, there are 11 customers without a CustomerID FK value in the orders table, but they will not appear in the result set because this is a right join listing ALL records in the orders table and only associated customers in the customers table. Notice that we do not have any blank values for the lastname, firstname, and address fields from the customers table, which means we have no orphaned records in the orders table.

lastname	firstname	Address	OrderDate	ShippingCost
Demarco	John	11 Lark Street	2012-06-10	34
Demarco	John	11 Lark Street	2013-06-09	40
Demarco	John	11 Lark Street	2012-11-07	34
Demarco	John	11 Lark Street	2012-03-23	49

(1000 row(s) returned)

CHAPTER 29 DISCUSSION QUESTIONS

1. What is the main purpose of joins in relational databases?
2. Why are the concepts of joins and normalization related?
3. Why do we relinquish flexibility if we do not know how to use joins?
4. What do we mean by the physical design of the database?
5. What is the usefulness of an inner join?
6. What is the purpose of a left join?
7. What is the rationale behind a right join?
8. How can we find orphaned records using joins?
9. How the concept of right joins is related to referential integrity?
10. What kind of a join do we need to use to find suppliers without products in our database?

CHAPTER 29 HANDS-ON EXERCISES

Chapter 29 Case 1:
Start SQL Server Management Studio. For each of the questions in this case create a new query (Ctrl-N) and name it as per the instructions in each question. Submit your work to your instructor as one text file that contains all SQL statements or as per your instructor's directions.

1. The sales director needs a list of sales representatives who have some orders in the orders table. Create a new query that contains the firstname, lastname, and address fields and satisfies the director's request. Use a subquery to achieve this task. Save the query as Chapter29_Case1_Q1.

   Your result should look like:

firstname	lastname	address
John	Anderson	32 Colonial Street
Mary	Teall	14 Highland Ave
George	Spicer	90 Lenox Ave
Phillip	Zensons	32 Camberland Street
Andrew	Simmons	16 Greenway Street

   (10 row(s) returned)

2. You need to achieve the same task as in question 1 but using a join this time. Create a new query and save it as Chapter29_Case1_Q2.

   Your result should look like:

First Name	Last Name	Address
Andrew	Simmons	16 Greenway Street
George	Spicer	90 Lenox Ave
Gerald	Williams	192 Tampa Ave
Jason	Vanderback	22 Woodville Ave
Jim	Baker	5 Ormond Street

   (10 row(s) returned)

3. The sales director needs a report that lists sales reps and their respective order information. He wants the report to include all sales reps whether they have orders or not. Specifically, from the SalesReps table he needs to see the lastname, firstname, and address fields, while from the Orders table he would like to see the orderdate and required date field. Create a new query that satisfies the director's request and name it Chapter29_Case1_Q3.

Your result should look like:

lastname	firstname	Address	OrderDate	RequiredDate
Teall	Mary	14 Highland Ave	2013-11-11	2013-11-21
Teall	Mary	14 Highland Ave	2013-07-30	2013-08-09
Teall	Mary	14 Highland Ave	2013-07-04	2013-07-14
Teall	Mary	14 Highland Ave	2014-12-19	2014-12-29
Teall	Mary	14 Highland Ave	2012-11-19	2012-11-29

(1000 row(s) returned)

4. This time the sales director needs a report that will list all orders and their related salesreps information. Specifically, from the SalesReps table he needs to see the lastname, firstname, and address fields, while from the Orders table he would like to see the orderdate and required date field. Create a new query that satisfies the director's request and name it Chapter29_Case1_Q4.

Your result should look like:

lastname	firstname	Address	OrderDate	RequiredDate
Teall	Mary	14 Highland Ave	2013-11-11	2013-11-21
Teall	Mary	14 Highland Ave	2013-07-30	2013-08-09
Teall	Mary	14 Highland Ave	2013-07-04	2013-07-14
Teall	Mary	14 Highland Ave	2014-12-19	2014-12-29
Teall	Mary	14 Highland Ave	2012-11-19	2012-11-29

(1000 row(s) returned)

5. The sales director wants you to check if there are any orders without an associated sales rep. As a result, she wants a list of orphaned records in the Orders table, if there are any. You must use a join to achieve this task. Create a new query that satisfies the director's request and name it Chapter29_Case1_Q5. HINT: See chapter 22 for help on this task.

Your result should look like:
(0 row(s) returned)

Chapter 29 Case 2:
Start SQL Server Management Studio. For each of the questions in this case create a new query (Ctrl-N) and name it as per the instructions in each question. Submit your work to your instructor as one text file that contains all SQL statements or as per your instructor's directions.

1. The inventory director needs a list of suppliers from which we currently have products in our database. Create a new query that includes the CompanyName, ContactName, and ContactTitle fields from the Suppliers table and satisfies the director's request. You need to use a join to achieve your goal and the

supplier names must appear only once in the result set. Use the tble_Products_JOINS table to create the join. Save it as Chapter29_Case2_Q1. Notice that although we have ten suppliers in the suppliers table, only seven appear in the result set.

Your result should look like:

CompanyName	ContactName	ContactTitle
American Foods, LLC.	John Marrey	Purchasing Manager
American Imports Inc.	Maria Hopkins	Sales Manager
America's Greatest Snacks, Inc.	Andrew Daves	Sales Manager
BayLine Farms Co.	Lisa Anderson	Sales Representative
Berkley Bakery Co.	Frank Baker	Marketing Manager
Home of Snacks	Pedro Adkins	Sales Manager
Mediterranean Foods, LLC.	Nick Papadopoulos	Owner

(7 row(s) returned)

2. The inventory director now needs a list of suppliers and their respective product information. She needs the list to include all suppliers whether or not they currently have products in the inventory. Create a new query that includes the CompanyName, ContactName, and ContactTitle fields from the Suppliers table and the ProductName, ProductUnitPrice, and UnitsInStock fields from the tble_Products_JOINS table and satisfies the director's request. You need to use a join to achieve your goal and the result set should be sorted by ProductName ascending. Save the query as Chapter29_Case2_Q2. Notice that there are three suppliers with no related product information.

Your result should look like:

CompanyName	ContactName	ContactTitle	ProductName
Nature's Food, Inc.	Tony Lebrant	Purchasing Director	NULL
Old York Foods, Inc.	Julia Ford	Sales Manager	NULL
Cape Cod Snacks Co.	George Casey	Accounting Manager	NULL
Home of Snacks	Pedro Adkins	Sales Manager	Almonds, Hickory S
Home of Snacks	Pedro Adkins	Sales Manager	Almonds, Roasted a
BayLine Farms Co.	Lisa Anderson	Sales Representative	Apple Cinnamon Ra
Mediterranean Foods, LLC.	Nick Papadopoulos	Owner	Artichokes in white

(52 row(s) returned)

3. The inventory director got word that there is a discrepancy in the products table. Specifically, she was told that some products do not have associated supplier information making replenishing impossible. Consequently, the director is asking for a report that will list the CompanyName, ContactName, and ContactTitle fields from the Suppliers table and the ProductName, ProductUnitPrice, and UnitsInStock fields from the Products table. She needs to see all product information whether or not they have an associated supplier. You need to use a join to achieve your goal and the result set should be sorted by CompanyName ascending. Save the query as Chapter29_Case2_Q3. Notice there are four products without associated supplier information.

Your result should look like:

CompanyName	ContactName	ContactTitle	ProductName
NULL	NULL	NULL	Cappuccino Almonds in 8oz. B
NULL	NULL	NULL	Chocolate Covered Cherries in
NULL	NULL	NULL	Chunky Pretzels
NULL	NULL	NULL	Chocolate Coconut Bar
American Foods, LLC.	John Marrey	Purchasing Manager	Chocolate Blueberries in 10 oz.
American Foods, LLC.	John Marrey	Purchasing Manager	Chocolate Fudge
American Foods, LLC.	John Marrey	Purchasing Manager	Chocolate Blueberries in 10 oz.

(53 row(s) returned)

4. You now know that there are four products in the tble_Products_JOINS table without associated supplier information in the Suppliers table. There are two logical possibilities: Some of the four products might have a SupplierID value which does not exist in the Supplier table and some of the four products might have a NULL value in their SupplierID field. Your task in this question is to identify those products with a SupplierID value which does not exist in the Suppliers table. HINT: Use a subquery and refer to chapter 22 for help. Create a new query and save it as Chapter29_Case2_Q4a.

Your result should look like:

ProductName	SupplierID	ProductUnitPrice	UnitsInStock	ReorderLevel
Chunky Pretzels	11	22.00	43	45
Chocolate Coconut Bar	11	26.00	37	45

(2 row(s) returned)

Your task now is to identify the products in the tble_Products_JOINS table which have a NULL value in their SupplierID field. Create a new query and save it as Chapter29_Case2_Q4b.

Your result should look like:

ProductName	SupplierID	ProductUnitPrice	UnitsInStock	ReorderLevel
Cappuccino Almonds in 8oz. Bag	NULL	35.00	32	30
Chocolate Covered Cherries in 8 ...	NULL	37.00	42	40

(2 row(s) returned)

5. Continuing from question 4, your task now is to create a report to list all products in the tble_Products_JOINS table without an associated supplier in the Suppliers table. It does not matter if they have a NULL value in their SupplierID field or a specific value. Create a new query and save it as Chapter29_Case2_Q5.

Your result should look like:

ProductName	SupplierID	QuantityPerUnit	ProductUnitPrice	UnitsInStock
Cappuccino Almonds in 8oz. Bag	NULL	30	35.00	32
Chocolate Covered Cherries in 8 o...	NULL	35	37.00	42
Chunky Pretzels	11	30	22.00	43
Chocolate Coconut Bar	11	15	26.00	37

(4 row(s) returned)

CHAPTER 30
WORKING WITH SUB-QUERIES

A subquery is a query nested within another query. Subqueries are primarily used to achieve results in a single step instead of using multiple queries. Specifically, subqueries are used in the following scenarios:

1. Find records in a table using criteria from another table
2. Find records in a table with no related records in another table
3. Find orphaned records
4. Find duplicate records
5. Return a single value
6. Create dynamic search lists with IN or NOT IN
7. Perform existence tests with EXISTS or NOT EXISTS
8. Perform dynamic aggregations with aggregate functions
9. Update records in one table using criteria from another table
10. Delete records in one table using criteria from another table
11. Create crosstab reports

Let us explore the scenarios above through practical examples.

280.   Find related records in a table using criteria from another table (using IN)
Find customers with orders in the fourth quarter of the year 2014
Discussion:
In this example, we will use the IN predicate with two date functions to retrieve customers with orders in the fourth quarter of 2014. We are looking for records in the customers table using criteria in the orders table.

Code:
```
SELECT *
FROM Customers
WHERE CustomerID IN
(Select CustomerID FROM Orders WHERE
(DatePart(q,[OrderDate])=4 AND Year([orderdate])=2014))
```

Result:

CustomerID	First Name	Last Name	Address	City
7	Robert	Demaggio	34 Princeton Dr	New York
9	Paul	Demarist	89 Mercer Street	New York
12	Jim	Devito	102 Lexington Ave	New York
13	David	Vanderback	91 Fifth Ave	New York

(60 row(s) returned)

281.   Find related records in a table using criteria from another table (using EXISTS)

Find customers with orders in the fourth quarter of the year 2014

Discussion:

We can obtain the same output with the previous example by using EXISTS.

Code:

```
SELECT *
FROM Customers C
WHERE EXISTS
(Select CustomerID FROM Orders O WHERE C.CustomerID = O.CustomerID AND
(DatePart(q,[OrderDate])=4 AND Year([orderdate])=2014))
```

Result:

CustomerID	FirstName	LastName	Address	City
7	Robert	Demaggio	34 Princeton Dr	New York
9	Paul	Demarist	89 Mercer Street	New York
12	Jim	Devito	102 Lexington Ave	New York
13	David	Vanderback	91 Fifth Ave	New York

```
(60 row(s) returned)
```

282.   Find unrelated records in a table using criteria from another table (using IN)

Find customers who have not placed any orders in the first six months of 2014

Discussion:

In this example our goal is to retrieve customers without orders in the first six months of the year 2014. Notice how we obtain that using the NOT IN predicate. As you can see from the result set, we have 86 customers with no orders in the first six months of that year. We can adjust our marketing efforts accordingly.

Code:

```
SELECT *
FROM Customers
WHERE CustomerID NOT IN
(SELECT CustomerID
FROM tbls_Orders
WHERE OrderDate BETWEEN '2014/1/1' AND '2014/6/30')
```

Result:

CustomerID	FirstName	LastName	Address	City
1	John	Demarco	11 Lark Street	New York
3	George	Demers	23 New Scotland Ave	New York
4	Phillip	Demetriou	22 Academy Road	New York
5	Andrew	Demichele	14 Glandel Ave	New York

```
(86 row(s) returned)
```

283.   Find unrelated records in a table using criteria from another table (using EXISTS)

Find customers who have not placed any orders in the first six months of 2014

Discussion:

We can achieve the same output with the previous example by using NOT EXISTS.

Code:

```
SELECT *
FROM Customers C
WHERE NOT EXISTS
(Select CustomerID FROM tbls_Orders O WHERE C.CustomerID = O.CustomerID AND
OrderDate BETWEEN '2014/1/1' AND '2014/6/30')
```

Result:

CustomerID	First Name	Last Name	Address	City
1	John	Demarco	11 Lark Street	New York
3	George	Demers	23 New Scotland Ave	New York
4	Phillip	Demetriou	22 Academy Road	New York
5	Andrew	Demichele	14 Glandel Ave	New York

(86 row(s) returned)

284.   Find orphaned records using a subquery with the NOT IN predicate

Find orders without customers

Discussion:

We can easily retrieve orphaned records using a subquery. In this example, we are looking for orders without customers. If we find any orders without customers, you need to delete those orders from the database and check the referential integrity setting for the one-to-many relationship between the tables Customers and Orders. In this example, we use the table tbls_orders where I put some orphaned records for demonstration purposes. As you can see from the result set, three orphaned records are found.

Code:

```
SELECT *
FROM tbls_orders
WHERE CustomerID
NOT IN (SELECT CustomerID FROM Customers)
```

Result:

OrderID	CustomerID	SalesRepID	ShipperID	OrderDate	Required Date
1500	250	11	2	2012-01-20	2012-02-04
1501	251	12	2	2012-11-18	2012-12-03
1502	252	14	3	2013-02-05	2013-02-20

(3 row(s) returned)

285.   Find duplicate records using a subquery

Find all duplicate records in a table

Discussion:

Our goal in this example is to find all duplicate records in the tbls_Orders table. Keep in mind that these records have identical field values and identical primary key values. So, they are exact duplicates. If you need to find duplicate records based on the values of one, two, or multiple fields but with different primary key values, consult chapter 22 where I list various scenarios for duplicate records. As you can see from the result set in this example, there are 11 duplicate records in this table.

Code:
SELECT *
FROM tbls_Orders
WHERE OrderID IN
(SELECT OrderID
FROM tbls_Orders
GROUP BY OrderID
HAVING count(*)>1)
ORDER BY OrderID

Result:

OrderID	CustomerID	SalesRepID	ShipperID	OrderDate	RequiredDate
8	71	3	1	2014-04-01	2014-04-16
8	71	3	1	2014-04-01	2014-04-16
45	93	1	3	2012-10-23	2012-11-07
45	93	1	3	2012-10-23	2012-11-07

(11 row(s) returned)

286.   Return a single value using the max() function in the subquery

Find the latest shipped order from the orders table

Discussion:

Let's assume we need to present the details of the latest order we shipped. We can use a subquery which first extracts the latest date using the max() function and then provides the details for the order.

Code:
SELECT *
FROM Orders
WHERE shippeddate = (SELECT max(ShippedDate) FROM Orders)

Result:

OrderID	CustomerID	SalesRepID	ShipperID	OrderDate	RequiredDate
4	165	2	1	2014-12-19	2014-12-29

(1 row(s) returned)

287.   Relate two tables on fields other than the primary and foreign keys using a subquery with EXISTS

Find customers who reside in the same city as that of sales representatives

Discussion:

Our supervisor is asking for a list of customers who live in the same city as our sales representatives. So, if we have a sales representative in Orlando, Florida, our supervisor wants us to identify all of the customers living in that city. We need to create a relationship between the Customers and SalesReps tables based on the city field.

We can accomplish this task using the following SQL statement. As you can see from the result set, we have 54 customers living in the same cities as our salespeople.

Code:
SELECT *
FROM customers
WHERE exists
(SELECT *
FROM salesreps
WHERE customers.city = salesreps.city)

Result:

CustomerID	First Name	Last Name	Address	City
1	John	Demarco	11 Lark Street	New York
2	Mary	Demania	12 Madison Ave	New York
3	George	Demers	23 New Scotland Ave	New York
4	Phillip	Demetriou	22 Academy Road	New York

(54 row(s) returned)

288. Find above average priced products using a subquery

Find products with prices above the average product price

Discussion:

In this example, we are looking for products with above average prices. We want the database to calculate the average price per product, compare every product price to the average price, and display only those products which exceed the average price. It looks like a lot for a single SQL statement, but it is possible. The essence of this SQL statement is in the WHERE clause where we ask the ProductUnitPrice to be bigger than the average ProductUnitPrice using the inequality predicate ">" and the aggregate function avg().

Code:
SELECT productname, ProductUnitPrice
FROM Products
WHERE (ProductUnitPrice) > (SELECT avg(ProductUnitPrice) FROM Products)
ORDER BY ProductUnitPrice DESC

Result:

productname	Product Unit Price
Pepper Cheese Box 3.75 oz.	50
Coffee biscuits	50
Pizza croutons	49
Chocolate Chip Cookies	49

(30 row(s) returned)

289. Retrieve the biggest orders using a subquery, EXISTS, GROUP BY, HAVING, and the sum() function

List order information with shipped invoices above $500

Discussion:

This time, we need to retrieve orders with a total of over $500. Our problem is that we need to list order information from the Orders table while making calculations on the ProductsOrders table where we keep product prices and quantities. We can achieve this task using a subquery with EXISTS and GROUP BY, which will run very fast as well.

The crucial part of this piece of code is in the GROUP BY clause. We need to group by OrderID in the subquery since in the ProductsOrders table the same OrderID appears multiple times because there might be multiple products in the same order. However, we want our subquery to produce only one OrderID per order. In addition, we use the HAVING clause because we do not know beforehand what orders have a total of $500 or more. By using the HAVING clause, we are telling the database to first calculate the order totals through the sum() function, group the results by order, and then, apply the filter (Sum([unitprice]*[quantity]))>500).

Code:
SELECT *
FROM orders O
WHERE EXISTS
(SELECT orderid, Sum([unitprice]*[quantity])
FROM ProductsOrders P
WHERE O.OrderID = P.OrderID
GROUP BY orderid
HAVING (Sum([unitprice]*[quantity]))>500)

Result:

OrderID	CustomerID	SalesRepID	ShipperID	OrderDate
308	196	3	3	2013-10-20
354	3	4	1	2012-04-28
404	101	4	2	2013-11-23
609	2	6	2	2014-05-09
944	106	10	1	2013-09-18

(5 row(s) returned)

290.   Retrieve non-discounted products using a subquery with the IN predicate
Find orders for which you extended no discounts for at least one of the products included in the order

Discussion:
Our business goal in this example is to retrieve orders for which we provided no discount for at least one of the products contained in the order. That is, for at least one of the products contained in these orders, the discount rate was 0. Keep in mind that there might be multiple products in each order. In addition, notice in the entity relationship diagram that the ProductsOrders table is the table that establishes the many-to-many relationship between the Orders and Products tables. Consequently, the logic should be to first look in the ProductsOrders table for all of the products with zero discounts. Using the OrderID from this result (the subquery) you will be able to find the corresponding orders in the Orders table. From the result, we can see that out of the 1000 orders in the Orders table, we provided at least one non-discounted product for 136 orders.

Code:
```
SELECT *
FROM orders
WHERE orderid
IN (SELECT orderid FROM ProductsOrders WHERE Discount =0)
```

Result:

OrderID	CustomerID	SalesRepID	ShipperID	OrderDate
2	184	2	1	2013-07-30
5	123	2	2	2012-11-19
7	165	2	2	2013-12-01
24	127	4	1	2012-03-12
25	23	4	1	2012-09-11

```
(136 row(s) returned)
```

291. Update records in one table with criteria from another table using a subquery

Update product prices in the products table using criteria from the suppliers table

Discussion:

Management has decided to increase the prices of products from suppliers from Boston and Dallas. This is because transportation costs from those cities have increased considerably lately. We need to update prices in the products table using criteria from the suppliers table. The subquery in this example needs to retrieve the SupplierIDs of suppliers in Boston and Dallas from the suppliers table. These retrieved SupplierIDs will be used by the main query to update product prices in the products table. Notice that in the products table, every record contains a SupplierID value.

Code:
```
UPDATE tbls_Products_Upd
SET ProductUnitPrice = ProductUnitPrice * (1+0.20)
WHERE SupplierID IN
(SELECT SupplierID FROM Suppliers
WHERE city= 'Boston' or city = 'Dallas')
```

Result:
```
(36 row(s) affected
```

292. Delete records in one table using criteria from another table

Delete order information in the orders table using criteria from the customers table

Discussion:

Our task is to delete orders from customers in Los Angeles and Orlando. These orders will be processed by another distribution center, and we do not want them to clutter our database and affect our reports. In essence, we are using a subquery to retrieve the CustomerIDs of these customers from the Customers table. Then, the main query will use these CustomerIDs to delete the orders for those CustomerIDs in the tbls_Orders_DEL table. Always remember to run a SELECT statement first before deleting records. (Check chapter 28 for a full overview of DELETE statements).

Code:
DELETE
FROM tbls_Orders_DEL
WHERE CustomerID IN
(SELECT CustomerID FROM Customers
WHERE city= 'Los Angeles' AND lastname = 'Orlando')

Result:
```
(6 row(s) affected
```

293.   Create a crosstab report using a subquery
Create a crosstab report that shows the number of products in every discount percentage category
Discussion:
In this example, we have a request from management to create a view that will list the number of products by order and by discount category simultaneously. For each order, management wants to know how many products were given a 0 discount, how many a 15% discount, and how many a 20% discount. Practically, we need to present the number of products using two dimensions: orderID and discount category. In the vast majority of cases in databases we analyze data using one dimension, for example, orders by customer. In this example, we use two dimensions. As you can see from the code below, we can use a subquery to create the discount category we want. We can include any discount categories we want and leave out the ones we do not want to appear.

Code:
SELECT OrderID,

(SELECT Count(*) FROM ProductsOrders P
WHERE O.OrderID=P.OrderID AND (discount = 0)) AS '0%',

(SELECT Count(*) FROM ProductsOrders P
WHERE O.OrderID=P.OrderID AND (discount = 0.15)) AS '15%',

(SELECT Count(*) FROM ProductsOrders P
WHERE O.OrderID=P.OrderID AND (discount = 0.20)) AS '20%'

FROM Orders AS O

Result:

OrderID	0%	15%	20%
1	0	0	1
2	1	2	1
3	0	2	2
4	0	1	0
5	1	3	1

```
(1000 row(s) returned)
```

CHAPTER 30 DISCUSSION QUESTIONS

1. What exactly is a subquery?
2. Name two scenarios in which we use subqueries.
3. When we use the IN or NOT IN operators with subqueries what are we trying to build?
4. Why is it so useful from a business perspective to be able to use subqueries to find related records?
5. Can we use a WHERE clause in the main query and a WHERE clause in the subquery in the same SQL statement?
6. Can we use subqueries to find orphaned records?
7. How can we create customized categories using subqueries?
8. What kinds of questions are answered by subqueries which return single values?
9. What extra functionality do subqueries provide to UPDATE statements?
10. Can we create crosstab reports with subqueries?

CHAPTER 30 HANDS-ON EXERCISES

Chapter 30 Case 1:
Start SQL Server Management Studio. For each of the questions in this case create a new query (Ctrl-N) and name it as per the instructions in each question. Submit your work to your instructor as one text file that contains all SQL statements or as per your instructor's directions.

1. The sales reps got word that there are orders in the tble_OrdersNS table without associated sales people in the SalesReps table. This fact results in lost commissions for them. They ask you to identify these orders so that they can get the appropriate commissions. Create a new query that includes all fields from the tble_OrdersNS table and satisfies the sales reps request. Save the query as Chapter30_Case1_Q1.

Your result should look like:

OrderID	CustomerID	SalesRepID	ShipperID	OrderDate	RequiredDate	ShippedDate	ShippingCost
957	168	11	1	2012-09-04	2012-09-14	2012-09-09	46
964	15	11	1	2014-03-20	2014-03-30	2014-03-25	47
965	31	11	2	2013-07-29	2013-08-08	2013-08-03	51
966	55	11	1	2014-02-15	2014-02-25	2014-02-20	40
967	59	11	2	2012-12-16	2012-12-26	2012-12-21	39

(9 row(s) returned)

2. Now, the sales director is asking for a list of salespeople from the SalesReps table who have no associated orders in the tble_OrdersNS table. Create a new query that includes all fields from the salesreps table and satisfies the sales director's request. Save the query as Chapter30_Case1_Q2.

Your result should look like:

SalesRepID	FirstName	LastName	Title	Address	City	State	Zip
8	Michael	Bernstein	Sales Reppresentative	21 Garden Ave	New York	NY	12189
10	Gerald	Williams	Sales Reppresentative	192 Tampa Ave	Dallas	TX	52347

`(2 row(s) returned)`

3. The sales director is back asking for a list of orders from the tble_OrdersNS table for which the shipping cost is greater than the average shipping cost of all the orders in this table. Create a new query that includes all fields from the tble_OrdersNS table and satisfies the sales director's request. Save the query as Chapter30_Case1_Q3.

Your result should look like:

OrderID	CustomerID	SalesRepID	ShipperID	OrderDate	RequiredDate	ShippedDate	ShippingCost
4	165	2	1	2014-12-19	2014-12-29	2014-12-24	48
9	194	3	1	2014-04-19	2014-04-29	2014-04-24	46
11	3	3	2	2013-06-07	2013-06-17	2013-06-12	47
13	53	3	3	2012-02-10	2012-02-20	2012-02-15	52
14	183	3	1	2014-09-10	2014-09-20	2014-09-15	47

`(504 row(s) returned)`

4. The sales director needs a similar report as in question 3 but one that only shows the number of orders whose shipping cost is greater than the average shipping cost of all the orders in the tble_OrdersNS table. Create a new query that satisfies the sales director's request. Save the query as Chapter30_Case1_Q4.

Your result should look like:

NumberOfOrders
504

`(1 row(s) returned)`

5. The sales director is finally asking for a list of products with sales above $3,000 without taking into consideration any applied discounts. Create a query that includes all fields from the products table and satisfies the sales director's request. Save the query as Chapter30_Case1_Q5. HINT: Quantities and prices for products sold are stored in the ProductsOrders table.

Your result should look like:

ProductID	ProductName	SupplierID	QuantityPerUnit	ProductUnitPrice
12	Chocolate Covered Cherries in 8 oz. Bag	2	35	37.00
50	Fudge Nut Brownie Cookies	7	25	44.00
19	Crispy Pears	2	20	33.00
39	Pizza croutons	5	20	49.00
17	Dark Chocolate Apricots in 20 oz. Bag	2	35	46.00

`(9 row(s) returned)`

Chapter 30 Case 2:
Start SQL Server Management Studio. For each of the questions in this case create a new query (Ctrl-N) and name it as per the instructions in each question. Submit your work to your instructor as one text file that contains all SQL statements or as per your instructor's directions.

1. The sales manager needs a list of sales reps from the SalesReps table with orders in the months of January, February, March, April, May, and June 2014 in the tble_Orders table. Create a new query that includes the firstname, lastname, and title fields from the SalesReps table and satisfies the sales manager request. Save the query as Chapter30_Case2_Q1.

Your result should look like:

First Name	Last Name	Title
John	Anderson	Sales Reppresentative
Mary	Teall	Sales Director
George	Spicer	Assitant Director of Sales
Phillip	Zensons	Sales Reppresentative
Andrew	Simmons	Account Manager

(10 row(s) returned)

2. The sales manager is back and this time she is asking for a list of sales people from the SalesReps table without any orders in the month of June 2014 in the tble_Orders table. Create a new query that includes the firstname, lastname, and title fields from the SalesReps table and satisfies the sales manager request. Save the query as Chapter30_Case2_Q2.

Your result should look like:

First Name	Last Name	Title
Phillip	Zensons	Sales Reppresentative

(1 row(s) returned)

3. The accounts receivable people need to know the details of the latest order that was input in the system according to the order date in the tble_Orders table. Create a new query that includes all the fields from the the tble_Orders table and satisfies the accounting people request. Save the query as Chapter30_Case2_Q3.

Your result should look like:

OrderID	CustomerID	SalesRepID	ShipperID	OrderDate	RequiredDate	ShippedDate	ShippingCost
4	165	2	1	2014-12-19	2014-12-29	2014-12-19	48

(1 row(s) returned)

4. The inventory people need a list of orders for which the shipping cost is greater than the average shipping cost of all orders. Create a new query that includes the OrderID, OrderDate, and ShippingCost fields from the tble_Orders table and satisfies the inventory people request. Sort results by OrderID ascending. Save the query as Chapter30_Case2_Q4.

Your result should look like:

OrderID	OrderDate	ShippingCost
4	2014-12-19	48
9	2014-04-19	46
11	2013-06-07	47
13	2012-02-10	52
14	2014-09-10	47

```
(505 row(s) returned)
```

5. The sales manager needs a final report. She needs a crosstab report from the tble_Orders table that lists the number of orders by sales person and by year for the years 2012, 2013, and 2014. You must use a subquery to obtain your result. Create a new query that satisfies the sales person request and save it as Chapter30_Case2_Q5.

Your result should look like:

lastname	'2012'	'2013'	'2014'
Anderson	0	37	40
Baker	34	34	33
Bemstein	2	34	37
Delaney	10	28	27
Simmons	53	44	47

```
(10 row(s) returned)
```

CHAPTER 31
STORED PROCEDURES

Stored procedures in their basic form are pure SQL statements. Yet, to these SQL statements we can add a series of characteristics like variables, data types, input parameters, output parameters, return values, conditional execution, and loops through which we augment geometrically their usefulness with respect to traditional sql statements. We have two types of stored procedures: system and user. System stored procedures are pre-developed ones through which we can achieve a multitude of tasks for administration and security. There is no meaning for me to waste your time with system sps since you can find everything about them here: http://technet.microsoft.com/en-us/library/ms187961.aspx. In this chapter we will look at stored procedures with respect to their usefulness in business problems.

Consequently, there are three main business reasons for which we use stored procedures: First, because we can achieve a lot more functionality with respect to pure SQL statements. For example, we can conditionally run multiple SQL statements. Second, since stored procedures are precompiled pieces of code it means they run faster than SQL statements. Third, and most importantly, we use stored procedures to enforce the business rules through which we run our business. For example, we might use a stored procedure to assign credit lines to customers based on their past purchases.

You can use the Query Editor you were working on till now to create stored procedures. Or within the database, click "programmability", right click on "stored procedures" and select "new stored procedure". In this book we will be creating all procedures in the Query Editor.

294. Create a simple stored procedure that contains only SQL code
Discussion:
In this example we create a stored procedure to retrieve a simple list of fields from the Products table. As you can see the sp contains only SQL code that will return all the products in the Products table.

Code:
```
CREATE PROCEDURE sp_GetProductData
AS
SELECT ProductName, QuantityPerUnit, ProductUnitPrice, UnitsInStock, UnitsOnOrder,
ReorderLevel, SKU
FROM Products
```

Execute:
```
execute sp_GetProductData
or
exec sp_GetProductData
```

Result:

ProductName	QuantityPerUnit	ProductUnitPrice	UnitsInStock
Almonds, Hickory Smoked - 12 oz. Bag	12	35	40
Almonds, Roasted and Salted - 18 oz. Bag	12	22	32
Banana Chips - 20 oz. Bag	12	27	25
Berry Cherry in 8 oz. Bag	15	30	50

```
(70 row(s) returned)
```

295.   Using input parameters with stored procedures

Discussion:

Here we assign the UnitsInStock field to be an input parameter field. Notice how we designate the parameter right below the CREATE statement and how we assign a data type to it. In the execution code, notice how we assign the value 15 to the parameter. The result set indicates that we have three products with 15 units in stock in our inventory.

Code:

```
CREATE PROCEDURE sp_Param_UnitsInStock
@UnitsInStock  smallint
AS
SELECT ProductName, QuantityPerUnit, ProductUnitPrice, UnitsInStock, UnitsOnOrder,
ReorderLevel, SKU
FROM Products
WHERE UnitsInStock = @UnitsInStock
```

Execute:

```
execute sp_Param_UnitsInStock @UnitsInStock = 15
```

Result:

ProductName	QuantityPerUnit	ProductUnitPrice	UnitsInStock	UnitsOnOrder
Dried Cranberries - 34 oz.	15	35	15	10
Chocolate Chunk Cookies, 9.5 oz.	34	48	15	20
Apple Cinnamon Raisin Cookies	30	27	15	20

```
(3 row(s) returned)
```

296.   Using multiple input parameters with stored procedures

Discussion:

In this example we assign the UnitsOnOrder and UnitsInStock fields to be input parameter fields. We designate them as parameter fields right below the CREATE statement and we assign the smallint data type to both of them.

Code:
```
CREATE PROCEDURE sp_Param_Multiple
@UnitsInStock smallint,
@UnitsOnOrder smallint
AS
SELECT ProductName, QuantityPerUnit, ProductUnitPrice, UnitsInStock, UnitsOnOrder,
ReorderLevel, SKU
FROM Products
WHERE UnitsInStock = @UnitsInStock AND UnitsOnOrder = @UnitsOnOrder
```

Execute:
```
execute sp_Param_Multiple @UnitsInStock = 50, @UnitsOnOrder = 0
```

Result:

ProductName	QuantityPerUnit	ProductUnitPrice	UnitsInStock	UnitsOnOrder
Berry Cherry in 8 oz. Bag	15	30	50	0
Artichokes in white sauce	20	22	50	0
Chocolate Chip Cookies	25	49	50	0

```
(3 row(s) returned)
```

297.   Using output parameters with stored procedures

Discussion:

The same way stored procedures accept input parameters, they can use output parameters to generate values which can be used by other consuming applications. For example, an output value for one procedure can be the input value for another. In the example below, we supply the stored procedure the input value for the ProductID and the stored procedure outputs the corresponding SupplierID for that product. As you can see from the code what differentiates an output parameter is the "output" or "out" keyword that follows its declaration.

Code:
```
CREATE PROCEDURE sp_Param_GetSupplierID
@ProductID int,
@SupplierID int output
AS
SELECT @SupplierID = SupplierID
FROM Products
WHERE ProductID = @ProductID
```

To execute the procedure we need to declare the output variable first. Then, we execute the procedure. Finally, we display the output value for the SupplierID using a simple select statement. As you can see from the result set, the SupplierID corresponding to ProductID=15 is 2.

Execute:
```
Declare @SupplierID int
execute sp_Param_GetSupplierID @ProductID = 15, @SupplierID = @SupplierID out
Select @SupplierID AS SupplierID
```

Result:

SupplierID
2

```
(1 row(s) returned)
```

298. Using conditional processing in stored procedures

Discussion:

A fundamental feature of stored procedures is their capacity to run conditional code. In this example, our sp contains two SQL statements and it accepts two parameters: @UnitPrice and @Discount. It also contains an IF ELSE conditional statement. The business goal is for the manager to enter a price point above which he has the discretion to provide any discount he sees fit. However, the manager's discretion will be applied only if the price point suggested is above the average product price in the Products table. If not, the manager's decision will be overruled by the sp and a 5% standard discount will be applied instead.

Code:
```
CREATE PROCEDURE sp_Cond_Inventory
@UnitPrice money,
@Discount decimal(2,2)
AS
IF @UnitPrice > (Select AVG(ProductUnitPrice) FROM Products)
  BEGIN
  Select ProductName, QuantityPerUnit, ProductUnitPrice as OriginalPrice, ProductUnitPrice* (1-
@Discount) AS NewPrice, SKU FROM Products
  END
ELSE
  BEGIN
  Select ProductName, QuantityPerUnit, ProductUnitPrice as OriginalPrice, ProductUnitPrice * (1-
.05) As NewPrice, SKU FROM Products
  END
```

Execute:
```
execute sp_Cond_Inventory @UnitPrice = 40, @Discount = 0.3
```

Result with @UnitPrice = 40 (above average):

ProductName	QuantityPerUnit	OriginalPrice	NewPrice	SKU
Almonds, Hickory Smoked - 12 oz. Bag	12	35.00	24.500000	PDKLS-2332
Almonds, Roasted and Salted - 18 oz. Bag	12	22.00	15.400000	PDKLSD-2344
Banana Chips - 20 oz. Bag	12	27.00	18.900000	PDKLSD-2347
Berry Cherry in 8 oz. Bag	15	30.00	21.000000	PDK-2589

```
(70 row(s) returned)
```

Execute:
```
execute sp_Cond_Inventory @UnitPrice = 10, @Discount = 0.2
```

Result with @UnitPrice = 10 (below average):

Although we put in a discount of 20% a standard discount of 5% has been applied.

ProductName	QuantityPerUnit	OriginalPrice	NewPrice	SKU
Almonds, Hickory Smoked - 12 oz. Bag	12	35.00	33.250000	PDKLS-2332
Almonds, Roasted and Salted - 18 oz. Bag	12	22.00	20.900000	PDKLSD-2344
Banana Chips - 20 oz. Bag	12	27.00	25.650000	PDKLSD-2347
Berry Cherry in 8 oz. Bag	15	30.00	28.500000	PDK-2589

```
(70 row(s) returned)
```

299.   Using update statements in stored procedures

Discussion:

In this example we use the sp to enter price increases for the products from various suppliers. The user will enter the SupplierID and the price increase percentage and the sp will do the rest. The cool thing about writing an sp for this task is that anyone and from any application can call it and use it. They will only supply two numbers, no need to write any SQL code.

Code:

```
CREATE PROCEDURE sp_UpdProducts
@SupplierID int,
@PriceChange decimal (2, 2)
AS
UPDATE tbls_Products_Upd
SET ProductUnitPrice = ProductUnitPrice * (1+ @PriceChange)
WHERE SupplierID = @SupplierID
```

Execute:

```
execute sp_UpdProducts  @SupplierID = 1, @PriceChange = 0.03
```

Result:
```
(10 row(s) affected)
```

300.   Error handling in stored procedures TRY CATCH

Discussion:

Sometimes procedures generate errors. For example, we might be looking for the supplier of a product but that supplier might not exist in the database. In other cases, procedures might violate constraints. For example, we might try to insert a quantity amount for the product inventory which is not acceptable by the system. Instead of letting the procedure generate a generic message and stop executing, we can use the TRY CATCH statement to provide feedback to the user or execute a separate piece of code. When we use the TRY CATCH statement, the code we have in the TRY part will execute first. If it generates an error, the procedure will execute the code in the CATCH part.

In the example below, we have the simple task to insert a new product in the Products table. We have the INSERT code in the TRY part. If just in case the user enters a SupplierID that does not exist the TRY part will stop executing and the CATCH part will take over.

Code:
```
CREATE PROCEDURE sp_ErrorHandling
@ProductID int,
@SupplierID int,
@ProductName text
AS
BEGIN TRY
INSERT INTO tbls_Products_sp (ProductID, SupplierID, ProductName)
VALUES (@ProductID, @SupplierID, @ProductName)
END TRY
BEGIN CATCH
PRINT 'Supplier does not exist '
END CATCH
```

Execute:
The value 11 for SupplierID does not exist in the Supplier table. This means we cannot use it as the foreign key for the SupplierID since this would create an orphaned record in the Products table. That is why the TRY part of the procedure stops executing and the CATCH part takes over to present the message we provide.

```
execute sp_ErrorHandling  @ProductID = 71, @SupplierID = 11, @ProductName = 'Chocolate'
```

Result:
```
(0 row(s) affected)
Supplier does not exist
```

Execute:
Instead, if we execute the statement below, it will run since a supplier with Supplier = 9 does exist.

```
execute sp_ErrorHandling  @ProductID = 72, @SupplierID = 9, @ProductName = 'Chocolate'
```

Result:
```
(1 row(s) affected)
```

CHAPTER 31 DISCUSSION QUESTIONS

1. Name two characteristics that differentiate stored procedures from pure SQL statements.
2. What are the two types of stored procedures?
3. What are the primary goals of system stored procedures?
4. Name one business reason for which we use stored procedures.
5. What is the primary business reason for which we use stored procedures?
6. If we run SQL code in a query or a stored procedure which one will run faster?
7. What is the reason for using input parameters in stored procedures?
8. Why do we need to use output parameters in stored procedures?
9. Why conditional statements in stored procedures are so useful in business operations?
10. What statement do we use for error handling in stored procedures?

CHAPTER 31 HANDS-ON EXERCISES

Chapter 31 Case 1:
Start SQL Server Management Studio. For each of the questions in this case create a new query (Ctrl-N) and name it as per the instructions in each question. Submit your work to your instructor as one text file that contains all SQL statements or as per your instructor's directions.

1. The sales people are asking for a report that contains the OrderID, OrderDate, RequiredDate, and ShippingCost fields from the Orders table. Create a new stored procedure in a query window that satisfies the sales people request and save it as sp_Chapter31_Case1_Q1. Execute the stored procedure.

    Your result should look like:

OrderID	OrderDate	RequiredDate	ShippingCost
1	2013-11-11	2013-11-21	36
2	2013-07-30	2013-08-09	39
3	2013-07-04	2013-07-14	34
4	2014-12-19	2014-12-29	48
5	2012-11-19	2012-11-29	40

    (1000 row(s) returned)

2. The sales people need a report that lists the ProductName, QuantityPerUnit, UnitsInStock, UnitsOnOrder, and SKU fields from the Products table. However, they want to be able to input the QuantityPerUnit themselves and then get the report. Create a new stored procedure in a query window that satisfies the sales people request and save it as sp_Chapter31_Case1_Q2. Execute the stored procedure with a value = 15 for the QuantityPerUnit variable.

    Your result should look like:

ProductName	QuantityPerUnit	UnitsInStock	UnitsOnOrder	SKU
Berry Cherry in 8 oz. Bag	15	50	0	PDK-2589
California Original Pistachios - 1 lb. Bag	15	35	0	PDK-2347
Dried Cranberries - 34 oz.	15	15	10	PDKLS-2347
Chocolate Coconut Bar	15	37	0	PDKL-2389

(4 row(s) returned)

3. The sales people are asking for a report that will include all the fields from the Orders table. In addition, they want to be able to input the CustomerID, SalesRepID, and ShipperID values themselves to get the report they need. Create a new stored procedure in a query window that satisfies the sales people request and save it as sp_Chapter31_Case1_Q3. Execute the stored procedure with a value = 3 for the CustomerID, value = 1 for the SalesRepID, and value = 1 for the ShipperID.

Your result should look like:

OrderID	CustomerID	SalesRepID	ShipperID	OrderDate	RequiredD...	ShippedDate	ShippingCost
97	3	1	1	2012-10-25	2012-11-04	2012-10-30	45

(1 row(s) returned)

4. The associate director of accounts receivable is asking for a process so that when he provides the database with an OrderID value in the Orders table, the database will return the corresponding CustomerID value. This will help them a lot with billing. Create a new stored procedure in a query window that satisfies the sales people request and save it as sp_Chapter31_Case1_Q4. Execute the stored procedure with a value = 728 for the OrderID variable.

Your result should look like:

CustomerID
10

(1 row(s) returned)

5. The sales department is asking for a new business rule to be embedded in the database. Specifically, for the orders in the month of December 2014 they want the shipping cost charged to the customer to be reduced by 50%. For any other interval in the system the shipping cost should remain as is. Create a new stored procedure in a query window with a parameter for the OrderDate field from the Orders table. The sp should output the fields OrderID, CustomerID, OrderDate, ShippingCost, and NewShippingcost from the Orders table showing the new shipping cost depending on the OrderDate. In addition, the first SQL statement in the sp should limit the orders retrieved to those in the month of December 2014 and the second SQL statement should limit the Orders retrieved to those from 1/1/2014 till 11/30/2014. Save the query as sp_Chapter31_Case1_Q5. Execute the stored procedure first with the OrderDate value of '2014-12-15' and then with the OrderDate value of '2014-11-15'.

Your result for '2014-12-15' should look like:

OrderID	CustomerID	OrderDate	ShippingCost	NewShippingCost
4	165	2014-12-19	48	24
58	72	2014-12-05	45	22.5
133	97	2014-12-07	38	19
165	120	2014-12-14	52	26
299	117	2014-12-03	40	20

`(14 row(s) returned)`

Your result for '2014-11-15' should look like:

OrderID	CustomerID	OrderDate	ShippingCost	NewShippingCost
8	71	2014-04-06	36	36
9	194	2014-04-19	46	46
14	183	2014-09-10	47	47
17	28	2014-10-19	45	45
27	186	2014-03-14	38	38

`(326 row(s) returned)`

Chapter 31 Case 2:

Start SQL Server Management Studio. For each of the questions in this case create a new query (Ctrl-N) and name it as per the instructions in each question. Submit your work to your instructor as one text file that contains all SQL statements or as per your instructor's directions.

1. The HR director is asking for a report that contains the FirstName, LastName, Address, City, State, and Zip fields from the SalesReps table. Create a new stored procedure in a query window that satisfies the HR director request and save it as sp_Chapter31_Case2_Q1. Execute the stored procedure to view the resulting recordset.

   Your result should look like:

FirstName	LastName	Address	City	State	Zip
John	Anderson	32 Colonial Street	Boston	MA	22459
Mary	Teall	14 Highland Ave	Boston	MA	22459
George	Spicer	90 Lenox Ave	Boston	MA	22459
Phillip	Zensons	32 Camberland ...	New ...	NY	12189
Andrew	Simmons	16 Greenway S...	New ...	NY	12189

`(10 row(s) returned)`

2. The HR director found the report in question 1 very helpful and now he is asking if it is possible to enter a zip code and obtain a report of sales people from that zip code. The report should contain the FirstName, LastName, Address, City, State, and Zip fields from the SalesReps table. Create a new stored procedure in a query window that uses the Zip code as an input parameter and save it as sp_Chapter31_Case2_Q2. Execute the stored procedure with a value = 22459 for the Zip code variable.

   Your result should look like:

First Name	Last Name	Address	City	State	Zip
John	Anderson	32 Colonial Street	Boston	MA	22459
Mary	Teall	14 Highland Ave	Boston	MA	22459
George	Spicer	90 Lenox Ave	Boston	MA	22459

(3 row(s) returned)

3. Knowing what is possible, the HR director is now asking for two parameters to obtain a report of sales people. He wants to be able to input the City and State as parameters. The report should contain the FirstName, LastName, Address, City, State, and Zip fields from the SalesReps table. Create a new stored procedure in a query window that uses the City and State as input parameters and save it as sp_Chapter31_Case2_Q3. Execute the stored procedure with a value = Dallas for the city variable and a value = TX for the state variable.

Your result should look like:

First Name	Last Name	Address	City	State	Zip
Jim	Baker	5 Ormond Street	Dallas	TX	52347
Gerald	Williams	192 Tampa Ave	Dallas	TX	52347

(2 row(s) returned)

4. The HR director is asking for a way so that when he provides the database with a last name from the sales reps table, the database will return the corresponding SalesRepID value. Create a new stored procedure in a query window with the lastname as the input parameter and SalesRepID as the output parameter and satisfies the HR director request. Save the new query as sp_Chapter31_Case2_Q4. Execute the stored procedure with a value = Anderson for the lastname.

Your result should look like:

SalesRepID
1

(1 row(s) returned)

5. The HR director wants to provide a work related bonus of 5% of the salary of the sales reps in the SalesReps table. However, those sales reps who were hired before 12/31/2000 will receive 20% of their salary as bonus. With such directions the HR director needs a process through which he will input the Bonus percentage such as 5 or 20 and the system will output the sales reps who are receiving this bonus percentage. Create a new stored procedure in a query window which will output the lastname, firstname, dateofhire, salary, and calculated Bonus fields for the appropriate sales people. Save the query as sp_Chapter31_Case2_Q5. Execute the stored procedure first with a Bonus value of 20 and then with a value of 5.

Your result should look like (Bonus = 20):

lastname	firstname	dateofhire	salary	Bonus
Anderson	John	1999-01-01	85000.00	17000.00000
Teall	Mary	2000-06-12	90000.00	18000.00000
Delaney	Kenneth	1995-05-10	90000.00	18000.00000
Bernstein	Michael	1991-05-25	150000.00	30000.00000

(4 row(s) returned)

Your result should look like (Bonus = 5):

lastname	firstname	dateofhire	salary	Bonus
Spicer	George	2004-05-15	105000.00	5250.000000
Zensons	Phillip	2001-06-10	118000.00	5900.000000
Simmons	Andrew	2006-05-11	190000.00	9500.000000
Vanderback	Jason	2001-05-12	120000.00	6000.000000
Baker	Jim	2006-01-10	105000.00	5250.000000
Williams	Gerald	2005-01-11	110000.00	5500.000000

(6 row(s) returned)

CHAPTER 32
TRIGGERS

A trigger is a special type of stored procedure that fires automatically on inserts, updates, and deletes of records. It is practically code that runs automatically when a record is inserted, updated, or deleted from the database. As such they are used extensively for checking data and enforcing the business logic of the corporation. For example, we might have a business rule that says "do not give more than 10K credit to new customers" and a sales person breaks the rule to get the big order in. In this case, a trigger can fire to email the rep and the rep's supervisor and reverse the action altogether.

In SQL Server 2012 we have two types of triggers: AFTER and INSTEAD OF. AFTER triggers are equivalent to the old FOR triggers and they will fire after update, delete, or insert statements and after any referential integrity or other constraints have been satisfied. On the other hand, INSTEAD OF triggers fire before any UPDATE, INSERT, and DELETE statements and practically replace those actions. For instance, if you have an INSTEAD OF trigger for updates on a table and an UPDATE statement is executed on that table, then the INSTEAD OF trigger will run instead of the UPDATE statement. We can have multiple AFTER triggers on a table but only one INSTEAD OF trigger for each of the INSERT, UPDATE, and DELETE actions.

The next item on triggers is the notorious NOCOUNT ON statement. When we set the NOCOUNT ON, any messages that count the number of records returned, updated, or affected will not be communicated to the client causing the trigger to run. This action will have a positive effect on the performance of the trigger. However, do not expect any tremendous increases in performance especially if the trigger just updates a single record or does some another simple operation. Maybe the best thing to do is to have NOCOUNT ON in the beginning of the trigger, let the trigger go through its operations, and then setting it off so that the final result of the trigger can be send to the client.

Another item I would like you to know about triggers is the ROLLBACK TRANSACTION statement. We use it extensively to undo the effects of an INSERT, UPDATE, or DELETE if they violate the business logic rules we included in the trigger. If we rollback a transaction in the trigger, all data modifications attempted will be reversed. If we have any code in the trigger after the rollback statement, that code will continue to run. In most cases however, the rollback statement is the last one in the trigger code. The ROLLBACK TRANSACTION, ROLLBACK TRAN, or simply ROLLBACK statements achieve the goal of reversing any attempted actions from the trigger.

Next, we need to know that the RAISE ERROR and PRINT statements are used to provide feedback to the user. The PRINT statement will simply return a text message to the client and its syntax is very simple. The message can be any text string we want allowing 4,000 characters for Unicode text and 8,000 for non-unicode text.

PRINT message

example:
PRINT 'This product is no longer in inventory.'

393

CHAPTER 32

Result:
```
This product is no longer in inventory.
```

We can include functions in the PRINT statement as in the example below:

example:
PRINT 'This product is no longer in inventory for the last ' + cast (DateDiff(d, getdate(), '2014/6/30') as nvarchar (1000)) + ' days.'

Result:
```
This product is no longer in inventory for the last 110 days.
```

The RAISE ERROR statement can provide more feedback to the client than the PRINT statement. Its general syntax appears below with the arguments explained:

RAISEERROR (message, severity, state) with option

message: a string up to 2047 characters long which can include functions as we have seen in the PRINT statement.

severity: a number from 0 to 25 specified by us. Numbers from 0 to 18 can be specified by any user while those from 19 to 25 by sys admins. A number between 20 and 25 will terminate the connection between server and client.

state: an arbitrary number between 0 and 255 specified by us. Its purpose is to distinguish among multiple locations of code that generate the same error.

option: it is an argument that takes multiple values from which the following two are the most useful for us:
1. **LOG:** this option will log the error in the error log
2. **NOWAIT:** this option will send the message to the client at once

example:
RAISERROR ('These products are available only in January', 0, 1)

Result:
```
These products are available only in January
```

In this example, we use the OPTION argument with the LOG value to record the error in the SQL Server error log.

example:
RAISERROR ('These products are available only in January', 0, 1) WITH LOG

Result:
```
These products are available only in January
```

Now if we open the SQL server log we will find this entry from raiseerror as you can see in the image below:

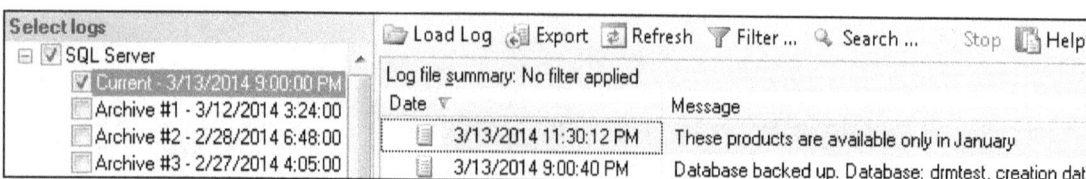

The last knowledge item for effective trigger writing is that of logical tables. In SQL Server we have the inserted and deleted temporary tables. Inserted temporary tables include any recently inserted or updated records while the deleted table includes any recently deleted records. Both logical tables are created automatically by the server so that we can use their contents in our triggers.

For example, we might want to check a recently placed order for the inclusion of products not available for sale this month. To achieve this in the trigger, we select the records from the inserted table to see if the sales rep put in sales orders for these products. If this is the case, we roll back the transaction. Another scenario, might involve the movement of deleted records to a historical table. Yet another scenario might involve the movement of recently updated records to an audit table. No matter what the business scenario is, we need the knowledge of logical tables in SQL Server to write effective triggers.

301. Trigger to prevent changes to a single column in one table
Prevent changes to the ReorderLevel column in the Products table
Discussion:
In this simple trigger we prevent changes to the ReorderLevel field in the tbls_Products_tr table. A product with any ReorderLevel can be inserted in the tbls_Products_tr table since this trigger will only fire for updates on existing products. Also, the trigger assumes that updates will happen one at a time through a front-end form and not through batches of changes between systems.

Code:
```
CREATE TRIGGER tr_ReorderLevel_NoChange
ON tbls_Products_tr
AFTER UPDATE AS
   If update(ReorderLevel)
   BEGIN
     RAISERROR ('The reorder level for this product cannot be updated.', 0, 1)
     ROLLBACK
     RETURN
   END
```

Result:
```
Command(s) completed successfully.
```

Test the action of the trigger:
Code
```
UPDATE tbls_Products_tr SET ReorderLevel = 50 WHERE ProductID = 1
```

Result:
```
The reorder level for this product cannot be updated.
Msg 3609, Level 16, State 1, Line 2
The transaction ended in the trigger. The batch has been aborted.
```

Delete the trigger before you go to the next example:
```
Drop trigger tr_UnitsOnOrder_DecemberOnly
```

302.   Trigger to prevent changes to multiple columns in one table

Prevent changes to the ReorderLevel or SKU columns in the Products table

Discussion:

With this trigger, we prevent changes to the ReorderLevel or SKU fields in the tbls_Products_tr table. Notice that if any of the two columns is updated the trigger will fire. Additionally, new products with any reorder levels or any SKU values can be inserted in the tbls_Products_tr table since this trigger will only fire for updates on existing products. Finally, the trigger assumes that updates will happen one at a time through a front-end form and not through batches of changes between systems.

Code:

```
CREATE TRIGGER tr_ReorderLevel_SKU_NoChange
ON tbls_Products_tr
AFTER UPDATE AS
   IF (update(ReorderLevel) OR update (SKU))
   BEGIN
      RAISERROR ('The reorder level or SKU value for this product cannot be updated.', 0, 1)
      ROLLBACK
      RETURN
   END
```

Result:

```
Command(s) completed successfully.
```

Test the action of the trigger for the ReorderLevel:

Code:

```
UPDATE tbls_Products_tr SET ReorderLevel = 50 WHERE ProductID = 1
```

Result:

```
The reorder level or SKU value for this product cannot be updated.
Msg 3609, Level 16, State 1, Line 2
The transaction ended in the trigger. The batch has been aborted.
```

Test the action of the trigger again for the SKU column:

Code:

```
UPDATE tbls_Products_tr SET SKU = 'PDLK-2139' WHERE ProductID = 1
```

Result:

```
The reorder level or SKU value for this product cannot be updated.
Msg 3609, Level 16, State 1, Line 2
The transaction ended in the trigger. The batch has been aborted.
```

Delete the trigger before you go to the next example:

```
Drop trigger tr_UnitsOnOrder_DecemberOnly
```

303. Trigger to prevent changes to a single column depending on a date condition

Trigger to enforce the purchasing month of products

Discussion:

The business goal here is to ensure that the products in the tbls_Products_tr table can be purchased only in the month of December. We assume they are seasonal products and they are useless for the rest of the year. If anyone tries to update the UnitsOnOrder field and the system date is not within the month of December, the trigger will not allow the update and will rollback the update. New products can be inserted in the tbls_products_tr table since this trigger will only fire for updates on existing products. Also, the trigger assumes that updates will happen one at a time through a front-end form and not through batches between systems.

Code:

```
CREATE TRIGGER tr_UnitsOnOrder_DecemberOnly
ON tbls_Products_tr
AFTER UPDATE AS
    If update(UnitsOnOrder) AND DatePart(m, GetDate()) <> 12
    BEGIN
        RAISERROR ('These products can be purchased only in December', 0, 1)
        ROLLBACK
        RETURN
    END
```

Result:
```
Command(s) completed successfully.
```

Test the action of the trigger:

Code
```
UPDATE tbls_Products_tr SET UnitsOnOrder = 10 where productid = 70
```

Result:
```
These products can be purchased only in December
Msg 3609, Level 16, State 1, Line 1
The transaction ended in the trigger. The batch has been aborted.
```

Delete the trigger before you go to the next example:

```
Drop trigger tr_UnitsOnOrder_DecemberOnly
```

304. Trigger to check that a quantity entered should be below a certain value

Discussion:

In this example we enforce an inventory policy that we do not allow more than 50 units in stock for any product. The trigger will run for updates as well as inserted records.

Code:

```
CREATE TRIGGER tr_CheckQuantityUnitsInStock
ON tbls_Products_tr
AFTER INSERT, UPDATE AS
   IF EXISTS (SELECT * FROM inserted WHERE unitsinstock > 50)
   BEGIN
      RAISERROR ('quantity entered for UnitsInStock exceeds 50 units.  Enter a lesser number', 0, 1)
      ROLLBACK
      RETURN
   END
```

Result:
```
Command(s) completed successfully.
```

Test the action of the trigger:
Code:

```
INSERT INTO tbls_Products_tr (ProductName, UnitsInStock) values ('New Product', 55)
```

Result:
```
quantity entered for UnitsInStock exceeds 50 units.  Enter a lesser number
Msg 3609, Level 16, State 1, Line 1
The transaction ended in the trigger. The batch has been aborted.
```

Delete the trigger before you go to the next example
Drop trigger tr_CheckQuantityUnitsInStock

305. Trigger to enforce the purchasing month of products for specific products (continues from previous)

Discussion:

The previous example is useful but limiting as well. For example, what if we would like to enforce a purchasing policy for December only for a couple of products? This makes a lot of business sense since not all of our products are seasonal. The trigger assumes that updates will happen one at a time through a front-end form and not through batches with multiple records. As you can see we select 1 record from the logical "inserted" table. In this case we create a trigger that will fire only for the products 'Crispy Pears' and 'Chunky Pretzels'